Healthtech Innovation

Today, over 500,000 medical technologies are available in hospitals, homes, and community care settings. They range from simple bandages to complex, multi-part body scanners that cost millions of dollars to develop. Yet a typical technology has a lifecycle of just 21 months before an improved product usurps it—the healthcare ecosystem is rapidly advancing and driven by a constant flow of innovation. And those innovations need innovators.

With $21 billion made available for investment in the digital healthcare industry in 2020 (a 20x increase on 2010), entrepreneurs, investors, and related actors are entering the healthcare ecosystem in greater numbers than ever before. Last year alone, over 17,000 medical technology patents were filed, the third highest of all patent types. Each of those has a dedicated team of entrepreneurs behind it. Yet with increasingly strict regulations and pharmaceutical giants growing more aggressive, many thousands of entrepreneurs fail before even the patent stage: just 2% secure revenue or adoption.

Healthtech Innovation: How Entrepreneurs Can Define and Build the Value of Their New Products is a down-to-earth survival guide for entrepreneurs struggling to secure a strategic position within the Healthtech ecosystem. Which is expected that by 2026, the global digital health market size will be around $657 billion. This book is designed to help innovators navigate this complex and newly volatile landscape. It covers business strategy, marketing, funding acquisition, and operation in a global regulatory context. It is written in simple language, evidenced by the latest academic and industry research, and explained using real-world examples and case studies.

Healthtech Innovation
How Entrepreneurs Can Define and Build the Value of Their New Products

Silvia Micalo

A PRODUCTIVITY PRESS BOOK

First published 2023
by Routledge
605 Third Avenue, New York, NY 10158

and by Routledge
4 Park Square, Milton Park, Abingdon, Oxon, OX14 4RN

Routledge is an imprint of the Taylor & Francis Group, an informa business

ISBN: 9781032347936 (hbk)
ISBN: 9781032347912 (pbk)
ISBN: 9781003323860 (ebk)

DOI: 10.4324/b23147

Typeset in Adobe Garamond
by KnowledgeWorks Global Ltd.

I dedicate this book with all my love to Morten. Who has always been with me, believed in me and supported me unconditionally. To him for being an extraordinary man and the best life partner. Without him, this would not have been possible.

Contents

PART THREE GROWTH

About the Author

Educated at the Autonomous University of Barcelona, **Silvia Micalo** is a biotechnologist with over 15 years of professional experience in different divisions (marketing and commercial, R&D&I and digital transformation). She has held managerial positions within high performance teams in the pharmaceutical industry at companies such as Wyeth, Novartis, Ipsen Pharma, Thea, Lundbeck and Johnson & Johnson.

Currently, she is CEO and founder of Sunshine Oxygen, an international healthtech company focused on the healthcare and healthtech ecosystems. Besides launching a pipeline of healthtech SaaS and digital therapeutics products, the company offers an advisory service to entrepreneurs in the healthtech community and runs an institution that teaches entrepreneurship skills to start-ups.

Highly focused on performance excellence, Micalo creates and develops value-innovative projects involving key stakeholders in the healthcare environment (the pharmaceutical industry, healthtech startups, public health authorities and patient associations), and she regularly shares her expertise as a global speaker.

Micalo excels at designing strategies and implementing profitable marketing tactics, and she has a broad experience in successfully leading business and brand roadmaps. She has driven multiple successful products go-to-markets and strategic re-launches, and she has redirected product life cycles in the healthcare and healthtech environments towards success, sharing her services with different pharmaceutical companies and private healthcare institutions.

As part of her career, Micalo has been an integral member of the Comité de Marketing Farmacéutico from the Club de Marketing de Barcelona and Associate Professor at the University of Girona. Also, she is a speaker for the Pharmaceutical Marketing Masterclass to students of the Master's in Management and Business Administration at the University of Girona.

In the entrepreneurship field, Micalo has been a jury member of a healthtech startup contest and participated as a board member in pharmaceutical laboratories and healthtechs acting as an advisor.

Alongside her entrepreneurship at Sunshine Oxygen, Micalo provides high-level strategic advice and acts as Board Advisor to several international pharmaceutical and healthtech companies at national and international levels.

Introduction

Today, over 500,000 medical technologies are available in hospitals, homes, and community-care settings. They range from simple bandages through to complex, multi-part body scanners that cost millions of dollars to develop (MedTech Europe, 2020). Yet a typical technology has a lifecycle of just 21 months before an improved product usurps it—the healthcare ecosystem is rapidly advancing and driven by a constant flow of innovation.

And those innovations need innovators.

This book is for those change-makers—you who are entrepreneurs, inventors, and disruptors of the status quo, who wish to build the future of healthcare. Your craft is healthtech, the state of the art in healthcare. You build software and technology that creates bridges of value between stakeholders in the healthcare ecosystem to improve health outcomes, advance patients' standard of care, and progress our society.

Yet yours is a competitive and volatile industry. Spurred by COVID-19 and the $21 billion made available for investment in the digital healthcare industry in 2020 (a 20x increase on 2010), entrepreneurs, investors, and related actors are entering the healthcare ecosystem in greater numbers than ever before. Last year alone, over 17,000 medical technology patents were filed, the third highest of all patent types including semiconductors and audio-visual tech (WIPO, 2021). Yet with increasingly strict regulations and pharmaceutical giants growing more aggressive, many thousands of entrepreneurs fail before even the patent stage.

This book is your survival guide for navigating this complex and exciting landscape of limitless digital possibilities. It covers business strategy, marketing, funding acquisition, and operation in a global regulatory context. And importantly, it is written in simple language, dispensing with the complex jargon so common in the healthcare, technology, and marketing environments. It picks crystal-clear expressions to teach valuable insights. Further, each insights is evidenced by the latest academic and industry research and explained using real-world examples and case studies.

Given how fast the industry advances, the book is also forward-looking. It covers the latest subjects and vanguard thinking to make the reader competitive in the emerging Healthcare 5.0 ecosystem, where the new normal is "no patient left behind".

This is an ecosystem where humans are at the centre, empowered by your technology. The circular economy drives sustainability in this system, meaning an autonomous and empowered patient earns early diagnosis and key prevention measures rather than depending on late-stage, costly interventions.

The idea is simple: there is no pathology burden if there is no pathology happening.

At no other time has the patient been so responsible for maintaining and improving their own health and quality of life. Yet it will be your technology that enables them to do so. Predictive and preventive medicine is becoming the major force in the sustainability movement, and healthtech entrepreneurs must learn how to engage with that narrative to thrive.

As with most talents, entrepreneurial hearts have much to say and big value to bring. This book is your guide to making successful contributions to the healthcare system—to becoming unstoppable drivers of progress focused on the wellbeing of tomorrow's patient.

When I think of innovative entrepreneurship, I often compare it with the clinical practice of a doctor. So often they seem to have a sixth-sense intuition when seeing a patient, coming up with an amazing and accurate diagnosis in just a few minutes. But what appears to be intuition is in fact a convergent judgement supported by thousands of experiences in clinical problem solving—a reapplication of lessons learned to a novel situation (Kahneman, 2013).

Looking at this healthcare professional, with their intuition and background of experiences—their personal sacrifices and lengthy journey in pursuit of saving lives—we find the foundation of the personalised and precision medicine of the future. And we find the foundation of healthtech entrepreneurship, too.

Such professionals have provided the clinical records of patient history, the blueprints for treatment, and the ethics of their craft. Their very career and the sum of their experiences plus those of countless other excellent healthcare professionals today form the big data on which AI-supported medicine depends to transform the whole healthcare sector (McKinsey, 2020).

Healthtech learns from our healthcare professionals, trying to combine, recreate and advance their expertise in the digital world. It brings intuition based on crowds of experience to give a truthful and reliable diagnosis, sometimes after a simple specialist glance.

But alongside the advanced technology, we must remember the more traditional elements of medicine in this emerging frontier. We remember the caretakers and caregivers, nurses and patient-oriented care communities that for centuries have given their time attending to and helping innumerable patients. Their work has perhaps had the most impact on individual lives and integrating their efforts into the technological advances of Healthcare 5.0 will be crucial.

Just as important to healthtech is the history of medicine. From the old sages of yesteryear and the inherited formulations of shamanic tribes to the invention of revolutionary drugs like Fleming's penicillin or the tech-enabled method for discovering new Active Pharmaceutical Ingredients (APIs) at high speed—all have contributed to the development of modern medicine and our current quality of life. And we can learn much from this history of innovation going forward.

So healthtech entrepreneurship must embody all three pillars of knowledge: the history of the craft, the experience of its professionals, and the technology of its future. It is therefore holistic (Auyang, 1999).

Nowadays, high-performance holistic medicine is enabled by the convergence of human and artificial intelligence (Topol, 2019). And nowhere was this more apparent than during the COVID-19 pandemic.

We were able to develop a COVID-19 vaccine in record time thanks to the current and prospective computational methodology (Hwang, et al., 2021). From the same technology, we can develop drugs and therapies for different diseases (Pigozzo, Macedo, Santos, & Lobosco, 2013). And more than this, we are starting to predict in-silico clinical trial results with no patients by testing the therapy options of digital twins of real patients to identify the individually optimal therapy (Schueler, 2021), (Nikles, Daza, McDonald, Hekler, & Schork, 2021). And technology is already determining the active ingredients responsible for the personalised treatments of the future, through technologies such as next-generation sequencing (Shah, et al., 2019).

So, ours is a revolutionary time to be a healthtech entrepreneur. Yet to innovate—to fly—we must have our runway secured and our flight chart prepared. We must know the ecosystem in which we will operate, its stakeholders, and its regulations, and we must know how to build our business in a way that is innovative, scalable, and secure. This is Healthtech innovation. How Entrepreneurs Can Define and Build the Value of their New Products. It is strategy, method, and growth—three parts.

Part One: "How to", or Strategy

"How to" forms the first part of the book. It provides the building blocks of a sustainable strategy for entrepreneurs to succeed in the healthtech ecosystem.

Chapter 1 introduces the landscape of the healthtech community, enabling you to orientate your business within the ecosystem and participate alongside its stakeholders. This involves an explanation of natural selection in healthtech—how companies emerge and compete among one another—industry growth, industry opportunities, and the major players in the industry. It also covers wider healthcare trends, such as the democratisation of healthcare and the circular economy.

Chapter two explores the person at the centre of the new landscape: the patient. Healthcare now operated according to the patient-centred healthcare model, meaning all your innovations must be built to offer the patient value first. The chapter also explores the technology enabling this patient centricity, the translational medicine model, and the building of the new patient profile in a digital world.

Chapter three considers the first steps of planning your business model and securing your strategic position in the ecosystem. It shows how to nurture and sustain a desirable relationship along the expansive bridges and alliances between the key stakeholders operating in the healthtech ecosystem. These processes, principles and techniques are much needed for consolidating our understanding of the particularities of the health business and its mode of operating.

Overall, the goal of Part One is to enable you to feel, think, see and speak in the new digital health ecosystem. You will be able to understand and make yourself understood. And consequently, you will be able to plan a key role in the disruption process because you will know how to add true value (Blokdyk, 2019) and locate yourself within the supply chain (Snyder & Shen, 2019).

Importantly, the how-to will allow you to align your potential value with real unmet needs in healthcare (Cahan, Hernandez-Boussard, Thadaney-Israni, & Rubin, 2019). You will get insights enabling you to navigate the healthcare ecosystem comfortably and safely, focusing on the procurement of a problem-solving methodology and strategic thinking. In other words, it should provide you with a solid strategic mindset to build your position in the ecosystem and contribute toward the new healthcare model's standard of care.

Part Two: "Learn", or Method

The second part of the book gives operational guidance for your entrepreneurial path. It is a breakdown of the core practical skills you will need to create your business and innovate your product.

Chapter 4 starts with the heart of your business: your value. This is what distinguishes your healthtech from those that will fail to secure success. Without true value, stakeholders in the healthcare ecosystem have no reason to engage with you, nor will patients demand your treatments. This begins with research and development and prioritising your investments. Then, when your value is defined and you are trialling products, you must build credibility among the community of stakeholders with evidence-based medicine (EBM). Finally, you must protect your value, through both patenting and other tech-enabled methods.

Once you have built your value, you must market it. No patient can use your healthtech to treat their pathology unless they are aware of and can access your product. Therefore, chapter five covers how to explain your value, monetisation, versatile marketing strategies, dressing your healthtech, social media, neuro-, inbound and data-driven marketing, and emerging marketing trends.

Closely linked to value and marketing is your stakeholder ecosystem. Part of creating and marketing your value is knowing to whom your product will be useful and know with whom you must collaborate and onboard into your circle. Accordingly, chapter six covers building a sense of community, mapping stakeholders, onboarding stakeholders, how to collaborate, and networking in the golden triangle.

In essence, planned for success, this second part of the book will enable you to implement the strategy. Thus, the book provides direct and indirect methodologies and tactics, extending a helping hand with the author's own stories and experiences, drawn from her extensive practical knowledge in the healthtech innovation area. And above all, the book offers practical case studies with which the reader can hopefully identify.

Part Three: "To Fly", or Growth

Having explored the core methods and techniques to start a healthtech company, Part Three looks to the bigger picture. Primarily, it offers inspiration for fulfilling global healthcare goals and expanding your business. To drive your enterprise to success, you need a bird's-eye view of the different continents and their optimal ecosystems, best-practice initiatives and ongoing projects with which you can engage.

This begins in chapter seven with expanding your vision and goals. This chapter covers some of the latest trends in healthcare, offering insights and possible avenues of exploration for you to travel down. It also covers advanced monetising, decision-making, building community and sustainability, continuous R&D, and growth drivers.

Subsequently, chapter eight covers fundraising and team building, two critical facets of sustainable growth.

Finally, chapter nine looks at the healthcare model from a global perspective, providing a regional overview of the latest projects and initiatives changing healthcare in different parts of the world. Digital Health Diplomacy is a core part of this overview.

The book then concludes with a call to trust your inner voice, your gut calls, and your purpose to push forward in creating valuable healthtech solutions. It emphasises a global vision of the present and future of healthtech built around sustainability and the circular economy.

I hope that this last part is the call to action that inspires your inner self. Indeed, the healthtech and healthcare environments—the future of health—need your contribution.

I hope you find success in Healthtech Innovation. How Entrepreneurs Can Define and Build the Value of Their New Products. I hope you recognise your own feathers and flaws, your courage and unique skills. With them, apply this new methodology and take flight within the digital healthcare ecosystem.

STRATEGY

I

Chapter 1

The New Healthcare Landscape

The goal of any country's healthcare system, privately or publicly funded, is to set up strategies and actions to improve the standard of health for citizens. Its institutions and services are the caretakers of the population, raising its life expectancy and quality of life.

Once, that model was mature. It was unidirectional and built around the traditional process of diagnosis and treatment of diseases, and it was dominated by the traditional major players: healthcare professionals, pharmaceutical companies and hospitals. Yet the model is rapidly changing as new technology enables patients to take command of their own healthcare journey, as prevention and early diagnosis replace pills and as healthcare moves from the hospital into our homes and our everyday lives.

As healthtechs, we are enablers of that change. We are companies spurred by advances such as automation, artificial intelligence, machine learning, blockchain, the Internet of Medical Things (IoMT), Big Data and other best-in-class technologies. Regardless of whether we are running a B2B, a B2C or a B2B2C or anything else, "we" as healthtechs operate in an environment filled with disruptive potential thanks to the near-limitless possibilities of the digital universe. For this, we should feel gratitude, opening ourselves up to all the possibilities of progress, but we should also feel a sense of responsibility—because we hold the future of healthcare in our hands.

It is irrelevant whether you are the owner of a healthtech, the owner of the key piece of technological architecture on which the potential of a healthtech relies or you are a front-end developer. You are on board for a major purpose: to change the game. And we—you, me and all of us—have a major responsibility to disrupt the healthcare model and push together for progress.

We face the very first stages of what could be called a rebirth of the healthcare environment, and we are bringing the necessary oxygen for it to survive and thrive.

But we already know this. And fortunately, we are not alone as innovators who depend on this technological revolution. Entrepreneurship constitutes a worldwide community growing every day. In 2020, Global Entrepreneurship Index (GEI) scores improved by 3% from 2019. These scores could add $7 trillion to global Gross Domestic Product (GDP) because institutions that support entrepreneurs also positively impact the economy (Acs, Szerb, & Lloyd).

DOI: 10.4324/b23147-2

We have also seen in 2020 a 22% increase in Product Innovation scores since the 2017 GEI, and an 11% increase in Startup Skills scores since the 2017 GEI. This suggests that the global population is becoming more educated and identifying more opportunities to create new products (Acs, Szerb, & Lloyd).

The general surge in entrepreneurship and innovation is being felt directly by the healthcare industry. In 2019, the global digital health market was worth an estimated $175 billion. With an expected compound annual growth rate (CAGR) of almost 25% from 2019 to 2025, the digital health market should reach nearly $660 billion by 2025. And over the last decade, investor funding in the digital health industry has increased significantly. In 2020, over $21 billion was invested in the industry, compared to around $1 billion in 2010 (Department, 2021).

And the phenomenon is global, though particularly advanced in the West. In the US alone, for example, the total market is predicted to reach $90 billion by 2022, of which around $44 billion is expected to be generated by the digital health submarket (Stewart, US Digital health Market Size by technology forecast, 2014–2024, 2018).

Europe, too, is one of the healthtech capitals of the world (Control, 2016), beaten only by the US. In Europe, healthtech has seen more than +25% growth since 2015 (SVB_Financial, 2019), representing around €120 billion in 2018 and 7.4% of the total expenditure in healthcare in 2018 (MedTech Europe, 2020). All in all, there are more than 32,000 healthtech companies in Europe, and 63% of the active ones have been built in the last five years (MedTech Europe, 2020). These European healthtech startups had a combined value of $41 billion (Stewart, Value of healthtech startups in Europe in 2021, by segment, 2021).

China, Saudi Arabia and in some cases India and Russia are becoming forerunners, too (Parmar, 2019). So, this is a global landscape that is undergoing significant change.

Such a thought might be daunting at first. We are building up a whole new health model that will truly impact the wellbeing of patients worldwide. We are all raising a new player, a new healthtech company or healthtech product or service, and this player must occupy and consolidate the right position within this hugely fluctuating healthcare framework. Only then can our healthtechs leverage their maximum potential and advance the current healthcare system (Press, 2002). First, then, we must understand the latest trends in the healthcare landscape.

The Circular Economy

A primary driving force of the new healthcare landscape is a desire to achieve a circular economy within the architecture of the healthcare model. Indeed, this has been a goal for the World Health Organization (WHO) since 2018, and it is one of the pillars of the current European Union (EU) guidelines. Unlike a traditional linear economy, which takes natural resources, makes them into products and then disposes of them as waste, the circular economy closes the loop, designing products from the beginning that are intended to be reused, recycled and redistributed within the economy to achieve climate change and sustainability goals.

Healthtech is impacting the whole healthcare ecosystem by reducing the costs, both financial and human, of advancing this sustainable future. We are breaking with the well-known vertical economy of pick up, produce and consume. We must therefore strive to grow sustainably, within a sustainable business model, as we play in a limitless ecosystem. The concept of a circular economy offers an avenue to sustainable growth, good health and decent jobs, while saving the environment and its natural resources.

When considering how the circular economy could be implemented in healthtech, a battery of concepts such as globalisation, recycling and sustainability arise that, at first sight, appear to have nothing to do with healthcare. Yet the circular economy on which we should base our business models is no more than a simple and common-sense model of efficient and sustainable production and consumption: give back the value you take and take only the minimum that you need. As the 2018 WHO guidelines state, the "circular economy of our healthtech business plans should pursue sustained growth over the time based on sustainable business models. In other words, early diagnosis, optimization of patient journeys and improved Real-World Evidence (RWE) of healthcare outcomes" (WHO, 2018).

As a healthtech, you should prioritise those three core concepts above all else when forming your business strategy. To do this we must shift from using solely key performance indicators (KPIs) to track the return on our investment, to also using sustainability performance indicators (SPIs). This last SPIs, for example in supply chain emissions goals, as it is the case of Global tech companies that need to achieve 100% renewable energy across their supply chain by 2030 (Greenpeace 2022).

Embracing multidimensional indicators is essential for expanding the circular economy's core values, which will include environmental, social and economic measures of sustainability (Saeed & Kersten, 2017). Sustained growth must increase output without using more resources, which is very difficult in other environments or markets where the resources are in most cases finite or single use. But in the digital and technological world, this becomes possible because resources are comparatively limitless.

But simple though the idea is, we need to think out of the box when we try to expand the sustainable value matrix of our products. They must align with a holistic approach and represent an immediate win-win for all the key stakeholders involved. Also important is the long-term win-win, considering the objectives of the health plans of the different regions. Some regions, for example, are prioritising early diagnosis, aiming to prevent pathologies rather than waste resources treating them (i-PROGNOSIS, 2021).[1] Bringing value to the system, including the public healthcare authorities and private institutions like insurance companies, means considering the payers as key stakeholders and containing global costs. That is so whether they are direct costs associated with the treatment itself, maybe through easing the way of administration or indirect like diminishing the burden of caretakers like nurses.

In healthtech, the prevailing commercial model is unfit. It is, as Boston Consulting Group puts it, "analogous to milkmen delivering milk in a world dominated by megastores". Indeed, according to Boston Consulting Group's recent research, the healthtech industry's outdated commercial model suffers from exorbitantly high costs hidden by other exorbitant gross margins. There is therefore considerable room for commercial development of the industry, pursuing a more sustainable approach. The most recent and important highlights of progress beyond the milkman model are value-based healthcare, digitisation and costs containment strategies including pricing, reimbursement and big changes in buying processes (BCG, 2013).

For example, companies can have a significant impact and increase revenues by 2%–3% annually by applying digital technology to a company's go-to-market model (Soderlund et al., 2012). Gartner, in 2020, conducted research on the "unprecedented commercialization model disruption" that life science companies were facing due to COVID-19 (Exeevo, 2021). Indeed, it suggests companies being forced to rapidly transition their digital initiatives from the planning stage to the implementation stage. And its Hype Cycle for Life Science and Commercial Operations,

[1] For example, i-prognosis.eu/# is an initiative towards this very early diagnosis adoption curve.

which tracks the maturity levels and adoptions rates of new technologies that it expects to yield the highest revenue growth and commercial efficiency gains, has undergone significant change. For example, it now highlights advanced decision support for sales, Artificial Intelligence (AI) in commercial operations, cloud computing, consent and preference management, conversational chatbots for analytics, data lakes, predictive analytics, remote patient monitoring and several other areas as key profiles of innovation in the next 10 years.

So what is the major problem? That the health authorities and health insurances cannot pay for all the health needs of all the citizens. Yet there is a new request for improved, standardised care and management of care across a patient's whole pathology lifecycle. In other words, new health-tech products need to bring value in lowering the total health expenditure costs while improving clinical outcomes. Consequently, the economy of health and the basis of the circular economy must be to optimise the patient journey, going from prevention and early diagnosis to a better prognosis. It is about, for example, detecting cancer when the first carcinogen cell appears rather than in the late stage.

Is this approach possible? In some cases.

In the example of cancer, we first need to develop the right biomarkers, those able to detect this carcinogenic cell (Badve & Kumar, 2019). They must become efficient enough so that they can label this cell in the very early stages of its development. However, the more important contributor to a circular economy model would be to enable an early diagnosis with a daily monitoring technology that we integrate into a home device for patients, creating in-home self-prevention diagnosis kits. This early monitoring and diagnosis saves expenditure throughout the treatment pipeline.

So, the circular economy will rely on patient journey optimisation, narrowing the gap between early diagnosis and improved pathology outcomes. Therefore, we must empower every single person so that they can become responsible for their own healthcare condition. Examples of strategies that can be applied to reach this goal are: AI healthtech-based self-referral, personalised outreach, behavioural change, AI facilitated care and device monitoring.

There is no better way to contain health expenditure than preventing the pathology. As Chapter 2 will explore, this movement towards optimising the patient journey is not only helping to create a circular economy, but it is also contributing towards a new healthcare model that places an empowered patient at its centre.

Digitalisation

Apart from a shift towards the circular economy, the healthcare ecosystem is experiencing a second seismic shift in its architecture: digitalisation. Cybercitizens or netizens (citizens of the internet) are growing in number. There are approximately 4.66 billion active internet users world-wide—59.5% of the global population. Of this total, 92.6% (4.32 billion) access the Internet via mobile devices (Statista, 2021). In other words, most of the worldwide population are potential new cyber patients—patients who are diagnosed by means of computer networks.

The COVID-19 crisis has revealed and catalysed this shift towards digitalisation (see Figure 1.1), with lockdowns and a global pandemic providing an urgent need for distanced healthcare. For example, while in 2019 telehealth represented 11% of overall healthcare, we are now at rates of 76% of interest in using telehealth going forward (McKinsey, 2021).

In overcoming these initial barriers—including the initial scepticism towards digital health-care that many patients had—we have seen how the industry can reshape itself towards the future,

Figure 1.1 Infographics explaining the jump of the healthtech ecosystem due to COVID-19 impact.

building capabilities for the next challenges. Indeed, tele-behavioural health has become an effective alternative to in-person care (Lazur et al., 2020).

As healthtechs, we are the vehicles for that change. As creators of this forward-looking industry, we must be more versatile, competitive and able to forecast disruption before it happens.

In response to the sense of urgency inherited from COVID-19, and in response to the explosion of technological advances in recent years including artificial intelligence systems, Big Data, virtual reality tools, wearable medical devices, telehealth and 5G mobile technology, many fields, including the healthcare system, have undergone a complete and rapid digital transformation. This is creating a huge demand for digital skills from all stakeholders operating in the ecosystem, including our healthtech companies. Such highly skilled people can understand the digital and technological languages, and they are becoming leaders in the industry.

Consequently, healthtech companies need to strategically enable their teams to thrive in this new digital landscape. We have a huge responsibility for building this battery of skills throughout the ecosystem to help reach the mature healthcare model.

Starting from the base, the key stakeholders in the healthcare ecosystem need to be able to understand the technological solutions that we are presenting. They need to become familiar with the new digital framework because it allows communication with one another easily and in a standardised way, steepening the adoption curve and letting industry players grow together quickly and keep up with the constant disruption.

In 2021, the European Commission presented a vision and avenues for Europe's digital transformation by 2030, evolving around four cardinal points: skills, infrastructures, business and government (Commission, 2021). For business, such as healthtechs, this includes targets that 75% of EU companies will be using the cloud, AI and Big Data by the end of the decade. To secure funding and a good strategic position in this emerging digital healthcare environment, your healthtech must embrace these targets and capitalise on these digital opportunities. For example, the European Commission expects 100% of citizens to have access to digital records; and it is already becoming a reality.

Importantly, much of the data already exists to enable these opportunities, and strategies are being enacted to promote their use. Such is the case of China, which has set a goal to complete a nationwide interoperable health information system that allows healthcare facilities to share residents' healthcare information (Owusu-Marfo et al., 2019). In Russia, Moscow's government launched the Unified Medical Information and Analytical System of Moscow (EMIAS) as a major project as part of its electronic healthcare initiative (EMIAS, 2021).

In the US, The Health Information Technology for Economic and Clinical Health Act (HITECH) sets meaningful use of interoperable Electronic Health Records (EHR) adoption in the healthcare system as a critical national goal and incentivises it. Nationwide Health Information Network (NHIN), an initiative for exchange of healthcare information, has been developed under the auspices of the US Office of the National Coordinator for Health Information Technology (ONC) (HealthIt.gov, 2021) (Sissel, 2021). The EU is also in line with the European Commission adopting a recommendation on a European electronic health record exchange format to unlock the flow of health data across borders (Commission, 2021).

Most countries are only just starting to integrate different adoption models to collect, fuse and use the data with AI. But they will accelerate their developments to track and optimise the standard of care and robotise the decisions currently taken by humans. All this will improve the patient's quality of life and present enormous opportunities for healthtechs.

But while free access to patient clinical records, population data and private information like genetic codes offers incredible potential, it is also difficult to manage. Healthtechs consequently bear great responsibility and must work closely with health authorities and regulators to ensure we are intelligently and safely processing the data within the IoMT after all, it is here to stay.

The IoMT is creating thousands of centres for data collection, bringing us colossal amounts of data that can be used to create services and products. This is geographically based, and so can be geographically targeted—again both a boon and a concern. We are bringing computation and data storage closer to the patient to improve response times and save bandwidth. But the more we collect, the more intelligent we must be to come up with smart conclusions. We are still not beyond the need for human interaction. Only when we can translate this data onto the right solution and strategically place it in the ecosystem to drive the progress healthcare does the value of data become clear.

Ultimately, continuous ethical decision-making is essential in disruption. Our healthtech businesses must continually strive to preserve our humanity. In the face of algorithms that increasingly try to make decisions for us based on efficiency and performance, we must more than ever remember the ethical side of the equation.

High-Value Care, from Smart Cities to Smart Health

Another important shift in the healthcare landscape, linked with the circular economy and digitalisation, is the new high-value care (HVC) standards. The growing demand for transparency around price, quality and safety is driving the integration of data-driven healthcare systems. It is estimated that by the end of 2025, a growth of 34% (since 2017) of global healthcare spending will be associated with some sort of value-based care models reaching $6.4 billion. (Singh A. et al. 2017)

These aim to connect smart cities, smart hospitals and smart healthtech environments (Health, 2021). HVC involves restructuring healthcare delivery towards the measurable, high-impact outcomes that matter most to patients. This is a transition from the previous healthcare industry orientation, which focused on paying for services rather than outcomes. HVC, however, would enable healthcare to embrace every person and onboard them onto the standard of care they deserve, leaving no patient behind. This broad network of public and private collaboration should elevate behavioural care in particular, which integrates knowledge in the biological, behavioural, psychological and social sciences into healthcare practices.

Smart Cities

We have many apps available on our smart devices. But imagine a whole network of seamlessly interconnected devices communicated and working together, built into the infrastructure of entire cities. This could make companies look beyond single-application wearables.

Currently, most healthtech solutions work as independent technologies, but what would happen if we could group all these services into clusters of integrated technologies? What if we could match different apps coming from different tools in terms of care? That is the dream, yet right now we have apps from the personal side, from leisure, bureaucratic platforms, lifestyle, career fields and other entities that work separately.

The new frontier will amalgamate the insights from these apps into one single platform that allows us to be holistically attended to on a full-time daily basis. This idea offers great possibilities, of course, but also drawbacks—data sharing or the monopolisation of care, for example.

Another major concern is the commercialisation of care. We, as normal people, go to the cinema, to the theatre, we spend our time gaming, we read books, we practice sport, we eat—all covered and provisioned by different kinds of independent services limited only by the consumer's wealth. The truth is that our own pocket is what conditions our freedom, and our access to high standards of healthcare, even in those countries with universal healthcare.

However, by clustering and grouping all these services to control networks of solutions, in an integrated way rather than monopolised by one company, governments might intervene and facilitate funding and regulation around this umbrella of services.

We are already used to attending virtual life events to receive care; this is a 1:1 human interaction enabled by technology. Further development in this area of information and communication technologies (ICT) could improve the standard of care, especially when integrated into municipal infrastructure and combined with mobile devices and machine learning.

Although best healthtech practices in smart cities are still unavailable, we can already look at maps of pathologies considering hot spots by number of social media posts published in certain timeframes and locations (Einspänner-Pflock et al., 2014). These are the infant steps of healthtech vehiculated by mobile health (mHealth), which is a medical practice enabled by mobile devices (Sasan, 2015). We could soon see upgrades to beacons[2] and commonly allocated ambient sensors managed by ambient intelligence (Mastorakis, Mavromoustakis, & Pallis, 2015), walkability[3] (Al-Qemaqchi & Abdullah, 2017), allowing smart city infrastructures (Cook et al., 2018) (De, Bharti, Technology, & Chellappan, 2015).

---

[2] A beacon or Bluetooth beacon is a hardware transmitter – a class of Bluetooth low energy (LE) device that broadcasts its identifier to nearby portable electronic devices. The technology enables smartphones, tablets and other devices to perform certain actions when in close proximity to a beacon.

[3] Walkability is how easy is an area for walking. It is directly related to health, environmental and economic benefits, as it directly impacts climate change. Walkability is a key concept of sustainable urban design for smart cities.

Overall, in a post-COVID world, this would see the improvement of healthcare effectiveness and containment of healthcare costs for smart city citizens. And it would promote equity of access to facilities via digitisation and the creation of smart healthcare hubs. For example, if we focus on walkability, which is directly related to health, environmental and economic benefits, small changes in main neighbourhoods could make a big difference.

We could, say, redesign congested streets to be walking-only streets according to each residential cluster, making the city as a whole less car-oriented and more bike- and walking-oriented. And there are many other changes that can be implemented in the near future (Kato H., 2021). This whole process, vehiculated by healthtech, would then snowball, speeding the adoption curves of healthtech solutions.

Some best practices are seeing implementation in founding smart cities like New York, along with wide standardisation (Smartcity, 2017). They are already implementing programmes such as Homeless Outreach & Mobile Engagement Street Action Teams (HOME-STAT) (Teams, s.f.) initiatives, which aims to completely solve homeless by partnering existing homeless response and prevention programmes with new innovations designed to better identify, engage and transition homeless New Yorkers to appropriate services and, ultimately, permanent housing.

Other examples include more healthcare-centred initiatives like the "Accessible mental health challenge" that aims to connect the NYC tech ecosystem, government agencies, local communities, mental health experts and global innovators to address the mental health needs of the city's most vulnerable communities (NYC, 2021).

Technology will drive the creation of these smart cities and our consequent healthier lives. Great advances will focus on the environment, replacing buildings with more eco-friendly ones, bringing plants and vegetation back to the city through implementing green fundamentals in construction. For example, in Europe, the European Commission has proposed a post-pandemic Recovery Plan for Europe focused on a greener, more digital and more resilient society with better preparation for the current and forthcoming challenges (Commission, Recovery plan for Europe, 2021).

This will come together with the improved management of street lighting, water quality and conservation, waste and air quality above all, making a direct, positive impact on the citizens' health.

Why not consider best practices such as the Swedish city Hyllie, the first Smart Prosumer District? Built around the idea of prosumers—people who are both consumers and producers—it is transitioning to a sustainable energy future by having homes both produce and consume energy. And it is linking them together on a micro grid and connecting them to a parallel digital infrastructure that enables different nodes of the energy system to share information with each other (Energy, 2017) (Technology, 2021).

Taking this as a conceptual blueprint, a healthtech might use new approaches like digital contact tracing (DCT) technologies over mobile phones and other smart infrastructures to create live health maps of the city during a pandemic or deal with new health challenges, setting a precedent for smart cities all over the world.

The core technology is already there. For example, Spain's Radar COVID App (DigitalMedical, 2021) was designed and directed by the Secretary of State for Digitalization and Artificial Intelligence to help prevent the spread of the coronavirus (COVID-19). The initiative was based on DCT that used phone apps to make contact tracing and notification between individuals. It has recently been proposed to be a plausible complement of manual contact tracing within the Test, Trace and Isolate (TTI) containment strategy (Rodríguez, 2021).

Another best practice example of using smart city technology to make healthcare smarter is the Singapore Smart Nation Health Program (Singapore S. N. Health, 2021). It is introducing robotics technology to reduce the burden of care for its elderly citizens, and it is promoting initiatives like the National Steps Challenge, which uses a mobile app and tracking technology to encourage healthy walkability across the city (Singapore S. N., 2021). These initiatives are transforming health on a citywide basis.[4]

Smart cities are already a reality. In essence, our whole existence is going to be integrated into smart cities. Our healthcare public buildings will connect with our wellbeing-driven houses, and our walkability initiatives will link in with e-transport systems. It will all come under the big umbrella of a smart city. It is a new model where everything has multiple sensor placements with an associated IP address that emits and collects data on a full-time and real-time basis. All this will impact the new healthcare status quo.

Smart Hospitals

Hospitals have traditionally and are still the centre of the health value chain. From in-hospital to in-patients, in-home or out-of-home integrated services, they remain part of an umbrella approach towards each individual lifestyle.

Yet we are on the edge of witnessing hospitals without walls, hospitals that constitute a digitally connected community rather than a localised physical space. This does not mean the death of the traditional hospital, though, since brand-new hospitals with high-tech infrastructures are also being built. They operate in a paradigm shift, from the IoMT towards the Internet of Beings (IoB) (Lawson, 2019)—the Internet conveyed onto a network of biometric devices, each one smaller and allowing greater interconnectivity (Iaione et al., 2019).

An example of an IoB device is an implantable cardioverter defibrillator (ICD), a small device that is placed in the chest or abdomen. Doctors use the device to help treat irregular heartbeats called arrhythmias and control life-threatening arrhythmias, especially those that can cause sudden cardiac arrest (SCA) (MedlinePlus, 2021).

In another example, AI-powered implants for epilepsy patients, approved by the FDA, significantly reduce the frequency of seizures (Foundation, 2021). Similar implants that can sense and avert impending negative health events could deliver remote monitoring and treatments, along with cost savings in patient care (Deloitte, 2019).

All these components in the shift towards smart hospitals will help fulfil the goals of the circular economy in healthcare, improving early diagnosis and reducing the cost of treating or managing pathology.

We and our partners in the tech and health fields must each collaborate and integrate with these new types of "hospitals". And overall, these shifting levels of care, which depend on huge quantities of patient data, must find purchase with regulators and healthcare authorities, such as the European Medicines Agency, that will ultimately establish the legal framework (EMA, 2019). And we must learn to navigate this landscape as healthtechs symbiotically with hospitals and their administrators.

---

[4] Also, South Korea, with the programme Smart City Korea (Ministry of Land, 2021), could be taken as a country's best-practice for fostering smart cities on behalf of the quality of life for citizens, enhancing the sustainability of cities, and fostering new industries by utilising the innovative technologies of the Fourth Industrial Revolution (Smartcities, 2020). Some national smart city pilots are the Sejong 5-1 Living Area (Ministry of Land, 2021) and Busan Eco Delta Smart City (Government K., 2021), having launched a smart city special regulations system for special cases.

In such an uncertain environment, a successful healthtech will focus on the patients' needs. It is a matter of covering the customer needs and improving their quality of life according to their lifestyle. Bluetooth low energy (BLE) locators, beacons, robotisation of procedures, sensors—all this will be on an integrative network that meets the remaining hospitals and integrates new smart hospitals and smart points of care.

In terms of coordination of teams, we must prepare our mindset for disruptive digitalisation within hospitals: the settling of units of integrated care, blueprinted data sharing, and data feedback integrated on a whole network of cloud computing.

Wearables and m-health, permitting patient support programs (PSP) that monitor patients daily, track, collect data, advise and recommend treatment and send reminders about upcoming appointments with the doctor, are already healthcare commodities in-use by hospitals.

Other m-health devices focus on screening, diagnosis and treatment like KardiaMobile (AliveCor, 2021), a device for taking a medical-grade electrocardiograms (ECG), clinically validated, that attaches to the back of mobile devices like iPhones and Androids. It tracks heart activity and transmits the activity to a mobile app through chest and finger sensors.

These healthtech solutions release the burden of hospitals and make them operatively optimised and more efficient. Another example is Owlet Bands, a new wearable band for pregnant women that monitors heart rates, kick counts and other neonatal indicators.

As healthtechs, integrating our solutions within this expanding realm of the "hospital" is crucial. Introducing care smart solutions to hospitals, pre-validated and integrating them in the hospital's standard functioning network will produce higher-quality healthcare with minimal service disruption.

And the traditional hospital building is also changing, seeing the introduction of advanced medical equipment and machinery. For example, along with digitalisation, robotisation is allowing doctors to perform many types of complex procedures with more precision, flexibility and control through robot-assisted surgeries. Such is the case of the Da Vinci Robot (Intuitive, 2021). Receiving FDA approval in 2000, it became the first surgical robot in the US.

So smart automation in hospitals is already taking place with a wide portfolio of ad-hoc solutions. One example is the concept produced by Siemens (Siemens, 2021). Seeking to reduce labour and operating costs, enable work and space efficiency and comply with changing regulations while bolstering patient experience, it is introducing smart hospital management systems that can monitor 800,000 data points enabling critical infrastructure to run smoothly, real time location services, energy performance technology and enhanced fire safety and security services. Siemens in turn is also the owner of Siemens Healthineers, a healthtech spinoff created in 2016.[5]

Another example is artificial Intelligence permitting AI-powered temperature sensors for screening staff and patients, such as the recent iThermo (KroniKare, 2021).[6] It reduces the need for manual temperature screening and saves time and manpower with the convenient, accurate and low-cost solution.

Primarily, these changes are impacting patient treatment. Smart hospitals are seeing new operating tools, such as intelligent intensive care units (ICU) for autonomous patient monitoring using

---

[5] A spinoff is the creation of an independent company through the sale or distribution of new shares of an existing business or division of a parent company. The spun-off companies are expected to be worth more as independent entities than as parts of a larger business (Investopedia, 2021).

[6] iThermo, is an AI-powered temperature screening solution. This solution was born from Integrated Health Information Systems (IHiS), the national HIT agency in Singapore, in partnership with local healthcare AI startup KroniKare to pilot iThermo – an AI-powered temperature screening solution that screens and identifies those having or showing symptoms of fever. URL: https://kronikare.ai/ithermo/

pervasive sensing and deep learning (Davoudi, et al., 2019).[7] With intelligent video feeds, they flag patient distress, enabling them to receive attention faster. It uses wearable sensors, light and sound sensors and a camera to collect data on patients and their environment. It then analyses the data to detect and recognise a patient's face, postures, facial action units and expressions, head pose variation, extremity movements, sound pressure levels, light intensity level and visitation frequency.

Aside from treatment, hospitals are advancing their customer service using healthtech. Conversational AI[8] is now used to explain procedures, as in the case of the Ada chatbot (ada, 2021),[9] which empowers businesses to provide personalised experiences at scale. Another example is Kore (kore.ai, 2021)[10] with use cases examples of how virtual assistants can drive cost savings and positively impact healthcare efficiency, improve access to care and reduce burden on clinicians. It can do this by providing smart appointment bookings and reminders that helps a hospital analyse patient behaviour and history to predict no-shows before they happen. It also helps hospitals and clinics to learn from the questions that patients ask to bots so that they can start to provide that information at the point-of-care, instead of forcing patients to search for the information later.

When we think about integrating our solutions into these smart hospital environments, we must vectorise our current silos of data to create new holistic ways of working in multidisciplinary high-performance teams—that is, teams the stretch from our own company to in-setting (in-hospital) stakeholders. In doing so, we can shorten the pathways between stakeholders acting on the patient journey. For example, the patient journey optimisation between the hospital and primary care is a priority, and innovators must push for real-time connection.

Much space for innovation and progress exists in the releasing of personnel from administrative tasks that can be automatised and perfectly digitalised. This will allow staff to spend more time with patients, working on the more traditional humanistic approach to the standard of care, permitting the recovery of lost empathy in the field.

Healthtechs can catalyse this shift from current to smart hospitals by creating solutions that are easily integrated into the wider hospital infrastructure and that staff can utilise without extensive training. The "sell" here is that although it will cost much in the short term to implement, the long-term benefits are exponential in terms of cost optimisation.

Better technologies can create homogeneity in diagnosis and equal access to care for citizens by narrowing divergences in the availability of health solutions. They can also stimulate the growth of more patient-centered jobs in the industry and allow patients to manage their own healthcare decisions, rather than being subject to the tick-box mentality of the current bureaucracy.

We are at the point where predictive technology can take a blood sample and forecast healthy lifespan from a genomic and proteomic perspective, allowing for more precise and personalised treatments. And we are optimising treatment delivery through a personalised dosage of medication and electronic dosing, contributing to a more efficient supply chain and the new model of the circular economy.

This new reality will come fully into existence when hybrid programs and solutions are directly developed and implemented in the hospitals. Starting from the problem and framing the solution

---

[7] https://www.nature.com/articles/s41598-019-44004-w

[8] Conversational AI combines natural language processing (NLP) with traditional software like chatbots, voice assistants, or an interactive voice recognition system to help customers through either a spoken or typed interface. They use large volumes of data, machine learning, and natural language processing to help imitate human interactions, recognising speech and text inputs and translating their meanings across various languages (Education, 2020).

[9] Ada. URL: https://www.ada.cx/

[10] Kore.ai URL: https://kore.ai/solutions/industries/healthcare/

in the hospital. Connecting in-person and digital interaction ending with a minimum viable product that will be tested in the field with a pilot sample and improved along the path.

This will be supported by all-embracing e-health and constant e-learning tools that provide the teams and the users, in this case the patients and caregivers, with the skills to interact through online communities. There, they can validate and obtain feedback on diagnoses, give support and follow up in terms of adherence to treatment.

This process will create a source of information that can act in acute and first-aid levels or with chronic, long-term approaches, helping stakeholders embrace the increasing importance of a healthy lifestyle and achieve a beyond-the-pathology normality (Hawkes, 2013) (Guardian, 2021).

For healthtechs, it is important to embrace the progress of hospitals into smart hospitals, which also means embracing all its smart subsidiaries.

For example, as the smart hospital expands beyond the traditional confines of the hospital building to create the in-home hospital, we must consider the supply chain. Now medicine has a new destination, which depends on new global marketplaces acting locally and requires intelligent shipping. And intelligent shippers are aligning their potential services and responding on a real-time basis to the emerging needs of the new hybrid healthcare systems. This mutual relationship is developing rapidly in some countries, like Ireland's recent intent to create a standardised unichannel shipment network through a drone service that is delivering medicine to the elderly in the region.[11]

Of course, we are still in the very early stages. Teams must be given time to grow, without being rushed, and allowed to make human mistakes while embracing the new technological approach by trial and error. We must permit and encourage pilots of minimum viable products being tested on a full go-to-live basis. Yet the hospital is an immensely promising field for healthtechs to engage.

Smart Information Environments

Alongside the transition to smart hospitals and cities, we find a supporting transition to new smart healthtech information environments based on social cohesion. A Smart Information Environment can be explained as integrated work processes of mediated information technology (IT) enabling a matrix of knowledge.

Thus, our healthcare environments must meet the standards of integrated technologically vehiculated contexts: in other words, crowds of information technology deployed in work processes that in turn facilitate changes in operational forms.

Any healthtech product, procedure and care delivery system can be considered a standard smart information environment, conveying into a matrix of data that results in a higher standard of care. In turn, this will define new health behaviours[12] and roles[13] in the new healthcare frameworks.

Besides, the aim of these smart information environments should be to promote social vitality, which is "the capacity to thrive and change in the pursuit of individual and social wellbeing, in ways that are inclusive and respectful of the needs and aspirations of diverse communities"

---

[11] Drones deliver medicines: https://www.youtube.com/watch?v=tXtX8gtH3oY

[12] Health behaviours can be smoking, physical activity, sleep, preventive health behaviours, illness behaviour, adherence to prescribed drugs, alcohol intake, reduction in stress or anxiety, sense of wellbeing in between others. Heath behaviours can be redesigned through good manage of smart information environments.

[13] New roles can be the intersection of tech and mental health, like offering personalised brain health as a reality for everyone, or to find in-network neighbourhood doctors.

(Canadian Council of Social Development, 2010). Also, good coverage of social vitality indicators (SVI), a measure of urban vitality with three main indicators: social vitality[14], economic vitality[15] and virtual vitality[16], will be the new tracking standards of the new smart healthtech environments (Kim, 2018).[17]

Social vulnerability indicators (SVuI),[18] in turn, can impact the healthcare capacity of universal coverage and its sustainability. An example of their use is the geo-location of health with tools like SVuI Interactive Maps, providing a snapshot of a regions' forecasted health vulnerability. Such is the case of the US interactive map provided by the Agency for Toxic Substances and Disease Registry (ATSDR)[19](ATSDR, 2018).

In parallel we are collecting genomic data that is already enabling products and solutions focused on precision medicine. And the evolution of the patient means they are becoming technologically empowered. This will push us towards communities of more organised patients who are more demanding and more able to manage their requirements and needs along their patient journey, requiring the best treatments and solutions to fill their needs of care.

This shift means interaction with healthcare professionals (HCP) is also changing. They will need to respond on a real-time basis at a high level to patients' highly informed treatment demands. This will narrow the gap between the patient and the HCP, pushing us towards a model of equity where no patient is left behind. Of course, nothing can replace the essence of a clinic-patient face-to-face interaction, so hybrid models will come to the fore.

Health information technology tools (HITTs) will be crucial to this new movement. They are products, services and systems related to information technology that are applied to health and healthcare. They are already facilitating the consolidation of the new smart-health environments not only in developed countries but also in sub-developed.

Such is the case of the Community Level Program Information Reporting for HIV/AIDS Programs (Evaluation, 2021)[20] lead by the MEASURE Evaluation Project (Evaluation Project, 2021)[21] and funded by the US Agency for International Development. The program seeks to improve information systems for community-level programs, supporting stakeholders in identifying their information needs, enhancing their systems for collecting information, and improving data utilisation to bolster program management and program performance. These types of

---

[14] Social vitality refers to walkability based on cell-phone activities.

[15] Economic vitality refers to smart economic transactions.

[16] Virtual vitality refers to WiFi access spots.

[17] Urban vitality is systematically measured in social, economic and virtual dimensions using big data. Although big data in smaller spatiotemporal resolution becomes available for researchers, the quantitative data is limited to understanding the urban complexities (Jacobs, 2011) and the rhythm of everyday life in particular space and time (Lefebvre, 2005). They could be fully understood with the observation of walkalongs, built environments, and atmosphere in various spatial and temporal contexts.

[18] Social vulnerability indicators (SVI) refers to potential negative effects impacting human health on a defined community. This effects can be caused by external factors including natural or human-caused disasters or disease out brakes.

[19] Agency for Toxic Substances and Disease Registry (ATSDR) is a federal public health agency of the US Department of Health and Human Services.

[20] URL: https://www.measureevaluation.org/resources/tools/hiv-aids/clpir.html

[21] The MEASURE Evaluation Project, funded by the United States Agency for International Development, had a mandate to strengthen health information systems (HIS) in low-resource settings. MEASURE Evaluation enabled countries to improve lives by strengthening their capacity to generate and use high-quality health information to make evidence-informed, strategic decisions at local, subregional, and national levels. URL: https://www.measureevaluation.org/about.html

programs drastically improve the quality of data in the healthcare environment, thereby enhancing healthcare professionals' ability to treat patients.

Ultimately, HITTs are embracing standardised remote patient monitoring and integrated electronic health records between all the stakeholders around the pathology and the healthtech environment, allowing data to be collected 24/7 in real time.

One important HITT is geographic information systems (GISs) used by healthcare professionals in the public system to analyse pathology trends (such as diabetes or cancer in the population). They also analyse who is accessing public health infrastructures, helping with the design of community health communication programs (Olofin et al., May 2020). One example is The Truth (Truth, 2021)[22], the anti-smoking public health campaign targeted to teens, which is funded by Truth Initiative, and working to get the facts around smoking (Initiative, 2021).[23]

The new smart healthtech information environment is already a big commodity. Beacons and IP physical devices are playing a key role along with the more technologically proficient profile of the patient.

This creates opportunities for healthtechs, especially in those countries facing digital poverty.

Health data poverty constitutes a risk of creating a digital health divide.[24] The scale of digital exclusion is still significant: in 2018, there were still 5.3 million excluded adults in the UK, 10% of the adult UK population (Statistics, 2021).

In a recent article published in the *Journal of Medical Internet Research*, the authors present a Digital Health Equity Framework in which digital determinants of health interact with other intermediate health factors. The article concludes that, to avoid duplicating the social stratification that exists in society at large, we need to ensure the meaningful involvement of people from marginalised and vulnerable groups in positions of digital health leadership, as health providers, and in codesign at all stages of innovation and implementation, including as stewards of their own health outcome data (Crawford & Serhal, 2020).

With such a need, data-driven digital health technologies have the power to transform healthcare. If these tools could be sustainably delivered at scale, they could provide everyone, everywhere, with equitable access to expert-level care, narrowing the global health and well-being gap (Ibrahim, Liu, Zariffa, Morris, & Denniston, 2021).

So, the barrier of missing data is available for jumping; now is the time to act if we are to counter the emerging digital health divide and build the data infrastructure that means that all parts of society can benefit from digital health solutions.

The New Commodities of Healthcare

One of the final trends affecting the healthcare landscape is a new understanding of what a healthcare commodity is and how it can be developed.

---

[22] The Truth is an anti-smoking 24/7 support network. URL: https://www.thetruth.com/. See also "The Singing Cowboy", The Truth community health communication program's most popular advert. URL: https://www.youtube.com/watch?v=g5CKSff19Ig

[23] Truth Initiative is a US national public health organisation. URL: https://truthinitiative.org/

[24] Health data is defined as personal data concerning health. It should include all data pertaining to the health status of a data subject which reveal information relating to the past, current or future physical or mental health status of the data subject (Consulting, 2021). Health data poverty is the inability for individuals, groups, or populations to benefit from a discovery or innovation due to insufficient data that are adequately representative (Ibrahim, Liu, Zariffa, Morris, & Denniston, 2021).

Standardising healthtech solutions and commoditising them equates to pushing the adoption curve, not only by the patient but also by the ecosystem. Standardising therefore means conforming to guidelines and adapting the new healthtech commodities to current patient lifestyles. For a healthtech solution to reach the status of commodity, it needs to have gone through technological and clinical trials that validate its true value.

Establishing and consolidating the new pillars of the healthcare systems requires speed of transformation and that governing healthcare institutions trust the healthtech solutions. The WHO[25] is the Master of Care. It is the United Nations (UN)[26] of care, and we must rely on its top-down guidelines that are in turn adopted by the institutions under its umbrella.

Governing institutions can push for our technological solutions and give them the seal of approval in the public eye. It is difficult to embrace the whole pipeline of new solutions and products, so what they do is validate the developer rather than every single solution.

This validation process works like a waterfall to cover all the high requirements at the speed requested. And it has a cascading effect on standardising commodities in digital care. When setting up a new digital healthcare commodity, we should consider a collateral cascade effect.

We are already in the governance process of standardising this precision and personalised medicine (Whitsel et al., 2018) (Prainsack, 2017). Let us imagine that we want to evaluate the impact of taking a single pill. Are there any secondary effects that could be diminished? Of course, in terms of precision and personalised medicine, there exists a specific active ingredient for each medical condition at a specific dosage that is the best for each individual.

Maybe the patient could have been prescribed with a different drug or a different treatment solution that could have fitted the overall biometric parameters of his whole body, analysed by biometric sensor technology, through a simple system of a wearable or hearable system. We could switch the treatment at the turning point when the secondary effects have not yet or have only partially arisen?

We are dealing with a level of precision medicine within treatments that was unthinkable a few years ago. Today, we can manage specific diseases or medical conditions at high levels of accuracy. A single pill is impacting the overall life health outcomes and in turn impacting the quality adjusted life years (QALYs). And more than this, we can forecast and predict this impact.

But approaching the available treatment with the perspective that a better cure option might soon be discovered also has a cost. It is a new element that impacts the economic value of healthcare, called "Scientific Spillovers," categorised by the ISPOR task force (Lakdawalla et al., 2021). This concerns the rates of viability of taking a certain pill, in other words, the pros and cons of taking a medicine. More than this, it concerns the rates at a certain stage of the pathology, and at a certain moment of the treatment options pipeline.

Translational medicine (TM) aims to improve the healthcare system (Mittra & Milne, 2013). It is an interdisciplinary branch of the biomedical field supported by three main pillars: benchside, bedside and community. The goal of TM is to combine disciplines, resources, expertise and techniques within these pillars to promote enhancements in prevention, diagnosis and therapies. Accordingly, translational medicine is a highly interdisciplinary field that pursues the coalescence of assets of various natures within the individual pillars in order to improve the global healthcare system significantly (Cohrs et al., 2014).

---

[25] World Health Organization (WHO) URL https://www.who.int/
[26] United Nations (UN) URL https://www.un.org/en/

TM fundamentals should accompany the healthtech entrepreneur in every single step of his journey, since the very first moment of conceptualisation of the product, to be able to understand how the new commodities of the future can be developed.

A core aim in the healthcare system is to reach excellence of care through TM. This means to fully personalise treatment, commoditise it, quantify its viability and adjust the dose on an individual patient level. Healthtech will enable us to reach the standardisation or commoditisation of the genomics and proteomics sciences while meeting the highest standards in prevention, diagnosis and treatment.

And what about having all the interdisciplinary data integrated and recorded in the same platform? With data orchestration, this is already happening. It enables combining and organising siloed data from multiple locations and makes it possible to be analysed, permitting automated and streamlined data-driven decision making (Segment, 2021). In other words, a cloud computing system of all the data collected from all the patients in a certain healthcare system, with immediate and simultaneous access to all the stakeholders involved in the patient journey, is no longer a distant prospect. It is now a reality. In essence, health technologies are already used in every single step of the patient journey and, more than this, in the whole healthcare supply chain automatising and improving resource planning in pharma and medtech, permitting TM and its commoditisation to start becoming a reality.

Chapter 2

The New Patient-Centred Approach

As Chapter 1 showed, the healthcare landscape is rapidly evolving towards the concepts of circular economy, digitalisation and the implementation of TM-based high-value care within our cities, hospitals and information environments. Yet we must also discuss perhaps the most important change to the healthcare environment, which is its new centre: the patient.

We are coming from a paternal, unidirectional model centred on the unique healthcare professional and his management of the pathology. But we are moving towards a new model with an empowered and self-managing patient at the centre.

Many are calling this the Copernican Revolution of medicine (Schutzer M.D, Grady-Benson M.D, Libert & Beck, 2017). The Copernican Revolution was a paradigm shift from the Ptolemaic model of the heavens, which described the cosmos as having Earth stationary at the centre of the universe, to the heliocentric model with the sun at the centre. In turn, the healthcare system was the centre of the previous model, acting as the provider. Now, the patient is the centre of the new model, acting as a customer or the "sun" in the Copernican approach.

Here, a bidirectional approach is the new status quo, and as the first chapter explored, an increasingly digital population is the key. Digital apps can now operate as care centres to patient management. And cyberhealth is transcending health cases management within a cyber-based environment (Busch, 2019). For example, we are now seeing early health coach guidance, and real-life continuous patient follow-up is becoming a new commodity vehiculated through IoMT.

A whole new battery and pipeline of solutions and products is arising and making up the new standard of care, enabling patients to manage their lifestyle and healthcare curves with new technologies. This means the customer is a more informed and empowered as a decision maker: a new stakeholder, impacting the outcomes of his own pathology.

This makes him more demanding. The patient requests and pushes his healthcare professional for access to the best and newest therapies in a kind of peer-to-peer conversation. This was not considered in recent years. It used to be that the doctor knew it all and the counterparty followed his suggestions. Of course, much of this stems from people increasingly using the internet for health information—turning to "Dr. Google" (Gualtieri, 2009).

DOI: 10.4324/b23147-3

And as the patient becomes more instrumental in the process of their care, so they are becoming important purchasers of healthtech solutions. Indeed, patients are adopting our healthtech solutions at an exponential rate. To the tech-proficient patient, new technologies are no longer novelties. They are considered mature products and services that respond to real healthcare needs. In turn, they are becoming commodities early and easily adopted by customers of health. What we are discussing here are medical devices that operate in real time on a 360° holistic basis, and they will be essential to patients' treatment outcomes and for follow-ups.

Consequently, in the new patient-centred model, a healthtech solution is inadequate unless it covers a real unmet need for the patient, rather than a need presumed by the developer. That does not mean a supposed unmet need that you as a healthtech entrepreneur figured out; it means a real patient need, and the only way to identify that is speaking to them. So, in this new healthcare environment, channels of communication direct to the patient will be essential.[1]

Our technology will address the management of chronic conditions, which is a big concern of the current healthcare system, but also key matters for acute conditions and ambulatory patients, which are another focus of the new healthcare reshuffle. For the former, treatment compliance[2] matters the most; while for the latter, treatment incisiveness[3] and speed of treatments key.

These remaining key patient management barriers can be overcome with health technology. For example, a healthtech solution that targets incisiveness helps overcome the barriers to treatment that arise just after a patient is properly diagnosed and properly prescribed. Besides, we are already close to better biomarkers some already digestible (Barh et al., 2017). With their upfront information, we can improve the administration route, or rather than this, evaluate the whole efficiency of the treatment while also considering the adherence to the treatment, bolstering patient compliance through monitoring it.

This is where we, as healthtechs, can bring real value. The first concern of a treatment, the efficiency and safety, relies on the construction of a patient-friendly improvement of the galenical of a medicine. Pushing for the easiest and most friendly administration possible requires the researchers and pharmaceutical industry, and our role here may be limited. But the second part, concerning patient follow-up and treatment compliance, is where we can play a big role.

To remind the patient about the administration of his personalised treatment, we are already engaging the IoMT to enable precision dosing and full-time monitoring of the patient.

In other words, our contribution as healthtechs will impact the whole patient journey, improving the overall health outcomes of the patient. In terms of the treatment, we aim to know if the drug has worked. And we now have the technology to evaluate the responder rates, track its efficacy and monitor for side effects on a real-time individual basis, generating digital notes, automatic digital medical records and performing digital tests.

More so, we can do this on a digital avatar, even before the real patient takes part in the treatment, reproducing a key part of their body or the whole body and forecasting the response to treatment in the virtual environment. Thereby, we can forecast the real response to treatment before it happens and discover the best adjustments to dosage, administration method, and therapeutic

---

[1] Also, onboarding patient communities, associations and centres of excellence around the pathology while we conceptualise our products and solutions is important. It can alert us to their real needs that technological medicine can solve, but we will address this in Chapter 6, on stakeholders.

[2] Treatment compliance, on the other hand is based on the idea that no pill or treatment works unless it is taken.

[3] Treatment incisiveness concerns the speed to control the pathology. It mainly aims to stabilise the patient in an acute state and get them to as near to a stable state as possible.

options for the patient. Thanks to our technology, this translational, precise and personalised medicine is already a reality (Medicine, 2018) (Halim, 2019).

Patient Empowerment

As the patient becomes the centre of the healthcare model and is empowered with the help of our technologies, we must ensure they receive the appropriate training. We must make people understand what is happening and why so they can become their own best health caregivers. That means using our healthtechs to improve their self-efficacy, self-esteem, knowledge, decision making and quality of life. Thinking back to the idea of a circular economy, this approach of early self-driven and training-empowered prevention and diagnosis can help us achieve outstanding rates of pathology reduction. A review of 118 pieces of research confirms that the evolution of the patient's health, through self-management, can be improved by increasing his empowerment (Galanakis et al., 2016).

In the same line, one study developed a 13-weeks stroke patient empowerment intervention (Health Empowerment Intervention for Stroke Self-management [HEISS]) to enhance patients' ability to participate in self-management. Those in the intervention group had a significantly better functional recovery than the control group (Sit et al., 2016).

The European Patients Forum defines empowerment as a "process that helps people gain control over their own lives and increases their capacity to act on issues that they themselves define as important" (EPF, 2021). Let us look at the example of diabetes to show how a healthtech can empower patients and make them understand their conditions and how to cope with it.

A diabetic patient needs to be able to live alongside their diabetic condition, adapting their nutritional habits, keeping an active lifestyle, exercising regularly and they need to perform glucose tests frequently and in a structured way or act fast when faced with hypoglycemia. An empowerment program performed with 208 participants' improved metabolic control of type 2 diabetes in Brazilian users (Cortez et al., 2017).

So, how can a healthtech assist? Well, the pharmaceutical company Roche's mySugar app is one solution.[4] This diabetes management app was made for people with diabetes by people with diabetes, and it permits storing all your important diabetes data from connected devices, integrations and manual entries, in one convenient place.

Also in the same pathology and concerning diabetes self-management, other programs exist such as Abbott's FreeStyle Libre system,[5] Dexcom[6] and Glooko.[7] Like mySugar, these are tracking apps that let the patient record their activities in the reader to unlock insights about what impacts their glucose levels. All are able to connect with NovoNordisk's smart insulins pens,[8] which are new smart insulin pens that automatically record insulin dosing information about each injection, so the patient or caregiver does not have to.

Another example of a healthtech promoting patient empowerment is in mental health. Patients with mental health issues often need self-guided programs for dealing with bad habits, self-esteem

---

[4] mySugr App URL: https://www.mysugr.com/en/
[5] FreeStyle Libre URL: https://www.freestyle.abbott/us-en/home.html
[6] Dexcom.URL: www.dexcom.com
[7] Glooko URL: www.glooko.com
[8] NovoPen 6 and NovoPen Echo Plus URL: https://www.novonordisk.com/our-products/smart-pens/novopen-6.html

and anxiety, something the healthtech app Intellect is providing to enable the redevelopment of traits, habits and behaviours.[9]

At the end of the day, it is about avoiding health ignorance and pushing for self-determination of patients. This will support early diagnosis and prevention, the twin pillars of a circular health-care economy.

How can we get to this? Make the patient responsible for their health destiny. And this applies during the pathology and before it takes place.

Also emphasise the importance of bringing medicine into the home. As Chapter 1 explored, the hospital is no longer the only place of care; the place of care is also the patient's home. The traditional hospital has become a centre of limited situations where the patient's condition needs to be attended by a super specialist. But before these limited situations happen, most can be pre-vented via patient empowerment.

What are we already doing? Bringing the hospital to the patient's home, through patient moni-toring, with the aid of IoMT, which are IP addresses[10] that emit and receive information, e.g. bea-cons and all sorts of devices. So, the doctor, without seeing the patient, can perfectly know their condition, as can the patient. And the doctor gets an alarm when their patient is going through an acute situation and can better anticipate when he is going to have it. So the patient is well taken care of from home.

Consider intelligent mirrors as an example of patient monitoring through the IoMT. As a recent article explains,

> An ordinary mirror can be transformed into an intelligent artifact, e.g., "smart mir-ror," by placing a semi-transparent sheet of glass over a digital screen and connecting this hardware to a computer with incoming data and a camera. On a basic imple-mentation, the screen can display real-time information about the weather or traffic patterns, alerts from emails, and calendars, as well as data collected via wearables.
>
> **(Miotto et al., 2018)**

The intelligent mirror recognises through facial recognition technology certain distinctive features that can be translated into whatever parameter that enhances health. For example, it can recognise low blood glucose, which is high risk for diabetic patients. And more than this, the person's health status, the physical characteristics and facial expressions, provide metrics that can be linked to health status, all of which can be captured by standing in front of the mirror. All this is monitored and submitted automatically to the platform for follow-up where a virtual doctor and a real one both have access.

Another user example of a healthtech smart mirror is Wize Mirror, which estimates cardio-metabolic risk and anxiety levels from anthropometric measurements of facial features (Colantonio et al., 2015), or Fit Mirror that helps people wake up as well as increase their motivation and activ-ity throughout the day (Yasmina Andreu, 2016).

Of course, it is not all about mirrors! Another example is the goods-to-person (GTP) robotic systems approach. An easier and less invasive approach to enforcing social distancing would be to keep the person in one place and then use human-virus-resistant automation, like robots, to move goods around: drones for drug delivery to the home, let us say. It is estimated that through 2023,

---

[9] Intellect URL: https://www.intellect.co/
[10] An IP address is an identifying number that is associated with a specific computer or computer network.

demand for robotic GTP systems will quadruple to help enforce social distancing in warehouses (Klappich et al., 2020). This shortcut in the supply chain skips wholesalers by taking drugs from laboratories to big marketplaces that bring the drug to the patient's home, again making them the centre of the healthcare system.

Patients as Communicators and Customers

The internet has played a major role in the shift to a patient-centred healthcare model, reshaping patient-physician communication and interactions (Martini & Bragazzi, 2021). AI in turn is permitting self-referral, behavioural change, data-driven self-diagnosis, personalised outreach, medical record collection, and AI-facilitated self-care functions (Foundation, 2021). And online patient communities are drivers of this patient empowerment (Johansson, Islind, Lindroth, Angenete, & Gellerstedt, 2021).

Through seeking information, guidance and a communal sense of belonging, patients are increasingly demanding the best quality of health. They can improve their quality of life by anticipating pathologies and preventing them through the adoption of good habits and better life standards. So they impact their own health outcomes and life extension rates.

A major novelty in this Copernican Revolution of medicine is the profound change associated with medical communication. Indeed, information and communication technology (ICT) is one of the elements of the new conceptual framework of P6 medicine, where the 6 Ps stand for "personalised," "predictive," "preventive," "participatory," "psycho-cognitive" and "public". (Downing Peck, 2017) (Bragazzi NL, 2013) (Bragazzi & Puente, 2013).

This increased ability to communicate with healthcare stakeholders is changing the role of patients in the overall healthcare economy.

Traditionally, healthcare's primary customers were not the patients, but the payers. These are parties other than the patient that finance or refund the cost of healthcare products and services. Payers can be government health authorities, administrators within health technology assessment (HTA) bodies, private medical insurance companies or even a pharmacist in a hospital who helps determine which drugs the hospital uses (Baily, 2020).

Now that they can communicate their needs so well and are becoming empowered, more and more patients are becoming the ones that buy health and consequently pay for it from their own pockets.

Other trends, too, are contributing to this shift, including, for example, fewer uninsured individuals in the US following passage of the Affordable Care Act (Holloway, Peterson, MacDonald & Pollak, 2018). And due to an increasing number of patients with high-deductible health plans, patients are now responsible for 30% of hospital revenues (Downing Peck, 2017). This is creating massive cost pressures in the healthcare system, with current economic conditions meaning people struggle to pay even modest balances.

So, healthtechs will play an important role in making healthcare affordable for the future generation of patient-payers (Bayley Matthew, Sarah, Levine Ed, & Monisha, 2021). And to bridge the self-pay gap, healthtechs must also help the healthcare system drive yield by engaging consumers: they must create billing transparency through online portals and facilitate risk-assessed and analytically derived payment plans (VisitPay, 2017).

As well as making healthcare affordable, healthtechs will also play a role in monetising more aspects of patients' daily lives. Consider, for e.g., mentioned smart-mirrors that monitor their facial features and give a popup health status every day, nutrition and fitness programs for patients to enrol in, and apps that offer health coaches to manage pathologies like diabetes. All these will encourage the patient to take responsibility for their health, but also to invest in it.

So, now more than ever, patients are "the sun" of the ecosystem, but now they play an active role, too: they are the new customers. The opportunity of healthtech companies to impact patient outcomes is huge. We are offering the first promising products and services of this emerging reality. As we create insights and richly divergent approaches, our work opens doors onto a broadening range of possibilities around economics of healthcare.

Precise, Personalised, Just-in-Time Medicine

With the patient at the centre of the ecosystem, we are transitioning from a mass patient approach to an individual patient approach. This means medicine that is more precise because it is more personalised, and it means the manufacturing and delivery of this treatment will transition to a "just-in-time" model where patients receive exactly and only what they need, when they need it.

As healthtechs, our role will be to facilitate the personalisation of every interaction between the patient and the healthcare provider, integrating it into a holistic digitally supported medical ecosystem.

The new mode of outreach will further patient empowerment, training them to self-manage and take responsibility for their pathology, even before it arises. By highlighting the possible range of pathologies to appear throughout the lifecycle, we empower the patient to monitor and use early diagnostic tools, helping to create a new generation of health-promoting citizens. Thereby, we are collaboratively participating in a circular economy in healthcare by forecasting the possibilities that certain pathology appears in the patient's life using precise, predictive medicine.

This transition will come through IoMT tools integrated into the patients' homes: smart devices, such as wearables and medical/vital monitors, personal emergency response systems (PERS), remote patient monitoring (RPM) and telehealth virtual visits (Alliance of Advanced Biomedical Engineering, 2021). But it will also come through app-based solutions. Examples include the Smiling Instead of Smoking (SIS) app (Hoeppner et al., 2017), enabling smoking self-monitoring. Or consider HealthKOS (HealthKOS, 2021)[11], an end-to-end patient-management system that improves outcomes for high-risk patients with remote patient monitoring. Its automated algorithms, real-time data and quality metrics involve patients in their own care and keep healthcare providers informed.

This constant flow of information, enabled by healthtech, will mean we will be able to switch to a just-in-time delivery system thanks to the instantaneous and continuous monitoring of the health outcomes.

Indeed, it enables the possibility of in-home delivery of correctly dosed encapsulated medication, for example like Amazon Pharmacy,[12] which is already offering the personalised service of Amazon Pill Packs and sending already dosed medication in "pill packs" properly labelled with the day and the time of administration. Pharmaeasy[13] is the same concept in India, or BookMyMeds.[14]

Along with a more demanding patient that claims a better quality of healthcare, instant access to care is already possible and resulting in improved healthcare outcomes. The empowerment of the new patient is essential when it comes to building the basis of the new healthcare model, and it relies on our ability to provide accurate, just-in-time healthtech solutions.

---

[11] HealthKOS URL: https://www.healthkos.com/
[12] Amazon Pharmacy URL: https://pharmacy.amazon.com/
[13] Pharmaeasy URL: https://pharmeasy.in/
[14] BookMyMeds URL: https://bookmymeds.com/

But to achieve this, we must improve the quality of available health information for problem-solving within the private-public citizen health alliance. Currently, there is a gap in health data accessibility. And that is hampering healthtechs, and healthcare generally, because patient data is the primary resource in our solutions. Smart solutions dependent on machine learning and Artificial Intelligence (AI) consume vast quantities of health data that must be made available safely and accurately. And it is not just any data: we need recent data. Studies show the "half-life" of clinical data relevance towards predicting future practices is just four months (Chen et al., 2017).

Indeed, the big data inaccessibility gap constitutes a "valley of death" for translational medicine (Hulsen, 2020). This gap is the difference between what is happening, we can estimate that we are living in a yottabyte[15] era with big barriers of non-usability of health data (Raghupathi & Raghupathi, 2014), and the ideal of what could be happening, maybe full healthcare big data accessibility meeting basic FAIR Guiding Principles.[16]

To reach this point, we need to first incentivise standard data sharing initiatives. Some examples are Personalised Consent Flow, a new consent model that empowers patients to control their personally collected health data and determine what they want to share and for what purposes. In Europe, the governmental Horizon 2020 Research and Innovation Programme of the European Union stimulates data sharing with companies. Also in the EU, the initiative 1+ Million Genomes involves 22 countries and hopes to combine one million genomes from small datasets into a big dataset to be accessible by late 2022 (Hulsen, 2020).

Health information silos therefore should be trustworthy. Data should be collected through blueprints that show all the methods by which data can be ingested and prepared, or help healthcare professionals to implement measurement-based care in their clinical practice through personalised approaches based on blueprints. And we will need tech-skilled collectors of information together with new data collection-enabling technologies such as pingbots[17].

This process will revolve around five pillars:

1. Patients placed in the very centre of the matrix of data collection and placed as the owners of their own health data and free-will providers of this data (NHS, 2009).
2. Protection and anonymisation of personal and collective health data, respecting data protection standards and policies.
3. Rewarded culture of open research, incentivising publishing full research completely and transparently, regardless of the results (Hulsen T., 2019).
4. A 4.0 data approach involving automation and data exchange in technologies, including cyber-physical systems, the Internet of things, cloud and cognitive computing and creating the smart healthcare environments (i-Scoop, 2021).
5. Avoiding the grey spots and blind spots in between groups of information (Hastie, 2009). Big data holds many unknown grey spots, which presents the first challenge of AI and machine learning to identify all those unknowns.

---

[15] A yottabyte (YB) is the largest unit approved as a standard size by the International System of Units. One yottabyte equals to 10^{24} bytes. There is nothing that can currently be measured on a yottabyte scale.

[16] The FAIR Guiding Principles for scientific data management and stewardship were published in 2016 and are based on four foundational principles—Findability, Accessibility, Interoperability, and Reusability—that serve to guide data producers and publishers as they navigate around the obstacles around data management and stewardship

[17] A pingbot is a proof-of-concept website monitoring or health-checking tool based on serverless architecture (GitHub, 2021).

Together, these pillars of data collection will secure patient empowerment, enabling well-informed patients to take their own decisions about their pathology management and care conditions. And health data will ethically secure the primary resource for healthtechs to create precise, personalised, just-in-time medicine: translational medicine.

In this new landscape of data-centricity and patient empowerment, patients are increasingly providing us with free information sources that can help build more accurate patient profiles, along with digital avatar twins of everyone (Pandey & Mann, 2000). This will go as deep as the biomolecular level: genomics, proteomics, metabolomics, metagenomics and transcriptomics. With individual biomarkers of disease being identified from these omic datasets and dataset analysis, we are reaching new frontiers of early diagnosis and personalised care (McDermott et al., 2013).

That privileged access allows precise medicine. We are going towards a model of translational medicine, where everything is about personalised treatments and precision medicine, helped by the building of supermodels—new avatar patient holograms that simulate key medical components (see Figure 2.1). In silico examples, built up computational methods that virtually recreate portions of a patient's physiology, are increasingly used in clinical trials (Brown, 2015) (Pouke & Häkkilä, 2013).

Along with the real-life patient approach, this is leading to avatar-based virtual environments. That involves wearable sensors and human activity simulations, conveyed onto new 3D virtual worlds realities (Pouke & Häkkilä, 2013).

Ultimately, the changing landscape of healthcare and the shift to a model of health provision with an expert patient-payer at the centre are democratising access to healthcare. Technology enables this, breaking old barriers of costs and locations. As Jasper Westerink, Market Leader of Philips Africa, writes, "Innovations in areas like telehealth and AI are already making a difference and are saving lives of people who otherwise simply would not have access to quality healthcare" (Philips, 2019). Our businesses, and all the key players of the ecosystem, should convey this new

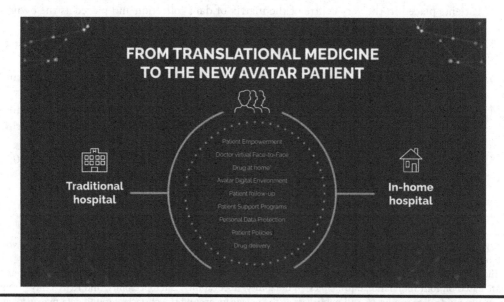

Figure 2.1 Representation of the bridges that are permitting an upgrade from translational medicine in the traditional hospital approach to the new avatar patient operating in a metaverse environment enabling in-home care.

approach throughout the ecosystem, since it can drop global healthcare expenditure while improving the standard of care.

A good example is Kenya's approach of national telemedicine. It is an initiative to improve healthcare access for the rural poor and the marginalised. The initiative will let rural patients and healthcare providers hold video conferences with experts at Kenya's main referral hospital Kenyatta National Hospital (KNH) (Net, 2015).

Such ICT should also enhance access to medical education, training and research by helping to address the lack of human resource capacity in rural areas. In general, the country is leveraging healthcare technology to increase interaction with the patient and thereby improve disease awareness and early diagnosis, putting the patients' needs in the very centre of the ecosystem.

As healthtechs, our role will be to facilitate that process. If we can cover the unmet need of the patient, on a real-time, real-life, in-home basis, this will directly and indirectly impact the healthcare outcomes by improving the treatment compliance and the response to the treatment and its follow up. By monitoring the patient, we change the old patient management approach taking place in the hospital. We move towards an in-home approach, leveraging the quality of life of the patient, and bringing him a life as close as possible to normality.

Chapter 3

Conceptualising Your Strategic Position

So, we are learning to fly. We are learning about the current, ever-advancing healthcare ecosystem in which we hope to operate. The "how" is simple. We just need to embrace the change: both the transition to a patient-centred model and to a landscape of high-value care, digitalisation and a circular economy (see Figure 3.1). We are on the edge of change, and this means that we also need to change. We must constantly reinvent our strategies to survive.

As US entrepreneur and CEO of General Electric from 1981–2001, Jack Welch, once remarked, "If the rate of change on the outside exceeds the rate of change on the inside, the end is near" (Quotes, 2021). It is our responsibility to catch these subtle indicators of change on the fly and include them in our strategies.

To do this, then, we must think strategically about not just our product, but about all the other factors that will influence the success of our business: the alliances we must build, the regulations by which we must abide, the teams and knowledge we must build and the capacity we must create for growth.

Our strategic position must be physical and digital, differentiated and firmly established in this ecosystem via our unique selling proposition (USP). That means it must have value in the eyes of the ecosystem's stakeholders (primarily the patient who is now the customer, but also all the other stakeholders in the ecosystem), which we will explore how to build in Chapter 4.

It also means that before you start creating your healthtech product, you must conceptualise your business model to fit this advancing healthcare ecosystem (see Figure 3.2). Get the right skills for you and your team to stay ahead of the technology curve and create a work methodology with a clear goal in sight.

If you consider snowballing at the proper speed and focusing on prioritising your core business goals from the beginning, capitalising on the right technology and incorporating the right talent into your team, you can prepare yourself for growing your brand and securing your position within the ecosystem. After you have that initial product out on the market, you can create pipeline extensions based on trial and error. This secures your future position, so do it no matter your budget (we focus on research and development in Part III).

But at first, it will be about that initial product and how you can get it to market.

DOI: 10.4324/b23147-4

Figure 3.1 Illustration of a healthy maritime ecosystem in equilibrium as a parallelism of a healthy healthcare ecosystem where all stakeholders occupy an optimum and sustainable operative role within the community.

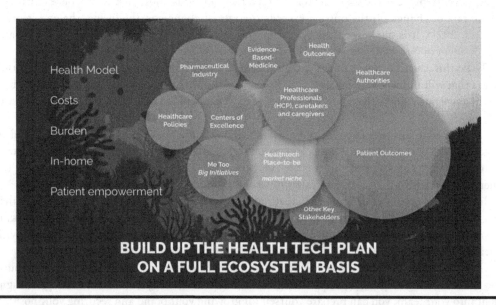

Figure 3.2 Illustration exemplifying a maritime ecosystem in equilibrium. Though the image represents the different key stakeholders operating in a Healthtech ecosystem. The size of the circles represents their influential weight. The circle in orange, leverages the healthtech place to be in the ecosystem as the starting point to build bridges of collaboration with the different stakeholders, and its settling is directly dependent on it.

Help this process with clear goals for meeting regulatory requirements, for growth, and for building collaboration and win-win alliances throughout the community, continuously networking. As we will explore, such connections—or backlinks—are the most common attribute of top-ranking CEOs, and they set you up for sustainable growth both digitally and in the real world.

As we move towards tech globalisation, we need to fight harder to establish our strategic position and protect it in the face of the broad trend of decentralising healthcare models, which in turn are the umbrellas containing the ecosystems in which we operate. Be sure that you understand the health sector deeply, learning the skills to understand specific science and the real-life health outcomes that you are bringing in.

Your Business Model: Prepare for Growth from the Get-Go

From the moment that we decide to start the journey, we must consider that playing in the healthcare ecosystem means more than launching a healthtech solution that covers a single unmet need like, for example, a product that tracks the administration and efficiency of medication. It also means optimising the discovery of efficient methods of pathology management, including early diagnosis, from the outset. In other words, it means integrating optimised solutions into the healthcare model so that key institutions will validate them.

Consider key leveraging points (KLP). These are either a touchpoint,[1] hot spot[2] or blind spot[3] regarding the management of the patient's journey, and they impact directly and indirectly the whole budget of the healthcare system.

This is because every improvement in a KLP can easily optimise the available resources allocated for a certain health goal, impacting the core healthcare plan of the different states or regions that manage their own healthcare expenditure.

As healthtech businesses, we start by retaining a key figure in our minds: the percentage of the gross domestic product (GDP) allocated to healthcare, the current health expenditure (CHE) (WHO, 2021). You must know this to optimise your impact in terms of the CHE. Getting this CHE rate to the lowest possible level while preserving and improving the standards of care will keep us as healthtechs alive and operating in this emerging, sustainable and global healthcare system.

So, pick a KLP and find out how you can develop it to lower CHE.

Remember that although in the digital world resources are limitless, they are not in the real healthcare world. Consider shortcuts and ways to reduce the overall burden and costs, and ensure scalability is possible in the future. Success is assured if our services and solutions contribute to obtaining better health outcomes, but do not forget a positive collateral impact on cost containment and patient journey shortcuts. Your solutions should optimise resource management to perfect the patient-centred healthcare journey. If you can bring value that optimises the whole pathology management, your solution will always be welcome.

---

[1] A touchpoint is any point of contact patients have with your healthtech product or service.

[2] A hotspot is an identified step within the patient journey where harm or near misses are alike to happen.

[3] A blindspot is an identified step within the patient journey that constitutes a blackbox. In other words, it is difficult to prognose the most likely scenario to happen and difficult to monitor aspects of care, for example, before admissions, after discharge or errors of omission.

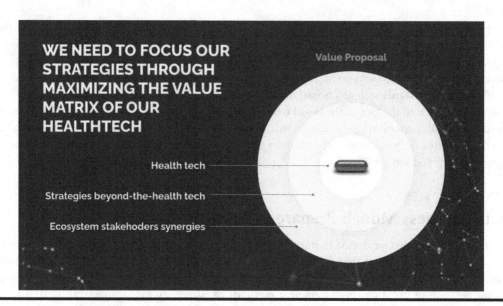

Figure 3.3 **Infographics representing the matrix of value of a healthtech and the levels to expand its value proposal.**

So, understand that healthtech is not only the single drug that is taken by the patient. It is all about the convenience of add-on treatments and associated pathology management tools—strategies beyond the single healthtech product's value (see Figure 3.3).

Besides, you can either have a good product or pipeline and a bad business model or the other way round a bad product or pipeline and a great business model. We are here to align both, conceptualising great healthtech products that cover true unmet needs in the healthcare ecosystem while forming sustainable business models.

Remember that either the product or the business can be redirected. Success at its core comes from the right entrepreneur or entrepreneurial team steering the ship's helm and adjusting its direction at the right moment. Of course, it helps to start out pointing in the right direction.

In the initial phases of the creation of your healthtech, you need to find out what is the long-term commercial model that you need, or you are willing to set up within your start-up.

Conceptualising a sustained and sustainable model is one of the first main steps. There is no secret to it other than using common sense. Do not complicate your life too early, so build it so you can do one thing at a time that, in turn, elevates your business to the next level. I would say take your time and do not rush. Sometimes a good easy beginning is a white paper that can clarify the different business models' viability for your unique story. In other words, you really need to know where you come from and where you are going.

There are different business models available, but they all revolve around certain core concepts. These concepts are circular economy, sustained and sustainable business model and scalability. In plain words, create curative, healthy and expandable business models.

Business-to-Consumer (B2C)

In this model, you sell directly to the patient in a direct to consumer (D2C) commercial model. Healthtech has witnessed a migration from the business-to-business (B2B) to B2C business model, with the new trend of the patient becoming not only the consumer but the new payer of health.

This model is straightforward. It relies on a conventional approach of selling directly to patients or end users. Caregivers or caretakers can also be examples of end users, who in some cases pay a subscription fee for, for example, IoMT patient support programs, AI articulated self-care apps, etc. Payment frequency may vary (monthly, annually, etc.) and some would pay with a pay-me-back scheme. Patients with this model purchase directly out of pocket. With disease management healthtech products, end users may acquire them through other marketplaces, like umbrella governmental health authorities' health marketplace platforms.

Despite requiring large marketing expenditure, this business model can be particularly successful in regions where the end user is used to paying for healthcare. For example, in the US, there are many examples of B2C healthtechs. On the other hand, in countries like Europe where universal public health coverage is common, the patient can be reluctant to pay for health out of pocket.

For newborn healthtechs, the B2C model can help you rapidly achieve strong cashflow so you can continue operating. Simultaneously, it allows you to get product feedback in the field that helps to iterate and improve from the very initial stages. It has big advantages due to the potential for high, quickly accelerating user adoption rates.

With B2C, initial barriers must be broken. These include regulatory hurdles considering the direct consumer of health and the customer is most often the patient who pays for health from his own pocket, usually digitally. That said, it is a common business model that achieves great turnovers even in the early phases.

Healthtechs selling a healthy quality of life are a good example of this model's success around preventive medicine. One example is TalkSpace[4], offering D2C preventive mental health services via a self-assessment. A key success driver for this model is the ability to care for the customer and its direct engagement with them. This enables them to gain the loyalty of big communities that share a common purpose.

Big marketplaces of health are also examples of B2C businesses, although they are addressed later in this book.

Another important barrier for B2C business models is the high costs that a company with direct sales to the consumer acquires. These are, for example, often related to the promotion of services through marketing actions that were initially contained. When the company gets going and acquires certain dimensions, these costs skyrocket and that is when the company may need to rethink its business model.

It is common that when the company reaches this critical point, it opens the doors to B2B collaborations to achieve leaps in billing and consolidate the structure and architecture necessary to continue the company itself. Then the business model becomes a Business-to-Consumer-to-Business (B2C2B), first selling to consumers and later, when they reach a critical target volume of consumers, transferring the sale to large payers and health purchasing centres such as insurers or government health institutions, hospitals, or hospital groups, among others.

Buoyhealth[5] is an example of this last approach, a disruptive healthtech that initially offered services of symptomatology diagnosis and best care options direct to consumer: the patient and caregivers. It transitions, and currently is also addressed to the business employers, health plans and other businesses like brokers and consultants.

---

4 TalkSpace https://www.talkspace.com/ [Last Accessed December 2021]
5 Buoyhealth. https://www.buoyhealth.com/ [Last Accessed December 2021]

Business-to-Business (B2B)

A B2B business model is selling to one or more businesses. In healthtech, it is a bit more complex than a business-to-consumer (B2C) model because the customer is another business or several businesses, and the initial investment and the timings of revenue streaming are longer.

For entrepreneurs, establishing the first synergies of collaboration in a B2B can sometimes be a critical challenge. You will need win-win partnerships with the key stakeholders, or you will fail. However, this first big barrier to entering the ecosystem can transform into long-term advantages when competitors arise.

With B2Bs, you will also see longer processes around the regulatory frameworks and bureaucracy, which can influence everything from operations to investment. If you can secure your position in a B2B, however, you can generate massive profits in the long term.

Business-to-government (B2G) and business-to-payer (B2P) are also included in this B2B group. These constitute the largest market in Europe and in the US. For example, the German Insurance Association (GDV) comprising the federation of private insurers in Germany has about 460 member companies offering health coverage and retirement provisions payers of health like private households, trade, industry and public institutions, through almost 454 million insurance contracts (GDV, 2020). Integrate your product into that network, and success is sure.

One of the key drivers of growth for this business model resides in which commercial model you decide to take. It must be versatile, and that is often achieved through a microservices approach.

1. A Device-like Commercial Model:
   This would be considered a "medical benefit" in, for example, digital therapeutics or Software as a Service. The healthtech sets the price for the solution, and the payer (a medical insurance company or healthcare authority) covers up to a certain amount as part of core medical benefits, and the patient pays coinsurance or copays.
2. A Drug-like Reimbursement Model:
   This considers the solution as a "pharmacy benefit" when it comes to reimbursement. The price is negotiated between the healthtech and the pharmacy benefit manager. Therefore, the solution is to be listed as one of the pharmacy benefits or on the digital formulary. The patient copays. Typically, a national code exists for the healthtech product or service.
3. Value-based Contracts and Risk Share Agreements Model:
   The healthtech contacts the payer, employer or organisation or group of healthcare providers. Contracts structured around improved healthcare outcomes or reduced costs (cost containment policies). They are generally paid on a per member per month basis. Payers most of the time require a pilot and/or robust evidence and return on investment (ROI) before adopting the technology. Contract renewal or payment is often based on usage or engagement key performance indicators (KPIs based).

B2B is an unusual first choice of business model for an entrepreneur just starting out. It is usually best applicable for big transformative healthtechs that impact the system. It works particularly well in Europe, for example, where digital therapeutics companies sell to governmental bodies or payers and self-insured employers. It becomes a challenging model when you plan to scale up.

Business-to-Business-to-Consumer (B2B2C)

B2B2C enables businesses (usually healthtechs providing health services) to understand and serve their end customers (usually the patient, caretaker or caregiver) by partnering with other companies offering the services under their umbrella platform.

An example of a best practice healthtech business using this B2B2C model is a healthtech that helps corporations take care of their personnel health affordably. Such is the case of Onsurity Technologies,[6] offering businesses benefits like telehealth, health diagnosis tests, health prevention programmes, as well as health, accidental, and life insurances for their employees.

Consumer-to-Business (C2B)

Consumer-to-business (C2B) is a business model in which consumers (individuals) create value and businesses consume and sell that value.

Healthcare datasets can be considered a commercial transaction between a consumer and a business. These businesses can sell processed datasets to a third party. This practice sometimes is performed by healthtech start-ups in the very initial phases of growth as they need turnover to continue funding investments into the development of other solutions. And why not? Health data is a great asset and a valuable product.

Consumer-to-Consumer (C2C)

In this model, consumers sell to other consumers through an intermediary, normally an online one, who charges a commission.

Healthtech group Clinic To Cloud is one example.[7] It offers a new approach for connected care, allowing the access, storage, and flow of healthcare information between patients and doctors, already having a payment gateway very close to finalisation.

Aside from these business models, different "business methodologies" ought to be considered when starting your healthtech. It is good to know them, and their implementation is key when you put your company's machinery to work and start to snowball.

- Pentagrowth Methodology: Pentagrowth is a methodology to design disruptive business models. Through the process, the organisation experiences the cultural transformation necessary to innovate and test prototypes of cocreated business models in the real world. It identifies five levers for exponential growth: connect, collect, empower, enable, and share. It is based on a study of 50 organisations that achieved over 50% revenue growth for 5 years running.[8]
- Agile Methodology: This methodology prioritises getting a working product into the hands of consumers as early as possible so that they can test it and you can improve it. That is all agile is: "discovering requirements and developing solutions through the collaborative effort of self-organising and cross-functional teams and their customer/end user" (Rally, 2021).

---

[6] Onsurity Technologies. https://onsurity.com/ [Last Accessed May 2022]
[7] Clinic To Cloud. https://www.clinictocloud.com/ [Last Accessed December 2021]
[8] You can access the full methodology free of charge here: https://www.ideasforchange.com/en/tools/penta-growth-report [Last Accessed December 2021]

You will aim to go to market with advanced but also adaptable healthtech solutions, developing your products and services along the way as you receive consumer feedback (Alliance, 2021) (Collier, 2012).

■ Purpose Launchpad: Purpose Launchpad is an agile framework to help people operate with the right mindset to successfully generate new initiatives and/or evolve existing organisations (start-ups or corporations) to make a massive impact. It combines lean start-up, customer development, agile, ExO and many other innovations to achieve high growth.[9]

■ Lean Start-up Methodology: The Lean start-up method is based on "validated learning"—that is, gradually verifying the hypothesis before having the final product (the definitive start-up) and starting to scale the business. The idea is to define and shorten the development cycles, launch different products for a period and obtain valuable comments from our potential customers or users, with which to improve the next final version of the product.[10]

■ Customer Discovery: It is a useful tool for entrepreneurs on how to create a company while avoiding the usual beginner mistakes and redirecting efforts towards the two main objectives of any company: the market and customers.[11]

ExO Attributes: The ExO framework argues that exponential organisations (ExOs) have at their core a massive transformative purpose (MTP). This is a foundation upon which the remaining 10 attributes for exponential growth stand. These 10 attributes are further divided into five external characteristics and five internal mechanisms: Staff on Demand, Community & Crowd, Algorithms, Leveraged Assets, and Engagement; Interfaces, Dashboards, Experimentation, Autonomy, and Social Technologies.[12]

Whatever methodology (or combo) you go for, remember: "Sometimes getting there is easy, and sometimes getting there is hard, but almost every successful entrepreneur has that 'eureka' moment that is part of his or her company's DNA" (Putrino, 2017). It will be that idea that is the most important element of your business and on which you will build a methodology.

Gaining Knowledge and Gathering Your Team

Continuous learning is a must. To be able to fly and thus survive, we must have before us worldwide instantaneous access to a massive amount of first-in-class possibilities of knowledge. This allows us to develop ourselves and our skills to become better, having real-time access from any remote part of the world.

Even more than continuous learning, the new employers and employees of the healthtech ecosystems need to perform strategic training daily. You must choose the right training to build up yourself and your path and prioritise and filter selected inputs of information above all. This is not easy, but it is the true key to success. Make your own careers continuously.

We need to be prepared to bring value into society, and this value comes from making yourself valuable and being brave at the same time. It is not only about integrating the capabilities and

---

[9] It can be accessed here: https://www.purposelaunchpad.com/ [Last Accessed December 2021]

[10] The principles of the methodology are found here: http://theleanstartup.com/principles [Last Accessed December 2021]

[11] Harvard Business School outlines the principles here: https://entrepreneurship.hbs.edu/Documents/Session%20Summary/HBSRock-Customer-Discovery-Final.pdf [Last Accessed December 2021]

[12] https://www.exo.works/home-01 [Last Accessed December 2021]

skills for the job itself, but it is about improving yourself in terms of emotional intelligence and life-work balance as well.

This requires competent leadership to communicate and onboard onto our mission, with the capability of self-control and self-management. Thus, we need to be able to keep calm no matter which situation we go through, and finally, but not less importantly, we must undertake self-learning to take responsibility for being prepared as well as possible. This also applies to our teams, which require continuous upgrading of capabilities and a must-learn attitude.

We all fly in the same sky, but we all have different skills for mastering how to learn to fly and then sustain flight over time. Thus, we must fly together, not alone. We must rely on different communities' networks of support in every single step that we take. Honest and worthy networking needs to be there, and this takes dedication and time. Do not remain static, but move—attend virtual conferences, summits and meetings. Be as up to date as possible.

Overall, to bring good and value to our society, we first need to become the best version of ourselves on a daily basis. And this can be achieved through knowledge. We must continuously upgrade our understanding of the world, the ecosystem and the environment in which we operate.

So first, devote your time to understand exactly what is happening in your niche—what processes, problems and existing solutions are present?

You cannot master all subjects. But we must fully know the subjects essential to our core business and understand the capabilities and limits of the software and hardware we are or want to manage. Not everybody needs to be able to code, but understanding the "whys", the "how's" and the "where's" is a must.

If you are struggling with this knowledge acquisition process, conduct a filtering exercise to identify the fields your business will interact with. Second, prioritise among those critical knowledge domains, and devote your time to studying news, research and company profiles operating in these areas. And remember, you can bring onboard people with mastery in other areas, so you do not need to do it all yourself.

Another daily technique to help you in these early stages is creating action lists. Consider what your biggest goals are, write them down, then plan out the linear steps you need to get there. Plot these steps into a timetable and follow it. Do not allow yourself to be distracted and remember to streamline the process to include only the activities that return the biggest bang for your buck. For example, you do not have to master the entirety of "digital mastering". But you can focus on creating a successful advertising campaign and easily build a roadmap to that.

Self-care is also critical

"The challenge is to take care of your brain to obtain sustainable performance over time, to guarantee a long managerial life", says Director of the Master's in High Performance Leadership at the EADA Business School of Barcelona.

Its High Performance Leadership Method focuses on four different balances to achieve high managerial performance: (1) physical exercise moments (Physical Exercise) & Moments of Rest (Sleep Time) Equilibrium; (2) Maximum Cognitive Activity (Focus Time) & Disconnection Activities (Down Time) Equilibrium; (3) Activities that involve interaction with other people (Connecting Time) & inner-self moments (Time Looking Inwards) Equilibrium and (4) leisure, fun and creativity activities (Play Time) & daily routines and disciplines (Routine Time) Equilibrium (EADA, 2018) (CAR, 2019).

So, you have started your knowledge acquisition and created a healthy routine and roadmap. Now, ask, "what is the team that I need to accomplish my goal?" Start from the vision and then work back, selecting the right people with the right skills.

We need to create highly talented teams to face different business cases and to break barriers and take advantage of the opportunities that the ecosystem puts in front of us. The people onboard your healthtech, and more than this onboard with the mission, vision and values of your healthtech, are the keys to success.

First, consider the size of your team. Depending on whether we aim to develop or disrupt, we need large or small teams respectively. A 2019 *Nature Research* publication analysing more than 65 million papers, patents and software products in the period 1954–2014 concludes that large teams develop and small teams disrupt science and technology. Large teams develop existing technologies as the attention to their work comes immediately and small teams disrupt science and technology with new ideas and opportunities impacting in the future of the company. Besides, the results demonstrate that both small and large teams are essential to healthtech progress. Therefore, we should support a diversity of team sizes (Wu, et al., 2019).

Though team building is sometimes a utopia, when it comes to deadlines and high levels of pressure that used to surround more traditional companies, teams did not operate on a normal human interaction basis and the environments used to become toxic. Above all, people must be willing to work in your healthtech. It sounds obvious, but nowadays positions in companies can be easily considered as positions to be occupied by volunteers. It is not salaries that pick up the talent but companies' sense of purpose. And more important than picking up talent is keeping it.

We are in an era of change where we can create our own workplaces. Our new business models can engage freelancers and can encourage their workforce by elevating the importance of work-life balance, creating family-friendly working models that start contributing to the system.

Sometimes, promoting Nordic-European models with 36.2-hour work week (Eurostat, 2021) and not expecting people to work beyond that ends up creating a far more productive work environment even though people leave office at 4pm (Danmark.dk, 2022).

We can offer parental leave and vacation periods, adopting a model of true work-life balance, where both have equal importance. This is a different perspective to entrepreneurship, and one we could have never thought in other times was going to be a new standard on the cutting edge of healthcare ecosystems and enterprises.

The entrepreneur Timothy Ferris in his book *The 4-Hour Work Week* (2009) states that a good mindset to help you create a healthy start-up is design your ideal lifestyle, valuing your time, managing work volume by deleting eliminable tasks—the ones that bring less return, outsourcing if it is necessary and prioritising what to do versus what not to do (Ferriss, 2011). It is a great approach that can help you to deal with your time management.

With the years you realise that what really works the most is to stablish morning affirmations that keep you in your goals path, a daily dose of physical activity, improving yourself with highly selected knowledge, and optimising and really understanding what can be done by others and, more than this, that can be done better than if you did yourself.

As humans, we have this spontaneous connection that is unexplainable when it comes to "connect" or "not connect" with each other. It becomes a reality and is irrational when we interact with each other, as it is something human and, from an anthropological point of view, is an inner skill for interaction between individuals. Follow this gut feeling while selecting your team members and surround yourself with good people.

This gut feeling that makes us get closer to one individual, and, by the same theory, pushes us far away from another, has no rational explanation. And this human matter should also be considered in your start-up's newly built teams; otherwise, they will not be able to operate effectively. It takes time to create high-performing teams operating to optimum effect. We all have skill gaps as individuals, but as a team, we can use this divergence to reach a comprehensive skill set and thus high performance. We can achieve a standard state of something akin to perfection.

Early Alliances

Start building bridges even before the pre-acceleration stage, while you are still conceptualising, to fill the subsequent needs and demands of your solution and bring value throughout the value chain in the ecosystem where you operate.

What do I mean by this? Onboard. Onboard everyone of significance. Call those with knowledge, ask, and knock-on doors. Collect the names of the key opinion leaders, the ones that pop up and are referenced in the pathology's journals, conferences, and press releases. Onboard them onto your project. Look to the reference centres, all those health centres and hospitals that are hotspots for pathology management. Find those who rise above their peers and lead the trends and upgrades to the pathology, the ones who drive the research and innovation in the field.

Networking activities can be anything. They can be a working lunch with an opinion leader of the pathology that you decided to onboard onto your project as a consultant. If you have chosen well, you will get a few tips that can turn your whole world upside down. Or why not sit for coffee with an informal contact—a friend of a friend that knows how pharmaceutical companies work or healthcare authorities work, or maybe how the next technological step for your solution works? There are a lot of good people in the world that, if they can, will be glad help you and contribute to your purpose just because they believe in it.

The only key guideline you need to follow is to construct your alliances on solid foundations and learn from the ones that already know. The newcomers walk around on their own 10 times slower and take a few curves along the way. If you can avoid taking these curves and speeding up your growth, just do it. But make sure that you are talking to the right person and not just a charlatan. Sometimes even people referred by your closest colleagues and friends end up being all smoke and mirrors.

Determine in advance the key strategic lines to the authorities in the field your solution fits best, and the stakeholders with whom it will work most closely. For example, say you want to develop a solution that can positively impact the goals of the chronics plan[13] of a region. That means you will need an alliance with the healthcare authority who is to publish and publicly back the plan, and they must be able to fit your solution into the plan as a key element of the strategy launched by health authorities of a certain region for a certain population.

Or in another example, say your healthtech solution adds value to reduce a hospital's bureaucratic burden of managing patients' Electronic Health Records through implementing a new big data architecture. You will of course need to onboard the hospital as a stakeholder in the process, but you should also consider the wider touchpoints of the solution. You could end up changing the bureaucracy of the whole country's healthcare system if you properly align your solution with the right alliances and deploy a scalable business model. For example, you might expand the pilot in a single hospital to a whole sanitary region or a whole country's EHRs. The first step to reach this expansion is to the pilot's show results and ally with the gatekeepers of the public authorities'

---

[13] A (five-year) chronics plan is a healthcare strategic plan that can be published by a healthcare authority. An example is the "The healthy Tasmania five year plan" that is ending this 2021, where the different healthcare lines of action are leveraged in the plan (Tasmanian, 2016).

strategies and action plans. Most times, these strategies, and who authors them, are transparent and open access (HealthIT.gov, 2020).

In fact, public healthcare strategies, especially government-backed plans, are a fertile resource for both business ideas and stakeholders with whom you can align your healthtech. Consider if your solution was an array of beacons that could facilitate the new in-home hospital approach for patients. A potential alliance will be with a key health institution, such as the American Hospital Association. If you look at their strategic plan, you will easily notice that they are pushing for acute care at home with their "Hospital at Home" program (Association, 2021). Other programs like the recently launched US Hospitals Without Walls can also bring opportunities to align your expansive healthtech proposal into the strategic plan (Models, 2020).

Think also back to the changing healthcare landscape and the evident trends. What are the stakeholders of such trends? For example, the shift of a country's municipalities and cities to smart cities can offer lines of health collaborative alliances.

Such is the case of the Austin Challenge (Austin_SCCFinal, 2020).[14] In the project, the Smart City team is working with many public-sector and community partners outside the transportation space, like Central Health and CommUnityCare, both for utilisation of data and information on health outcomes. One of the goals is access to healthcare, community by community, and missed healthcare appointments, clinic by clinic. If you can demonstrate that your healthtech is the vehicle by which cities can achieve this goal, you will build powerful alliances and secure a market for your solution.

And why not knock on the door of leading pharmaceutical companies? They can be the owners of a certain pill that is still innovative in a certain ecosystem, the ones that really bring value to the treatment of the patient and that could be somehow attached to your solution. Look for them because they will be investing on behalf of the progress of the whole pathology itself. They are investing in continuous medical training. They are the providers of e-learning and platforms that can become essential in terms of knowledge.

Partner with anyone who improves the overall pathology outcomes.

Here is an example.

Imagine that a certain pharmaceutical company is willing to launch a first-in-class drug[15] to a certain market where you are also willing to operate, or that maybe you think is the right ecosystem for your product to be exploited to its maximum potential.

Imagine also that your solution is a wearable or a dispositive expected to be located in the home of the patient. It monitors the data of the patient and, in particular, tracks a parameter that is key for demonstrating that the pharmaceutical company's drug or medical solution is efficient, or can show that it is less invasive or has less of a certain secondary effect that is key for the health outcomes of the patient. Whatever it is, you are bringing value to a translational medical approach for the new drug.

The pharmaceutical company will of course be open to at least hearing you. And maybe, who knows, you can find a win-win alliance and collaboration that can upgrade one of their clinical trials—perhaps help them follow up with the patient and monitor the data with the aid of your healthtech solution. You may even get onboard one of their clinical trials and secure real-world evidence (see Chapter Four) of the performance of your product and their drug.

---

[14] Austin Challenge. URL https://www.austintexas.gov/sites/default/files/files/Transportation/Austin_SCCFinal_Volume1_5.25.pdf

[15] First-in-class drugs are pioneers for presenting a different and unique mechanism of action, usually perceived as revolutionary for bringing novelty and better outcomes to the treatment of a certain medical condition.

Maybe you could both present together the value dossier from a joint-venture perspective to the health authorities and both win a strategic position in the healthcare system. That is surely a win-win-win for all three parties involved. For you, the win is demonstrating that your solution is a top-class one contributing to the overall pathology management. For the laboratory, the win is demonstrating that their drug brings value. Finally, for the healthcare authorities, the win is gaining improved cost-efficiency around the pathology, which impacts their overall healthcare budget expenditure.

It does not matter if your solution is an e-health standard development, distributed technology like blockchain, telemedicine, or anything else. Whatever you do, you need to be able to convey your value to a panel of key stakeholders in simple bullet points to get them onboard. Show how you fit in their healthcare system's strategic plans, and how you can help to improve healthcare outcomes and save expenditure. We will explore exactly how to do this in Chapter Six of Part II, but you must have in mind potential stakeholders and alliances as you conceptualise your business idea.

Finally, consider these interactions with the key personas or institutions, these touch points, as key insights to build within your business model. Learn from every single interaction.

And I repeat, listen, ask for help, feel the trends of the market and anticipate them. Surround yourself with knowledge of pathology and the market. And please, be proactive with self-learning and staying up to date; do not let the changes surprise you. You must be the change-maker. Look overseas, across disciplines, and up and down hierarchies. Some of the best ideas can be found in the most surprising of places.

Ultimately, you should build your own advisory board from the alliances that you make because you will never have all the answers, and ten minds are better than one. Fill your board with people you trust and who have a vested interest in the success of a treatment—not just the company directors, or your team, but the outsiders not belonging to your organisation or profession. And reward honesty: sometimes it can be shocking, but it will always be educational.

Regulation and Reimbursement

In the healthcare framework, regulation is key. It is there for a reason, and it is based on authorities and regulatory bodies adopting technologies through evaluating their credibility. Above all, regulation is our way to show responsibility and reliability in fitting our healthtech innovations into the global framework. Through registration, the governmental bodies ensure that healthtech products meet the requirements relating to quality, safety and efficiency in accordance with current legislation, thus ensuring the safety of citizens.

In Europe, we have a European directive on public procurement of innovative solutions and also pre-commercial procurement. A typical pathway is as follows:

■ Pilot phase of the trial
■ Input from early adopters
■ Contracts with payers and providers
■ Universal reimbursement

In every step forward, you are reaching out to a bigger number of stakeholders, proving efficacy and safety and, importantly, that you solve the new stakeholders' core unmet needs.

In the US, the main regulatory compliance checks are the Health Insurance Portability and Accountability Act (HIPAA) and the National Institute of Standards and Technology (NIST). They are part of the Department of Health and the Human Services Department and constitute legal codes of conduct to secure healthcare IT information and its management by parties such as healthtechs.

Enacted by the US congress, HIPPA is a framework of federal regulatory standards that outline how protected health information may be legally used and disclosed in the US. Meanwhile, NIST fights for healthtech innovations to meet the highest standards. As a result, the NIST agency ensures good practices in the healthtech industry by promoting and providing a measurable framework for medical devices, clinical diagnostics, imaging tools and the characterisation of complex biotherapeutics. NIST recently launched a guidebook to help to implement HIPPA rules.[16]

If you want to start-up and scaleup your healthtech innovations and business, you should consider these two US-based compliance frameworks from the get-go. The guidelines are easy to follow and will insure you against potential liabilities down the line.

Of course, alongside regulatory approval, you must secure engagement from the appropriate health institutions, patients' associations, healthcare professionals, and pathology associations. Only then can you reach reimbursement: when you embrace health technology assessment bodies, from the very first moment of your solution, and work in awareness with key stakeholders and payers along the journey hand by hand at every phase of the project.

If you decide to register your healthtech products or services and look for a reimbursement from health authorities, remember that bodies are continually changing and consolidating. So do your research into the latest state of play. At the very least, to be eligible for a reimbursement request, you must meet certain requirements:

1. Cover an unmet clinical need
2. Prove clinical efficacy
3. Secure regulatory affairs approval
4. Demonstrate real-world evidence vs a benchmark (or similar standard technology)
5. Demonstrate cost-effectiveness improvement vs benchmark (or similar standard technology)

Obtaining reimbursement for your technology and therefore its inclusion in the public healthtech portfolio requires above all data that validates your technology and its quality and the potential for high user adoption. Follow these steps:

Phase I: iteration and pilot study phase.
Phase II: early adopters' program (to get certification).
Phase III: contracts signed with independent healthcare providers, local or regional payers, health or hospital clusters.

Only when the number of customers or users is high and the clinical and technological evidence is backed by hard data will you achieve universal reimbursement for your health technology.

We must remember we are playing in an environment with many advantages and many privileged sources of information that other fields like retail or mass markets lack. It is easy to get access to the names of these huge companies and public institutions that are effectively vendors of health

---

[16] https://www.nist.gov/programs-projects/security-health-information-technology/hipaa-security-rule

data and information. We will need this information about our customers, patients, caregivers, HCP, and institutions to build our solutions and prove their effectiveness, and it is generally easy to access.

But we must be careful of the policies that surround and control our zones of operation and our access to information. Each country has a unique regulatory environment. We cannot all do whatever we want—our customers are patients, and we shall remember that patients are humans who have a disease and who have rights around their privacy.

We can be innovative, disruptive and game changing, but we are not playing in a free environment. We are playing with health, which is a significant responsibility, in a very restricted environment. There are increasing numbers of ad-hoc rules to regulate disruptive business concepts to ensure and preserve the health and wellbeing of our patients. Thus, security and legal compliance are critical considerations when designing and implementing health solutions.

Patients rely on us to efficiently meet their needs, to improve their pathology outcomes, and to make their lives as near normalcy as possible. To get there, and to get there ethically, we need unified interfaces to ensure data legality and optimisation to provide personalised value. This is especially true regarding the integration of the IoMT and AI. Despite 25% growth in IoMT devices per year, 90% of healthcare data is lost (Statista, 2021). Neither we nor our patients can afford this.

With so many new solutions being presented and the regulatory landscape so complex, you would be forgiven for being overwhelmed. Yet regulators are now validating the developer on an umbrella basis, rather than the individual innovation, to cope with the huge number of requests that they are experiencing. This can be a considerable boon to our own processes as innovators—we can innovate a solution under an existing umbrella of regulation.

The Three Steps to Regulation

1. Lose the Fear

Failure to comply with a standard framework like the General Data Protection Regulation (GDPR) may result in significant fines of up to EUR 20 million or 4% of your company's global turnover for certain breaches (Union, Data Protection under GDPR, 2021). Certainly, regulatory matters can be scary. But when you start diving into them, you realise they share a commonality: all are rules matrixes based on common sense ethics put at the service of the patient. That is sometimes a tricky maze to navigate, but the first step is to lose the fear and happens by staying well informed.

Regulatory frameworks apply depending on the location of your company and where it operates. Consider the registered headquarters of your healthtech as the county of reference and the legal frameworks that apply to country-by-country regions (US, EU). You should be covered by sticking strictly to them. It is also important to consider the scope of applicability, in which countries you are operating, and which are the most restrictive rules in them.

An international homogenous regulatory environment is still far off. Yet already, first steps have been taken with the creation of an international program, the International Medical Device Regulators Forum (IMDRF) (IMDRF, 2014). IMDRF constitutes a group of medical device regulators from around the world that have voluntarily come together to harmonise the regulatory requirements for medical products that vary from country to country.

Current IMDRF members represent official medical device regulatory authorities in:

Australia - <u>Therapeutic Goods Administration</u> (Administration A. T., s.f.)
Brazil - <u>National Health Surveillance Agency (ANVISA)</u> (Government B., 2021)

Canada - <u>Health CanadaExternal Link Disclaimer</u> (HA & Canada, 2021)

China - <u>China Food and Drug Administration</u> (MDChina, 2021)

Europe - European Commission Directorate-General for Internal Market Industry (MD.EC, 2021) Entrepreneurship and SMEs

Japan - Pharmaceuticals and Medical Devices Agency and the Ministry of Health, Labour and Welfare (PMDA, 2021)

Russia - <u>Russian Ministry of Health</u> (Government R., 2021)

Singapore - <u>Health Sciences Authority</u> (Government S., 2021)

South Korea - <u>Ministry of Food and Drug SafetyExternal Link Disclaimer</u> (MFDS, 2021)

United States - <u>US Food and Drug Administration</u>

Besides, the World Health Organization (WHO) is an Official Observer. The Asia Pacific Economic Cooperation (APEC) Life Sciences Innovation Forum's (LSIF) Regulatory Harmonization Steering Committee, the Asian Harmonization Working Party (AHWP), and the Pan American Health Organization (PAHO) are regional harmonisation initiatives with IMDRF. Later in Chapter 4, we will address some of the IMDRF guidelines to digital therapeutics regulation.

In the US, if you are a healthtech providing a mobile health (mHealth), health information technology (IT), wearable devices, telehealth and telemedicine, or personalised medicine, your regulatory framework will be based in the Digital Health Centre of Excellence from the food and drug administration (FDA) and its rules (FDA, 2021).

For example, if you are developing a mobile health app in the US that collects, creates, or shares consumer information, use the tool on the Federal Trade Commission's website to find out when the FDA, Federal Trade Commission (FTC), or Office of Civil Rights (OCR) laws apply.[17]

Here are the laws most likely to apply to your solution:

■ The Health Insurance Portability and Accountability Act (HIPAA), which protects the privacy and security of certain health information and ensures notifications of health information breaches.

■ The Federal Food, Drug, and Cosmetic Act (FD&C Act), which regulates the safety and effectiveness of medical devices. It focuses its regulatory oversight on a minority of health apps that could represent a higher risk.

■ The Federal Trade Commission Act (FTC Act), which prohibits deceptive or unfair acts or practices in or affecting commerce, including those relating to privacy and data security, and those involving false or misleading claims about apps' safety or performance.

■ The FTC's Health Breach Notification Rule that requires certain healthtechs to provide notifications following breaches of personal health record information (FTC, 2016).

The FDA has also developed a Digital Health Innovation Plan (FDA, FDA Food and Drug Administration. Centre for devices & Radiological Health Digital Health Program., 2018). This is an agile pilot model for regulating software and constructing a regulatory framework that rests on three core capabilities:

---

[17] You can easily obtain information about which laws do apply to your healthtech app by answering 10 yes/no questions in the immediate response questionnaire tool that you can find in the following link: https://www. ftc.gov/tips-advice/business-center/guidance/mobile-health-apps-interactive-tool# [Last Accessed: December 2021]

1. The Regulatory Development Kit (RDK): SaMD developers likely could benefit from regulation 11, reimagining digital health, which gives timely information on FDA requirements and guidance on how to interact with the agency to get their products to market.
2. FDA Pre-Cert: here, eligibility is determined based on a company's ability to demonstrate a culture of quality and organisational excellence (CQOE).
3. The Multi-Stakeholder Real World Data Capability: this operates from highly distributed to extremely centralised and can be especially effective when individual companies, industry stakeholders, patients, and appropriate governing bodies work collaboratively to develop a solution. An example is the Medical Device Innovation Consortium's (MDIC) National Evaluation System for Health Technology (NEST)[18] (Dhar, Delone, & Ressler, 2018).

In Europe, if you are a developer of a medical device or software as a service, you should consider official regulatory validation using CE marking. This is the manufacturer's claim that a product meets the General Safety and Performance Requirements (GSPR) of relevant European Medical Device Regulations. It is a legal requirement for taking a product to market in the EU.

Besides, Regulation (EU) 2017/745 of the European Parliament and of the Council (EU, 2017), also called MDR, will apply to any class II medical device under Regulation (EU) 2020/561 of the European Parliament and of the Council of April 23, 2020 (eur-lex, 2020). It applies to any healthtech solution and to any size of healthtech company, including small and medium. At the same time, MDR is a big step towards the alignment of EU and US frameworks (Garcia Perez, 2020).

Once you have identified the regulatory bodies that will impact the growth and adoption of your healthtech, you must, of course, adhere to their guidelines as you build your business. But you can also consider regulators as possible allies with whom you can build strategic alliances. After all, they are stakeholders in the ecosystem as well. Primary market solutions, based on "essential healthcare", need to be re-established. So, let us work together with the regulatory entities from the very beginning. This collaboration can be official or nonofficial in the first interactions or meetings, as it all helps build the right win-win alliances to secure official validation in the near future.

Authorities are trying to make new regulations less bureaucratic and more open, trying to give room to the new healthtech solutions of the future. They are more committed than ever to fostering innovation. The launch of new alliances such as the recent EU Commitment to ensure "systematic and structural cooperation" between the European Innovation Council (EIC) and the European Institute of Innovation and Technology (EIT) are the vanguard (EC, 2021).

We are all part of innovation hubs and accelerators, surrounded by talent support, and we all ultimately want to build up and co-create to advance our healthtech companies for the good of the present and future of healthcare. There is a movement towards private-public bridging institutions that can face the unmet need of the healthcare system and objectively validate health technologies safely and cost effectively to ease the public adoption of private technologies. And this favours our newborn healthtech companies.

One example is a recent UK government initiative with Genome UK, where the UK government attempts to incorporate the latest genomics advances into routine healthcare to improve prevention, diagnosis and research. The governmental program also goes through cross-cutting

---

[18] NEST is a voluntary network of data partners assembled to "apply an inclusive, patient-centred approach to increase the responsible use of Real World Evidence across the total product life cycle (TPLC) for a diverse set of stakeholders in a cost-effective and sustainable manner".

themes positioning the patient in the centre and vehiculating the advances through the latest technologies. Thus, British genomics constitutes one of the leading platforms in the world (Government, 2020).

2. List the "Hot Spots"

For an example, let us say you are the owner of a blockchain technology and are planning your regulatory path.

Social and ethical responsibility typically prioritises individual privacy. The management of data is the main source of energy in the healthtech environment, and from it arises conceptualisations such as blockchain. Blockchain brings the possibility of protecting data while making it shareable among stakeholders without breaking any safety, compliance, or legal barriers. As such, blockchain has the potential to be the foundation for a safe, global health information exchanges (HIE)—even if it probably will not see mainstream adoption until 2030 (Exeevo, 2021).

So, where are the regulatory hotspots? Clearly, they are in data collection. So that you would then consider data ownership principles established by the EU GDPR and US HIPAA (other interesting compliance frameworks to start with can be ISO 27001 and SOC-2). This might require you to give data owners the ability to control third party access to their data and to be compensated for data sharing.

As the relationship between blockchain platform and user now becomes a commercial transaction, it is regulated by consumer laws as well as privacy ones. Therefore, you should consider all regulatory frameworks around data monetisation.

Your healthtech company as the provider of the online service that commercially exploits users' data must provide sufficient information, in the registration process, about the commercial value of data and the commercial purpose pursued. In other words, ensure that the citizen understands what he or she is consenting to already in the registration process (Union, Data Protection under GDPR, 2021).

You would also need to consider the country's wider strategic plans relating to data collection. In America, this would be found at the US. Office of the National Coordinator for Health Information Technology, which pursues nationwide health interoperability under the Health Interoperability Outcomes 2030 (HealthIT, 2020).[19]

3. Set a Roadmap

Set a roadmap with actions to take, with clear deadlines, and assign them to skilled employees who will be responsible for ensuring all these tasks are carried out successfully and on time. And more than this, include each action within your budgeting to remove unpleasant surprises.

Hiring a data protection officer (DPO) for the company is a good idea. A DPO is responsible for monitoring how personal data is processed and to inform and advise employees who process personal data about their obligations. The DPO also cooperates with the data protection authority (DPA), serving as a contact point towards the DPA and individuals (Union, Data Protection under GDPR, 2021).

---

[19] https://www.healthit.gov/topic/interoperability/health-interoperability-outcomes-2030

Be Adaptable to Change

Before you start your journey, you should have roughly sketched out what business model you will use. You should have acquired sufficient knowledge about the field you are entering and built a team around additional knowledge requirements. You might also know which stakeholders will make for useful allies and what regulations will apply to your work.

Ultimately, remember that you and your entrepreneurial mind have the power to change the whole healthcare system as we know it and help create the new healthcare model.

So, your solution is part of something much bigger than itself or your company. It is part of breaking and remaking the healthcare system, and thus you must help yourself and your business find the right place within the bigger picture while helping to upgrade the new horizon of healthcare.

Recently, somebody asked me, "Why me? Why my enterprise? Why will my healthtech succeed above others? And how can I bring value when all of us are bringing value?"

My answer was this. Think about how to solve the unmet need in the bigger picture of the future. Think about our healthtech world in five years and prepare your solution and yourself to fly in a scalable and sustainable way by then.

We are experiencing a digital natural selection. We are moving from a model of prevention to a model of patient empowerment, from patient support programs to digital holistic health, and from treatment to early diagnosis (see Figure 3.4) (Membrillo, 2021).

Charles Darwin stated, "It is not the strongest of the species that survives, nor the most intelligent, but the one most responsive to change". (Darwin, On the Origin of Species By Means of Natural Selection, 1859), as illustrated in Figure 3.5. And we need to see ourselves as the bridges that will help the healthcare industry transition onto the path of this digital evolution.

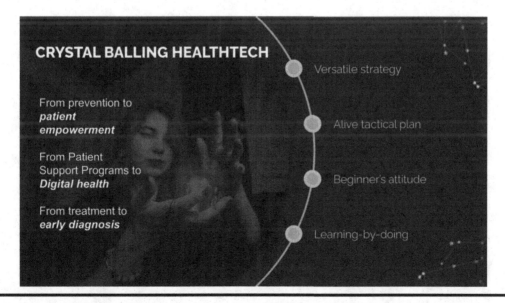

Figure 3.4   Representation of main future umbrella trends in healthtech and its tactics towards implementation.

Figure 3.5   Charles Darwin, natural selection theory quote.

We need to envision reaching equity in the new healthcare model. That means that all the people can achieve their maximum potential in terms of health, having access to high-quality healthcare no matter their social position, where they live or their wealth. Our goal should be reaching the point at which all the healthcare resources could be assigned to any individual in the world according to their needs.

METHOD

METHOD

Chapter 4

Defining and Building Your Value

Once you have come up with your business idea and have conceptualised your strategic position within the emerging healthcare landscape, you must begin to take the first concrete steps towards building your first healthtech product. That means you must define and build value.

A 2019 Special Task Force report (ISPOR task force) identifies and defines a series of elements that warrant consideration in value assessments of medical technologies (Lakdawalla, et al., 2021) (Lakdawalla, et al., 2018). It does so with the aim of broadening the view of what constitutes value in healthcare and spurring new research on incorporating additional elements of value (as illustrated in Figure 4.1) into cost-effectiveness analysis (CEA).

So, as healthtechs, the primary way to create value is to improve healthcare outcomes through:

- QALYs: The ISPOR task force concluded that quality-adjusted life-years (QALY) remains the most accepted measure for capturing the incremental benefit of a treatment for use in population-level decision making. One quality-adjusted life year (QALY) is equal to 1 year of life in perfect health. QALYs are calculated by estimating the years of life remaining for a patient following a particular treatment or intervention and weighting each year with a quality-of-life score (on a 0 to 1 scale).

   You can simply express the benefit in health outcomes with them, considering how many 1, 3 or more QALYs the patient earns on average with your technology.
- NET Costs: To exemplify what NET costs are, let us use the monetary value of a QALY. The Institute for Clinical and Economical Review of the US estimates a QALY costs between 50,000 and 150,000 dollars. Imagine that you can pharmacoeconomically demonstrate if your technology improves 1 QALYs per patient in a population like that of the US of approximately 330 million people (census.gov, 2020) and with a prevalence of 10.5%, as is the case of diabetes (Services U. D., 2020). Then your solution will represent an additional value for almost 35 million patients that will improve their QALYs with a consequent economic impact that will oscillate between 1,750,000 and 5,250,000 dollars of containment of health spending.

DOI: 10.4324/b23147-6

Elements of Value

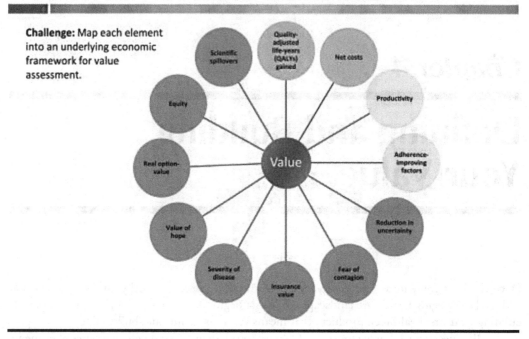

Figure 4.1   Elements of value in healthcare.

When you are trying to pitch your solution to the payer or other key stakeholder, the economics are, unfortunately, as equally important as the health benefits. This dual value can be extrapolated to any health asset that we deal with in health technology. You can even turn health datasets into QALYs and monetise them.

■ Productivity: The added health that a healthtech solution can bring to the workforce translates directly into productivity gains for a country or region. In an inverted population pyramid where the population of working age is increasingly reduced, this concept is an important element of a value dossier.

A clear example is the lack of health equity that is translated in a loss productivity in the US of 42$ billion and 1.4% cost of GDP in EU. With the unique goal of commitment towards health equity between and within countries, in September 2021, at the World Economic Forum the Global Health Equity Network (GHEN) was presented (Brown et al, 2022).

■ Adherence Improvement: In essence, you add value if your technology can contribute to adherence and persistence in treatment, which translates into health results. It is also a convenient factor and is easily quantifiable.

■ Reduction in Uncertainty: Uncertainty is usually reduced following a precise diagnosis. Reducing uncertainty is valuable because it reduces risk and therefore translates into improved health outcomes. Consider a treatment with poorly known effectiveness. In this instance, even a slight quantifiable increase in certainty assumes a high value. When the pathology's progression cannot be predicted in advance, any help provided by technology will be of great value.

- Fear of Contagion: With the recent global pandemic impacting every home, this parameter acquires a very high importance. If your technology can add value by reducing fear of contagion, quantify it and put it as one of the first bullet points of a value dossier.
- Insurance Value: Chronic diseases are expensive for health insurance companies. If your solution can impact the cost of treatment or improve the management of chronic conditions, insurance companies will prioritise it. The disease ratio in a population or morbidity is directly related to the value of the health coverage that the citizen receives. Here we could include the quality of universal public coverage in those cases where it applies.
- Severity of Disease: This value is sometimes controversial. For example, a patient with a worse prognosis but with better health coverage may have additional QALYs compared to a patient with a better prognosis and poor healthcare. At this point, health technology can contribute and is contributing a lot of value in the continuous follow-up of the patient journey in all its stages, creating better health results.
- Value of Hope: The value of hope can be defined as the preference for higher-risk solutions for the chance of a cure even if the probability for success is fairly low. Stated otherwise, "Many severely ill patients may be willing to trade off some survival (e.g., undertaking a risky procedure) for a chance at a "cure"—even if only for a small probability of that much longer expected survival or cure. Technologies that provide an opportunity for a cure would thus be more valuable to many patients, and a payer, acting as their agent, would be willing to pay more on their behalf" (Lakdawalla, et al., 2018).
- Real Option Value: Future advances in medicine will occur, but when and precisely how are uncertain. Patients must endure this uncertainty, but a solution that extends life improves the chances that a patient can enjoy future advances. This is known as "real option value".
- Equity: Refers to any technology that brings us closer to the concept of equity, universal access and democratisation of health. Offering access regardless of social status or economic capacity is a factor of high value for the health systems of the future and their new operations. Thus, considering the applicability and scalability of technology not only in first world countries but also in low-to-medium income countries (LMIC) can be a good starting point when conceptualising the technologies of the future.
- Scientific Spillovers: The value of this parameter lies in the impact that technology can generate today on future generations of patients. This can happen in very cutting-edge technologies that, despite being patented, can represent a basis or premise to establish or achieve the optimal technology in the future. They are, essentially, building blocks. If you can demonstrate that, then you are adding scientific spillover value.

It is that Simple.

The ISPOR task force ranks these elements of value. It classifies QALYs and NET Costs as the core elements of value. It considers Productivity and Adherence Improvement Factors as common but inconsistently used elements of value. Finally, Reduction in Uncertainty, Fear of Contagion, Insurance Value, Severity of Disease, Value of Hope, Real Option Value, Equity and Scientific Spillovers are labelled by the task force as potential novel elements of value.

Keep in mind that the cost-effectiveness of any healthtech product is taken from other existing benchmarks and similar technologies available in the market.

When you present your solution to healthtech authorities, to the payers, or to any potential stakeholder, follow the ranking of the elements of value: put QALYs and Net Costs first and foremost. Also consider that the ISPOR task force states that QALYs, Net Costs and Adherence

Improving Factors are value elements included in the traditional payer or health plan perspective; and the rest of the elements of value are also included in the societal perspective.

So first off, discard your ego—only amateurs cling to the idea of being the next unicorn. Prioritise improving the QALYs of each citizen and patient alongside optimising the patient journey, narrowing the window between early diagnosis and better prognosis which in turn translates into NET costs impact. We must also do this sustainably: maintaining a rate of growth with a simple, high-level of focus on the health outcomes. This means not creating significant collateral problems for future generations and keeping grounded by focusing on the circular economy as the basis of healthtech businesses from the beginning.

As healthtechs, we can easily bring benefits to the system and contribute to a more sustainable and circular economy by enabling the following:

- Faster and more equal access to services.
- Lowering the burden of oversized healthcare expenditure costs.
- Early prevention, real-life, continuous non-invasive screening and early diagnosis ideally resulting in a non-appearance of the disease.
- Short- and long-term QALYs extension.
- Interoperability and coordination between stakeholders, thus upgrading output delivery.
- Vertical and horizontal healthcare costs containment.
- Shortcuts and optimisation of the value chain.

We also create value by commoditising technology in terms of products and services added to the medication itself. This is possible if you do not think of it as an isolated item but more as an item that impacts patients and interacts with them within a bigger picture in a "tech-normalised" way.

Overall, if I really had to leverage a key field and decide where to focus, considering the whole healthcare system's trend towards reaching a standardised and sustainable model, I would say, focus on the early diagnosis. Let us integrate easy access to preventive medicine and early diagnosis into the lifestyle of citizens, which would improve life extension standards. And this should be one of the main goals that entrepreneurs pursue, if we pay attention to the bigger picture and if we really want to bring value.

We are already at the point where the patient can buy QALYs, or healthy ageing.

As healthtechs, our solutions are the digital health products and services they acquire in the big marketplaces that operate as digital supermarkets. Through us, they buy the health of the future, on a basic system of supply and demand, in a retail environment. As we have explained in Chapter 2, this supply and demand market is starting to emerge already, in which the customers pay from their pockets and become new actors in the ecosystem.

Citizens are the new consumers of health, and thus starting to be the new payers. This used to be the role of governance institutions and insurance companies. Now, however, as payers and consumers of health, citizens are contributing to the healthcare system, keeping healthier lifestyles and in turn impacting the overall cost-effectiveness picture of the current healthcare systems. But they will not pay for a solution unless you can demonstrate its value to them.

This requires training, which makes patients take responsibility for their own health and embrace the healthtech offered in their lifestyles.

Getting the patient to comprehend their real needs through early exercises, before they may experience the health problem, will be the new starting point for future health marketing and consumer healthcare. Consequently, all business strategies should point towards brand localisation

(Voser, 2018)[1] within the consumer's lifestyle. So that all your product or service strategies operate in the new healthtech ecosystem. That means pursuing the needs of a targeted patient, or more often a healthy citizen and healthy lifestyle, and anticipating the occurrence of the pathology. In other words, the new core of the value flower is looking after health and fostering early diagnosis before the pathology arises.

Building the Patient Profile

QALYs, and the new model of healthcare in general, centre on the patient. So, to create value for the patient, we must first understand the patient. Indeed, the new patient profile is more demanding, empowered, powerful, educated and updated than we could have ever imagined. We must stay on top of defining the patient to provide valuable healthcare solutions. Thanks to all the data currently available to us, healthtechs can target the specific "moment" of the patient journey that we want to impact, and we can create a much stronger picture of healthcare outcomes.

What I mean with this is that we must not only understand the patient pathway, but also their behaviours and the reasons they exist as patients in the first place. Understanding those is the key to creating value. Above all, we must know their true needs and what really matters for them in terms of healthcare outcomes for them to buy into our solution.

Consequently, patient involvement is a must in the process of obtaining these value insights, which we should rank by importance. Without doing this simple exercise, it is not possible to reach high-performance technologies and healthtech solutions. It is a must to co-create along with patients, to both educate and learn from them the best practices at individual and global levels, and at all the leveraging points of the chain of care and of healthcare.

To perform this co-creation, we must understand what is going on in terms of our patients, so we apply social listening. A recent Forbes article stated that the social determinants of health (SDOH) account for a larger portion of overall health outcomes than medical care determinants (Das, 2019). Thus, in the article, they predict increasing utilisation of "social determinant" data in making risk assessments, patient outreach and business decisions. This equates to building up focus groups that can produce this information, which we use to improve our services. Setting up these patient communities, or getting access to them, is therefore critical.

Ethnography is a must when we speak about understanding the anthropological behaviour around a pathology. It is deep-diving into the lifestyle, behaviours, thoughts and opinions of patients, always analysing the cultural phenomena from their perspective. After all, they are the customer.

Also, ethnographic studies are carried out to understand thoughts and opinions around a certain product or service, as well as a pathology.

Medical and digital ethnography are expanding areas of this discipline applied to the methodology of focus groups and ethnographic studies.

An ethnographic study for healthtech can be easily performed in low-resource settings through a focus group of patients, healthcare professionals, caretakers or caregivers. Use patient videos, self-reports, or SMS diaries or role-play in sessions to obtain ethnographic understanding (Fernandes, et al., 2021).

---

[1] Brand localisation is a buzzword in the marketing industry, essentially meaning taking the brand or a product and outfitting it for operating in a new market.

Performing a focus group study is easy.[2] The difficulty is in knowing who is speaking truthfully—because participants often lie. They lie because they feel pressure from whomever is conducting the study and do not want to compromise, or they do not want to be judged, or for the simple fact that they would like to please. So, the more warm and relaxed you make the environment in which the study is conducted, the better. Aim to elicit a response that is visceral, spontaneous and the closest to reality as possible—not compromised by external factors.

You can carry out an ethnographic study yourself or you can outsource it to a third party that will do it for you. If you lack experience, this second option is the best approach. I have spectated many ethnographic studies from behind a one-way glass. From time to time, the moderator I had hired would come out to me asking for feedback. How was the focus group going? Should it be redirected or investigated differently? This kind of observation and modification is important to achieve the best results.

Implementation is not as important as preparation. Rigor and structure are key when preparing. To well prepare an ethnographic research essay, I suggest you first define what behavioural questions you really want to answer. What is it that you do not understand, and you really want to about your customer of health? Take time to identify this.

Afterwards, decide where you want to conduct the study. Ideally, it will be in a place that is non-intrusive and impacts people's usual form of communicating and experiencing as little as possible.

A simple meeting room with a one-way observational glass window will suffice. You can rent these in most large cities easily. Sometimes a simple interview in a hotel room, recording the session to later analyse it in detail, is enough.

Consider: who will lead the meeting? They may play the role of an integral member of the community or the role of a leading moderator. Have you considered the ethics of their role? How will questions be posed? Have you eliminated bias from them?

Always aim for whatever is the least invasive. You can also conduct an observational study with real immersion in the field.

Taking notes for an accurate and detailed report of what happens in the study is very important. Sometimes, having an expert who knows how to read between the lines, such as verbal and non-verbal language, is also beneficial for reaching objective conclusions that help optimise the products and services of your healthtech for the benefit of the patient.

A broad spectrum of ethnographic studies exists, and methodologies are constantly improving and being adapted to the healthtech industry. So do your research.

For example, a significant recent improvement is the digital performance of ethnographic studies. Usually, we implement these when the target participant size is much bigger, since the primary value of performing a digital ethnographic study lies in the large quantities of data collected at a high speed. With datafication, we take data collected by objects connected to an IP address (IoMT) and anonymise it for social analysis. In this way, datafication offers new cultural spaces of data collection—in-home, on-app, etc.—where human behaviour is better understood and even shaped thanks to the synergy between Big Data and ethnographical methodologies (Paoli & D'Auria, 2021).

An example of this digital ethnography and Big Data intersection is FitBit. The commoditised smartband had 31 million active users in 2020 (Statista, 2021).[3] FitBit datafies your physical

---

[2] A good guide to the process is Liamputtong, Pranee. *Focus Group Methodology: Principle and Practice* (SAGE Publications, 2011).

[3] FitBit URL: https://www.fitbit.com/

activity from each day (Elliott, 2013). All this Big Data can be ethnographically processed to understand human behaviours and reach smart conclusions about what customers value.

These smartbands are, by now, well-known examples of holistic patient-generated health data (PGHD) collectors. They have the potential to transform healthcare by supporting and evaluating health in everyday living for several reasons. They are familiar to most people; are increasingly available as a consumer device; enable near-real-time continuous monitoring of physical activity and physiological measures; support tailored messaging and reminders; enable communication between patients, family members and healthcare providers and allow for in situ observation, mini-surveys and behaviour verification using sensor-based measures (Reeder & David BS, 2016).

Without patient input in the development of mobile health devices, healthtech tools will fail to meet patient needs and to keep patients motivated to continue to capture and share PGHD with clinicians and researchers (Services, 2018). PGHD collection needs to meet patients' essential daily patterns of behaviour and keep high standards of patient quality of life.

As this section has explained, ethnographic studies through focus groups enable customer understanding. But also, they are useful in product design, from modelling engagement to finally building a valued customer experience and an optimised health journey.

For example, you can already perform ethnographic research with wearable cameras by taking real-time pictures according to changes in the user's environment detected by sensors. Then, you can analyse the metadata to create a time-activity matrix, activity maps, artefact interaction maps and other visualisations that can inform your healthtech innovations and help you construct value (Thoring, Mueller, & Badke-Schaub, 2015).

Social studies like this enable us to build an empathy map through integrating all the blueprints allocated in datasets and translating them onto a holistic understanding of patient attitudes and reactions (Gray, 2017) (Pontis, 2018).[4] This would allow us to understand what they feel, think, visualise, say, do and listen to and consequently design proper strategies for a better standard of care.

By using ethnographic studies to build hubs of patient profiles and create these empathy maps, we can align our healthtechs with the humanised model of healthcare. That is healthcare that involves "respect for patient's dignity, uniqueness, individuality, and humanity, as well as adequate working conditions and sufficient human and material resources" (Busch, et al., 2019).

Primarily, it will do this by helping you identify pain points along the patient's journey (Shewan, 2020) that technology can help with. These are problems that prospective customers of your business are experiencing. Pain points can be many things, and if we focus on healthcare, a common pain point that patient need to deal with are the unbeloved waiting rooms. So, building a solution around alleviating that pain point is a great way to secure value. Another pain point could be data breaches, so healthtechs could build a solution around protecting health data.

This ethnographic approach goes hand in hand with Patient-Reported-Outcomes (PROs). PROs put together two terms ("patient-reported" and "outcome") and—according to D.L. Patrick—they mean "any report coming directly from patients, without interpretation by physicians (Refolo, et al., 2012) (Patrick, et al., 2007). To truly connect with the patient and build something they value, you will need to understand and engage with their PROs. These hubs of patient profiling can come up with different patient experiences and well-defined needs within the same clinical condition. Thus, ethnographic panels are in-depth ways to use User Design and Design Thinking to understand the needs of the final users.

---

[4] You can find a template for an empathy map here, URL: https://medium.com/the-xplane-collection/updated-empathy-map-canvas-46df22df3c8a

And remember to think holistically: this kind of study can address all stakeholders in the healthcare ecosystem (patients, healthcare professionals, caregivers and payers) to help you build a valuable solution.

Safety and Security Around Patient-Generated Content (PGC) and Health Data (PGHD)

When we talk about patient-generated content (PGC) and patient-generated health data (PGHD), we mean the expert sessions, 24/7, 365-days-of-the-year data recording, patient testimonials and voluntary patient reports. Seventy-three percent of the EU citizens want to share health data under the precondition that data is secure (ICU, 2020) (see Figure 4.2). Thus, when it comes to patient data protection, security really matters not only in our healthtechs themselves but also in the providers we work with. Security and compliance practices must be there. We must face data breaches that impact our access (Smith, 2016).

One of the primary ways companies collect PGC is via ad hoc websites designed specifically for patients. Examples include PatientsLikeMe[5] for people with medical conditions, Myhealthteams[6] for chronic medical conditions and TheAsianParenting[7] as a pregnancy and parenting solution. All are communities that help patients share their experiences and guide them through their difficulties in decision-making.

Cybersecurity is the new fundamental concept to secure a future for your tech enterprise and yield positive outcomes. Normal people are scared to express their opinions freely. The rise of trolling is one reason for this, and it is something that we as healthtechs must deal with as well.

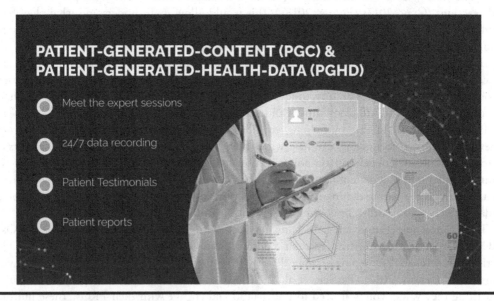

Figure 4.2   The main sources of patient generated content (PGC) & patient-generated- health-data (PGHD).

---

[5] PatientsLikeMe. URL: https://www.patientslikeme.com/
[6] Myhealthteams. URL: https://www.myhealthteams.com/
[7] TheAsianParenting URL: https://sg.theasianparent.com/

We must deal with signing up with fake domains and emails, email-based links compromising security, etc.

Consequently, we need to earn this information from the customer. We really need to be trustable and deserve all this information that the patients freely share with us. This will help give a new, more positive face to the healthcare and pharmaceutical industry.

It is important to determine which of the available technologies have been assessed to determine this trustworthy health data.

MedMij constitutes a best practice case of PGHD. MedMij[8] is a Dutch initiative that wants to implement personal Electronic Health Records in the Netherlands, ensuring anyone can have instant access to their own health data in a personalised health environment. Patients can keep their personal health records private or decide who to share the information with, no matter if it is the healthcare information system of a hospital, the physician, the clinic, or the pharmacy. Considerable value can be derived from this form of data collection, but it simultaneously protects the patient and gives them autonomy over their data.

Build Your MVP with Needs-Based R&D&i

We need to be versatile and constantly disruptive to open new doors and establish partnerships and alliances that allow us to settle and consolidate our strategic position in the ecosystem. Consequently, having understood the needs of our patient and built a patient profile, we must get a solution into their hands quickly, before it becomes outdated, that can be upgraded using an iterative approach.

So, we must target a minimum viable product (MVP) first, then perform line extensions of the master product, reaching for standardisation based on a continuous go-to-market model. An MVP is a version of a product with just enough features for early adopters to use, who can then provide feedback for future product development. According to most definitions, it must have three qualities: enough value in its initial form for people to buy; enough future benefit to retain early adopters; the capacity to garner feedback from the user to guide future development. These are solutions that meet patients' needs, get good shares of the market and at least temporarily solve the problem.

We can get an MVP through the agile methodology we discussed in Chapter 3. And we can do it within a week, aiming to cover priority issues.

With agile methodology, you can develop software and establish operational steps using the principles of the Manifesto for Agile Software (Alliance, 2021). These constitute a mindset: development focused on coding as a social act, software that works rather than overdocumentation, close collaboration with customers and versatility towards change. Ultimately, the agile method is about rapidly validating and iterating products based on what the final user thinks of them.

You should also consider the lean development principles from Chapter 3, together with Agile Model Driven Development (AMDD) and continuous independent testing (Ambler, 2008).

To achieve an MVP, you must eliminate the nonessential and the timewasting—everything that does not contribute to creating the final product, which is what you want to achieve in record time.

Take the creation of a Software as a Service product. The main goal you need to pursue as a newborn healthtech is to get an essential product element—an MVP—that meets basic healthcare

---

[8] MedMij. URL: https://www.medmij.nl/en/

needs as fast and as well as possible. This process is one of divergence towards convergence via iteration, where key steps could be:

1. Investigate and frame the problem.
2. Conceptualise the MVP.
3. Launch of a working product.
4. Continuously updated product deliveries.

The adoption curve of major technologies is much faster than it has ever been. This dramatically impacts how products (either digital therapeutics or Software as a Service) are conceptualised and built—everything is now about rapid developments, implementation and in-field testing. From the very first moment, we must be embracing and integrating user inputs into our development process.

We aim to solve the burden across all the leverage points in the system, but we need to consider technology also as a burden across all the dimensions of the healthcare system. Easiness and simplicity must come above all. By optimising and accelerating the adoption curve of technology towards standardised commodities, we can reduce this burden.

But first things first, start with the healthcare outcomes your idea or technology can achieve. You need to be able to think outside the box and start from the end with the solution in mind. Then move back until you can conceptualise the MVP, supporting it with a suitable position in the pathology's ecosystem. And really think about how your solution can become the main choice for customers—a seemingly simple concept that is difficult to accomplish—and then every stakeholder in the ecosystem. This will enable win-win alliances and should impact your design choices along the way.

A good way of testing the water for a potential MVP is an easy exercise of A/B testing. And this testing can easily be performed on social media (SoMe) during the conceptualisation process. To perform A/B testing—also known as split testing—you separate your audience into two random groups and show a different variation to each one. You then compare the responses to each variation to determine which is most effective based on your chosen metrics.

A/B testing can really help when it comes to getting initial consumer reactions, for branding and even building an audience for a prototype testing. The A/B test is a very simple test of a real population sample, offering critical real-world feedback for product development. You can perform it digitally and noninvasively, for example via an app or online survey on a social media site. Participants can swipe right if they like the idea (variant A) and left if not (variant B). You will know easily and quickly if the prototype/idea has potential, since you gain massive amounts of feedback very quickly through voting. And it is trustworthy for being so intuitive.

Once you have your MVP, build up the basis of a solution that addresses the whole pathway of the pathology, a solution with potential for sustained growth over time. Think of a master pathway that will uplift the core business of your healthtech model.

Sometimes you will get lucky, bumping into a lateral-thinking best-in-class solution that you were expecting to have to push for when you started the journey. Serendipity sometimes allows us to come up with a very positive upgrade from nowhere, but it is usually the result of a continuous pursuit of innovation. So, if you cannot be lucky, innovate through disruption.

1. The first wave is to diverge, and later converge. Disruptive innovation means coming up with five solutions for each unmet need, rather than one, then choosing the best and pushing for that the MVP while embracing the expertise of others and teambuilding with them. Trust your peers and do not be so sceptical of comparable healthtechs around you.

2. Define the MVP carefully to fit core needs. And above all, try to fit your MVP into the healthcare plans of the public systems. As the guidance and policy documents governing these systems are public and free, research them thoroughly and find out which key points or key lines of action are pursued by those with a helicopter vision of the whole pathology ecosystem.

The healthcare authorities, healthcare insurances and governmental healthcare institutions (traditionally the payers, and still so in public systems) are the ones that have already carried out social, burden and pharmacoeconomic studies within a certain area, within a certain pathology. They have already come up with crystal-clear lines of action that cover many unmet needs still in existence in the field, thus expanding the patient journey and opening paths of collaboration towards the aim of a sustainable healthcare model.

So, try to build around this. Take advantage of their good work and build up your MVP solution around key healthcare plans. Find common goals in the plans of the different states and regions you are acting within.

Forecasting Your Success

When innovating a new solution within the new healthcare standard of care, first forecast the overall impact of the technology before going to market.

An easy way to do sales forecasting is through the technique of crystal ball projection. This is more than guessing; you can predict outcomes three to five years from now in an excel sheet with the aid of tools like Oracle Crystal Ball (Oracle, 2021). This is an application for risk management and reporting that depends on Monte Carlo simulation, time-series forecasting and optimisation.

A benefit of this tool is that you do not need a benchmark. It involves knowing key single point estimates for inputs. You can use a range, and these inputs can vary over time. The model comes with a gallery of probability distributions (common graphs used in basic statistics), in which you need to define the key data points. Finally, when you get the estimated forecast, it is important to look at key parameters like the mean of the simulation or the standard deviation rate to consider the reliability of the forecast.

The Oracle Crystal Ball will estimate the most likely scenario. More advanced models will also include the best and the worst scenarios. However, no forecast is fully accurate. So, remember to build the costs of forecasts inaccuracy into your budget, vary the timeframe (usually from 6 months up to 10 years), and frequently update the forecast using real-world data.

Proper forecasting can help you understand upcoming business trends, the potential of your product and the likely direction of the market. Based on these readings, you can adjust your business strategies. Through forecasting the impact of technology, you will be able to develop powerful viable business analytics to plan your business life cycles, use real-world datasets to customise your healthtech needs and finally improve and foster the decision-making process of standardised business models. Forecasting can also help you to explain your business vision numerically to an investor (I do explain how to deal with funding later in the book).

Once you have forecasted the future environment you will operate in, think outside the box with deep tech possibilities that respond to real needs and are adaptable to the change. To do so, we do need to make our mindset more flexible and agile—focused more than ever on the customer. That requires co-creating with the key stakeholders, those who know what the real customer needs: the pharmacist, the patient, the physician, the caretaker, the caregiver, etc.

Build Your Team, Lead Your Company

Conducting R&D&i and developing an MVP also requires that you be a good team leader, which means doing whatever it takes to drive your business towards success.

The first step is to take care of your people. Deal with mental health concerns promptly and assign the appropriate load to each person in your company. You will become the new lean laggard by overworking your team members. Doing so results in high staff turnover, burnout and poor or disappointing innovation. Coming back to the Lean Methodology explained in Chapter 3, cope with these matters and improve workplace efficiency by applying the five key Lean principles (Crawford, 2016):

1. Define value (how your healthtech solution covers the unmet needs of the customer).
2. Map the value stream (present on a single sheet of paper the optimised key steps in the process of creating the MVP).
3. Create flow (clear the way for the process to run smoothly by anticipating potential interruptions and avoiding blockages).
4. Prioritise the delivery of working products.
5. Pursue perfection (implement a continuous lean mindset in the company culture).

Innovation is all about the user experience. When we innovate, we should provide a familiar but enhanced user experience through simplicity. We do not need to invent a panacea. It is a matter of "just providing health technology that fits inside a lifestyle". This concept could easily be translated to "on-demand" instantaneous personalised healthcare, as is the case of on-demand telemedicine (Sterling & LeRouge, 2019). Other examples are IoMT healthtech innovations such as Omron Evolv,[9] which allows you to check your blood pressure anywhere and anytime, and Netatmo Healthy Home Coach, which acts to keep your home healthier—the monitor measures what matters with its sensors, highlights potential problems and tells you how to fix them.[10]

Ultimately, design thinking plays a key role in how to present the solution beautifully for a perfect user experience, so onboard a designer early in the process of prototyping. User experience is the area that is least impacted by regulation, which is great news for building MVPs. However, do consider standards around usability, meaning how easy things are to use, and accessibility, which relates to how a disabled individual uses something.[11] A good resource for this is the Laws of UX for user interfaces.[12]

Finally, engagement is key. We need to engage through gamification, through innovating around visual, auditory and kinaesthetic channels, while defining the prototype that later will convey onto a viable MVP to go to market. Here the adoption of the technology is key, and it means humanising the technology.

In this sense, to develop an MVP in a healthtech start-up or small or medium enterprise (SME), try to create an optimised Health Technology Team (HTT). This should comprise the following (all of whom should have extensive prior experience in the role):

1. UX and Design Team, with highly skilled Design Specialists including User Interface (UI) and User Experience (UX) Specialists.

---

[9] Omron Evolv URL https://www.omron-healthcare.fr/fr/tensiometres/EVOLV.html

[10] Netatmo Healthy Home Coach URL https://www.netatmo.com/en-eu/aircare/homecoach

[11] Here is an example of usability standards set by the UK government. URL: https://www.usability.gov/get-involved/blog/2013/01/accessibility-and-usability.html

[12] https://lawsofux.com/

2. Development Team, including Software Developers, Software Architects, Software Engineers.
3. Project Management Team, including a Use Case Manager who builds the use case with the team and a Project Manager or Operational Manager.
4. A Product Manager, managing the product marketing and its lifecycle, but also performing the ethnographic studies and focus groups together with the UX & Design.
5. A Medical Director, who oversees regulatory affairs and can perform clinical trials and submit registrations and patents. They also ensure the clinical effectiveness and safety of the product, including the interaction with clinical centres that carry out clinical studies and manage RWE publications.
6. A Commercial Director, who is not only responsible for preparing the land for future sales but also for researching initial grant money and opportunities.
7. A Public Relations Manager and an Institutional Relations Manager, who handle the company's external relationships.

Initially, you can outsource some of these functions. Outsourcing is a good approach if you start alone or with a very small team and very little budget (like most of us start). If you do this, it is important that you cover the value of the company's property by signing non-disclosure agreements (NDAs). These ensure that the collaborator will maintain strict confidentiality.

In parallel, sign contracts that ensure that the two parties agree on the commitment to collaborate for the company for a specific function within a larger project that is and will remain the property of the company. It is essential to have these things agreed on from the very beginning, and the only way to do this is in writing and signed—verbal agreements are rarely valid.

Although outsourcing works initially, gradually incorporate the different members of the team into your company staff. They will quickly become indispensable, and leaving them as external functions is a risk.

When all the team members are in the company, R&D&i is an easy flow of:

1. Defining the supposed healthcare need.
2. Understanding through asking the users.
3. Learning from their real healthcare needs.
4. Confirming that this need can be covered by the technology.

In this process, co-creation from all members of the team in an AI- and Big Data-empowered workshop is important. But much more important is the co-decision making. Prioritise feasibility and high-impact projects, remembering that the input of the final user is essential to future engagement and adoption of your solution.

As mentioned, after the divergence stage, where you come up with many solutions, you will perform the convergence exercise to define the MVP. This requires development and testing. So always have the user, the customer, in your head when you push for a prototype. It is essential that you have their input from the very first moment, as it is the equivalent to the engagement with your MVP. But also onboard the experts at the very initial phases of the development—not only the patients, which are essential in this stage, but also the healthcare professionals, caregivers and stakeholders around the pathology. They have pre-existing knowledge you can capitalise on, and they will provide you with valuable proof of patient engagement and satisfaction rates.

Ultimately, building an MVP is about converging a prototype into an operating product, learning from failures in a process of iteration. In other words, ensure the construction process ends in an operational software or product. That's it. Develop and deploy through implementation and testing so when you launch the product it is a product that works. And only then scale up, maintaining your healthtech product and expanding your product lines. We cover growth in Part Three.

And finally, perform cost effectiveness and cost impact studies. These will give you the profitability rates to evaluate the viability of the go-to-market from the very beginning.

To Patent, or Protect?

While developing and conceptualising a new solution or product, a particular dilemma commonly emerges. What product innovation protection do you want to go through? There are two different solutions: knowledge preservation, or patenting. Both have pros and cons.

Patenting protects you for an average of 20 years before anyone can access and copy your solution freely, meaning about 10-15 years of exclusivity in the market (assuming that the corresponding annuities are paid). That is an eon of time in the healthtech field.

Your solution will be public but protected—you will own it. And that protection can earn you substantial funding when you go public. This is a good route for health software solutions and healthtech, as it preserves the value and extends its ownership. Of course, to go through patenting, you need to be exclusively "new" in your innovation and be its sole developer and owner; this is essential.

On the other hand, if you decide to go through know-how preservation, you will endeavour to keep the solution and the technology you are using secret. This takes considerable planning, often using advanced cybersecurity to ensure your employees can work collaboratively but without opening vulnerabilities in your system. Ultimately, the solution technology will have restricted access—it will be private. But it will only be private so long as you have trustworthy partners and employees.

Importantly, hiding your solution does not grant it legal protection from being plagiarised, nor from being understood and copied via reverse engineering or industrial espionage.

Overall, which is the best solution to protect innovation? It depends on your business model, so do the research and contrast it with experts in the field.

Build Credibility with Evidence-Based Medicine

If understanding your patient's needs and learning to scale an MVP are the two foundations of a valuable healthtech solution, evidence-based medicine (EBM) is the way to validate that value and give it creditability in the eyes of the healthcare stakeholders that matter most. Use EBM drawn from real world evidence (RWE). Get results from clinical trials and centres of excellence. Submit your healthtech to prizes, awards, collaborations and recognitions. Strive for credibility above all.

I cannot claim a health outcome with no evidence supporting it. What RWE can I obtain to achieve success? Here, use technology to your advantage. For example, for RWE and health economics and outcomes research (HEOR), we can leverage AI to mine and analyse real-time data from EMRs, patient-reported data and other sources. As a recent report finds, this can help us "to assess real-world efficacy of drugs and medical devices and correlate to outcomes. This function may complement or even substitute for clinical trials and could ultimately lead to better targeting of specific drugs to individual patients" (The Rockefeller Foundation, 2018).

Clinical Trials

To claim that our health technology has a specific value, we must demonstrate it in a strict clinical trial framework, just as one would with a vaccine or a drug.

Using the analogy of a drug or vaccine, we can assume that the active ingredient of a medicine, in health technology, would be equivalent to the software; and the excipients of the medicine would probably be how this software is presented either through an IoMT device, a wearable, a digital avatar, etc.

We need to clinically prove to the payers of the healthtech:

1. Evidence of the claimed value.
2. Effectiveness of the solution.
3. Evidence reported from the healthcare professional.
4. Demonstrate coverage of the unmet need.
5. Adopt the solution.
6. Demonstrate the cost-efficiency and viability of the solution (using a pharmacoeconomic study).

Besides this, for the healthcare professionals, nurses and caretakers, we need to:

7. Provide proved better clinical management tools.
8. Adapt the solutions to the daily clinical practice not the other way round.
9. Show the impact in the patient journey.
10. Demonstrate overall healthcare outcomes.

Let us use the example of digital therapeutics, as Gartner's recent research forecasts suggests they will become mainstream between 2025 and 2030 (Exeevo, 2021). Digital therapeutics are considered and regulated worldwide as a software as a medical device (SaMD). In Europe, new Medical Device Regulations replace the EU Medical Device Directive (MDD), representing a much more restrictive framework for the validation of new healthtech innovations, asking partner companies that are responsible for carrying out device audits commonly known as notified bodies for greater exigency and demand.

Following the already mentioned IMDRF guidelines, when planning the process of a clinical evaluation to prove effectiveness, safety and performance of a SaMD, you must prove two things. First, prove there is a validated clinical association between the output of a SaMD and the targeted clinical condition. Second, prove the SaMD provides the expected technical and clinical outcomes.

There is only one way to get all this clinical evidence and that is by conducting one or more clinical studies.

It depends on your professional background, but you will probably not be the person responsible for conducting the clinical trials needed for the validation and future register of your MVP. Usually, the person leading clinical research from the healthtech, and the contact person to the clinicians and researchers of the hospital or multiple centres performing the clinical trial, is the Medical Director. They normally obtain the help of the different members of the company and sometimes use an external agency called a Contract Research Organization (CRO).

Regardless, to perform a clinical trial for digital therapeutics, first carry out a pilot clinical trial. Then perform a bigger trial with a bigger sample population. Then conduct post-marketing follow-up. Here is what these three steps look like in detail:

1. *Pilot Clinical Trial*

    A pilot clinical trial (involving 5 to 10 patients) brings in the first evidence of whether it makes sense to further develop a solution. The main goal of performing a pilot clinical trial is to obtain evidence on the efficiency of the product and get first feedback and impressions from the user, usually the patient.

    In broad strokes, the key steps to perform a pilot clinical trial are.

    Step 1: Submission of a dossier containing the informed consent of the participants, the justification of the study, and the clinical situation that you want to study with all the details on the structure of the clinical trial for validation by the hospital's pharmacotherapeutic commission and ethical committee.

    Step 2: Get the first outcome. You can do this quickly, from a period of 12 weeks to 6 months depending on the patient profile and diagnostics used to test the digital therapeutics.

    Step 3: An analysis data plan will be performed by the healthtech or in the hospital or in some cases by an external clinical statistics specialist. This is a roadmap for how you intend to organiser and then analyse your trial data. It should help you answer your top research questions.

    In most cases, results should also inform a diffusion plan (how the new solution will be accepted by the market). Usually, this type of quick trial using small patient sample studies is published in an online journal such as BMC.

    After this pilot clinical trial, you may decide to conduct a full product development phase. That would mean using the results obtained from the pilot clinical trial to review and improve the product (digital therapeutics or Software as a Service (SaaS)) with the aim of nearing a final version. In this improvement phase, strategic, commercial and environmental aspects such as sustainability are also considered.

2. *Randomised Controlled Clinical Trial (RCT)*

    As explained, a clinical trial is done to demonstrate the benefit of a healthtech product, usually to get approval from regulatory authorities and get reimbursement.

    Following the pilot is typically a Randomised Controlled Multicentre clinical trial (including more than one centre or hospital) involving a representative sample of a minimum of 100 patients (this number can vary and be much bigger depending on the statistical significance needed).

    Follow the same steps mentioned of submitting the informed consent and justification of the study dossier to the ethical committee. The same step needs to take place in the different hospitals selected for the study.

    The study will take more time than the pilot, as all the patients will need to be recruited. The participating physicians' researchers will need to recruit the patients that meet the criteria of inclusion in the study. Plan for at least a year duration, but hedge for double that.

    Publish the results via an article in a high impact scientific and technology journal.

    With all this clinical evidence that you will get, the medical director can start to apply for the registration of the healthtech product and its price consecution and reimbursement.

3. Post Marketing Follow-Up

Finally, once the product is on the market, you can closely monitor its real-world use to validate its safety, identify possible adverse effects and reveal areas of improvement. Do this on as large a scale as possible.

All this RWE has to do with obtaining data that additionally validates clinical results. This includes (1) safety (tolerability and health) risks that often appear due to improper use of the healthtech product or software failures; (2) effectiveness, or the improvement in health results and its impact on values such as quality of life or as we have mentioned before QALYs; (3) economic impact, such as cost-effectiveness, budget impact, pricing points, etc. This last pharmacoeconomic parameter is usually consolidated after obtaining safety and effectiveness results.

RWE data related to the patient's experience can also be collected as (1) testimonials collected by users that validate its operation, or their (2) degree of satisfaction translated into user experience results, together with for example (3) user engagement and loyalty with the healthtech product.

Centres of Excellence

According to UNESCO, a centre of excellence could embrace a variety of national, regional or international institutions able to provide services at a standard sought by Member States or regions, and a satisfactory rationale for investment in their activity by interested customers. A centre of excellence could be a research or training institution, a university or one of its departments, a laboratory, science museum or library, etc. A national centre of excellence need not necessarily be a public institution, though by virtue of the profile of the centres that may be associated with International Basic Sciences Program (IBSP), this will probably be the case (UNESCO, 2021).[13]

When considering which is the right centre of excellence to onboard onto your project, choose the first-in-class for the focus pathology in your operating ecosystem. If you are creating a solution for sleep apnoea, find who is leading the trends and making advances in the pathology, nationally and internationally. And do the same for key opinion leaders (KOLs) that lead the strategic department and are the heads of the progress of the pathology inside this Centre of Excellence (Barcelona, 2021).[14]

To onboard a centre of excellence can mean many things. In essence, it means that the Key Opinion Leader that leads the study of the pathology (the person behind why the centre is known worldwide), and his/her team believes in your healthtech product.

It also means getting the centre of excellence to be the main centre or hospital that performs the first pilot of a clinical trial and the later randomised clinical trials that you plan to perform to validate clinical outcomes of efficacy and safety of your technology. Ideally, any follow-up studies should also involve the centre of excellence as well as the leading centre.

---

[13] "The International Basic Sciences Programme (IBSP) is an international multidisciplinary programme established by UNESCO Member States in order to reinforce intergovernmental cooperation and co-operation between partner organisations in science to strengthen national capacities in the basic sciences and science education. The Programme focuses on fostering major region-specific actions that involve a network of national, regional and international centres of excellence or benchmark centres in the basic sciences" (UNESCO, UNESCO, 2017).

[14] The right Centre of Excellence will depend on the pathology and field of expertise you are focusing your healthtech solutions on. Some examples of reference Worldwide Centres of Excellence are the Karolinska Institute https://ki.se/en; Mount Sinai https://www.mountsinai.org/locations/mount-sinai; Barcelona Clinical Hospital https://www.clinicbarcelona.org/en/assistance/about-clinic.

Finally, onboarding can mean that you can validate the RWE patient experience in the centre of excellence, collecting engagement, satisfaction levels and patient testimonials that will help you to build the credibility of your solution.

Why should you onboard the centre of excellence? Its value is in being at the heart of the worldwide attention on the pathology—its validation of your solution is recognised throughout the ecosystem of the pathology, especially by regulatory bodies.

Prizes and Awards

Put yourself in a position to continuously win awards. Pitch your start-up or healthtech in contests and be there personally to accept awards. Start adopting the position of a winner. Enter all the competitions and contests that can add value to your company and solutions. Why not participate in a hackathon raised by a public institution or a Centre of Excellence? Public or private awards give you credibility and reliability.[15]

For example, say that you get Breakthrough Device status designated and granted by the FDA official body. This can change the reliability onto your product not only for healthtech B2B business partnering but also help reach a retail B2C market supported by healthcare authorities (Breakthrough Designation, s.f.). Winning such awards can also ease the regulatory path your business must take. For example, the FDA validation gives businesses prioritised review of their devices. For these reasons, targeting official validations and working towards winning top awards can be a perfect early goal to set up.

Collaborations, Compliance and Recognition

Clinical validity is a must, thus submitting your products and services to standard key framework evaluations to get validations should be mandatory. Get society's seal of approval for your products or validation for being compliant, or what about a CE conformity marking?

It is also important that you consider this recognition, leveraging your partnerships and collaborations. Why not, when you sign a contract of a win-win strategic alliance, go public, as both of you will win? Keep connected, in a regulatory and compliance manner. Thus show the world the regulatory and compliant validations you achieve along the way.

The regulatory environment in healthcare can initially be scary, but as Chapter 3 explained, it is just about reading the regulatory framework and understanding them in relation to your healthtech product or service. It is nothing else than this.

Compliance enables growth and scalability. More than ever, you must fit into legal and regulatory frameworks from the start. It is not just a matter of having true values for your company. They are important. But you need official validation from the key institutions that determine the legal framework and set up the guidelines.

The digital age is one of the main strategic pillars of the European Commission on its 2019-2024 strategic plan (Union, 2021).[16] Thus, the healthtech niche is a big part of this strategic plan, and you will need to learn how to operate within this framework if you wish to succeed.

New regulations are popping up, too, as for the first time a common set of rules on intermediaries' obligations and accountability across the single market will open up new opportunities

---

[15] Here are three examples: EuroPriSe: https://www.euprivacyseal.com/EPS-en/Home; Official ISO 27001 CERTIFICATE; HIPAA Compliance.

[16] You can see the priorities here, URL: https://europa.eu/european-union/about-eu/priorities_en

to provide digital services across borders, while ensuring a high level of protection to all users, no matter where they live in the EU (Commission, 2021).[17]

Such is also the case of a regional recent law (Gazette, 2020)[18] published in Spain and pushed by the recovery funds provided by the EU called "Next Generation EU". It simplifies the bureaucratic procedures to be able to modernise and digitalise the Spanish healthcare system.

As part of the European Digital Strategy, *Shaping Europe's Digital Future* (Commission, 2021),[19] it was announced that the European Commission would upgrade the rules governing digital services in the EU. The European Commission proposed two legislative initiatives: the Digital Services Act (DSA) (Commission, 2021)[20] and the Digital Markets Act (DMA) (Commission, 2020).[21]

The DSA and DMA have two main goals to create a safer digital space in which the fundamental rights of all users of digital services are protected and to establish a level playing field to foster innovation, growth and competitiveness, both in the European Single Market and globally (Commission, 2020).[22]

Along with the big techs facing a barrage of new rules, new regulations for healthtechs are also emerging. Fairness in open digital markets and services are being prioritised to advance the speed of growth of the field and ensure safe and accountable online environments (Gold, 2021).[23] If you, as a healthtech, meet these regulations and use them to guide your development of an MVP, you will create value and that value will easily secure validation from the most important stakeholders in the healthcare ecosystem.

Seek Validation for Sustainability Standards

Thinking back to the notion of the circular economy, you should get validated by official sustainability standards. The United Nations Sustainment Development Goals (SDG)[24] (General Assembly, 2015) could be a good starting point. Focus your business on sustainability and link to companies with the same social purpose. It is an exercise of building on top of what is already built.

---

[17] URL: https://ec.europa.eu/info/strategy/priorities-2019-2024/europe-fit-digital-age/digital-services-act-ensuring-safe-and-accountable-online-environment_en

[18] Real Decreto-ley 36/2020

[19] https://ec.europa.eu/info/strategy/priorities-2019-2024/europe-fit-digital-age/shaping-europe-digital-future_en

[20] https://digital-strategy.ec.europa.eu/en/policies/digital-services-act-package

[21] https://ec.europa.eu/info/sites/default/files/proposal-regulation-single-market-digital-services-digital-services-act_en.pdf

[22] https://ec.europa.eu/digital-single-market/en/digital-services-act-package

[23] https://www.linkedin.com/news/story/big-tech-faces-barrage-of-new-rules-4992884/
Official EU Web Page: https://ec.europa.eu/info/strategy/priorities-2019-2024/europe-fit-digital-age/digital-services-act-ensuring-safe-and-accountable-online-environment_en
https://ec.europa.eu/info/strategy/priorities-2019-2024/europe-fit-digital-age/digital-markets-act-ensuring-fair-and-open-digital-markets_en

[24] Note: The Sustainable Development Goals (SDG) or Global Goals are a collection of 17 interlinked global goals designed to be a "blueprint to achieve a better and more sustainable future for all". The 17 SDGs are: (1) No Poverty, (2) Zero Hunger, (3) Good Health and Well-being, (4) Quality Education, (5) Gender Equality, (6) Clean Water and Sanitation, (7) Affordable and Clean Energy, (8) Decent Work and Economic Growth, (9) Industry, Innovation and Infrastructure, (10) Reducing Inequality, (11) Sustainable Cities and Communities, (12) Responsible Consumption and Production, (13) Climate Action, (14) Life Below Water, (15) Life On Land, (16) Peace, Justice and Strong Institutions, (17) Partnerships for the Goals. Source: (General Assembly, 2015).

The higher you aim from the start, the easier scaling up will be. Adopting the rules of the country is important, but it is also important to be aligned with the global standards.[25] For example, this would be looking for official validations by using tools such as the certification of a B-CORP[26] Accreditation Corporation to make an auto analysis of the healthiness of your healthtech. Or join up to the SDG Action Manager tool,[27] built by the United Nations to be able to track the contribution of the companies to the new Sustainable Development Goals (SDG).

Doing this can be a quick win for your company. But you also need to differentiate your healthtech by sustainability, which, translated to healthcare language, means early diagnosis, prevention and prediction in most of the cases. Sustainability could also mean to build or produce under demand and adopt policies of communication based on transparency, trustworthiness and sense of common purpose (Gennari & Navarro, 2019).

Data Collection: The Key to Value

"The volume of data produced in the world is growing rapidly, from 33 zettabytes in 2018 to an expected 175 zettabytes in 2025" (IDC, 2021) (Commission, 2020). Currently, it relies to centralised data and computing centres an 80% of all cloud data science activities, while a remaining 20% is "edge computing" or in IoT close to user. A significant upgrade in this framework is expected by 2025 (Panetta, 2016).

Analysis of the population's health is critical for every country to be able to improve healthcare outcome rates and equity. Real-time, quality health data is key to this progress. The WHO is already providing roadmaps that countries and its official partners are implementing in order to consolidate health information systems and strengthen support for data-driven policies (Organization, 2021).

As healthtechs, we know that we derive our value from the data we can access. With data collection, the big question is, where are the limits? We need to build business models operating through high-performance teams in the ecosystem of a pathology that can also address ethical matters. With data collection a major asset for AI-dependent healthtech business models, companies are seeking alternative cash-flow revenues by selling patient data to third parties like a pharmaceutical company, a medical device company or SaaS healthtech. These incomes of cashflow can serve as an earlier milestone before the full deployment of the technology takes place.

This presents a major concern. The moment we unlock and unleash data is a sensitive one, and we really need to play with trustworthy stakeholders, strategically chosen and operating in the ecosystem. But if we can do this, every single piece of data brings value to the whole healthcare framework if you can think of the big picture. For example, why do we not identify or create an

---

[25] Consider, for example, guidance provided by the UN. Let us say your healthtech undertakes drug testing, the UN provides an "introduction and practical guidance to national authorities and analysts in the implementation of method validation and verification, and also in the calibration/performance verification of laboratory instrumentation and equipment within their existing internal quality assurance programmes." You can find the guidance here, URL: https://www.unodc.org/unodc/en/scientists/guidance-for-the-validation-of-analytical-methodology-and-calibration-of-equipment.html

[26] B-Corp Certification for a Corporation. "Businesses that meet the highest standards of verified social and environmental performance, public transparency and legal accountability to balance profit and purpose". URL: https://bcorporation.net/ [Last Accessed December 2021]

[27] SDG Action Manager https://www.unglobalcompact.org/take-action/sdg-action-manager [Last Accessed December 2021]

open data platform for sharing datasets relevant to AI in global health? It could be a first attempt towards fostering healthtechs to sustainably collect and share data.

So, why not get engaged with public health authorities as providers of data, or why not provide them with data? The key is the quality and usability of the data. In other words, what can be generated from that data? But above all, we must remember the overarching risks and counteract them before we unite our clouds of information.

While entering the matrix of data, who-is-who becomes important. Who is the owner? Who is responsible for protecting it? Who is the manager of the data? And who provides the significance to the data science? Sometimes, controversial topics can arise around who owns and who protects the data simply because parties have different goals.

When working with data, ensure you meet different countries' data privacy and data security standards, especially for sensitive and personal data. Main global frameworks to consider would be the EU's General Data Protection Regulation (GDPR) and the US's National Security Agency (NSA). Other countries have their own specific data standards. Let's deep dive into this main two.

In Europe, to support the age of computing and cloud, the European Cloud Federation has a framework for keeping European data European.

The GDPR (GDPR, 2021)[28] is a regulation in EU law on data protection and privacy in the European Union and the European Economic Area. It also addresses the transfer of personal data outside the EU and European Economic Areas (EEA). Considered an international standard of privacy, it represents one of the most developed regulations on this subject matter worldwide.

There are over 500,000 types of medical devices and In Vitro Diagnostic medical devices (IVDs) on the EU market (Commission, 2021). X-ray machines, healthtech apps or 3D printed hip replacements are examples of medical devices that need to be GDPR compliant. Thus, compliance with the GDPR is likely to imply compliance with other less rigorous regulations, although localisation and clearance are still required.

In turn, a new applicable EU regulation on medical devices, known as Medical Device Regulation (MDR) was launched in 2021. It entails a shift at the regulatory level in the healthtech sector, in which practically any healthtech application will required to be MDR compliant. Consequently, many software solutions are most likely being considered class IIa medical devices under the new regulatory framework, e.g., medical devices considered less dangerous than those that require control by the notified bodies.

Medical Devices are classified by risk into four categories: Class I is self-certification; Class IIa, Class IIb and Class III are certified by an accredited notified body. All are based on the basic assumption that CE mark is needed to define the regulatory requirements.

Nevertheless, if your healthtech application is not MDR compliant, and if it collects personal data, then it does not meet the GDPR standards. Or in other words, MDR compliance for healthtech applications requires GDPR compliance.

In this line, GAIA-X is a federated data project for the development of an efficient and competitive, secure and trustworthy federation of data infrastructure and service providers for Europe, which is supported by representatives of business, science and administration from Germany and France, together with other European partners (GAIA-X, 2021).

The other major data policy to consider is the US NSA policy framework, by which data collection is legally mandated (NSA/CSS, 2021). The 2020 NSA Cybersecurity Year in Review report published by the NSA states that NSA's new Cybersecurity Collaboration Centre worked

---

[28] European Union's General Data Protection Regulation GDPR URL https://gdpr.eu/what-is-gdpr/

throughout 2020 to forge the foundation for new bi-directional cybersecurity partnerships between industry and government in Public-Private Partnerships (PPPs).

In this regard, the most public aspect of NSA's support to protect the COVID-19 vaccine development efforts was a joint product issued by the NSA, Department of Homeland Security's Critical Infrastructure Security Agency (CISA) and partners in the United Kingdom (UK) and Canada to warn of Advanced Persistent Threat (APT) 29's targeting of organisations engaged in COVID-19 vaccine research in the US, UK and Canada. Finally, NSA is responsible for ensuring that the U.S. Government (USG) IT owners can secure their most valuable information that resides on National Security Systems (NSS)—systems that handle classified information or are otherwise critical to intelligence and military operations (NSA, 2020).

In the US, medical devices, for example, are classified as in the EU—based on risk. Class I goes through the regulatory path of general controls and the FDA oversees registration and listing. Class II goes through a pre-market notification path. Finally, Class III utilises a required pre-go-to-market approval and a rigorous and exhaustive process for application to marketing.

Every country has launched some sort of data privacy laws to regulate the frameworks on how information is collected, how data providers are protected and what major governmental authorities control data affairs once the information is transferred. Therefore, it is already a reality that Health Authorities have taken action and are approving these urgent measures to upgrade and modernise public administration for transformation, resilience and recovery.

The US has hundreds of different state data privacy laws safeguarding data availability, accessibility and breaches. For example, on the West Coast, the California Privacy Rights Act (CPRA) is already creating new industry requirements, consumer privacy rights and enforcement mechanisms, establishing new obligations for businesses as healthtech that will come into effect on January 1, 2023 (Bonta, 2021). Or on the East Coast, New York has its "Stop Hacks and Improve Electronic Data Security (SHIELD) Act", which is amending the existing data breach notification law and creating higher standards of security data requirements for collection of information from New York citizens.

In the US, the NSA/CSS Freedom of Information Act Program aims to release as much information as possible, consistent with the need to protect classified or sensitive information under the exemption provisions of these laws (NSA, 2004).

So, do your research. Ensure you know exactly what regulations are in effect for the technology you are using, the people who are your customers and partners, and the data you are collecting. Get familiarised with not only GDPR and HIPAA but also with SOC-2, ISO27001 and others. Select which are the compliance frameworks that can be worth it to implement for covering a broader umbrella of compliance mandatories.

Count on a B-corporation that can act as a reliable compliance audit partner. In turn, can help to get an easy initial objective readiness assessment of cybersecurity, availability, confidentiality, processing integrity and privacy. Later, speed up an output report and rely on a higher expertise level of guidance that can really support transversally your team members until getting the beloved compliance accreditation. So you do not have to do-it-all yourself, as many times harbours delays in time and effort not to mention repetitive bureaucratic work. Either outsource an external audit or onboard a compliance officer if you lack the expertise and headcounts needed to do this yourself.

Open Access Data

Open access data will be critical to your ability to build value (it will also be critical to gather information for marketing purposes). The more that members of society use the new integrated systems of the healthcare system, the more data becomes available and the stronger it becomes as a resource for healthtechs.

Most healthcare systems in different countries already have the clinical history of each patient in the cloud—the integrated Electronic Health Records of the citizenship. Most of the time, the countries that own this data have already anonymised it, and they open it up to third parties like private healthtechs, research centres and many other institutions. This data is your strategic starting point for your projects and business lines of action.

With access to key open datasets, your healthtech company can:

- Manage datasets responsibly to help to drive healthcare progress.
- Accelerate innovation by identifying unmet needs in the population.
- Accelerate the adoption curve of innovations by adapting to patient lifestyles.

For example, the WHO has a data observatory API available with accessible, free and open datasets.[29] It constitutes an open repository of health data, systematically organised from its 194 member states. You can get information on morbidity, mortality, about different pathologies and health systems, the burden of a certain disease and other risk factors.

On the other hand, in the Registry of Open Data on AWS,[30] you can freely access data such as genome sequencing, biomolecular modelling, COVID-19 datasets and many others. There are also guidelines and example use cases for the datasets.

The registry collects legacy datasets from entities such as The Cancer Genome Atlas,[31] Foldingathome COVID-19 Datasets[32] and Facebook Data for Good,[33]. And it includes tools built from de-identified data as well as tools developed from satellite imagery and other publicly available sources. The NASA Space Act Agreement,[34] for example, opens up high-value NASA science datasets. These and the many other useful datasets available on the Registry of Open Data on AWS, when used responsibly, can drive healthtech progress and save lives.

Google also collects public data in Google Public Data Explorer,[35] where you can find datasets like World Development Indicators from sources like the World Bank, with data from fertility rates of different countries, or data about Infectious Disease Outbreaks with datasets from healthmap.org and Harvard Medical School. Also consider Google Dataset Search,[36] where with a simple keyword search you can obtain a list of datasets hosted in thousands of repositories on the web.

The US, under the OPEN Government Data Act Program, required government data to be made available in open, machine-readable formats, ensuring privacy and security.

And it puts at the service of the citizen the website data.gov, with more than 337,304 datasets, including the recent launch of coronavirus.gov and its data tracker.[37] The United States Census

---

[29] World Health Organization (WHO) Data API available link: https://www.who.int/data/gho/ [Last Accessed May 2022]

[30] Registry of Open Data on AWS available link: https://registry.opendata.aws/ [Last Accessed May 2022]

[31] The Cancer Genome Atlas. URL: https://registry.opendata.aws/tcga/ [Last Accessed May 2022]

[32] Foldingathome COVID-19 Datasets URL: https://registry.opendata.aws/foldingathome-covid19/ [Last Accessed May 2022]

[33] Facebook Data for Good. URL: https://registry.opendata.aws/collab/facebook/ [Last Accessed May 2022]

[34] NASA Space Act Agreement. URL: https://registry.opendata.aws/collab/nasa/ [Last Accessed May 2022]

[35] Google Public Data Explorer. URL: https://www.google.com/publicdata/directory [Last Accessed May 2022]

[36] Google Dataset Search. URL: https://datasetsearch.research.google.com/ [Last Accessed May 2022]

[37] US Covid-19 Data tracker. URL: https://covid.cdc.gov/covid-data-tracker/#datatracker-home [Last Accessed May 2022]

Bureau[38] is a dataset dissemination platform where you can access demographic and economic data from the US Census Bureau.

In the same line, the European Union has launched the Official Portal for European Data,[39] putting into service more than 1.3 million datasets from 36 countries. Health has its own site in the portal where you access European Union, national and international health data.[40] You can search datasets by category, keywords, publisher, etc.

Likewise, UNICEF datasets[41] are open, offering categorised data with an easy dataset search tool[42] that lets you get the datasets by type, topic and year. Some datasets here can be very useful to prepare your healthtech innovations for Low to Medium Income Countries (LMIC).

Open data sources like this should always be your first port of call. They are free and often more than sufficient. However, you will find sometimes that key datasets are proprietary. This will entail partnering with the owners: healthcare authorities (local, regional or global), private companies, or healthcare insurance companies, etc. Always double check, when accessing a dataset, that you are compliant and ethical.

Security and Cybersecurity

A major component of data collection is security. A Clark School study states that every thirty-nine seconds a hacker attempts to steal personal information from people and businesses around the world (Cukier, s.f.). Consider this and let us prioritise security: we are dealing with healthcare data, the most sensitive data that a human can have.

Security in healthtech products and services relies on compliance. For example, healthtech facilitators like the Open Web Application Security Project (OWASP),[43] a non-profit foundation that works to improve the security of software best practice, can help you with guidelines for apps and web-based solutions. Meanwhile, existing accreditation regimes such as Cyber Essentials and ISO 27001 are relevant, and the need to demonstrate "security by design" and suitable vulnerability testing is also becoming key.

The EU Agency for Cybersecurity (ENISA), created in 2015, is working closely with the cybersecurity community across the EU, which has, in a short period of time, become a real priority. This institution serves us in watching over the wellbeing of our new emerging businesses. It suggests some baseline considerations we should all take into account, like implementing network segmentation by separating your company networks.

Overall, it is a matter of prioritising cybersecurity in your healthtech (BITSIGHT, 2021).[44] Push yourself to meet high cybersecurity standards by going one step further from the very

---

[38] United States Census Bureau. URL: https://www.census.gov/data.html [Last Accessed May 2022]
[39] Official Portal for European Data. URL: https://data.europa.eu/en [Last Accessed May 2022].
[40] Health site in Official Portal for European data. URL: https://data.europa.eu/data/datasets?categories=heal& page=1&locale=en [Last Accessed May 2022]
[41] UNICEF Datasets. URL: https://data.unicef.org/ [Last Accessed May 2022].
[42] UNICEF Datasets search tool. URL: https://data.unicef.org/resources/resource-type/datasets/. [Last Accessed May 2022].
[43] Through community-led open-source software projects, hundreds of local chapters worldwide, tens of thousands of members and leading educational and training conferences, the OWASP Foundation is the source for developers and technologists to secure the web. URL: https://owasp.org/
[44] The Urgency to Treat Cybersecurity as a Business Decision, 12 February 2020, Paul Proctor GARTNER is a registered trademark and service mark of Gartner, Inc. and/or its affiliates in the US and internationally and is used herein with permission. All rights reserved.

beginning. How? Why not establish a vulnerability management process to monitor and address vulnerabilities of ICT products and services?

Let us look at the example of a cutting-edge hospital. With so much digital technology at the core of its operations, it could be highly vulnerable to cyberattack. This healthcare organisation may consider including a requirement for the Bill of Materials (BOM) to be used in acquired systems or products to help track vulnerable systems in their infrastructure based on publicly available vulnerability information (ENISA, 2021).[45]

Easy-implement actions such as establishing strong Wi-Fi passwords or making a two-factor authentication obligatory in healthtech medical devices, remote patient devices, user identification systems or cloud services can be really efficient to avoid cyberattacks.

Healthtech suppliers should also ensure that they track the transmission of data, at least for a predefined period, to avoid data loss to face interoperability cyber security matters such as system failures, human errors or malicious actions.

At some point, to determine minimum security certification requirements for suppliers for different types of procurement, for example for the supply of security services, the supplier must be ISO 27001 certified (Commission, 2021).

Medical devices such as PET/CT scanners, surgical robots etc. should also be physically protected. ENISA again suggests as a cyberattack procurement guideline establishing physical access control measures for medical device facilities, like access using biometrics.

Overall, when you establish a contract with any vendor that will bring value for your company, you need to make the contractual obligations in terms of cybersecurity explicit. It is as simple as this. It is about more than the responsibility of the cybersecurity of your company, as it also has to do with the responsibility of your third parties and collaborators.

---

[45] The practice of having a vendor publish a Bill Of Materials (BOM) of the actual software and hardware used in a system allows any third party to track independently whether a certain device may be susceptible to a certain known vulnerability. It is common for such BOM information to be disclosed to the Notified Bodies, so that the Notified Bodies may disclose advisories about certain medical systems and devices. However, it may be beneficial for healthcare administrators to also have access to such information in order to track vulnerable components across their infrastructure. URL: https://www.enisa.europa.eu/publications/good-practices-for-the-security-of-healthcare-services

Chapter 5

Marketing Your Value

When building our marketing plan, we must first keep in mind our company's purpose, "the why" (see Figure 5.1). Having built and defined the value of your healthtech solution in the previous chapter, you should by now know what problem you are solving and for whom you are solving it, whether the patient or another stakeholder in the healthcare ecosystem. This is your "why", and it is what you must successfully communicate to the world.

More than ever, healthtechs are in the public eye, and so proper public relations and marketing are the new gold standard. In today's politicised environment, your company's marketing will be intimately bound up with your reputation for corporate social responsibility (CRS). To market successfully, both must serve the stakeholders of the pathology ecosystem. Make this explicit in all your marketing communications, actions, and plans. Create interactions based on clear key messages, aligned with the goals of the core business.

This is critical to prevent the healthtech industry, and your company, from inheriting the dark image that once belonged to the pharmaceutical industry (Times, 2021). This moniker of "the bad guys" came from ethically questionable practices and the population's perception of pharmaceutical companies deriving considerable wealth from patients' lack of health. Although nowadays such companies are revising their practices, with most following strict codes of conduct, operating under increased regulation and meeting high compliance standards, they still carry the stigma from the past.

We, as healthtechs, are inheriting this bad reputation simply for selling health. There is a negative connotation towards business success on behalf of the health of others. By this cultural perception, you can make a business in any field you want but choose health and there is a perception you should be a non-profit organisation.

Therefore, we need to reassure the public of our CSR and create in their minds a benign reputation from the offset (Singh & Misra, 2020). We are the disruptors. The healthcare model's sustainability depends on us. It needs our cutting-edge products and solutions. Yet change, particularly innovation around health, can easily cause fear and concern if it is poorly understood. Indeed, healthcare systems operating in developed countries suffer major barriers to the implementation and diffusion of novel initiatives (Berwick, 2003).

A wrong step in terms of bad practices, poor communication, or a failure in a product can turn out to be fatal, cementing stereotypes and sinking your company. From the very first moment, we must develop our company's reputation through coherent marketing strategies that speak to the

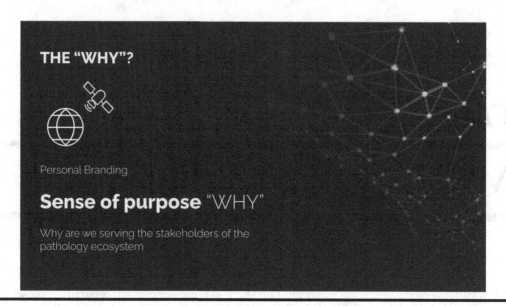

THE "WHY"?

Personal Branding

Sense of purpose "WHY"

Why are we serving the stakeholders of the pathology ecosystem

Figure 5.1 **Infographic representing the key bullet points to keep considering the importance of the sense of "why" in all the phases of our healthtech companies.**

evidence of our product's effectiveness, and which capitalise on our skills as innovators to generate interest in the product through our social networks. As one study has found, innovators themselves are often the most powerful agent of dissemination through their role as product champions (Barnett, 2011).

Healthtechs can also use social issues to leverage their sense of purpose and the values of the company. I am tired of seeing companies walk all over their own, not embracing social, ethnic, and gender diversity. Think of something as simple as awareness days. The 7 April is Worldwide Health Day, the 21 May is World Day for Cultural Diversity for Dialogue and Development, and there are hundreds more pathology-specific days like 1st of December, which is World AIDS Day, and the 25 April, which is World Malaria Day.

Companies that do not publicly show their support for these global health awareness days, and on other matters of social interest, can be wrongly perceived as tacitly opposed to such causes. No longer can companies avoid taking a public stance on social issues—they have become inherent to the success of the brand.

That may appear scary. But think of it as an opportunity to build the image of the company and communicate publicly what your values are, and which causes you support. In doing so, you can create and cement loyalty among customers.

Remember, though, that to gain trust you must be consistent with what you claim, support, and communicate. And, as this chapter will explore, you must do this in a humanised way—communicating with an approachable, individual persona—rather than through stiff, corporate statements. Commit yourself to social matters as much as you do to health outcomes.

At its core, your marketing as a healthtech should explain how you solve your customers' needs. Do this successfully and you will create a community of believers, or what we call ambassadors of your company. These are key stakeholders and influencers, and we rely on them for the task of diffusing our value through word of mouth—either digital or physical—which remains one of the best ways to generate brand awareness.

Of course, your ambassadors' aspirations must match yours as a brand. Everything they do will impact your branding directly or indirectly, regardless of your intention. Once you have a public image, it is out there forever, and it will start to snowball. But if you find a true ambassador that matches your purpose, they will guide that snowball in the right direction, amplifying what is known as your Share of Voice. This is the percentage your company spends on media versus the total media expenditure for the product, service or category in the market.

Ambassadors are also essential in dealing with stigmas against technology adoption based on misinformation about your technological firm.

So, when marketing, prioritise branding above all, and align it with your stance on social issues. Keep faith in your sense of purpose. And align clear calls to action with the USP of every product or service your healthtech offers.

Humanising the Patient

Key to marketing is the ability to understand the patient. After all, it is they who are at the centre of the new healthcare model, and it is they who will be buying your product primarily.

When we open conversational marketing channels, when we create avatar-based virtual environments, when we post on social media (SoMe), or when we run personalised patient support programs, we must remember that the patient is a human being.

This may sound simple, but it can easily be forgotten. We know, for example, that data is critical to marketing—it can help narrow our target market and focus our initiatives (as illustrated in Figure 5.2). Yet although we deal with anonymised data much of the time, we must avoid treating the patient as a mere object or deal, or merely as a set of data points within a cloud of information.

This is not just data; these are life journeys, lifestyles and living beings, which deserve respect. When we manage all the massive amounts of data that we are allowed to deal with, we need to

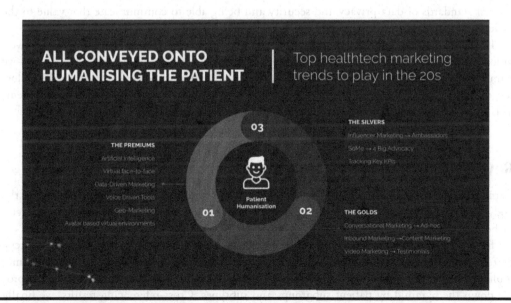

Figure 5.2   Top healthtech marketing tends to operate in the 2020s, focused on the humanisation of the patient.

elevate our sense of responsibility, respecting the patient and their privacy. In other words, we should ensure the ownership of artificial intelligence operates on an auditable and trustable basis, and we should fully comply with the regulatory frameworks that preserve patients' rights.[1] This is especially so in sensitive matters, for example the recent contact tracing tools for COVID-19. It is through this respect for data privacy that we humanise our marketing.

To do this, we pair evidence-based medicine (EBM) with values-based medicine (VBM) in daily practice. In our marketing, we aim to educate the target on both. And we fine-tune our educational interventions to create demonstrable changes in attitudes and practices in favour of our products. So, what values to we communicate? A recent study found that the three most important values to uphold were personnel-patient relationships, empathy, and respect (Sueiras, et al., 2017).

That sounds complex, but what it really means is this. We need to build our healthtech solutions and deliver health outcomes around a particular lifestyle. And we must try to preserve or enhance that lifestyle holistically, not just by treating an individual symptom. From a marketing perspective, we can also humanise how we connect with the patient by using data to tell stories, which subsequently humanises our healthtechs as well. We can build pathology journeys from symptom to diagnosis to treatment for real patients through the unique data we can collect as healthtechs. And we can rely on that knowledge in our marketing campaigns.

This mentality must exist in our staff but also in our solutions. For example, in machine learning, where we train machines to learn by themselves by trial and error, we must instil the ability to learn about lifestyles and behaviour as much as it learns about symptoms and other traditional health datapoints. We must design self-learning and funnel-effective strategies while embracing the patient as a human being. From natural language processing to image recognition, we can analyse patterns in a huge amount of democratic cloud data to recognise the life journey of our target user.

For all our technological skills with this data, a strong aspect of humanisation in our marketing strategies is regulatory compliance. These exist to protect the patients. So rather than considering them a barrier, consider them a guide to your interactions with the customer. Meeting the highest standards of data privacy and security and being able to communicate that value to the patients is a valuable marketing asset.

In prioritising humanisation, we now have the right mindset. Yet when we open these conversational channels—whether through social media, chatbots, or even traditional advertising—we bump into the issue of targeting and outreach. And the question is, how can you reach those clusters of humans? How can you find the humanised target that you really want and engage them? This is still a challenge, but it begins with what I call reverse capillarisation (see Figure 5.3).

Reverse Capillarisation Targeting

Capillarisation is the formation and development of a network of blood vessels to a part of the body. In a marketing context, it means the penetration of the market and the ability to target a niche patient profile through a particular network.

Before digitalisation, businesses targeted customers using a pyramidal capillarisation process. Starting from the top with no idea of who our target patient was, we defined a master customer profile based on deep, laborious business intelligence research. And later we expanded the profile down the pyramid by patient subgroups and subtypes. Cross-referencing results, we finally

---

[1] Please refer to the preceding chapter for more information on regulatory compliance around data.

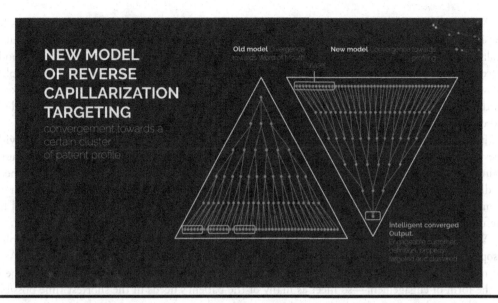

Figure 5.3   New model of reverse capillarisation targeting, converging the outreach to clusters of patient profiles.

reached the desired patient profiles, and then we focused our strategies on them. This process used to take us a lot of time and financial investment and left doubt over whether the patient subtypes selected were the right ones on which to focus our efforts.

In other words, we targeted our customers through an outreach exercise of divergence from a convergent, hypothetical starting point.

Thus, starting from a unique patient profile used to be the marketer's goal. You went from a defined target that you made loyal and engaged with your product out to a broader patient profile.

This old approach has changed. Now we are operating with a reverse pyramid or reverse capillarisation to profile the customer. We start from a crowd of divergent data points, containing a vast number of communities, geographically distributed, with different traits spread over a broad network, sometimes many networks. Then we start to itemise, group, and scale up positions in the pyramid until we reach the right target. This way, aided by artificial intelligence, we converge from our data onto the perfect customer profile.

A recent study explored the potential for the practical application of such cluster analyses to segment a local General Practice-registered population. It worked with primary and secondary care datasets to create a database of 79,607 patients, including socio-demographic variables, morbidities, care utilisation, cost and risk factor information. The study shows that cluster analysis can segment the population into distinct groups with unique health and care needs, providing useful intelligence to inform local population health service planning and care delivery (Nnoaham & Cann, May 2020).

Being able to find those segments is critical because it is to them, we can bring the most value, so invest resources and effort into this type of reverse capillarisation targeting. It will ensure that groups of human beings with common traits and, above all, common needs emerge from the data and can be met by our healthtechs. This is the new state of the art, where the digital clusters of humans represent real clusters with the same potential needs and who request a different set of services from other clusters.

When we talk about humanisation, we can integrate this concept into the targeting process by considering more than just medical data points. Potential customers of a diabetes-monitoring wearable healthtech solution, for example, are more than a set of traits (such as regularly reported high blood-glucose levels). And they are more than their symptoms (excessive thirst and tiredness, for example). They are also people with sets of behaviours that can be targeted and integrated into our later marketicised customers. For example, they might be people who struggle with diet or keeping active. And so, an educational outreach channel of communication would help onboard such individuals.

But to identify that, we must occasionally mix medically irrelevant correlational data with relevant data. We can help ensure a causal model that can define our target patient profile by auto training the model to find correlations in very broad and diverse data sets that may not appear medically related. So, search far and wide for your data (as we explored in chapter 4), incorporate as much as you can into your target analysis, and ditch the preconceptions about what will be useful and what not.

When building customer experiences and marketing, we must also remember time. The philosopher Theophrastus said that "Time is the most valuable thing we as humans can spend". And we are more aware of this every day. When marketing, we must have compensation for time spent in the form of engagement—so meet as many of the patient's needs in the shortest time possible through a good segmentation.

Considering the reverse capillarisation model above, we need to follow a particular marketing funnel to prioritise our time. This funnel should be designed to bring your value closer to the target segment with as little effort as possible. And at each step, you should be able to easily answer the question, "What am I doing here?", and "What *should* I be doing here?", based on your core business goals.

For example, artificial intelligence can help marketers to better understand the behaviour of the patients, thus make more timely and informed decisions (IBM, 2021). But when we interact with our customer through a chatbot, we must ask ourselves, are we really bringing value to the patient? Are we really embracing the "expert patient figure"?, gaining their attention by meeting their needs? Or have we sunk considerable resources into producing an annoying, poorly communicating piece of software with a limited and rigid decision tree?

Marketing Funnels

The specifics of your marketing funnel will depend highly on your business model. What is needed? Maybe a crowd-learning site to empower patients, filled with relevant content and calls to action. Maybe something else. But whatever it is, it should aim to change the patient's mindset; for changes in their mindset produce changes in their behaviour—this is our biggest incentive. Right now, this is the generic funnel:

1. Start with word of mouth. This is the concept of creating noise around a solution and awakening a sense of interest. This word of mouth can be face-to-face, online or offline or by testimonials and opinions. Begin with yourself as the solution's champion.
2. Then, expand the conversation to key stakeholders. Use social media or influencers that can continue driving this interest/attention.
3. Once you have built noise, hone the conversation. Establish for yourself a strategic position within the pathology's ecosystem by posing your solution and your information as the answer to the problem you have generated noise around. This is where you can really

conceptualise your business and establish your clear position and sense of purpose, driving the customer to the right source of information. Rely on confidence and trustworthiness. You only get one shot.

4. Onboarding. This is when the customer interacts with the concept, registers on the website, follows you on social media and develops sustained interest in the overall project. This customer engagement is the launchpad.

5. When you begin to get engagement, focus on the customer experience. Every single click must drive the customer to the right place, and here more than ever arises the importance of backlinks and SEO. These drive the customer journey from the edges of your healthtech ecosystem to its centre.

6. Conversion. Convert all these visitors and leads into customers, which in the end are health outcomes. The ones that leave the marketing funnel are also important. Resources spent analysing why people leave are rarely wasted. Most exits from the funnel happen at the transition from the free to paid version of your service/product. Bridging this is as smoothly and consistently as possible is critical.

In today's marketing environment, website funnels especially are key. Since we are in a continually moving sector, we must be versatile and able to create updatable, interactive experiences for potential customers on our websites. Where do you want them to go? Create ad-hoc ways, different journeys, and personalised escorts. Do it for every single customer that enters the webpage—because the age of the static webpage is dead.

When customising, base adaptable pages on your patient profiles and test your funnels for efficacy! Here, we come again to the concept of "focus groups", as they are perfect for this. Create these mini advisory boards based on real potential customers following your funnel. Track where they are or drop off and adapt accordingly.

A common reason for customer drop-off is a lack of value-add at each stage of their journey through the funnel. Whether new educational content, product information, or simple entertainment, you must give the customer something of value after every click. For healthtech marketing specifically, the value we add is in advancing the dynamics of the pathology: shortening time-frames of diagnosis, improving treatment follow-up, and improving health outcomes. We should be upgrading the number of valuable interactions that pull and push the patient, each time getting closer to the point of sale.

Beyond websites, we must also locate and interact with patients in their community—within the hubs of the pathology, whether digital or physical. This depends on your team's ability to map and onboard stakeholders such as centres of excellence and networks of healthcare professionals, which we cover in the next chapter.

Above all, we as nascent healthtechs are agile. We need to use that to our advantage, constantly redefining our marketing plans, keeping them alive and progressing according to the different data that we get and the ones we can afford as a company.

While we home in on the perfect patient profile through our targeting, we also need a holistic overview of the patient no matter where they are in real life and the digital world. We should know their location on the patient journey. That means knowing when to provide valuable information and when (and when not) to create a call to action.

Overall, remember that your marketing funnel is an experiment. Forget about all the commonly touted solutions and "marketing hacks", and focus on "learning-by-doing". Be brave, try different things and analyse their return on investment. Always create a marketing budget, split it according to each marketing project or initiative, and build in room for cost overruns.

Inbound Marketing, or Content Marketing

Content (or inbound) marketing is a strategic approach for creating a new ecosystem around our business model. It focuses on making and distributing valuable, relevant, and consistent informational content around the pathology to attract and retain a clearly defined target patient and ultimately drive profitable customer action.

In comparison to outbound marketing, which interrupts customers with unwanted content (like generic adverts), inbound marketing reverses the relationship between the customer and the company. It allows an integrative and holistic approach, overall creating the perfect moment to impact the patient with the right coverage of their unmet needs, while leveraging and filling the gaps in the patient journey.

Content marketing means understanding the patient behaviour and journey, framing key leverage points along the latter, and defining the patient profile in relation to each product and health solution. Vice versa, it is conceptualising the right product and service for each patient or customer and finally efficiently stimulating customer loyalty and preventing customer loss.

Ultimately, content marketing is how we add the value to each step in our marketing funnel.

Consumers want novel deliveries in what we come up with and what we post. The trends in the omnichannel change constantly. One day the trendsetter is one platform, and the next day it is another. But what does not change is the value and sense of purpose of the content we provide on these platforms.

A key matter to address when we consider the return on investment of an inbound marketing strategy is the call to action. Around the content we give away freely, we need to pursue a positive response (not necessarily a commercial transaction). And we must pursue this for every interaction along the patient journey. We must recognise that the customer will respond to everything we do, whether we want them to or not, and the response will either be helpful or unhelpful to our marketing purposes. Thus, it is better to be proactive and anticipate this response by being transparent and showing the customer why we are calling them to action.

Ask, what do we want from the customer? And understand that the customer asks the same thing the moment they visit our website platform, read our email, or interact with our post on Twitter. What do they want from me?

So, show it explicitly. Clarify the call to action in the first place. Do you want them to click on the link below, read this article, or follow our newsletter? Do you want him to join our community, or be part of the #learntofliers movement? Or do we just want a testimonial and for the customer to share their experience? Perhaps we want feedback—for the patient to tell us how to improve our services or products. Or maybe we want them to attend our next event or learn something about their pathology. Whatever it is, show it clearly.

When producing content, make it understandable for everyone. This means translating complicated matters into easy words, providing different language options for different regions and keeping the message or key takeaways from each piece of content short and consistent.

Once you have done this, then just be straightforward with what you want from the customer. They will respond to what you ask them to do. They may or may not do what you want, but they should at least understand their choice. They should know what you are claiming about your healthtech solution and how they can be part of the ecosystem of your company, helping you and its members grow.

When you are creating content for your inbound marketing, integrate customer relationship management (CRM). This is a discipline with a wealth of tools to compile data and extract the patients' needs, ensuring you send your offering to the right person, at the right moment. Done properly, CRM draws on your whole ecosystem: your website, telephone, email, live chat, and social media. And will help you tailor your inbound marketing with insights about your target audiences—how to meet their needs, retain interest and engagement, and ultimately drive sales.

You can develop and manage a CRM either in-house with your team of engineers or developers, or you can outsource. Often, the dashboard or results screen will be more intuitive if you build your own ad-hoc CRM. The third way is to opt for pre-existing CRMs such as Veeva CRM or Salesforce HealthCloud—two of the best. And maybe build an internal parallel system that allows you to view the data better according to your specific needs. The same companies will offer you this service and even data analysis as well. Whatever you choose, it is all about getting a good cost-benefit agreement that meets your strategic and budgetary needs.

A CRM system will allow you to integrate web content management (WCM). This can positively impact your workflow and help you store your customer data while meeting high standards of security, manage emailing, automatise recurrent to-do's, automate suggestions to customers, engage and attract new customers, and reduce customer drop-out. It can also help you maintain your B2B relationships, enabling you to provide partners with reports on customer satisfaction and so on. You can also use it to organise the customers or patients according to your segmentation requirements. And they can be a good source of knowledge for in-home continuous training courses for employees and customers when it applies.

Overall, a CRM gives you full, 24/7 access to any information that you might need, horizontally and vertically, within your business insights. And it gives you a fully personalised dashboard almost instantaneously with a screenshot of your business.

Of course, to obtain all these insights—to create a successful customer journey—you first need to know what options you have available as a communication tool. And the most important, currently, is social media.

Social Media: The New Healthtech Must

For healthtechs, social media is the primary communication channel to create this engagement, build up this community of believers, and onboard stakeholders. It begins with the aim of maximising your business potential, expanding the value matrix of your product and services through Facebook, Twitter, Instagram and other emerging platforms.

Start with simple actions on social media: regular, informative posts and community interaction. Uphold the main principles of advocacy in healthtech, which would be sense of purpose, cybersecurity, data privacy, equality of access, patient empowerment and humanisation of healthcare. Advocacy, in turn, is known to promote equality, social justice, social inclusion and human rights, aligning your business with your social reputation.

Considering these main principles, start building the tactics and actions around your healthtech advocacy, designing one key line of action for each main principle. Then channel them through the Big Four: Facebook, Instagram, LinkedIn and Twitter.[2]

Key questions to bear in mind are: is our content responding to real needs? Where are the links, the likes, the shares? How are we analysing our return on investment (RoI)?

---

[2] Later, you might consider disease-specific platforms. This can be the official site of the country's medical society of reference in the pathology, or just any other platform with strong presence: some of the public health authorities' platforms can give real credibility and validation if engaged with.

It is not about doing everything possible but putting value into every shot we take and ensuring it impacts the core business. Do not get stuck on the quantitatives of key performance indicators (KPIs) over the qualitatives.

As with any marketing campaign, preparation is key. Research what really brings value to patients. Know what they are really looking for in customer service and online interaction. Find where your customers congregate—what chat rooms, what platforms, what Facebook groups—and study how they communicate. You will likely find they want answers, advice and information about a brand, about the problem they are suffering from, and about the solutions available to them. Meet those needs, and you will get the engagement.

If it suits the tone of your business, you can also combine organic engagement with "growth hacking". For example, you might create a gamified onboarding process for the users, a referral system, or a sense of urgency with a prize contest or discount? There are plenty of simple methods to promote yourself online and gain followers but start small. Piloting your product to a very targeted, segmented subgroup of users or patients can help you to expand into other groups and grow at high rates later. If you need help in this, hire a professional: there are plenty of social media wizards called community managers out there who can help create a whole strategy for online engagement, and even run it for you as well.

Where Do I Post? (Opening Channels)

From Twitter to Facebook to general online communication, opening channels permits us to create a dialogue among patients, caregivers and doctors. It is also largely free to publish, so maximises the marketing RoI. This simple opening of channels might be enough to position us according to how we want to be seen by this community.

So, how do you open a channel? Hashtags are a great start, including strategic words like #healthcare, #health, #tech, #digitalhealth.[3] They connect us with like-minded individuals who are actively seeking new content in our ecosystem. Another tactic is to live-Tweet conferences or public events or share articles on a subject using hashtags.

You can also make push and pull with influencers. If you can find key influencers online who operate in your target customer's ecosystems, you can drive word of mouth through them. It has to do with onboarding ambassadors with a common sense of purpose and mission to your company (see Figure 5.4). Let your product or service be promoted by those who push on behalf of the progress of the ecosystem in which the pathology is placed.

Ensure that you are putting effort and resources into getting engagement that serves your larger purpose of creating an ecosystem in which your customers can reside. Otherwise, your social media account will become just another advertising channel. This is not the intended purpose of these channels.

We see much value in turning on comments in open channels because there are often things that your community can say that you cannot say. For example, they can elevate your product reputation without you saying a single word. Indeed, you can collect a lot of information from open channels and open comment fields on your site or service.

When engaging with customers, use tags and labels. These allow you to categorise conversations and provide context to those replying to messages (Slack, 2019). For example, when responding in a thread, you can mention that person with an @ in front of the name and the person will

---

[3] New, popular hashtags are always cropping up, and you can find a list here, URL: https://www.symplur.com/healthcare-hashtags/ ; https://top-hashtags.com/hashtag/healthtech/

Figure 5.4   Infographics representing "the hows" towards building a sense of community around your healthtech.

be pinged. Or if you are discussing a particular topic, you can tag the keywords and make the discussion more findable for search engines.

You can use labels and hashtags on open channel outlets to better understand trends and active players in the ecosystem. You rarely define the label yourself. But you can use it to gain an overview of the community and, if you are fortunate, what they are saying about your strategy or product. If you structure your tags and labels well, you can create a news feed that displays them to you—this is great for keeping on top of the conversation about your healthtech.

If you are uncertain how to engage with customers, follow the recommendations of an external communication agency or have a member of your communication department respond. Always follow their advice and double-check your post before you press the publish button.

What Should I Post? (Content Strategy)

Reset the landscape to zero. Start over with how you want to be seen, not how you are seen now. Then think deeply about how you want to build the ecosystem and the perception around you and your tech solutions. Build the publication roadmap around the business objective, identify tactics and only then implement.

Videos of patient testimonials are a good place to start. They validate the reliability of our products and services without costing much to produce. They do not need to be long, just micro-videos but true and reliable. These testimonials will leverage the credibility and reliability of your products and services with the same effectiveness as validation through clinical trials—they can garner way more attention despite being qualitative outcomes.

Social campaigns are another powerful type of content to spark social conversation. Such is the case of Canadian's Bell's annual Let's Talk Campaign,[4] which helped the telecommunications

---

[4] URL: https://letstalk.bell.ca/en/

company to engage in the global mental health conversation. During the one-day advertising campaign, the company donated money to mental health funds according to how many social media interactions were made with the branded hashtag, #BellLetsTalk. The campaign generated $121 million for mental health in Canada—and over 1.3 billion interactions on social media. Importantly, it was so successful because it drove value for the patient/customer by raising awareness and helping combat the stigma around mental health. This was a one-time positive contribution to the ecosystem that we could take as a best-practice.

With content, the idea is to build a community. And you can brand your solutions or not. An effective tactic is to build an unbranded community comprised of a very specific, highly targeted audience, and then to invigorate this community. Creating a community of patients like this can be a premarketing action where you do not even mention the medical solution, product or service before launch, and it can really work. But you must have a clear goal, which is to reach out to and offer the community of patients' valuable content that responds to their real needs. You must be able to answer positively to the following questions:

- What do you want to get from that post?
- How do you want the reader to react?
- Are the contents aligned with your mission, vision and goals as a company?
- Are you premarketing a near-future launch? Thus, preparing the landscape for your core business's next step?
- Are you onboarding, making loyal and thus empowering your community of believers?

After posting, reap the reward. If done successfully, you should be able to answer these questions:

- Is the interaction genuine? And are you using the proper metrics to measure the interaction and determine its quality? What is the highest-quality audience and the lowest-quality audience?
- Have you used any digital acceleration models? If so, did they work?
- Is the investment worth it? Is it giving the expected return? Which platforms justify your social media investments?

Overall, post content with strategic value and genuine information. Ensure you are impacting the right audience, mapping them properly, geolocating them, and targeting the correct ecosystem. Each shot within your digital action plan should target whom you want to impact and build loyalty with your customers with valuable content. Select the channel with which to do it, the medium that allows you to be sustainable over time with a cost-effective strategy.

Understanding the Right Metrics

Social media marketing is useless without the correct monitoring, and that requires the right key performance indicator (KPI). Without it, we have no measure of campaign success and therefore marketing efficiency.

In the iceberg of KPIs (see Figure 5.5), the tip is the quantitative data. It is asking how much impact, how many conversations, and how much must I invest for how many impacts. It is a simple calculation of income distribution by number of posts.

But as mentioned earlier, measuring quantitative figures—likes, views, etc.—is only the surface level. Measuring quantity is important, but we need to leave the surface to pursue a "deep

Figure 5.5 The image represents healthtech SoMe metrics redefinition and the main cost-effective leveraging points to be aware of.

dive", getting to the deepest part of the iceberg where the most valuable nuggets of information lie about the quality of impact we are generating. These are where we find the qualitative insights that maximise the growth of our business and optimise our investments.

Instead of "how many", ask "who?" Who is liking, who is sharing, who is commenting? The one who downloaded the post must be who you really want them to be. Here, more is not necessarily better. Fewer downloads by the target that you are pursuing, that influencer who is a true thought leader in your field, is better than more downloads by out-of-target users. They will not convert to sales.

Of course, it is important to not get lost in the metrics. Sometimes it is a matter of taking a step back and seeing the overall picture from a helicopter perspective. You can begin with a marketing pilot that is well prepared on the back of research and polish along the way, creating a true method for sustained value and consequently growth.

Artificial Intelligence in Marketing

While social media will likely form a key tool of your marketing activities, there are many other tools that you should consider. While it is not possible to detail them all—several good books have been written on this subject already[5]—one of the most important drivers of success is AI. We as healthtechs are riding the waves of disruption, enabling a sustainable transformation. We are helping a global economy deliver healthcare innovation. Because of the speed of that disruption, we need versatile marketing strategies (as illustrated in Figure 5.6) driven by smart machines.

---

[5] Shailendra Tripathi. *CRM in Pharmaceutical and Healthcare Marketing: Creating a long-term partnership over transactional relationship* (Clever Fox Publishing, 2020); Thomas, R. K. *Health Services Marketing: A Practitioner's Guide* (Springer, 2008); Eric Berkowitz, *Essentials of Health Care Marketing* (Jones & Bartlett Learning, 2016).

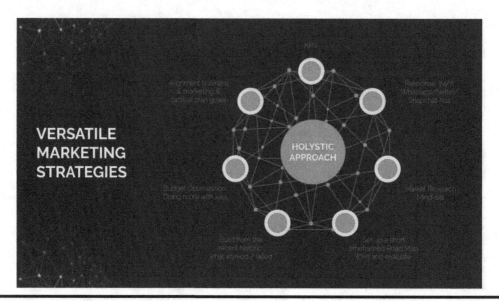

Figure 5.6 **Infographic representing the main adaptive and adaptable marketing strategies that the new 2020s recall from healthtech businesses.**

AI is a combination of reasoning, problem-solving, knowledge representation, planning, creativity, social intelligence, and many other subcategories. It has the potential to deliver additional global economic activity of around $13 trillion by 2030, or about 16% higher cumulative GDP compared with today (McKinsey Global Institute, 2018).

AI-driven marketing is already seeing successful implementation. Among others, this comes in the form of conversational AI that mirrors human-to-human interaction, predictive analysis, voice search optimisation, content generation, personalised user experience or operational efficiency (by automating the known, handing off the unknown).

IBM's value survey for AI in marketing ranks these as the most valuable applications: (1) to manage the omnichannel customer experience, (2) to manage marketing attribution, (3) to manage leads, (4) to manage/create customer-focused content, (5) to develop and manage marketing plans, (6) to understand market trends, (7) to integrate and scale use of first-party data and (8) to understand customer preferences (as illustrated in Figure 5.7) (IBM, 2021).

Overall, in healthcare as in marketing, we are still in the very early phases of exploiting AI potential. While we are working a lot with machine learning, natural language processing, deep learning, computational processing power (cloud processing), there is significant room for development that could positively impact the healthcare field. The COVID-19 crisis accelerated the integration of technology at high-performance levels. Yet we need to remember that we are operating in a more restricted environment than others, and as we deal with the citizens' health and privacy, we must meet higher compliance standards.

Consequently, show patience and consider different speeds for implementing AI into your healthcare marketing. Healthtech companies are becoming so competitive that they are all clamouring to jump aboard the AI train at the speed of light. And often, companies invest into novel solutions that, while they sound impressive, are misaligned with their marketing objectives. Indeed, less than 40% of companies see gains from their investment in AI. This is often because they ask the wrong question, so AI solves the incorrect problem. Or they fail to understand the

Marketing's application of AI across functions

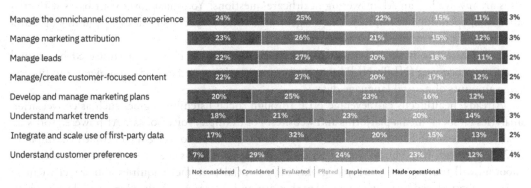

	Not considered	Considered	Evaluated	Piloted	Implemented	Made operational
Manage the omnichannel customer experience	24%	25%	22%	15%	11%	3%
Manage marketing attribution	23%	26%	21%	15%	12%	3%
Manage leads	22%	27%	20%	18%	11%	2%
Manage/create customer-focused content	22%	27%	20%	17%	12%	2%
Develop and manage marketing plans	20%	25%	23%	16%	12%	3%
Understand market trends	18%	21%	23%	20%	14%	3%
Integrate and scale use of first-party data	17%	32%	20%	15%	13%	2%
Understand customer preferences	7%	29%	24%	23%	12%	4%

Source: IBM Institute for Business Value AI value survey. 2020. Note: Percentages may not total 100 due to rounding.

Figure 5.7 (IBM, 2021) shows IBM's value survey for AI in marketing across functions. We can easily appreciate the emergence of most of them and recognise that understanding customer preferences would be the most commoditised pilot function of AI applied in the marketing field.

strengths of a particular AI solution—such as its ability to make highly frequent, granular decisions (Harvard Business Review, 2021).

While ethical concerns should be paramount, the way we embrace the data that we own as a healthtech and the smart conclusions we draw from it will bring value to our marketing. In a near future this will show us how to improve and get closer to the patient's real needs. For example, cognitive computing environments allow human-computer collaboration at the speed of thought. This will revolutionise intelligence collection, accelerating and enhancing planning and direction, collection, processing and exploitation, analysis and production and dissemination. It will become the new status quo in marketing, fully leveraging the vast quantities of health data available.

Only when you have understood the data should you change to lightspeed. This shift up is essential, too, since not being the first mover in the healthtech market is expensive both economically and in terms of securing your market position.

One of the core areas in which AI is impacting marketing is user engagement. Consider the AI engaging initiative carried out by Sensely,[6] a US healthtech company that uses AI to engage users on their terms. Its empathy-driven conversational platform uses AI to enhance the member experience, elevate brand preference and influence behaviour, taking their preferences into account, on the channel of their choice, in over 30 languages, via text or voice to meet their needs.

And in your case, from your healthtech's perspective? Have you thought about how you are going to engage the users or even approach them? What is going to be your rate of engagement success? Who needs to be involved in making these decisions? Are you going to train your potential customers? And what about retaining those already on board? Knowing the answers to these customer service questions is part of your healthtech's core business, and AI will help find those answers and drive success.

On the simplest level, AI can help solve two major issues in healthcare marketing: a massive audience with individual health requests and limited time to answer them.

Automatic healthcare Q&A through well-trained bots can automatically answer most of the requests that patients have, and they can do it instantly, 24/7. This is a great way to drive brand

---

[6] Sensely. URL: https://www.sensely.com/

loyalty by providing valuable content to your customers. But how is compliance managed? What risks are involved in an AI answering healthcare questions? You must cover your bases with trial after trial, operating within the relevant legal framework, or AI can just as easily put in jeopardy a company as it can elevate it above its peers.

Social listening is the new trend in AI marketing, and it is being spearheaded by natural language processing (NLP). NLP leverages computer science and artificial intelligence to process large amounts of natural language data.

Already, healthtechs can leverage NLP through social listening engines such as conversation analytics on social media platforms and websites. For example, voice bots are AI-powered software that can understand natural language and synthesise speech to converse with people (Voximplant, 2020). They can help you to outbound call campaigns of any scale or even perform intelligent inbound call routing, ensuring you gather all potential customer enquiries and direct them to the agent best placed to answer them. Another option is Interactive Voice Response (IVR), which lets humans interact with a computer-operated phone system using voice and dual-tone multi-frequency signalling tones (DTMF).

Decisions can be made easy through NLP and NLU tools, which identify insights and patterns for us. For example, IBM Watson has a new standardised tool that uses Deep Question and Answer (DeepQA) software and Apache UIMA (Unstructured Information Management Architecture) framework implementation. This computing system can answer questions easily by processing huge amounts of data, posing it as natural language using evidence-based reasoning. As its website states, "With a question, a topic, a case or a set of related questions, DeepQA finds the important concepts and relations in the input language, builds a representation of the user's information needs and then through search generates many possible responses" (IBM, 2021).

In other words, this technology can help to prioritise through clustering information around main subjects and deciding which matters to create content from, optimising SEO and scaling the ranking of positions.

Other examples of commoditised mass-market solutions include automated speech recognition (SR), enabling users to ask their smart speaker questions related to health, manage IoMT devices or simply performing daily administrative tasks. Popular commercial voice assistants include Apple's Siri, Amazon's Alexa, Microsoft's Cortana and Google Assistant, and they are available for healthtechs to leverage (Hoy, 2018).

Indeed, already we are seeing voice assistants help conduct surveys and clinical trials or solicit and collect feedback. These can all help customer (patient) retention and in creating more engaging and impactful marketing campaigns. Such innovation is already seeing regulatory acceptance. Alexa, for example, is now compliant with the Health Insurance Portability and Accountability Act (HIPAA), so it can work with health developers that manage protected health information (Penn, 2021).

A core component of AI marketing is data. Massive inputs into accessible datasets are driving marketing insights and significantly impacting our decision making as healthtech before we even deliver healthcare outcomes. In the face of large, unstructured and disparate datasets, we are seeing increasing private-public collaboration. Many governments are standardising their permissions around access to databases towards a common goal of improving the healthcare system and consequently its fair marketing. An example is sharepoints, where shareable data is input and to which access is provided free thanks to government-to-citizen (G2C) and government-to-business (G2B) initiatives.

We are also shifting from a mixture of free-access platforms (external) and enterprise (internal) data to a single cloud of information, brought together by a combination matrix and integrative cloud technology. This is beneficial, but we must also use it properly and take care of the data. It is our raw material for building our customer experience and patient engagement, and above all our marketing strategies and healthcare solutions.

Consider the example of AI in geographical analysis. We are already able to analyse spatial data with the aid of mapping software and in turn design digital maps with geographic data and other data sets. COVID-19 has shown us that geographical information systems (GIS) in combination with contact tracing tools allow us to map and control the hotspots of a contagious disease. Despite the ethical issues, which can be mitigated, according to the research, this can enable better decision making (de Jong BC, 2019). For example, Emirati authorities track people who test positive for COVID-19 and require them to wear electronic wristbands (Serkel, 2021). In the wake of the pandemic, healthtechs will increasingly look to use GIS and geo-clustering to market their solutions, matching them with real-world communities that share traits.

This allows us to create geoproducts, geoprices and geopromotions for local targets. Granularity in the GIS will be important to target customers specifically enough with our localised healthcare commodities.

Clearly, new marketing models are data-driven! Thus, unboxing data will be key. This is where we use advanced analytical techniques—AI—to decode the ins and outs of data, decomposing the results of these complex models back to the inputs to better understand and quantify how the input parameters contribute to overall output.

If we can use AI to properly analyse this data, we will gain insights into consumer behaviour. A well-crafted inbound marketing strategy can help determine prospects, and AI techniques enable us to construct emotions and connect spontaneously, like a human. Organisations that leverage customer behavioural insights outperform peers by 85% in sales growth and over 25% in gross margin (Gallup, 2021).

Our behaviours as humans are already framed in patterns, characterised and standardised by advanced computational algorithms and integrated into smart devices. For example, we have cameras able to capture multiple aleatory expressions in a facial recognition system. This is creating an emerging trend in healthtech: neuromarketing. And it is starting to impact "how" we sell to the customer. Using AI, we are now able to pick up physiological and neural signals from customers and learn their motivations, preferences and decisions.

Here is a new term: "mirror neurons". They are neurons that learn by imitation, and they are why we as humans learn by copying. They can also reproduce in us the feelings of others—empathy. But mirror neurons could also be responsible for making customers perform an action by imitating others doing the same action (MedicalNewsToday, 2021).

Think of the success of real testimonial campaigns or humanised happy-faced patients in the adverts for certain products. They are conveying their feelings onto real patients, mirroring themselves with healthy patients (Lacoste-Badie & Droulers, 2014).

We can assume that happy experiences create more happy thoughts (Speer & Delgado, 2017), while unhappy ones can create a cascade of negativity (Bhatia, 2020). Neuro-linguistic programming (NLP) shows us that if I tell you, "do not think of a pink elephant", you will probably be able to think of nothing but a pink elephant (Ready & Burton, 2008). Daniel Kahneman, in *Thinking, Fast and Slow*, states that "if you take a pencil between your teeth, having the rubber at your right and the pencil tip in the left, forcing you to smile, you will probably have a more positive judgement" (Kahneman, 2012). AI can use all these tricks to model behaviour and market healthtech solutions.

We are highly influenced by environmental visual, kinaesthetic and auditory stimuli (Ready & Burton, 2015). This same phenomenon is why behaviours are becoming so polarised in an online environment—so much of our behaviour parallels a sense of belonging (McCarty, 2020).

We mirror ourselves on what is familiar according to what our pre-acquired programming has taught us. An example of this polarisation is the recent emergence of the antivaccine movements regarding COVID-19 across different social media platforms, despite public information campaigns promoting their safety (Burki, 2020).

The internet acts like an echo chamber, and that is something that AI can leverage but that we must also be wary of.

As healthtechs, we have a responsibility to preserve individuals' freedom to choose their health. But we also have a responsibility to educate patients about all their choices so they can make informed decisions. And through informing patients effectively with accurate healthcare information, delivered at just the right time in a humanised manner thanks to AI-driven insights, we can change their behaviour and, ultimately, secure their engagement with our product.

With digital marketing, design simplicity and closeness to customers are important. It takes your brain 50 milliseconds to create a first impression of a website or digital solution. Indeed, our subconscious—that primitive fight-or-flight binary—determines 95% of our buying choices and brand loyalty (Google, 2021). Consequently, healthtechs must use more than logic in their marketing campaigns and tech adoption approaches. They must use behaviour and address three main stimuli:

- **Visual** language is a system of communication that uses visual images, like symbols or design.
  Visual language-based technologies for healthtechs include eye tracking or ocular follow-up, or new image-based search technologies. Colour code studies (Shrivastava, et al., 2014), pricing or interface layout are used in healthtech marketing. In social media infographics, reels or videos posts are proven to be processed faster than text as the information transmitted to the brain is visual.
- **Auditory** language is a system of communication that uses auditive stimulus as a preference. Healthtech technologies including virtual assistants can already enable computers to understand spoken or typed remarks. This communication system is also used to tell stories and provide accurate health information or diagnosis in spoken form, for example, user-friendly, trustworthy explanations of your solutions. These voice-activated assistants and speech recognition platforms are creating better experiences by expanding patient access to information, cutting transcription costs and delays and improving the quality of health records. Usage of chatbots and natural language processing would also be included in this group (Burroughs, 2021).
- **Kinaesthetic** language is a system of communication that uses the feel of the message being transmitted.
  Kinaesthetic behaviours include decision paralysis, emotion response analysis (ERA), mirror neurons and loss aversion attitudes. At the same time, AI marketing involving kinaesthetic language includes gamification with reward and punishment and even galvanic responses (emotional arousal).

These are only a few in a spectrum of AI marketing tools that can turn to turn formerly untouchable qualitative data into touchable quantitative conclusions.

Whatever marketing routes you choose, know that understanding your patient's human behaviour is key to strategically positioning ourselves in the healthcare ecosystem and placing the patient at the centre of our business models (Nunez, 2021). It is the key to marketing success.

Chapter 6

Your Stakeholder Ecosystem

Building a healthtech is about more than simply creating a valuable product and marketing it effectively. To succeed, we need to integrate our healthtech businesses into the healthcare ecosystem. We need to reinvent our strategies to build bridges of collaboration and synergy with all the stakeholders of the pathology. Put the patient in the centre and define where, through value paths, you can link all the parties.

It is not only us as a solution, as an independent healthtech. It is all about building these win-win alliances with the rest of the ecosystem stakeholders and our versatility to be able to adapt to their needs and, in turn, the patient's needs (Shortell & Kaluzny, 2011). Ultimately, all we are doing is co-creating and enlarging the value of our healthtech and ensuring our "sense of place" in its ecosystem. This sense of place is a multidimensional, complex construct characterising relationships between us and other people, but prioritises authentic human attachment and the exchange of value (W. Caves, 2004) (Casey, 2010).

Consequently, our healthtechs must create improved healthcare outcomes that impact the whole ecosystem, not just the patient. We must build everything around these key stakeholders, who constitute the ecosystem network. That includes our business objectives, our core pathology, our tactical plan and the roadmap that we are building—we must design each with the goal of occupying the right position in our ecosystem to touch all the stakeholders.

This is all about collaboration: building the community and coworking teams to cocreate value that translates into healthcare outcomes across the whole pathology, from diagnosis to aftercare.

We should also remember that the overall healthcare ecosystem is being impacted by volatility, uncertainty, complexity, and ambiguity (Gläser, 2021). If COVID-19 showed us anything, it is that the ecosystem is in flux. It is like a maritime ecosystem, with weather-influenced fluctuations and changing streams of water, and we need to be prepared for that in all our strategies and future marketing plans. This means building multiple value-bridges to stakeholders as a way to mitigate sudden changes in the ecosystem.

Selecting stakeholders that will constitute your ecosystem is the essence of market segmentation. In this process, you decide who is who, and more than this, where they land in the hierarchy of value to your healthtech. Ask, which stakeholders will occupy the position of key customers, key influencers, key opinion leaders, and key allies of favourable growth?

DOI: 10.4324/b23147-8

This process is essential as you can design a favourable ecosystem or a hostile ecosystem in which to expand. And, as in nature, your healthtech's survival depends on how well you fit your ecosystem.

In a natural habitat, a favourable maritime ecosystem provides the correct physical properties of light, temperature, waves, currents and chemical composition, as well as different ecological organisations and a distribution of organisms.

We can extrapolate the same concept to the ecology of the healthtech industry, where light, temperature, waves, currents and chemical composition would be the potential of the regulatory frameworks, the funding possibilities, and the infrastructure of the ecosystem, and the different types of ecological organisations and the distribution of organisms would be the mapping of stakeholders we select to constitute our ecosystem and how we are able to onboard them.

Stakeholders play a strategic role, with direct and indirect influence over our success and market position. They must become convinced and independent ambassadors of your solution, so that when they change or the ecosystem changes, you are brought along.

Your stakeholders must understand and know about the solutions that we are offering as healthtechs. Thus, educating them is important.

And we should establish synergies, not competitions. Set up win-win agreements with all stakeholders of the pathology. That is, value-based contracts (VBC) (I, 2021). Also known as success-based contracts, these are a type of contract model that ties the price of a healthtech product to how it performs, and in turn to the improvement of direct and indirect healthcare outcomes. Sometimes referred as risk-sharing agreements (RSA) for being outcome-based, they constitute an innovative payment model that brings together two key stakeholders, i.e., healthcare payers and a healthtech company, to improve technology adoption among patients (Drummond, et al., 2020) (Espin J, 2010).

To create these types of win-win alliances, we must onboard our stakeholders by presenting clear value dossiers—something this chapter will explore in detail. In these, you will show that you are not creating a single solution for a single problem. You will show how you can be part of an ecosystem inside a pathology, with a solution that is impacting the day-to-day of the patient, of the healthcare professional, and of the healthcare payer. And you will show how you impact the costs of the pathology's overall expenditure framework.

Remember, the "lone wolf" entrepreneur no longer works. Avoid fragmentation and start embracing all the players and onboarding them, which in turn means engaging them in your business plan.

Framing and conceptualising the ecosystem in which to operate requires state-of-the-art know-how, experience and above all capacity as an institution. More than this, it is not a one-time job but a continuous labour of building and preserving the ecosystem, like maintaining an aquatic ecosystem in a fish tank.

Coexistence in a self-sustaining ecosystem takes trial and error, time, and resilience. But it is possible if you identify the key stakeholders and establish healthy alliances and collaborations with them. How? Through adding value at all the leverage points and meeting the unmet needs of the value chain.

Mapping Key Stakeholders

When creating your ecosystem, you need not be big, but you need to be clever. And that comes from keeping the balance and becoming the best in your field. Consequently, you must discover

Figure 6.1 **Infographic representing table chess in which each key stakeholder occupies the right strategic position in the ecosystem and interacts with each other in a game of key strategic moves.**

which are the true partnerships that will help you—those who know where to start and who can provide you with the proper network.

You should brainstorm potential stakeholders and rank them by what they can provide to your business concept needs. Can they open your doors? Can they become a strategic ambassador or partner? A common sense of purpose must exist. It can be as simple as a shared interest in the progress of a pathology, or a simple burden release, or why not the common pursuit of a simple jump in the quality of life of a citizen living in the umbrella of a smart city?

It is like in chess, where ordering the pieces is the first step before starting the game. Also, know on which side you will play—private or public, or maybe both, through a hybrid business model. In chess, each key stakeholder occupies the right strategic position in the ecosystem and interacts with other figures in a game of key strategic moves. Unbeatable could mean always drawing, or always winning. Until today, chess does not have an unbeatable set of moves (see Figure 6.1). The same is true in a healthtech ecosystem.

Ensure you are asking and actively listening to the right stakeholders by mapping and classifying them with a who-is-who approach. Below, we run through some of the key stakeholders you should be mapping and planning to onboard into your ecosystem.

The Pharmaceutical Industry

They are the big fish. They have the pill, the pathology solution, and we have the service that brings value and upgrades the healthcare outcomes across the whole ecosystem.

Why not knock at their door and ask them to extend a helping hand so that we can work together, through a win-win strategic alliance? They can really embrace our project, and we can really bring them the value that they lack. Let us start onboarding them onto our projects and solutions.

And why not, at a certain point, maybe co-create and innovate together on joint projects? Some examples of pharmaceutical industry initiatives to enable this collaboration are:

■ Bayer G4A,[1] which helps digital health funding and partnerships.
■ Novartis Biome,[2] which is a catalyst for impactful digital collaboration.

There are also accelerator programs that push for healthtech progress:

■ Innovation Centre,[3] led by Merck.
■ Startupbootcamp,[4] owned by Sanofi Aventis.
■ Baselaunch,[5] funded by multiple pharmaceutical companies pushing biotech ventures.

These initiatives are useful if you are starting, you want to scale up fast or you simply need a push through partnering or network. PhRMA's Medicine Assistance Tool (MAT) is a useful a search engine designed to find resources available through the various biopharmaceutical industry programs.[6]

On the other hand, there are accelerators lead by technology companies:

■ Philipps Healthcare with its Philipps Ventures:[7] giving you the chance to gain industry insight, connections and resources that can help you to become a start-up partner and to turn some ideas into a scalable reality.
■ Siemens Technology Accelerator:[8] building many innovative businesses based on Siemens's inventions and addressing highly valuable applications in markets which are not covered by any Siemens entity.
■ Microsoft Accelerator:[9] works closely with market-ready start-ups and provides the tools, resources, knowledge, and expertise required to succeed. The goal of this accelerator is to help start-ups mature into enterprise-ready companies by scaling every aspect of their business.
■ General Electric (GE):[10] with the GE Healthcare Division, is launching a new start-up accelerator for artificial intelligence in Europe.
■ IBM Hyper Protect Accelerator 2021:[11] If your start-up collects and stores sensitive healthtech data, you must find the right cloud program to secure it. The IBM Start-up Program is providing to select start-ups access to the IBM Cloud Hyper Protect Services powered by IBM's LinuxONE server.

---

[1] Bayer G4A (formerly known as Grants4Apps), URL: https://www.g4a.health/
[2] Novartis Biome, URL: https://www.biome.novartis.com/
[3] Innovation Centre, URL: https://www.merckgroup.com/en/research/innovation-center/accelerator.html
[4] StartupBootCamp, URL: https://www.startupbootcamp.org/accelerator/digital-health-berlin/
[5] Baselaunch, URL: https://baselaunch.ch/
[6] PhRMA's Medicine Assistance Tool (MAT), URL: https://www.medicineassistancetool.org/; URL to members https://www.phrma.org/about/members
[7] Philips Ventures, URL: https://www.usa.philips.com/healthcare/innovation/philips-ventures
[8] Siemens Technology accelerator, URL: https://new.siemens.com/global/en/products/services/technology-accelerator.html
[9] Microsoft Accelerator, URL: https://www.microsoft.com/en-in/about/empowering-startups-msaccelerator.aspx
[10] GE Healthcare Accelerator, URL: https://thehealthcareinsights.com/ge-healthcare-launches-a-new-startup-accelerator-for-artificial-intelligence-in-europe/
[11] IBM Protect Accelerator 2021, URL: https://community.ibm.com/community/user/ibmz-and-linuxone/blogs/kavon-badie1/2021/04/30/ibm-hpa-applications-2021

Big pharmaceutical companies and big technological firms also have knowledge of the ecosystem. They have been there for many years, and they have consolidated departments that work on the cutting edge. They will have whole departments concerned with market access, legal matters, medical affairs, regulation, business intelligence, privacy and security affairs, and they are all working towards a globally shared goal in healthcare: the achievement of improved health outcomes and extension of QALYs.

The Healthcare Authorities

Healthcare authorities have been major players in the ecosystem for a long time, and they remain central to economic considerations. They have always been the payers, and they still are. With your healthtech solution, you are impacting their 5- or 10-years healthcare plan in the different regions, nations and countries.

In some countries, the authorities are private: we are speaking about private health insurance companies. In some counties with public healthcare systems, they have decentralised healthcare budget management per region. In other cases, the country works as a big octopus that intelligently manages the whole country's expenditure and budget, delivering the resources from a centralised position to each region that sometimes have governance of health expenditure, like in Spain.

So, how do you, as an individual, reach these seemingly unreachable entities? First, ask for help. Some healthtech hubs and accelerators can help you to channel or convey this first contact with top pharmaceutical companies or governmental health bodies. For example, some accelerators or healthtech hubs organise journeys where members of a certain laboratory come by one day and listen to pitches from members of the hub related to a certain subject—for example, "AI that can optimise the patient journey". Find the hubs and accelerators specialising in your field and become a member to access these opportunities.

Another option is cold calling—knocking on the right door with the right speech through, for example, LinkedIn. Surprisingly, the figures that are higher in a company's pyramid, if they are the right people, are usually open to listening to things that respond to their unmet needs. You may not reach them directly, but the right pitch will get their agent to pass along your details. So be brave, open your own doors. When you do not know where to start, a simple call to a large organisation or governmental body can help you solve months of key stakeholder management work, directing you to the right person. Although each company works in its own way and has its own doors of communication, be positive they will always swing open for the right person or pitch.

And when you ask for help from the right authorities and regulatory bodies, come prepared with a high-value dossier full of (1) trustable data, (2) real-world evidence, (3) health outcomes and (4) quantified burden impacts within the pathology where you operate (we discuss how to build this in more detail later in the chapter). Prepare well, then re-prepare—you will often only get one chance to be considered. Bring in clear data on the direct patient optimisation pathways and their correlated expenditure and more than this, show how you can contribute to contain such health expenditure. For example, why not prepare a pharmacoeconomic study that brings you real data of all the value that you are creating in the system?

Also make sure that you present the hidden value, the indirect and valuable health outcomes: costs, burden, citizen productivity, wellbeing, etc. In other words, make sure that you leverage the indirect added value that is not obvious at first. Make sure that you translate all this value and present it in terms of improved healthcare outcomes. You can use qualitative or quantitative data but please, make sure that is genuine and trustable. Your credibility depends on this.

Above all, health authorities are enablers, and we need to see them this way. We must get them onboard and deal or negotiate with them from your experience, from your company's validated value proposition and the provision of services.

We include here the Ministry of Health from the country, the states, communities or regions into which the country is divided or organised. We mean all these regions that manage their own healthcare budget expenditure, and finally the hospitals that sometimes also act as centres of healthcare, in turn regions where key hospitals are the reference for other hospitals in the same area and depend on them and their policies.

These key authorities provide guidelines for the procedures and good practices for the whole pathology, and all the healthcare professionals in the region will embrace these rules. Getting them onboard is essential to establish your position into the ecosystem, so bear in mind where and how you bring them value. Think about how your product or service can be integrated into these regions' validated recommendations and timeframes for healthcare strategic plans, which are usually reviewed every five years.

Connectivity and alignment with these critical ecosystem stakeholders are key. We as healthtechs should aim to fit the role of a specific partner with infrastructures in place to accelerate solutions and create value faster. Public-private collaborations—in a favourable legal framework—will drive the future of healthcare (Madir, 2020).

In this group, we could also include the official review institutions for healthtech solutions. Here, we mean institutions with worldwide recognition and value such as the English National Health Service who publish the top recommended apps, or the Ministry of Health from any key country that you are focused on that recommends the use of some apps for optimising pathology outcomes. Consider that a good recommendation or review from their side is 1,000 times more valuable than a hundred other recommendations with no trustable entity behind them, though you should collect as many recommendations from as wide an array of authorities as possible.

Target these key authorities proactively. Prepare evaluations from these institutions before their output is published. This evaluation of the available health technologies most likely to be standardised and validated must be done using the right information; it is your job to provide this to the health authorities before it is too late. Most important of all, it is a matter of informing them that you exist; otherwise, you will never appear in their picture.

Here arises an opportunity for private-public collaborations, where it is important to choose projects that catalyse innovation throughout the ecosystem. We must be close to the healthcare authorities, the public and the private managers and thus to the different healthcare systems to articulate the healthcare system's upcoming disruptive change. In other words, bring consistency and internal structures, bring organisation and cohesion to the healthcare system.

When presenting to these authorities your healthtech product or service in a value dossier, make sure that you use real-world evidence (RWE) based on clinical practice and Health Economics and Outcomes Research (HEOR). Multiple resources exist detailing what constitutes RWE and how to obtain it (Administration, 2021) (Agency, 2021) (Cave, et al., 2019).[12] Make sure that you accomplish the evidence standards framework for digital health technologies, i.e., if your company is allocated in England, accomplish the standards of NICE (NICE, 2021).[13]

---

[12] RWE for FDA, URL: https://www.fda.gov/science-research/science-and-research-special-topics/real-world-evidence
RWE for EMA, URL: https://www.ema.europa.eu/en/events/technical-workshop-real-world-metadata-regulatory-purposes
[13] NICE Evidence standards framework for digital health technologies, URL: https://www.nice.org.uk/about/what-we-do/our-programmes/evidence-standards-framework-for-digital-health-technologies

You must articulate to the health authorities the value of your solution, give bullet points covering the main key areas, provide clinical evaluating data such as adherence or cure rates, evidence economical medical resource utilisation, and demonstrate a humanistic relation to quality of life. In particular, compare new with existing data. Thus, RWE complement randomised controlled trials (RCT) to generate supplementary new evidence.

Through RWE, we can generate robust value dossiers that allow us to quantify a real-world and healthtech-product-specific value compilation. You must frame the natural status of the disease and forecast its progression. Define real unmet clinical, social and human lifestyle needs by characterising the burden of the illness based on local and global treatment patterns and approaches.

The key is to quantify all the associated costs of the standard of care and translate it onto a crystal-clear value proposition: how to improve health economic models based on an improvement of the standard of care.

Governmental health institutions and private parties are also sometimes owners of big, centralised accelerators that push for progress of healthtech:

■ In Europe, EITHealth,[14] co-founded by the European Union, promotes European centralised acceleration at any phase for the most promising start-ups.
■ Also, initiatives like SeedCamp[15] exist, which invests in early in world-class founders attacking large, global markets and solving real problems using technology.
■ In the US, the city of New York drives technology with the New York Digital Health Innovation Lab.[16]
■ Newcomers include the Ocean Hub Africa,[17] an accelerator based in Cape Town and started in 2020.
■ An example of a government institution in China pushing healthtech innovation is the National Development and Reform Commission, which helps development of medical device technology.[18]
■ In Taiwan, Be Capital Accelerator[19] has launched Health for All,[20] a virtual start-up community to engage and potentially establish long-term collaborations with Taiwanese corporations.

Centres of Excellence (COE)

Do you know the centres of excellence for your pathology? The ones that are driving the research and the outcomes of the pathology? Do you know which hospitals and healthcare professionals are significantly contributing to the present and the future of the pathology? If not, get to know them.

You must be intimately familiar with their work, and they with yours. They will be the diplomats for your healthtech solution, your ambassadors who believe in it and push for it. Consequently, early adoption from customers will be easier to gain. They are the experts, so get them onboard from the start, as we explained in the clinical trials section back in Chapter 4. Have them include

---

[14] EITHealth, URL: https://eithealth.eu/
[15] SeedCamp, URL: https://seedcamp.com/
[16] New York Digital Health Innovation lab, URL: https://digitalhealth.nyc/
[17] Ocean Hub Africa, URL: https://www.oceanhub.africa/
[18] China National Development and Reform Commission. https://www.ndrc.gov.cn/xxgk/zcfb/tz/202007/t20200715_1233793.html
[19] Taiwan Be Capital Accelerator https://www.beaccelerator.com.tw/
[20] Health For All https://www.healthforall.tw/

your device onto their clinical trials, and gain from them RWE, giving your solution a pack of trustworthy data validating its health outcomes in front of regulatory bodies and others.

If anyone will help you, they will; they are the ones pushing the pathology outcomes for the sake of patient wellbeing—for no other reason than value.

So, work hand in hand with them. Onboard them to the healthtech world as another player in your ecosystem. Co-create and co-build with them—because you need them, and they also need you. And above all, the patient needs this alliance to achieve their deserved future healthcare model.

Well-known centres of excellence include the Karolinska Institute,[21] a research-led medical university in Solna within the Stockholm urban area of Sweden; Mount Sinai Hospital[22], founded in 1852, one of the oldest and largest teaching hospitals in the United States, located in the New York City borough of Manhattan; and Moorfields,[23] from UK which constitutes a centre of excellence in the ophthalmology area.

Overall, your aim should be to target this centre of excellence around the pathology and acquire evidence-based medicine (EBM) validated by trustworthy data. They can perform the randomised clinical trials (RCT) necessary to validate the efficiency and effectiveness of the solution and understand its cost-effectiveness through EBM.

The difference between efficacy, efficiency and effectiveness are key. As the latest research explains, "Efficacy, in the health care sector, is the capacity for beneficial change (or therapeutic effect) of a given intervention (for example a drug, medical device, surgical procedure or a public health intervention) under ideal or controlled conditions. Effectiveness links to the notion of external validity, in that it refers to patients who are visited by physicians in their everyday practice. Efficiency is doing things in the most economical way. It is the ratio of the output to the inputs of any system (good input to output ratio)" (Burches & Burches, 2020).

Most healthtechs suffer from a lack of real-world evidence substantiating their claims about their product. RWE regarding efficacy, safety and user testing is necessary to achieve successful market access and product uptake. RCTs are necessary, but the reality is more complex; you must understand reality from the patient's perspective.

Thus, demanding evidence of benefits and risks in a real-world setting is a baseline requirement. You cannot claim your enterprise, your healthtech, brings healthcare outcomes without having validated data behind these affirmations. And centres of excellence are how you achieve this.

Finally, healthtechs have a responsibility to co-work with centres of excellence in developing frontline technology and leading the operation of the best healthcare solutions. And more than this, they will need to speed the adoption curves of this technology.

Centres should bring flexibility and scalable methodologies that others can model. And this relies on a win-win alliance between the two of you, with the intention that they become best practices for other centres with your solution at their core.

Advancing centres to this standard requires us to provide continuous technological training programs, opening the doors to our up-to-date knowledge and onboarding the key stakeholders from these centres of excellence to our research, development & innovation (R+D+i) programs.

---

[21] Karolinska Institute. URL: https://ki.se/
[22] Mount Sinai hospital. URL: https://www.mountsinai.org/locations/mount-sinai/your-visit/locations
[23] Moorfields Eye hospital. URL: https://www.moorfields-private.co.uk/

Healthcare Technology Innovation Centres (HTIC)

They are mission-driven entities that work with higher education institutions to research, develop and innovate in the technological field. They are found within the centres of tech companies, constituting accelerators and shuttles. They exist in the key cities and capitals worldwide, full of talent able to create and advance new technology. We need to onboard them and rely on their accelerator programs and funds.

Also consider the reference HTICs in your country that are bringing together technologists, engineers, healthcare professionals as well as industry and government stakeholders to develop healthcare technologies for the country. All of them have one common aim when it comes to healthtech: accelerating the progress of healthcare through technology. We can build with them, creating key partnerships, and they in turn can help us to elevate and push our pipelines.

Worldwide, the top tech reference centres include:

■ Silicon Valley Innovation Centre,[24] which is the United States' centre for innovative technology companies, being home to many of the world's largest technology companies including Apple, Cisco, Google, HP, Intel and Oracle.
■ The European Institute of Innovation and Technology (EIT).[25]
■ The China International Technology Transfer Centre (CITTC) in Beijing, Shanghai and Shenzhen is firmly established as China's leading tech hub.
■ Azrieli Center in Tel Aviv, which is home of the country's biggest tech companies.[26]

Legal Institutions and Regulatory Bodies

Remember that you act in a regulated environment. Know the limits. Study the legal frameworks, and scale in a way that respects those limits. For healthtechs, this mostly comes down to data and the national institutions regulating such data. We have covered this extensively elsewhere (Chapter Four).

Comparables or Follow-Ons

Comparables or follow-ons refer to those companies that are similar to a pre-existing company. Do not fear them or treat them as competitors. But I would suggest, embrace them.

Network with any business like your healthtech or with a similar product—those big initiatives that have similar business models to yours, or prototypes that structurally or functionally seem to mirror your solution with only very slight changes.

They may be comparable, but remember, they are neither competitors nor enemies—they should be your friends. We must learn from one another to succeed. We must embrace similar solutions. You will achieve more that way.

---

[24] Silicon Valley Innovation Centre. URL https://siliconvalley.center/events/category/healthcare URL https://siliconvalley.center/education/standard-programs/transforming-the-healthcare-industry
[25] European Institute of Innovation and Technology (EIT) URL: https://eit.europa.eu/our-communities/eit-health
https://ec.europa.eu/programmes/horizon2020/en/h2020-section/european-institute-innovation-and-technology-eit; EIT Health. URL: https://eit.europa.eu/our-communities/eit-health
[26] https://restofworld.org/2021/tech-hubs-tel-aviv/

Sun Tzu, in *The Art of War* states, "If you know others and you know yourself, not in a hundred battles will you be in danger; if you don't know others, but you know yourself, you will lose one battle and win another; if you don't know others or yourself, you will be in danger in every battle." (Tzu, 2018).

Healthcare Professionals, Caretakers and Caregivers

The WHO reports that for every medical doctor there are 3324 people in Africa, 1239 in South-East Asia, 989 in Eastern-Mediterranean, 533 in Western Pacific, 417 in the Americas and 293 in Europe (WHO, 2021).

It also estimates that by 2030 the world will be short of 9.9 million doctors, nurses and mid-wives (WHO, 2021). This statement confirms that healthcare professionals are essential. And more than this, healthcare professionals are the key ambassadors of our healthtechs (see Figure 6.2). They must be onboarded from the very beginning. They are the reference contact for the patient, also for the caretakers and caregivers, and for the new professions we are creating through our healthtech solutions.

Healthcare Professionals (HCPs) have direct, daily patient contact. They know the particularities and insights of the patient's journey and the pathology's pathway. They know the patient's profile in the first place and are the ambassadors of their true needs.

They are becoming early adopters of healthtech, on behalf of improving their daily clinical practice with easier and better diagnosis, permitting a more humanised patient approach and cutting-edge medical practice (Empresarial, 2021).

They must be onboarded in our products and services from the beginning, from the seed conceptualisation until the up-to-market and later escalation. Their feedback is key. So onboard them in panels of experts, in advisory boards or more than this in becoming the very first testers of the technology as individuals giving feedback or in a clinical trial.

Figure 6.2   The importance of the healthcare professional in all the business decisions your healthtech considers.

As healthtech innovators, our work directly impacts the status quo of these patient-facing stakeholders every day. We must consider their needs and help them to cover the needs of their patients.

We need to get the healthcare professionals' points of view and acknowledge them in our projects and solutions because they are the ones that are in the field. They know the pathology, and more than that, they know the patient first-hand.

Healthcare professionals need better tools to support their patients, an efficient fit-to-care practice, and an impact on the care pathway. Indeed, we need to be able to provide better telehealth tools, AI-supported diagnostics, chronic patient follow-up platforms, acute-phase upgraded prognosis and prediction tools, robotic precision surgeries, etc. We are the enablers of their improved daily practice.

Healthtechs might engage clinicians and caregivers in the development of their solutions as they are the patient reference and have the knowledge of the clinical field. For example, say we wish to involve the National Association of Clinical Nurse Specialists in the conceptualisation of a healthtech digital therapeutics or service as a software. Specifically, imagine you want to build a collaboration agreement under which they onboard the project, helping to fine tune and validate our approach to patient humanisation.

They would bring their valuable experience (in-field feedback) to your healthtech product and its operation. Their contribution can directly impact the delivery of your solution, improving patient adoption and integration into the patient's daily life while respecting their quality of life.

And more than that, collaboration with the association would give insights into how your technology can improve these nurses' working conditions in their day-to-day life and in the quality of patient care. Only they can know this part, as they are the ones who are directly involved in it.

For this and other reasons, it is essential to onboard those with field experience like key reference societies of healthcare professionals, midwifes, and patients. Their value-add to your project will be unique and something you cannot obtain elsewhere or in-house.

Some of the healthcare professions are becoming digital or are already digital. So, we are impacting their day-to-day, and we need to have them in mind and train them with our solutions to build the new healthtech ecosystems. Computers will replace physicians for many diagnostic tasks, citizen science will give rise to citizen medicine, and enormous data sets will give us new means to attack conditions that have long been incurable (Topol, 2016).

In a recent article published in *Nature*, authors confirm that the value of an AI clinician's selected treatment for sepsis is on average reliably higher than human clinicians. And mortality was lowest in patients for whom clinicians' actual doses matched the AI decisions (Komorowski, et al., 2018).

As this shows, AI has the potential to transform everything that doctors do (Topol, 2019), and consequently healthcare professionals need to be transformed too. That means healthtech upskilling. The clinical decision-making process must be improved with the help of technology and the synergy of doctor and technology.

Clinicians do not need to understand the ins and outs of the technology, but they do need to understand how to operate it—not everyone needs to know how to write code. But understanding it at a minimum level is necessary so that they can bridge the clinical role they are occupying at the moment and the one they will need to occupy alongside the technology.

For example, this upskilling healthcare practitioner will undeniably need stronger technological skills to understand how AI works at a certain level of detail, and the data scientists and engineers will need some basic medical knowledge and strong communication skills to help them translate clinical requirements into technology solutions. All staff will need both digital and genomics literacy. This means practitioners will need ongoing expertise and guidance to evaluate new technologies, based on real-world evidence and their understanding of data validity and accuracy (AHA, 2021) (NHS, 2019) (eHI & Cerner, 2018).

All immediate clinical decisions that do not have to be deeply thought are going to be taken by robotics. HCPs and most of their daily work will be assisted by a computer, alleviating the high burden of their jobs from the past. Their new professional roles will need continuous interaction with the tools that the system and governments provide to them. Their decisions will be primarily validating diagnoses that the computing systems are already doing, or making difficult decisions—risk decisions and ethical matters, etc.

Everything is going to be roboticised. Automatisation will be the new status quo. Everything that now requires only a superficial semi-automatised thought from our human brain will be a decision automatically taken by a machine. We cannot be sceptical about embracing all these new game-changing possibilities, therefore, that the digital world is bringing. We must embrace all aspects of the new technology despite our inherent resistance to change. This is true on our end and for HCPs. Indeed, most HCPs cling to a traditional healthcare model, but we must disrupt that with a culture shift. We must teach, train, and equip—building the healthcare pyramid anew.

Healthtech will be crucial to this transition. We must face resistance with open arms, breaking down barriers and hesitancy with transparency and honesty—revealing our core values to all and upholding them so they can onboard to our mission.

Indeed, new educational initiatives are already emerging. For example, free e-training and crowd-learning platforms exist to give access to many more valuable training and development opportunities for healthcare professionals. Such is the case of the e-learning portfolio boosted by Health Education England (HEE) for the health and care workforce. It partnered with FutureLearn.com to provide short, free courses to the National Health Service (NHS, 2021).[27]

Crowd learning is another leading field. Medscape[28], for example, is a free platform for healthcare professionals and caretakers like nurses that provides guides for decision making, clinical information on medications and their identification.

The Patient

The patient is the core of all we create and of our entire ecosystem. If you cannot onboard the patient, you have no hope of success as a healthtech. Our products and services directly impact them and the course of their health outcomes. Therefore, we must fully associate ourselves with them; empower them through high-quality, genuine training and knowledge that helps them decide on their own health.

The expectations of patients and families are continually evolving with increasing consumer requests coming with the democratisation of healthcare. The "expert patient figure" (Bipolar, 2017),[29] though, is a new emerging figure. They differ from the individual patient because besides their disease-specific expertise, they have technical knowledge in R&D and/or

---

[27] Future Learn, URL: https://www.futurelearn.com/
[28] Medscape, URL: https://www.medscape.com/
[29] NoSome patients, known as expert patients, strive to improve the performance of the health care system. The precise nature of their activities, skills and personality traits are unclear, however, which could compromise their recognition.

regulatory affairs through experience (Costanza, 2020). The expert patient is one with chronic conditions who is knowledgeable enough to make informed decisions about and manage the care of the pathology.

A study conducted in France identifies the activities that an expert patient figure engages in and concludes that their core competency is "to improve the management and/or prevention of the illness." The expert patient is a core element of the new healthcare decision-making process—a hybrid between the conventional "top-down" approach and a newer "bottom-up" approach. In the same study, expert patients referred to themselves as "lobbyists" in improving the wellbeing of their peers, "patient trainers" and "medical researchers", too, or "user representatives" on various committees, defining the lobbying activity as occupying the major part of their time.

Also, expert patients actively participate in the democratisation of health. Under the credo "participate, act and influence", these patients sit on advisory boards where they represent not only their own disease but also constitute the heroes who defend the interests of an entire community of patients, setting aside their personal history and acting as a spokesperson. (Gross & Gagnayre, 2014).

Expert figure patients are enrolled in other important activities, like ensuring the progress in the management and results of their disease. Through continuous study and the continuous updating of knowledge, they are often able to suggest new innovative treatments and even support their use by the medical community. They also help the community of doctors by enrolling as training patients for doctors to learn about.

Not all patients do all these activities at the same time. Most focus on a specific area and, broadly speaking, there are two groups of expert patients: (1) those whose activity is directly related to the treatment of the disease, and (2) those who are more focused on the health system, social issues, and the daily management of the disease. This result helps us understand the nature of expert patients' actions and their contribution to the healthcare systems, making the expert patient figure easier for traditional actors to identify and recruit, as recommended by the World Health Organisation. They could also be used as pedagogical benchmarks in a potential (self-) training process (Bipolar, 2017).

The figure of the expert patient can support your health technologies, but first you have to know them—through clinical trials, as discussed in Chapter 4.

Along my career I have had the chance to bump up into reference expert patient figures, some of them amazing human beings. One example is, who in that moment was president of the patient's association Mundo Bipolar (Bipolar, 2017)[30] and a role model for the community that is still fighting for the good of bipolar disorder patients. She is also a RECOVER-E[31] project partner and leads communication and dissemination activities in the project. She is an example of the perfect expert patient to onboard into your stakeholder ecosystem and collaborate with to advance the healthcare outcomes of the pathology.

Patients are increasingly informed and empowered. Thus, we must provide the correct type and amount of information to explain our products and services. We cannot stay on the surface when we are explaining our solutions because they are already well prepared and highly demanding. They acquire much information, so we must fully explain our solutions in easy ways and with comprehensible language so that anyone can perfectly understand their entirety.

---

[30] Patients Association Mundo Bipolar (translation: Bipolar World) URL http://mundobipolar.org/
[31] RECOVER-E is a European Commission Horizon 2020 project with 16 partners from 11 countries; the project complements numerous ongoing efforts in mental health service delivery transformation and innovation in Europe. URL http://www.recover-e.eu/

You must include patients in focus groups, and more than this ask for feedback from the community of patients—after all, they are your true customers.

Influencers (Key Opinion Leaders and Key Stakeholders)

Influencers are the ones that have enough weight to carry out a potential impact in the ecosystem, with a positive opinion or positioning towards your solution, through opening doors, pushing to jump obstacles or break barriers, bring in opportunities, etc.

They, sometimes, are the ones that lead the innovation and drive the performance of the pathology.

Key opinion leaders (KOLs) are one type of influencer. They are professors from top universities, reference hospitals and Centres of Excellence. They have the key expertise, and they have spent all their lives driving the treatment of a particular pathology towards life extension and patient wellbeing.

Key stakeholders include clinical practice stakeholders and the figure of the health manager. He or she can be defined as a Medical Director of a Centre of Excellence or a hospital of reference for the pathology, a Hospital Manager, Pharmacy Director, a Primary Care (PC) manager, a PC pharmacist, etc. All of them in turn impact and influence large communities. These figures play very different roles depending on the country or sometimes in different regions of the same country. They also can have different nomenclatures. Consider them while you map stakeholders.

Marketplaces

Marketplaces are digital retail sites (in other words, digital supermarkets of products and services). Depending on your sort of healthtech product, if you cannot onboard them, you will not be able to sell your product. They can deal with Over the Counter (OTC), sanitary products, medical devices, healthtech products, SaaS and prescription drugs.

They include wholesalers and legitimate parallel exportation pharmacies (Vega, 2003) and all sorts of healthcare-derived businesses. They are anywhere that the customer can purchase health, giving them the best products and services at the best price. In the pharmacy field, we have CVS Pharmacy,[32] Walgreens[33], Walmart[34] and Costco.[35] And as digital marketplaces offering healthcare services, we could leverage Amazon Care[36], where you can connect to a team of medical experts dedicated to providing Connected Care attendance to your needs, and Ali Heath.

These platforms operate at a macro level with different pathologies and leading health matters. Their backlinks are essential to help you to scale up positions in the SEO ranking, in terms of what used to be the old product placement. They will help you to position your product around the environment and succeed with your visibility.

---

[32] CVS Pharmacy URL https://www.cvs.com
[33] Walgreens URL https://www.walgreens.com
[34] Walmart URL https://www.walmart.com
[35] CostCo URL https://www.costco.com/pharmacy/warehouse-pickup
[36] Amazon Care URL https://amazon.care/

Building a Value Dossier

French fashion designer and businesswoman Gabrielle Bonheur "Coco" Chanel once said, "Dress shabbily and they remember the dress; dress impeccably and they remember the woman".

The dressing of the product, how you present it digitally and physically, can have a big impact in stakeholder adoption. How customers perceive us is everything, so it is important to dress your solution by expanding its value matrix. This means enlarging your value proposition through strategies "beyond the healthtech": best practice recommendations, clinical trials, patient support programs (PSP), in-home approaches, and a comprehensive holistic and integrative digital health outlook for all stakeholders.

To get stakeholders interested, you will need to address each of their needs in a comprehensive value dossier. A value dossier should also contain key global outcomes in terms of burden and costs based on pharmacoeconomic studies and a bibliography that supports all this value for them as payers. It does not need to be thick, nor filled with flashy colours—just black and white, with sound evidence, and comprehendible in the first few pages of key bullet points that summarise the content of the dossier in a nutshell (McKenna, 2020).

While presenting how you meet the needs of the other party, whether they wish to alleviate the burden of the pathology or are simply looking to support and invest in a healthtech that can disrupt the whole healthcare system, you must present the data using common sense. More data does not necessarily mean better data.

Consider your data the "what". You must present it so that it can communicate *what* you really want it to: the value. Show your value in an easy and understandable way to everyone with comprehensive proposals covering the personalised and precise unmet needs of your customers.

And remember, who offers everything, turns out to offer nothing.

Sometimes it is a matter of conveying all your knowledge into a practical Clinical Cases Study (CCS) or similar structure that makes the technology comprehensible and explains how it addresses the customers' unmet needs. Just as if it was a CCS standard, we should follow the same methodology when presenting real-life cases, defining a clear value proposition.

An excellent value proposition should present "the why of your product or solution". To make it simple, we can approach presenting with a CCS structure, such as:

1. Initial situation (practical case starting point = patient initial status)
   A point-of-situation, regarding the environment, the place to start, and the whys without a judgement—just a helicopter global vision of the common sense "why's" that foregrounds the unmet need.
2. Problem diagnosis (practical case problem = pathology diagnosis)
   What is or are the "unmet need or needs"? Here you should just need to confirm what the customer already has in mind if you did a good pre-work with stage one.
3. Healthtech solution (the best healthtech solution = treatment prescription)
   By doing what you claim to do, what solutions do you bring which solve the "practical case" leveraged "why's" highlighted in the "initial situation"?
4. Healthcare outcome improvement (practical case approach = clinical case resolution)
   Proof or evidence of what you claim your health technology does by quantifying its impact on the system with quantitative and qualitative health outcomes.

The last step and the most important one is to sell the value that you bring, taking this "value proposition" and starting from the most generic global benefit, such as reducing the economic burden of the pathology for the governing institution, and bringing it to the most specific benefit possible, such as a concrete health outcome for the patient.

This method of explaining your value in a clinical case format needs to be understandable and aligned with what the third party pursues. And it is your job to do the preparation work and know what the wants and needs are.

Finally, it is essential that the key points are covered in the value dossier, with practical cases based on real world evidence.

A Value Dossier for a Health Authority

This should be an executive summary containing key bullet points of tailored value covering the unmet needs of their healthcare plans. Present briefly, and face to face, but accompany the presentation with a comprehensive dossier of data that validates these claims—the thicker the better. Create a cover page containing an executive summary, explaining each of the value bridges of the collaboration in no more than three pages.

A Value Dossier for a Fundraising Round

When in front of a fundraising round, present the key potential of your core business briefly with a visual pitch deck. This should perfectly tease where you are, where you are going to be very soon, why, and how you will overcome upcoming challenges. Be prepared to answer any obvious and out-of-the-box questions and have good documentation and enough copies on hand to share on demand with attendees after your presentation.

A Value Dossier for a Big Pharmaceutical

It is perfectly fine, that after introductory calls, present your value dossier with a big pharma digitally via a video conference meeting to the right stakeholders.

Present a project of partnership or collaboration towards a common goal. That can be a patient quality of life improvement, a patient support program, or a facility in patients' daily lives that gets them as close as possible to a normal life. In a meeting like this, it would be very welcome to invite the president of the pathology association or a well-known key opinion leader healthcare professional and specialist that knows the pathology's most inner particularities first-hand.

A Value Dossier for Investors

Investors—the pharmaceutical industry, public or private healthcare systems, or business angels in top lists of the most influential people in tech that invest their own money—really know their stuff. So, it is important to present clear ideas that you have already filtered and make explicit the value of your business, product or services for them.

In essence, when the investor is the pharmaceutical industry, they will probably be firstly interested in synergic collaborations for better health outcomes. If it is public or private healthcare systems, the goal is to come up with cost-efficiency results and pharmacoeconomic results. If the investor is a business angel, they will be interested in your proposal—whether you want a loan or a joint venture, about percentages and return and above all a good financial plan behind the business plan.

A Final Word of Warning

Albert Einstein once said, "If I had an hour to solve a problem, I'd spend 55 minutes thinking about the problem and 5 minutes thinking about solutions". You should go about creating your value dossier in the same way.

All in all, put on top of the table the potential of your healthtech and the faces of the ones that are driving the project in the first place. Execution is 90% of the success of the project, and it relies on the people who drive the boat. The 10% leftover is innovation.

Set up ambitious goals, and more than anything, use common sense while presenting the project. Would you invest in it? Would you set up a bridge of collaboration if you were in their place? If you would, so would they.

Make sure that all parties win with the alliance. A win-lose makes no sense if you want to build a sustainable ecosystem that supports you over time.

An important tip for engaging with stakeholders and networking in general is maintaining your sensitive data. Once one general manager, while signing a Non-Disclosure Agreement, told me it should be very easy to comply with an NDA by just keeping one's mouth shut. And I could not agree more.

When asking for advice or trying to present your value, you will be vulnerable and maybe susceptible. You could bump into big deals or, at a certain moment, decide to share or not share your inner sensitive information. But always play with layers of information. Perhaps start with sharing the two first layers of your business, but always keep for yourself the core information of your inner business.

Please be really cautious. When networking, most advice does not depend on the info you provide; it is more the info that they can provide. If you share the whole knowledge of a certain product, it is the essence of that certain product. The same goes for the development of a solution. You need to share precise and certain information, not the core information of the company just for the sake of sharing or trying to prove value. So, keep the information in different folders, the one that is shareable and the one that will never be shared.

GROWTH

Chapter 7

Expanding Your
Vision and Goals

So far, we have covered the strategy and methodology of establishing your healthtech. To recap key points:

- Think of maximising the value matrix of your healthtech.
- Define an avatar patient profile, with all this data we have and be sensible and sensitive.
- Keep your healthtech roadmap alive. Build it for the short term and continuously update it.
- Set up KPIs to measure the quantitative data, but deep dive onto the KPIs and consider qualitative impact on your business. Remember Sustainability KPIs (SPIs) as well.
- Build up your ecosystem, onboarding all key stakeholders through deep and strategic stakeholder mapping—know who is who.
- Trustworthiness is a must. Build it with evidence-based medicine, and genuine and trustable data.
- Invest according to return of investment (RoI) for the immediate future and the long term.
- Humanise the patient. Get closer to them than ever.
- Centre everything you do on the unmet needs you can meet.

Remember that we are game changers in the healthcare environment (see Figure 7.1). All that we know is changing—what we think we know, we do not and what we think is going to happen can happen one thousand times faster or on a greater scale than what we think is possible now.

Indeed, the rules of healthcare have changed. According to the survey, in July 2020, 42% of Brits believed that digital technology is currently making the problems caused by the pandemic "a lot" or "a little" better, although it also highlights a fell to 37 % by December 2020 (Stewart, People's perception about the use of technology in response to COVID-19 in UK in 2020, 2021).

We are now in a world of digital Darwinism; those who cannot adapt will fail. So, we must be creators of versatile healthtech businesses and the trend setters of the new model. Post-COVID -19, we are building the healthtech ecosystems of the future. And as this third part of the book will explain, this means we need to prioritise our own growth and our ability to continually research, develop, upgrade and collaborate.

DOI: 10.4324/b23147-10

Figure 7.1   How the healthtech world will change.

The Future of Healthcare: Global and Collaborative

Our future will probably entail a digital hub for every pathology, both in terms of a community patient experience and clusters of co-marketing. For marketing especially, these digital hubs will enable us to co-market products and services in an approach of cross-ambassador cooperation and cross-selling. So, embrace it, and embrace it together.

Together with all the stakeholders of pathology, we will be fighting towards one common goal: the consolidation of the new sustainable healthcare model. And this new model will create healthtech environments integrated in smart cities, smart hospitals, smart transports and smart homes of the future.

This post-COVID world of healthcare is emerging, but the currently operating health system is still a conservative environment, being in a process of total disruption. It is pursuing the goal of universal and equal access to circular economy sustainable healthcare for everyone. Those who have grown alongside the change—permitted themselves to change in the first place—will succeed in this digital selection

Patients play a key role in the transformational urge as they demand better healthcare quality and access. They, more than ever, are organised and driving change. Thus, citizens play a major role as permitters and providers of high-quality health information.

What used to be sanitary areas—groups of care centres and regional hospitals led by a major centre or reference hospital—are becoming clusters of information where workflows are shared. This microwork can be expanded to other clusters of hospitals or points of care to become more efficient. Throughout this integrated data sharing platform, patient electronic health records can be recorded, and patients and practitioners can have simultaneous access no matter where they are or their circumstances. The new centre of care will be the patient's home, and AI systems along with IoMT can come up with ways for HCPs to embrace and optimise this remote treatment.

Currently, we still have gaps of collaboration between different levels of the process of care, as simple as the coordination and collaboration between primary care and specialists. This is already being standardised to provide better patient care.

We must capitalise on the already-working algorithms along with the blueprints that the system permits, which process information around a certain patient with its own clinical condition. Democratisation of information is the new standard.

So, this change brings us towards the future healthcare model.

And the future of health brings us hope.

Personalised and precision medicine together with translational medicine are already the new standard of care. And this means a better quality of life with an extension of the standard of longevity, for us all and our families, ending up with life extensions and higher rates of quality of life from the starting point of expanding healthcare equity between diverse populations.

Sometimes the barriers to equity come from social status, and other times it is simply the language. When the patient does not speak English, Spanish or French, what do healthcare professionals do then?

Disparity will also be reduced, with the patient as the very centre of care.

The first step towards the materialisation of the future of healthcare is the change of mindset from top-down to bottom-up in all the healthcare systems, and this means coordination and collaboration at all levels.

Global approaches are already happening, especially when it comes to data sharing (Corporation, 2021). Cerner,[1] for example, is bringing solutions across regions and populations. It uses data to resolve clinician burnout, improve health equity and enhance clinical, financial and operational outcomes. A best-practice initiative, Cerner's EHR-agnostic insights platform HealtheIntent helps health systems and other provider organisations create and operate high-performing networks across regions and populations.

Enli Health Intelligence,[2] in turn, enables care teams to perform to their full potential by integrating healthcare data with evidenced-based guidelines embedded in provider workflows across the population and at the point of care. For example, Enli makes social determinants of health (SDOH) data actionable for care coordinators by incorporating it into Enli Central Worklist care coordination programs.

These are some of the many existing examples of companies covering the unmet need of this digital global mindset change (echalliance, 2021).[3] And digital transformation permits this spontaneous coordination and collaboration of integrated procedures. Thus, the new healthcare model has no intermediaries in the value chain; it is a mere conveyance of continuous digitisation and disintermediation. Consequently, the value chain is more optimised than ever.

Overall, this change is optimising and personalising treatments, driving precision treatments to emerge and settle based on 24/7 care and the follow-up of treatment compliance. In-home treatments and care, telemedicine, chatbots and voice tech tools are already the new present.

Stay in the Latest Game

To survive and thrive in this future of healthcare, healthtechs must know how to grow sustainably. Simplifying R&D&i processes, speeding up timeframes and continuously conceptualising

---

[1] Cerner. URL: https://www.cerner.com/
[2] ENLI Health Intelligence. Linkedin URL: https://www.linkedin.com/company/enlihealthintel/
[3] In Europe in particular, we have platforms like The Global Connector: European Connected Health Alliance (https://echalliance.com/) and The Digital Health Society (https://thedigitalhealthsociety.com/) that promote this transformation.

excellent products are critical for our healthtech companies' progress. We cannot discover a new best-in-class solution daily. But we can optimise our processes, principles and methodologies.

Let me suggest you base your healthtech's R&D&i departments on an ancient Japanese concept, the Kaizen.

By Kaizen's main principle, change for the better comes from continuous self-improvement.[4] The core guidelines are to not settle and be open to continuous improvement.

Here are a few tips for its easy implementation,

- Get rid of defective products and services that require reworking.
- Go to market with the concept for the minimum viable product (MVP).
- Do not waste time in definitions, and redefinitions, before you know what works and what does not; there is no time for it, optimise development flows.
- Prioritise sustainable products and services, having in mind the circular economy.
- Enable reuse, particularly with software (Mili, et al., January 1998) (Mäkitalo, et al., 2020), to avoid the duplication of effort, decreasing testing and the cost of the redevelopment.

In the process of research, avoid "paralysis by analysis", where overthinking and overanalysing can impede forward motion and prevent decision-making (CrystalLinks, 2021). Base your prototypes and services on business intelligence data analysis. Buy data, keep your own data and manage both intelligently to improve your continued business research. Remember that your data is your major asset. Here, tokenisation of the available data plays a key role to protect customer privacy and abide by regulations [Consulting, General Data Protection Regulation (GDPR), s.f.]. This means turning meaningful pieces of healthcare data, such as a clinical outcome linked to a single individual social security number, into a random string of characters called a token that has no meaningful value if breached.

Taking advantage of these possibilities around the availability of data, while preserving the privacy of citizens and in turn patients, we can conduct research into the real unmet needs that the healthcare industry of the future is urging us to cover. Through tokenisation we can reach the point of converting the available data into accessible data in the very near future.

Seek out the technologies. Do not wait for them to find you or your business. Get out there and look for the next technology to embrace. AI is already in a mature state (Goasduff, 2020), and in the healthcare environment we are currently using machine learning. With a combination of AI with data, analytics and automatisation, you can wholly transform your business into a competitive business that can scale up in the healthcare system.

For this, you need a more integrative vision than ever. There is a need to have a holistic overview of everything, a helicopter vision. Take a global view of the whole business concept to see the gaps and improve and optimise your marketing tactics in line with the strategy.

Also, internally, there must be a site, a cloud for the company that links every action. This must have an accurate history, and common location that all the internal stakeholders can access.

We must also examine industries that are one step ahead of the healthcare ecosystems. Their regulation is often laxer or more standardised, and we can learn from how they have developed. Indeed, we can take advantage of cross-field innovation to spur development in our healthtech, considering what is working in other markets. Of course, we have a different and more restricted

---

[4] Kaizen is a Japanese term meaning "change for the better" or "continuous improvement". It is a Japanese business philosophy regarding the processes that continuously improve operations and involve all employees. Kaizen sees improvement in productivity as a gradual and methodical process.

environment, but we need to flow with the mainstream of innovative digitalisation and improve and learn from the others, through modelling our companies on their best practices.

Regarding the products and services our healthtechs offer, we must account for two big distinctions in the customer: the prescriber of the product and service, which is normally the healthcare professional or caretaker, and the buyer, which is commonly the health authority or insurer, or in other words the payer. However, as we have already explored at length, increasingly, the customer is also the patient, and in some pathologies his caregiver.

At a higher level, the hospital or the sanitary area would be the prescriber and the healthcare authorities and private insurances the payers. The healthcare professional usually pursues technical treatments of the product and service that improves or leverages their medical practice, while the patient nowadays is an empowered expert of the different available and highly valued products or services.

We are facing an environment of continuous outdated technology. What emerges with the intent of being best in class is soon an apprentice struggling to learn how to emulate another leading tech. How can we stay current? Here are few tips:

- Onboarding new insights daily, not looking for new big changes but working on a daily basis on our R&D&i and continuously updating our companies.
- Working with high-performance teams, with the best multidisciplinary teams with world-class skill sets, with younger members providing novelty and elders providing common sense and years of health environment experience.
- Spearheading technology use, helping HCPs gain new purpose in their roles, and integrating it into the patient community.
- Do not forget the tactics in the field—in-house know-how is important but also insights from the environment and the competitors that have the same goals and challenges.
- Practice forecasting and envisioning market trends and upcoming advances in technology, something that is possible if we all work as a community and join efforts. Why not share code and best practices?
- Updating our business models regularly. Why not adopt a hybrid model? This is a new trend also emerging. Or a totally disruptive new business concept? For example, going-to-market with multiple products or within an umbrella of 100 business, embracing many versatile possibilities rather than just one. This is a way of making sure you do not put all your eggs in one basket, as is the case when you go to market with one MVP and one business model.

Continuous Upgrading Within a Healthtech Business Model

Continuous training means speeding up the adoption of technological and emotional intelligence skills within up-to-date excellent operating teams. And on top of this, it means improving their major talents, allowing all of them to progress along with the company.

People need to be onboard with this high-speed evolution of the whole healthcare system—they must be active players. Not only healthcare professionals and all the healthcare personnel, but also all the teams that are inside expanding healthtech companies need to be able to embrace change.

We are facing a new era of knowledge. Free training is already available, and it relies on individuals taking responsibility for their skillset and grasping the educational opportunities available. The best universities in the world, the best innovation centres and the best healthcare role models all offer such free resources.

Some governments are already launching initiatives to address the deficiency of tech knowledge. Such is the case of Singapore's government, which is leading the program Smart Nation Singapore.[5] This entails the launch of an online channel to help continuous tech e-learning, with free courses on basic coding, video conferencing, and the latest digital trends from tech professionals.

You can also get best-practice cases explained by key tech role models on YouTube, up-to-date technological events, summits, and meetings providing best vanguard trends. And there are platforms and apps offering top free and low-cost courses in various fields, like Coursera,[6] Khan Academy,[7] LinkedIn learning[8], and Udemy. There are also more specific single-field training options like Dataquest,[9] where you can learn Data Science. The World Health Organization also democratises learning with WHO Academy.

Even top-tier universities are doing it. Massachusetts Institute of Technology offers OpenCourseWare, making their training materials free to everybody.[10] This disruptive mindset among industry leaders unlocks knowledge and permits the training to be available for anyone around the globe.

Facilitate and train your teams on the latest code, fill them with best-practice examples, and push them to break their knowledge barriers. Permit them to learn new languages of healthtech, so they can speak the same language as the highest technology players in the healthcare business. And why not give them room and space in their daily journeys for learning? It is just a matter of investing one hour a day—by the end of the year, this will aggregate to a significant skill increase.

Helping others to understand what is going on empowers them as active agents of innovation. Why not push your team to identify or create an open platform for sharing code relevant to AI in global health?

Of course, education is a two-way street. From our healthtech's side, we can for example assist governmental bodies towards the implementation of electronic health records in their systems. Or we can analyse care and health workers' data to predict and plan for resource needs. Why not incorporate AI into advanced analytics to review medical records plus patient-generated data to automatically execute claims processing or retrospectively analyse previous clinical decisions, indicating where errors may have been made given the patient context, as key input into quality and efficiency improvement efforts (Foundation, 2021). These educational initiatives will help spread knowledge throughout the ecosystem and, importantly, prepare the ground for technology adoption.

Continuous Research and Technological Development

Position yourself for continuous research and technological development (RTD). What today is a trendsetter is stale tomorrow. Snowball your RTD to constantly transform the new healthcare world.

On a funding level, initiatives like Horizon 2020 can help your research advance. It is one of the world's biggest multinational research programmes, having distributed €74 billion (US$90 billion) to more than 150,000 scientists participating in 31,000 projects or grants (Abbott, 2020).

---

[5] Smart Nation Singapore initiative #SmartNationTogether online channel, URL: https://www.smartnation.gov.sg/

[6] Coursera. URL https://www.coursera.org/

[7] Khan Academy URL https://www.khanacademy.org/

[8] Linkedin Learning. URL https://learning.linkedin.com/

[9] Dataquest. URL https://www.dataquest.io/

[10] https://ocw.mit.edu/courses/mit-open-learning-library/

To improve your organisational performance and help you to snowball, an excellent approach is the improvement cycle method, also known as the plan–do–check–act or plan–do–check–adjust (PDCA) method (W. E, 2004). As we will now explore, it is an iterative design and management method used in business for the control and continuous improvement of processes and products.

This dynamic approach combines four steps:

1. Plan, which is about setting objectives and indicators for an experiment and predicting the results.
2. Do, which is about carrying out the plan while documenting problems and unexpected observations.
3. Check, which is about analysing the results, comparing the data, and respecting disaggregated data (PAHO, 2021)[11] to build equitable healthtech solutions.
4. Act, which is about taking action to implement changes, improve the process and prepare the next cycle.

The PDCA method enables you and your team to achieve improved outcomes through multiple iterations of the cycle until you reach a solution to the problem (Langley, et al., 2009).

The examples on how you can position yourself for continuous RTD are multiple, though it does not only rely on us as independent healthtechs to foster innovation; it also has to do with each country's RTD agenda.

This is highlighted in a report published in 2021 (Bijker, et al., 2001). The article states some of the core arguments for countries' RTD, suggesting that:

■ "Science and technology are crucial for a long-term and stable development of a country."
■ "Precise aims for scientific and technological development should be specifically formulated for each country".
■ "The formulation of these specific aims should be based on a proper insight in the present situation of the country and its planned future development: this insight is offered by a RTD Diagnostic Study".
■ "Carrying out a RTD Diagnostic Study means to engage into a process of policy dialogue in which the developing country (and its many internal parties) and donor countries jointly formulate objectives, strategies, and means to support the development of that country".
■ "A constructivist perspective on the role of science and technology in society is most adequate to guide this policy dialogue and carry out these diagnostic studies".

To give you a global overview of this worldwide RTD situation, in 2017, research and development constituted an average 1.7% of global GDP, according to UNESCO Institute for Statistics. The split by region was a 2.5% for North America and Western Europe; 2.1% for East Asia and the Pacific; 1.0% for Central and Eastern Europe; 0.7% for Latin America and the Caribbean; 0.6% for Arab States; 0.6% for South and West Asia; 0.4% for sub-Saharan Africa and finally 0.2% for Central Asia (UNESCO, 2020).

Approach constant upgrades of your healthtech solutions using cycles of improvement. First, think carefully about your key role inside the ecosystem. How is this role carefully upgraded and at the same time preserving the equilibrium of the company?

---

[11] Analysing disaggregated data permits us to predict results of our healthtech products and solutions that can have a positive impact on the big equity barriers (like age, economic status, education, location or gender).

Then, think about revamping your healthtech by shifting to a hybrid business model that embraces the mentioned RTD patterns to iterate solutions and innovations.[12] Now more than ever, the pattern for upgrade is having a healthy healthtech business model that permits RTD. We really need to optimise our pipelines to be cost-effective patient vendors. The pressure to cover large health demand expectations in a highly competitive market means differentiation by continuous RTD transformation is the key.

The Latest Trends in Healthcare

Of course, while continuous upgrading and R&D&i is essential, this requires hard decisions to be made about where you invest your resources. For strategic and budgetary purposes, Environmental, Social and Corporate Governance (ESG) helps us to manage the limited resources of our companies. We must optimise and distribute them internally and externally. Ultimately, we must do more with less. And that means staying abreast of the latest trends and judging which will be worth engaging with and which can be safely ignored.

So, ask, what are your healthtech's priority technology investments? Where are we investing the most? Are you achieving sufficient return on investment (ROI)?

And strategically speaking, are we focusing our efforts and investments onto the customer experience? Are we learning and bringing knowledge and oxygen from the best practices of other markets that act under a less restricted environment? Have we really done this exercise? Not only benchmarking our environment but also looking for other inspirational markets. Cross-market innovation is critical to create a unicorn.

We must ask, is investing in the trendiest and newest tools and technologies really worth it? Will that trend augmented reality suite truly benefit your patient and drive down costs? Are you technically proficient enough to make the best use of quantum computing?

We should learn from the retail, automotive, food industry as from many other pioneering environments. Absorb from integrated and integrative marketplaces rather than remain inside our bubble with no vision for expansion and adaptation. Approach customer experiences as an omnipresent model. Ultimately, getting the patient engaging in a consumer-centric healthcare model will secure your strategic position.

Your ability to forecast future trends is essential.

Think of George Orwell's *1984*, published in 1948. He was a future thinker, predicting many of today's mostly negative trends around surveillance and state interference in personal liberty. We must think similarly. Visualise our future incoming years and try to anticipate and be able to reverse its impactful outcomes with a more optimistic approach—this is how to prioritise the basic human values and find progress.

Much will happen in the next five years, so we must be prepared and be able to rely on our strengths as healthtechs. Create high-performance teams, with well-educated operators to address and take wins from all these opportunities around. For opportunities only appear for a split second. And you must be able to break barriers and jump obstacles to change the status quo and create the new healthcare model focused on early diagnosis.

According to the Pareto principle, 80% of the impact comes from 20% of the actions. The same concept can be applied onto the action plans that we decide to implement. You need to boost

---

[12] Business Model Patterns are reusable business model architectural components. The business model innovator can use one or more of these patterns to create a new business model.

that percentage in favour of impact. To repeat, it is time to do more with less, and new technologies allow us to do so in a standardised way. This means to filter and select those actions that can bring us the maximum potential results in our core business. Here are the key trends to keep an eye on in the next decade.

Artificial Intelligence (AI)

Machine learning, deep learning and neural networks are becoming a priority for our healthtechs, consequently impacting the whole healthcare model's status quo (Chebrolu, et al., 2020).

But how can AI really bring value to the customer of health? By improving early diagnosis and prognosis of the pathology. An early mover in this regard is BioMe,[13] an initiative linked to Mount Sinai's EHRs. It enables scientists to rapidly and efficiently conduct genetic, epidemiologic, molecular and genomic studies on large collections of research specimens linked with medical information. By combining traditional clinical measures, genetics, and new blood biomarkers with AI methods, they are improving efficiency in early diagnosis (System, 2019). For example, artificial intelligence can now predict one of the leading causes of avoidable patient harm, acute kidney injury, up to two days before it happens (Tomašev, et al., 2019).

In breast cancer, AI tools can quickly analyse the radiological images of potential lumps (Cancer.Net, 2019).[14] And, using machine learning and pattern recognition, it can identify areas of potential cancerous growth and provide a diagnosis of potential cancer within each sample. This tool provides easy early diagnosis with no need to double or triple check from human doctors.

For another example, Flomics Biotec[15] is offering a complete range of services for Next Generation Sequencing (NGS) and launching a screening product, "liquid biopsies". Using a simple blood extraction, the company's in-house protocols and machine learning algorithms create accurate and clinically useful diagnostic tests.

We can imagine a future in which population-level data from wearables and implants will boost our understanding of human biology and of how medicines work, enabling personalised and real-time treatment for all (Health, 2020). But it will need AI to interpret it.

Therapies are already being progressed towards a model based on smart translational medicine,[16] along with AI-supported precision medicine. In other words, defining personalised treatments for every single patient profile on an individualised approach.

Today, we can already test drugs virtually in human twins, or in other words in digital avatars of patients, that soon will let us predict with precision how the body of the patient will respond to a certain medication administered at a certain dose and adjust it to the optimum. The AI in these solutions is predicting the secondary effects and efficiency rates of a certain therapy with the intent to find the perfect therapy in an advanced personalised and translational medicine setting.

Yet AI faces two major challenges when it comes to low- to medium-income countries (LMIC) that present us as healthtechs problems to solve. These problems concern access and include (1) inputs: structured data and unstructured data; (2) processes: main and subprocesses; (3) outputs: conclusive valuable outputs. Other problems in LMIC concern infrastructure. We need to be

---

[13] BioMe. URL: https://icahn.mssm.edu/research/ipm/programs/biome-biobank

[14] However, please note that the only way to confirm whether a cyst or tumour is cancerous is to have it biopsied by a doctor.

[15] Flomics Biotec. URL: https://www.flomics.com/

[16] Translational medicine is defined by the European Society for Translational Medicine (EUSTM) as "an interdisciplinary branch of the biomedical field supported by three main pillars: benchside, bedside, and community".

building a valuable structure that lets us manage the computing resources to train, test and deploy AI algorithms that can serve to produce (1) state-of-the art outputs that can be translated into (2) improved healthcare outcomes and (3) drive healthcare progress impact (Foundation, 2021). And this should leave us food for thought.

Ethical Concerns

Technology will ultimately help create "citizen health passports" complete with their medical history, enabling the forecasting of health issues using prospective data—creating predictive health supported by statistical likelihoods.

This, of course, leads us to forecasting of conditions based on DNA, and even the potential to rank individuals by health or future health potential, creating a whole range of ethical challenges around hierarchising our human value via our health status.

Such a process is already operating in a simplified version in countries with their own platforms for smartphones that allow access to an individual's health data, such as COVID test results or vaccination status. Examples of the "vaccine passport" during the COVID-19 pandemic were the "Digital Green Certificate" (Commission, 2021) in Europe, or platforms like Denmark's Coronapas (Commission, 2021) or Israel's "green passport" (Congress, 2021). In the US, New York's Excelsior Pass worked by tapping into state immunisation records. But database errors can cause problems, especially if there were data entry errors at vaccine sites (Review, 2021).

Health passports are just one aspect of the ethical concerns that predictive smart health is creating. Ethical issues in healthcare could be summarised, based on four common, basic prima facie moral commitments—respect for autonomy, beneficence, nonmaleficence, and justice—plus concern for their scope of application (Gillon, 1994). These ethical trends will only grow more pressing in the years to come, so healthtechs that can offer solutions to them will benefit.

This is why humanisation remains central to the development of the healthcare system. We need to humanise healthcare and avoid the emergence of new social hierarchies, not categorising or ranking individuals by their predicted potential as members of society. Progress in healthcare impacts the different anthropologic segments of the population, sometimes separating them by the quality of health they can achieve. Therefore, healthtech entrepreneurs must prioritise equal access to prevent the hierarchisation of society.

Implementation at the point of care is fraught with challenges. Matters like ensuring that AI in healthcare is trustworthy and equitable are still being overcome. Such was the case of a recent artificial intelligence prediction tool for minimising patient "No-Shows". The model was meant to suggest potential "no-shows"—which are a major source of waste in US healthcare—and enable the scheduling of an additional patient in the same timeslot.

Based on an AI built into EHR datasets model, the algorithm included biases.[17] The "black box" of the AI ended up translating these into discriminatory practices against marginalised

---

[17] Note: Biases in the predictive model, where based on more than the decided to potential for explicit discrimination personal data such as ethnicity, financial class, religion and body mass index that, if used for overbooking, could result in health care resources being systematically diverted from individuals who are already marginalised, and consequently this data was removed. Still the model was likely to correlate with socioeconomic status, perhaps mediated by the inability to cover the costs of transportation or childcare, or the inability to take time away from work. Likewise, a patient with obesity who struggles with mobility may make it to their appointment only to find it overbooked, and their clinician thus overworked and distracted.

members of the community (Wigmore, 2021).[18] Its outputs disadvantaged marginalised members of the population with fewer resources to deal with day-to-day barriers to attending an appointment.

This result highlights the questionable reliability and ethics of AI currently in use. Indeed, the inputs for the training of the model had sensitive personal characteristics deleted yet doing so was unable to remove the biases. We must never assume, therefore, that simply preparing datasets and anonymising data is sufficient to prevent an AI contributing to inequity of access to healthcare (Sara, et al., 2020).

When everything is based on prediction statistics, everyone should count equally in the eyes of healthcare. Consequently, we still need to test input selection methods and the "black boxes" originating ethical matters.

Other predictive models can have a nocebo effect. It occurs when the negative expectations of health can cause negative effects on an individual, reproducing the symptoms of a disease that do not currently have. And we can see how forecasting lifespans and percentage chances of future diseases might stimulate these negative expectations.

We must consider these issues and foreground ethics within our healthtechs, promoting them also within the industry foundations. This human element will become increasingly important as AI-enabled robots start making mechanical decisions. What do I mean with this? I mean AI will be predicting pathology needs and improving healthcare outcomes for everyone, and upgrading quality of life, but it will only offer equity and universal access if humans combat algorithmic biases and discrimination when decisions are made.

Machine Learning

This branch of AI has great potential to elevate the standard of care when combined with appropriate technology. Machine learning is computer algorithms that improve automatically through self-experience, or "learn". The algorithms identify patterns that enable forecasting of healthcare outcomes.

Through machine learning, we can already take most medical decisions automatically, with minimal human intervention. DeepMind Health is an example of a tool that can give doctors a 48-hour headstart in treating acute kidney injury (AKI) (Tomašev, et al., 2019), a condition that is associated with over 100,000 people in the UK alone every year (NHS, 2021). Equally, Moorfields Eye Hospital NHS Foundation Trust is already able to use thousands of anonymised eye scans to train algorithms to identify signs of eye disease and recommend referral or treatment, making the correct referral decision for more than 50 eye diseases with 94% accuracy (Fauw, et al., 2018). In the same line, AI can automatically recognise complex patterns in imaging data and provide quantitative, rather than qualitative assessments of radiographic characteristics (Montagnon, et al., 2020).

This frees up HCPs for the more complicated cases where ethics and human responses/emotions are meant to play a key role.

---

[18] Black box is a term widely used in AI predictive methods to define any artificial intelligence system whose inputs and operations are not visible to the user or another interested party, in other words we do not know how the system operates to get to certain outputs.

Data Management and the Health Lakehouse Solution

Healthcare data—such as information from clinical trials, disease registries, electronic health records (EHRs), and medical devices—is growing at a compound annual growth rate of 36% (Osti, 2021). Healthtech entrepreneurs must consider ways to use metadata management initiatives at scale to deliver business value (Simoni, 2018). Healthcare institutions are generating big amounts of data, at rates of nine petabytes (PB) ranging from EHR, medical images, genetic code sequences and beyond (Donovan, 2019).

When we speak about huge silos of healthcare data that we need to store, we must push for cost-effective approaches. And, as healthtechs, we need to be able to bring together all healthcare institutions', patients' and operational data in a unified, open and compliant platform for both traditional analytics and data science at scale.[19]

Here is where a new solution comes in: the data lakehouse. A data lakehouse is a form of data management that combines the best elements of data lakes (a system or repository of data stored in its natural/raw format, not yet processed or assigned a purpose) and data warehouses (a repository for structured, filtered data that has already been processed for a specific purpose). It can implement data warehouses' structures and management trademarks for data lakes. An open data management architecture that combines the flexibility, cost-efficiency, and scale of data lakes with the data management and ACID transactions[20] of data warehouses, enabling business intelligence (BI) and machine learning (ML) on all data.

Health lakehouses process, reorganise and activate these big, varied datasets for analytics and machine learning at scale to leverage smart patient insights in the cloud (Lorica, et al., 2020).

Open data formats used by data lakehouses make it very easy for data scientists and machine learning engineers to access the data in the lakehouse, facilitating the possibility of forecasting health trends, early diagnosis of patients, and exploiting the full potential of the available and accessible data.

Folksonomy and Tokenisation

Alongside managing data, a significant trend will be the goal of making it all open access.

Folksonomy, a user generated system allowing the association of metadata like electronic tags, permits the organisation and classification of all this data by labelled categories. This process allows us to make the available data accessible, by deleting the compromising parts of the data, and making it sellable.

Imagine a private consultancy operating in the last 30 years. It would have vast amounts of EHR data that machine learning could process, enabling us to identify patterns of accurate diagnosis within a certain pathology and local population. But the data has names and surnames of the patients, and certain DNA sequencing-associated information. We can strip identifying points, keeping the main part of the information, and assign an aleatory-personalised way of labelling the data. This retains its usefulness in a medical sense while keeping the anonymity of the individuals and accomplishing the data protection required by law.

---

[19] Health Insurance Portability and Accountability Act (HIPAA) Compliant in the case of the US, and General Data Protection Regulations (GDPR) Compliant for Europe.

[20] In computer science, atomicity, consistency, isolation, durability (ACID) is a set of properties of database transactions intended to guarantee data validity despite errors, power failures, and other mishaps.

Tokenisation is a core part of this process. It is substituting a sensitive data element with a non-sensitive equivalent (a token) without extrinsic or exploitable meaning or value. In healthcare, this permits us to break barriers in sensitive data usage just by replacing the sensitive part such as primary account numbers (PANs) (Kagan, 2020), electronic protected health information (ePHI), and net primary production (NPP) data collection by non-sensitive values. Anonymising the data makes it easier to share data from one location to another—currently, you still cannot share specific data from a certain region in Europe to the US. And more than this, tokenisation helps us build patient-centric products, solutions and healthcare models.

Let us consider an example of tokenisation used to safeguard sensitive data involving medical records or personal identification information. This data can later be easily transferred and held by intermediaries, such as private insurance companies, hospitals, healthcare organisations and at a certain point the pharmaceutical industry, which in turn can reduce the overall cost of the patient's medical treatment.

Such is the case of Swiss-based dHealth network[21] by HIT foundation, a not-for-profit foundation established under the laws of Switzerland and registered in the commercial register of the state of Zug, a distributed and community-owned network for healthcare-related transactions that powers a global data-driven healthcare ecosystem. They are leading a best-practice project of a public Blockchain Infrastructure for Healthcare that aims to connect clinical researchers with individuals willing to share their medical data.

Other best-practices are Hu-manity,[22] a healthtech that empowers consumers, corporations, and countries transitioning to a consumer-inclusive data economy. TimiHealth[23] is another. It empowers people to secure, control, and monetise what they already inherently own: their genomics, health, and fitness data. And Emrify[24] empowers citizens to be the owners of their own data, an accelerated path to showcase the Utility Token model in healthcare. All of them explore blockchain tokenisation to place patients at the centre of the healthcare ecosystems.

These are best practices that highlight how blockchain is an enabler in the healthtech ecosystem, with many potential applications that can make care more patient-centric by helping patients own their data. E-Estonia is an example that uses blockchain technology to address major healthcare system problems, with three major projects, e-healthtech records,[25] e-ambulance[26] and e-prescription.[27] In Estonia, KSI Blockchain[28] technology is being used for the system to ensure data integrity and mitigate internal threats to the data.

AI-Driven Computer Vision

We can already understand the world by images being processed and transformed into computing languages. This enables us to leverage utilities in the medical field, with robotics capable of

---

[21] dHealth Network. URL: https://dhealth.network/
[22] Hu-manity. URL: https://hu-manity.co/
[23] TimiHelath. URL: https://timihealth.com/
[24] Emrify. Emrify is launching a decentralised Personal Health Record platform on top of the Ethereum public blockchain to deliver trusted health information to the right hands at the right time anywhere in the world. URL: http://www.emrify.com/hit.
[25] E-health Record. E-estonia. URL: https://e-estonia.com/solutions/healthcare/e-health-record/
[26] E-ambulance. E-estonia. URL: https://e-estonia.com/solutions/healthcare/e-ambulance
[27] E-prescription. E-prescription. URL: https://e-estonia.com/solutions/healthcare/e-prescription
[28] KSI is the name of the copyrighted KSI user model of blockchain owned by E-Estonia

recognising and processing pathologic patterns and automatically coming up with an accurate diagnosis.

This in turn provides AI datasets that permit delivery of AI-driven products and solutions by providing world-class AI expertise and tooling for computer vision applied to medical technology. In other words, training computers to replicate human sight.

This visual pattern recognition technology is being applied to elevate the precision and earliness of diagnosis, for example in cancer patients. Deep learning's ultimate technique in computer vision is being able to read and visualise 3D spaces from 2D images. That enables healthcare professionals to achieve a deeper understanding of a patient's clinical framework. An example is tomosynthesis. Breast imaging has advanced from traditional 2D mammography to 3D tomosynthesis or 3D mammography, which allows radiologists to capture images at multiple angles and display tissues at varying depths (Care, 2021).

Quantum Computing in Healthcare

Quantum computers apply quantum theory through a simplified method of superposition and association, which generates two states for the qubit (quantum bit). While it is in superposition, the quantum computer and specially built algorithms exploit the power of both possible states of the qubit.

Quantum computing might bring us huge advances soon with supersonic drug design, using "in silico" clinical trials on digital avatar human profiles. In other words, with "live" simulated virtual humans, quantum computing can accelerate the pharmaceutical industry's drug discovery process while improving patients' healthcare outcomes (Cao, et al., Nov–Dec 2018).

Aqemia[29] is already embracing this technology. It uses in silico drug discovery, combining AI and its own structure-based affinity algorithms to quickly discover innovative therapeutic molecules with better success rates. Another example is the Singapore's Entropica Labs,[30] which builds cloud-based quantum computing software and algorithms for bioinformatics, including multi-omics datasets and phenotypic measurements with cutting-edge classical-quantum and machine learning methods.

A recent IBM Institute for Business Value report highlights three major areas of quantum computing use cases in healthcare:

1. Diagnostic assistance: Diagnose patients early, accurately, and efficiently. For example, through early diagnosis of colon cancer, survival rates increased, and the treatment costs decreased by a factor of 9 and 4 respectively. The key to early diagnosis is to classify cancerous from normal cells. After modern diagnostic procedures, datasets are combined and several techniques applied through quantum computing, linked to machine learning, to enhance such classification. This could boost single-cell diagnostic methods.

2. Precision medicine: Keep people healthy based on personalised interventions and respective treatments. Personalised and precision medicine is also leveraged through quantum computing in, for example, the biomarkers discovery field. In essence, when new biomarkers need to be classified, it is important to be able to analyse big and complicated pools of datasets and at the same time match and combine results from disciplines like omics, genomics, transcriptomics, proteomics and metabolomics. From another side, quantum computing can help

---

[29] Aqemia. URL: https://www.aqemia.com/ [Last Accessed December 2021]
[30] Entropica Labs. URL: https://www.entropicalabs.com/ [Last Accessed December 2021]

match and find correlations between treatments and outcomes personalising treatments. Knowing exactly at a cellular level how a drug will perform in a certain individual and their sensitivity to it is a significant leap forward.

3. Pricing: Optimise insurance premiums and pricing (Flöther, Murphy, & Murtha, 2021). When contracting an insurance plan, the pricing strategy is a key factor considering many parameters. By risk assessment, quantum computing can help to fix a price for certain insurances price standardisation. At a population level, quantum computing can forecast the risk that a population as a whole can have towards a certain healthcare condition or pathology and rates of recovery. The overall objective, though, more than establishing a price, is to optimise price strategies and offer reduced prices of premium plans with lower costs associated for all the parties—the patient that pays for the insurance, the country's healthcare plans and the private insurance company.

Quantum computing thus can bring us precise and accurate healthcare forecasts and prognosis. This is a whole new edge to predictive medicine, early diagnosis and cost contingency transparency plans that will end up impacting the whole cycle of the circular economy and finally permit sustainability in healthcare.

Quantum computing is already emerging as Quantum Machine Learning (QML). Quantum computing increases the number of calculation variables machines can deal with, thereby enabling faster smart health decisions, which is what we really need.

There is still work to do in binding the best of the two technologies of machine learning and quantum computing. Yet we must really rely on all these new technologies. They are improving at the speed of light and increasingly securing adoption. These high-speed rates of deep learning, and autonomous learning, will enable us to handle and interpret vast quantities of soloed and unstructured data to upgrade our decision making and advance medical treatments and processes.

Telehealth

This segment of virtual health assistance was estimated to be worth $5.6 billion in 2019 and is expected to grow until 2025 at a compound annual growth rate (CAGR) of 24% in a world pre-COVID-19. It is forecasted that this segment will thrive even more in the next few years (Caselli, 2009).

Telehealth is here to stay. Patients' value telehealth, and it is already a commodity adopted and standardised to articulate and vehiculate the current patient journey. Not only does it connect the patient with the physician digitally, but also with the whole care team.

We need to analyse the pre-visit and the post-visit to the healthcare professional, while considering face-to-face interaction as always improvable. This could be through training videos projected during the session that can mentor the patient's progression, empowerment, wellness and support them through the pathology, thus extending the next appointment to the doctor.

And how can we transform consumeristic healthcare into free healthcare and ultimately provide universal coverage using digital technology?

We can consider best-in-class solutions like the Chinese AI One-Minute Clinics booth for diagnosis, Ping An Good Doctor (PAGD). Each PAGD One-Minute Clinic booth includes an AI Doctor, trained to collect data on patient symptoms and medical history through voice and text input, after which one of Ping's human doctors provides remote diagnosis, medical advice, and immediate online prescriptions (GBV, 2021).[31]

---

[31] Ping An Good Doctor (PAGD). URL: http://www.pagd.net/.

Meanwhile, the traditional face-to-face goes from being a one on one to a one on many—even one on 10 is the new normal in some places.

Here, innovation should improve patient empowerment, in the line of making the healthcare systems more sustainable. An example is including ad-hoc training sessions in the middle of tele-health calls with the healthcare professional. As a result, the overall cost of the patient follow-up drops thanks to better deployment and treatment compliance.

Other best-practice solutions include the Swedish Doktor.se,[32] offering both digital triage and treatment, Medadom,[33] offering teleconsultation via terminals or booths, or Healthily[34] from Reckitt Benckiser, a self-care app that empowers the patients through training so they can gain the knowledge, skills and confidence necessary to manage their health to the best of their ability (Healthtech, 2021).

We can also perform diagnosis over the phone, recognising image patterns and emotions associated with illness during telehealth calls and supporting the physician's diagnosis.[35]

However, in telehealth, we need to consider the elderly and young populations as the two big groups with different behavioural patterns, and therefore different early adopters of the technology. Telecare thus is differently perceived depending on the segment of the population. For a working citizen, it could mean no need to lose one day off and skip the waiting room for attending a consultation for them or their family for whom they care, which often means "no-shows". For a pensioner, it could mean losing his social time or the chance to change his lonely routine at home by having a nice chat in the waiting room of the consultancy.

Nevertheless, in both cases we are improving disease awareness, diagnosis and treatment, as we are reducing the costs of infrastructure and personnel. Primary care will be the form of care mostly moved to remote, but secondary care and concentrated hospital care will still see changes.

Home remote care, though, is an opportunity for public private partnerships (PPP) and alliances for healthtechs. An example is the case of GluCare,[36] allocated in the United Arab Emirates, making telehealth available 24/7 to help patients understand their body, keep up with their care plan, or get them back on track. It is a best-practice integrated model of care that allows holistic treatment for diabetes, including the best of traditional and remote care. This reduces the overall costs and improves healthcare through a more meaningful, patient-centric approach. It is a good example of interoperability between multiple stakeholders.

Rwanda has also recently created a PPP involving telehealth to address the 1:10,000 doctor-to-patient ratio that the country is facing, with a 10-years partnership between Babyl[37] and the Rwandan government. The project's goal is to stop high rates of self-diagnosis and self-medication by enabling free access to doctors.

The project already processes an average of 3,000 consultations per day with 30% of the overall adult population registered. The PPP constitutes a leading step towards the first African universal primary care initiative, positioning Rwanda as a best practice to follow (Team, 2020).

---

[32] Doktor.se. Founded in 2016 and is one of Sweden's biggest providers of digital healthcare and also has physical healthcare clinics across Sweden as well as digital operations across the world. URL: https://doktor.se/

[33] Medamom. URL https://www.medadom.com/

[34] Healthily. URL https://healthily.com.au/

[35] https://www.researchgate.net/publication/251931989_Face_recognition_system_to_enhance_E_Health

[36] GluCare. URL: https://glucare.health/

[37] Babyl, is the largest digital health service provider in Rwanda. URL: https://babyl.rw/

Voice Tools

These are voice recognition, voice interaction with robotic solutions, and voice communication conveyed onto health services. They create high engagement and commitment as an empowering communication tool. Also, they are highly patient-centred.

For example, robotic advisors empower patients, encouraging them to direct their own care and manage their own pathology outcomes, follow-ups, and surrounding lifestyle. This brings high value because HCPs cannot manage everyone's daily monitoring needs (Andrus, 2015). Well-designed bots can imitate human behaviour successfully, uncovering and responding to patients' human needs automatically over extended and repeated interactions.

Speech Recognition

Another important trend is the utilisation of speech recognition (SR) for registering patient data into electronic medical records. A recent study explored the value of using SR for clinical documentation tasks within an electronic health record system, involving thirty-five emergency department clinicians who completed a system usability scale (SUS) questionnaire. It concludes that the addition of an SR component to an EHR system can lead to a significant reduction in terms of usability, primarily due the sub-element of learnability (Hodgson, et al., 2018).

This technology is already helping HCPs focus on human interaction with the patient rather than spending most part of the patient's visit using a computer screen and checking whether the keyboard is clear. The technology is likely to impact primary care, as well as outpatients and emergency departments in hospitals (NHS, 2019).

Avatar-Based Virtual Environments

We can predict the secondary effects of drugs using virtual avatars of each patient. The avatar experiences the effects, allowing us to make adjustments to personalise the dosage and other variables.

Embracing this technology can create opportunities—could it have been used in the COVID-19 vaccine development process, for example? It comes from uniting the considerable efforts of researchers digitally. We can use the shared data between public and private fields to create predictive models. Indeed, we are on the edge of having our own tri-dimensional avatar twins built in high detail, enriched with biometric parameters, and modulated through different approaches and models. This will advance translational medicine, allowing stakeholders to coalesce healthcare knowledge to improve predictive maintenance, bioproducts and the precision and personalised nature of medicine.

Virtual and Augmented Reality

Virtual reality[38] simulators are becoming powerful tools that help stimulate and predict health outcomes. With them come totally immersive experiences in a real-time activity simulation, making the new technology interesting for healthtech solutions focused in major areas like medical and surgical training among professionals (Huang, et al., 2018).

---

[38] Virtual reality (VR) is a simulated experience in a virtual framework that can have similarities or disparities to reality. Some examples using virtual reality are videogames, military and medical simulated training or virtual avatar environments used in business or virtual meetings and events.

Augmented reality[39] and VR tools are leading the possibility of empowering patients, like the initiative Nixi for Children.[40] It is a clinically tested solution that uses virtual reality to reduce preoperative anxiety in children.

The technology works using 3D viewers that are constantly converting data into virtual AR. Such is the case of AED4EU,[41] a downloadable iOS and Android tool which shows automated external defibrillators (AEDs) currently available near you.

Microsoft's Hololens[42] and Google Glass[43] are also becoming standardised for medical education and training. Hololens 2, in turn, is involved in a project between Mount Sinai and Ugandan surgeons who, though 7,000 miles away, work together in real time, bringing life-saving expertise to rural communities (Microsoft, 2021).

Google Glass is a major asset in the Empowered Brain[44] wearable system that has been used by hundreds of children and adults with autism spectrum disorder (ASD), where each software module connects to Brain Power's cloud-hosted portal where artificial intelligence (AI) algorithms produce insights and predictions in real time (360, 2018) (Wire, 2017).

3D Printing

3D printing in healthcare entails recreating 3D models of anatomical parts with the aid of a printer, designing customised tools and devices. Orthopaedic implants are already part of the IoMT, 3D printing or design printing, generating ad-hoc solutions for the right patient at the right time. Soon we will be able to print the shape and size of a personalised pill, advancing the fields of precision medicine for everyone.

Bioprinting is a healthtech's next step in traditional 3D printing. Bioprinting can produce living tissue, bone, blood vessels and what we call organoids—a stem cell derived 3D tissue produced in vitro with key features of a realistic organ.

An example of bioprinting is Wake Forest Institute for Regenerative Medicine (WFIRM) where physicians and scientists engineer laboratory-grown organs that are successfully implanted into humans. In the same line, disruptive healthtech Biopixlar[45] is an all-in-one bioprinting platform capable of printing single cells with high precision and reproducibility, allowing them to print tissues at will—with single-cell precision and at the same time constructing relevant tissue and disease models.

Extrapolating a Growth-Share Matrix for Your Healthtech

As well as navigating the regulatory environment and innovating in mainstream healthtech products to cover healthcare unmet needs, we should prioritise our healthtech pipelines to sustain growth (see Figure 7.2). This means that we need to be able to keep an eye on every single product

---

[39] Augmented reality (AR) is our reality augmented with digital data. The digital data can be in the form of text, pictures, videos, 3d assets, or a combination of all of the above. (Wikipedia, 2021)

[40] Nixi for Children URL: https://nixiforchildren.com/en/

[41] AED4EU shows known AED's near you. URL: https://www.layar.com/layers/sander1

[42] Microsoft Hololens 2 URL: https://www.microsoft.com/en-us/hololens

[43] Google Glass Enterprise Edition 2. URL: https://www.google.com/glass/tech-specs/

[44] Empowered Brain by Brainpower. URL: https://brain-power.com/empowered-brain/

[45] https://fluicell.com/biopixlar-3d-single-cell-bioprinting/?gclid=CjwKCAjwmeiIBhA6EiwA-uaeFSYLvTxxJR_R8E0mgrXIeKjQItefY–5JTr5pCOC12KJySorLqROaBoCwIYQAvD_BwE

Figure 7.2 List of commoditised technological options in where to choose prioritising investment.

and solution alongside the one with which we decide to go to market. Stay informed with their trends and validate growth opportunities to uniquely capitalise on the identified white space—appropriately sizing and developing a clear selective strategy for frontline products and mature products.

A good tool to use is the widely known Boston Consulting Group (BCG) matrix (see Figure 7.3). In the BCG matrix, products are classified by "cash cows", "dogs", "question marks"

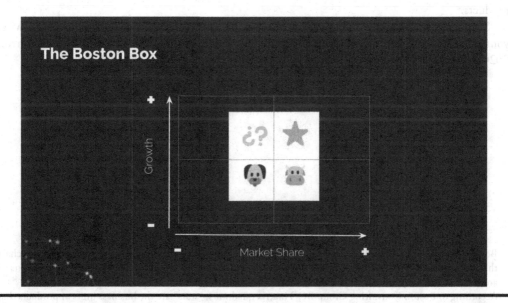

Figure 7.3 The Boston Box.

and "stars".[46] Milk (cash) is produced by cash cow products, that funds star products and helps with the question mark products, which themselves are aimed at becoming cash cows in the near future. This BCG matrix is a well-known tool of growth-share categorisation and can be translated to the healthtech field, helping to manage our healthtech pipeline.

Cash cow products are low growth, but high market share. In healthtech, they could be commodities and standardised technologies and products with a consolidated place in the market, already adopted by the user. These cows are the products of the healthtech pipeline that give us cash flow to invest in innovative solutions and products. These products are neither the most innovative nor the ones that grow the most. However, such commoditised and mature products (like consolidated telehealth solutions, or commoditised, standardised operating algorithms) create massive revenue for the company, and for this reason are essential to keep the fund innovation elsewhere.

Dog products, in turn, are low growth, low market share. These healthtech products have not yet found and consolidated a strategic position in the ecosystem with a good growth trajectory and are still facing barriers of positioning in the market. Unless they are accomplishing some other key goal for the company, eliminate these as soon as possible if you cannot convert them into a cash cow, since they are not profitable.

Question marks have high growth but low market share. They are products with uncertain potential. They might fail, or, over time, they could gain market share and become stars or cash cows. They need good investment and strategy to succeed.

Star products are high growth, high market share. In healthtech, they are the products with the highest revenue for the company and that drive the company to become a unicorn in the immediate future. The hope is that stars become the next cash cows and commoditised technologies. A way to ensure this is by sustaining their success until a time when the market's growth begins to slow.

You should evaluate your portfolio of products to categorise each product, plan a strategy for it, and then execute. A good starting point may be through an exhaustive analysis of budget optimisation and risk analysis of each product, forecasting frontline products and safe backup products.

Such categorisation into four product types enables you to prioritise your resources, growing your value around core viable products or services—or around the stars of your company (Martin, 2020).[47]

---

[46] Boston Box, BCG-matrix, Boston matrix, Boston Consulting Group analysis, portfolio diagram) is a chart that was created by Bruce D. Henderson for the Boston Consulting Group in 1970 to help corporations to analyse their business units, that is, their product lines.
[47] According to Boston Consulting Group BCG matrix quadrants, "stars" are the business units or products that have the best market share and generate the most cash, thus they are considered stars.

Chapter 8

Fundraising and Team Building

Most healthtechs are accelerated, getting help in the development of their idea from the very beginning with seed funding or angel investment. Seed funding is the initial fund that enables the planting of the idea, which will grow into a tree or fully-fledged company. Investors with a high tolerance for risk—venture capitals—are the ones that usually provide the funds. Friends and family often do too.

Some healthtechs even get help in the pre-seed phase. The environment presents a problem, and they get these monetary steppingstones to develop a solution or MVP from the outset. From there, they can start their penetration of the whole ecosystem.

Following seed funding, investment progresses in stages: Series A, Series B and Series C funding rounds to grow the business. Series A funding rounds represent the first steps to turn an MVP or idea into a disruptive global company (Reiff & Mansa, 2021).

However, the real jump comes in the later series B and C, which are only productive if we design our companies to be scalable in the beginning.

Sometimes, there is a lack of push in this second phase. It is already difficult enough to get the business going—all our efforts are on the base, be able to create, be viable, get to market. But our healthtechs' real need from the very beginning is not only to grow based on sustainability, but also grow in a sustained way over time. This means having scalability in mind not only when we need it but always to be able to survive.

You can have ambitious goals of becoming a unicorn. Fair enough, but before that you need to prepare the environment to be able to grow. Scalability in the healthtech world is difficult. You need funds. But still, the most important thing is to understand what is going on around you. You need to understand the market, the patient, your position in the ecosystem, and which role are you playing within the whole picture.

Health outcomes are a must for scalability. "Walk the talk": start from the point of what I claim that my healthtech solution brings, validated by experience and by the pilot that you have already completed. Now is the moment of truth, where you can be cannibalised—you can be easily copied by a better solution with a better strategic positioning and a consolidated network within the whole ecosystem, helped by better alliances.

So, to avoid this, we need forward thinking. We need to have in mind the vision of the company and clarify the "sense of purpose" from the beginning. This is what is going to help us

DOI: 10.4324/b23147-11

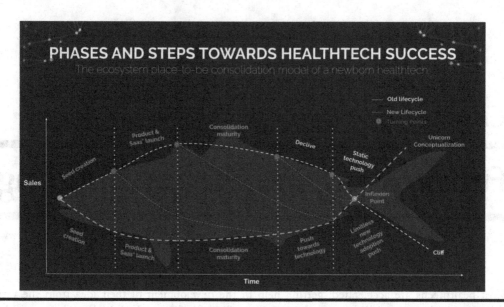

Figure 8.1 **The new lifecycle for healthtech products, digital therapeutics, and software as a service towards success with key turning points leveraged in red, where a switch towards the success path is possible.**

overcome the real challenge, which is to become mature companies, and finally consolidate and sustain our flight over time.

The scalable phases in the healthtech business models have changed (see Figure 8.1). We used to have a copy-paste projection model of a lifecycle based on five stages: launch, growth, maturity and decline. Now it has become a more optimised flow based on go-to-market, early growth, late growth, consolidation, and continuous internal R&D&i updating of the healthtech solution to sustain growth.

Before, the go-to-market used to be the challenge. Now we face a challenge at every stage.

And while help and mentors are plenty, and business angels and funds exist, you are ultimately alone in achieving this unicorn goal.

So, first things first, the world and the future of healthtech will not be built in one disruptive year. It is a matter of long-term vision, of continuous skill adoption and learning-by-doing. And I repeat, we need to grow as a community. More than ever, we must be generous with our colleagues, with our competitors, and help each other to consolidate this healthcare environment of the future. There is room and market share for all of us, so let us help each other.

I think we are witnessing a change in the healthtech model into a concept of pathology hubs of co-marketing, and this means alliances and partnerships. It is ultimately about making friends with every stakeholder in the ecosystem—above all with the health authorities and regulators. They really need us, and we also need them to avoid the fragmentation of the last century. Remember, we are on the cutting edge, and here we all fly together.

Choosing a Funding Source

Building the ecosystem means building the right partnerships. Specifically, it means reaching out for the proper funds that can support and advance your scaling process. From continental funds to national funds, to private funds, business angels and finally self-funding, not all possibilities are right. You must first think big to define the next milestone of your business. Only then decide the funds you need, who will lead the capital injection, and most importantly, when is the most suitable moment to search for and secure these funds (usually 6 months before they are really needed).

So, how to choose your big brother for each step? Who is that entity that will help you fly? Who shares your company's mission, vision and values? And how can you create a win-win alliance from the beginning? You need to find a funding partner that wants to support a high-potential opportunity of growth that can change healthcare, and be open enough to permit you to attend for underserved populations around the globe.

Consider whether you need to sell your business pipeline. Do you really need to give the project to those better suited to scaling at the pre-acceleration point? Do you need to wait until it becomes more mature, or until just after you hit the first barriers to breaking into the market? To answer these questions, commit to clear milestones and defined objectives for each stage, then weigh these against your current capabilities. Look for more than money; look for business expertise, healthcare expertise or those with the best industry contacts.

In Europe, there are many examples of accelerator programs:

■ G4A[1] from Bayer for young digital health startups.
■ Accelerated Assistance[2] from Eithealth from the EU.
■ DigitalHealth.London[3] for digital health companies with a product or service that has high potential. to meet the current challenges facing the NHS and social care today.
■ Health2Baccelerator[4] as a Free, 0% Equity, Virtual Healthtech Accelerator.
■ Rockstart health program[5] for driven entrepreneurs or teams working within healthtech and med tech with a scalable business idea.
■ Baselaunch[6] that is partnering with scientists and entrepreneurs to help launch and grow. exceptional biotech companies developing cutting-edge therapeutics.
■ Open accelerator[7] from Zambon that is a fast-track accelerator program dedicated to life sciences and digital health with a focus on central nervous system and respiratory diseases.
■ Accelerace[8] for pre-seed startups that want to scale up.
■ Healthtech Venture Lab,[9] which is an accelerator driven by a powerful network of healthcare. industry leaders, universities, organisations and alumni.

In the US, there are also many accelerators and funding sources:

■ Rock health,[10] supporting companies improving the quality, safety, and accessibility of our healthcare system.

---

[1] https://www.g4a.health/about/strategic-partners
[2] https://eithealth.eu/what-we-do/eit-health-accelerator-programmes/accelerator-assistance/
[3] https://digitalhealth.london/programmes/accelerator
[4] https://www.f6s.com/health2baccelerator2020
[5] https://www.rockstart.com/health/health-program/
[6] https://baselaunch.ch/
[7] https://www.openaccelerator.it/
[8] https://www.accelerace.io/accelerator/
[9] https://hvlab.eu/
[10] https://rockhealth.com/about/

- Startup Health,[11] investing in health transformers to unite them into a global army and broadcast their progress.
- Blueprint Health,[12] a community of healthcare entrepreneurs, helping build the next generation of healthcare IT companies.
- Healthbox,[13] with a team that draws from a diverse background in digital health, enterprise strategy, clinical operations, and strategic investing to deliver a unique suite of services.
- Texas Medical Centre Accelerator,[14] focused on clinical partnerships to improve healthcare delivery and outcomes.
- Startup Here Toronto,[15] (Canada) helping you to get your business moving by connecting you to funding, mentors, advisers, a place to build your product, or helping you just to see what your options are.
- New York Digital health Innovation Lab,[16] scaling innovation in health technology.
- StartupBootcamp,[17] which helps to gain access to the most relevant connections, supporting startups with direct access to an international network of the most relevant mentors, partners and investors to help them scale.
- Smarthealth Catalyzer,[18] which is accelerating the commercialisation of therapeutics, diagnostics and medical devices being developed at US Midwest universities and research hospitals that diagnose, prevent and treat life-threatening diseases.
- McKesson Ventures,[19] which can help you as a healthtech entrepreneur to build and scale your business when it tackles some of the toughest challenges in healthcare.

Asking for resources is something few enjoy, as it can be perceived as asking for charity. But it is essential to scale—we need resources to build and expand. The resources come from cashflow, and with cashflow we have options that we would not otherwise have.

You can be brave and invest in yourself with your own capital, or that of your friends and family. We can get grants, loans, accelerator aids, crowdfunding, or look for venture capital (VC) funding when we want to grow quickly. Each has benefits. For example, VC is a form of private equity investors provided to startup companies and small businesses that are believed to have huge growth potential. Not always is this private equity economical; sometimes it has to do with bringing value in terms of business mentorship or technical advice.

For the first phases, pre-seed and seed, I would say the best approach is to obtain the easy free money: grants and public aid. These early-stage funding opportunities typically mean you do not have to transfer control of your company or explain your actions as much to, for example, new stakeholders. However, you must ensure you meet the inclusion criteria when applying for these funding opportunities. Often, they are very specific, and you can spend hours and hours—as I remember doing—preparing business plans and technical plans only to end up in the slush pile because my company was not correctly aligned with the contest requirements.

---

[11] https://www.startuphealth.com/
[12] https://www.blueprinthealth.org/
[13] https://www.healthbox.com/
[14] http://www.tmc.edu/innovation/innovation-programs/tmcx/
[15] https://startupheretoronto.com/startup-support/
[16] https://digitalhealth.nyc/
[17] https://www.startupbootcamp.org/
[18] https://www.smarthealthcatalyzer.com/
[19] https://ventures.mckesson.com/

Another popular option is angel investment. This can be a quick and fairly easy way to gain significant capital injection into your company, but it is not always the right option.

I remember when an angel investor offered me €2.5 million on the table. I almost fell out of my chair when I thought of all that I could achieve with this amount of money. Although, after cold studying the pros and cons of the small print with the help of an economist friend, I finally decided to take the not-so-easy path and postpone the investment later for the health of the company. The angel investor wanted too much in return.

Instead, I chose slower growth and to self-fund my company for a while. Then, not long after, a second investor offered me a smaller amount with a different agreement, although in this case it was a loan instead of a joint venture. Even though the amount was lower, the conditions were much better, and the company was in a much more consolidated state to get the most out of this amount.

A much smaller investment can drive you towards the next milestone and, after six months, enable you to create a healthy base, focusing on the real deal, and being much more prepared for the future.

People or entities that invest in a healthtech company in the very initial phase are comfortable with high risk. This can mean a high return in some cases and in others, the total loss of their capital. Often, they will invest in you as much for your conviction as for your ability to evidence your value. So always be confident in your abilities. First and foremost, ensuring the identity and veracity of those who want to invest is important.

All in all, when we think of investors, we must remember stakeholders that are aligned with the core values of our healthtechs: the "project's core value" and above that, the shared 'whys' of the project. These two aspects, value and purpose, should be taken into account when considering investors: the big techs, e.g., Google Ventures, and the pill developers—the global big pharmaceutical industries. Both types of investors can also play a key role in promoting out healthtechs, as well as offering a long-term investment focus.

Remember, they as investors choose you. But also, you should choose the best investors – those with long-term views, with no short-term pressure, that understand that growth takes time. Avoid those who would push you down *their* path, not *your* path. Investors must be able to help you, understand the environments, and give good advice to your venture team.

Also remember that the best funders are your healthtech members—the people that you hire. They must be the best in their fields and be able to bring value to the company; they must always be better than yourself in their own areas. These talents will be your best investments. Thus, it is key to spend time interviewing and looking for the right team, and replacing the talent when it is necessary, to create a team with high potential and performance. In other words, hire the best talent and get rid of mistaken talent as soon as possible; do not wait to take the decision.

Those pieces of the team that are not 100% committed to the project and passionate about the companies' mission and goals are not in the right place. It is a matter of an equilibrium, 50%-50%, of what they bring to the company and what they get in return from the company. If this is not fully aligned, it is not a win-win for the company and the employee and it will not work. These individuals have a perfect place, but it is not in your team or company.

But first things first. More important than looking for funds is looking for funds in the right moment of your healthtech lifecycle. Taking on funding too early at too high of a cost—shares in your company or direction over it—can stunt your growth potential and ultimately jeopardise the business. Once you give away those shares or ownership, you can never regain them. Strike a fair deal, when it is right for you—not simply because the funds are offered. For example, ensure you have positioned your company for rapid scaleup, otherwise the funds will go unused.

Sometimes, advisors and investors become cannibals of small companies. And in others they are drivers of growth and accelerators of the company and its talent. Thus, youth or startup juniority must not be understood as foolishness. You need to preserve your integrity and value because it will be translated into the integrity and value of your company.

And speak from the same level as the investor you have in front of you. Maybe they are offering you €3 million for a small part of your company, and, in this particular moment, this will be a big push for your business. But think with a cold perspective. Take your time and really focus on the true value to you. Maybe you are offering something worth €15 million that will be easily sold for €3 million. And soon, you will have to split more shares of your company at rates that are not worth it.

Remember, sometimes appearances are deceiving. Think about the win-win from your own deeply studied case, and avoid involving yourself in win-lose deals from the get-go. They will not help you scale. Believe me, soon you will need another one or two digits on that figure to scale up your company if everything goes as you planned; in phases C and D you will really need help.

We must deeply evaluate each of the projects that we are working on, each of the bridges and alliances that we have created onto the whole pathology community. And from each one, analyse deeply the achievement/assets accomplished up to the moment, and the performance issues.

Scalability also means supporting our business with growth drivers and basing our next steps on the few past successes we have as a new company. As immature companies, our first steps into the ecosystem will be mixed—some will have worked, some have not. So, home in on what does work using intelligent analytics, and prioritise it through replicating your own best-practices.

The latest trends show an increase in public-private partnerships (PPPs), suggesting fast-growing, scalable ventures must be based on innovative public-private win-win contracts. Thus, why not embrace and suggest disruptive changes to public healthcare from your position as a private entity? Also, when it comes to the touchpoints with the public system, if you have evidence that some part of the ongoing healthcare system is no longer valid, suggest areas of improvement, being proactive and brave. This is also part of the win-win alliance and the value that you are bringing as a healthtech and as the game-changer you are meant to be.

Institutions like the World Bank Group offer many resources for those considering the establishment of a PPP through their legal resource centre (PPPLRC, 2021). There, you can find downloadable samples of PPP agreements and concessions, checklists and sample clauses, terms of reference, risk matrices, standard bidding documents developed by government agencies and sample PPPs and sector legislation and regulation.

In funding there are several stages:

■ A series funding: Most of us will end up on A-series funding. This is where we can get with hard effort and well-worked pitches. It follows initial seed capital and brings in figures in the 10-million-dollar range. You will only want this after having demonstrated a viable business model with strong growth potential. Consider this option if you have a plan to expand but lack the cash, and use the funds for hiring, inventory, equipment and R&D&i. Financiers at this stage often gain considerable controlling interest in the company.

■ B–C series funding: Expansion and scalability continue in the series B funding round. You will already have an established user base, but this is about expanding market reach. It is in the moment where you really need to go from 100 users to 10,000, and from 10,000 to 1 million users. We are now in the moment of truth. Will you be able to make your company grow at scale? This is where you show which part of the market you will penetrate and own.

The B–C stages are not about finding the solution, they are about developing it. The challenge is getting to this second phase in a position with measurable potential and projected growth rates. Here, growth trajectories should be easily identifiable. For example, for a line extension of the products and services that you are offering based on your acquired experience. And sometimes, here arises the possibility of expanding into emerging markets and countries with potential and buying other solutions that share a purpose with your core business.

■ D series funding: D series is the last big jump on the flight path. Not all companies decide to fly to this height because, to go for D-round funding, you must want to operate or expand "also" into another market (country or homologous healthcare ecosystem). It is also a good strategy to grow the value of your healthtech before the jump of going public.

This D-round can fail—it is commonly known as the "down round" for not meeting the expectations of growth, with shares sold for less than during the previous round.

Enticing an Investor

So, now you know what the stages of funding are and the different types of investors. But how do you get these investors wanting to invest in your company at fair rates?

■ Common sense. Would you invest everything you have because you really believe in it? If the answer is no, we have a business problem that we need to redress. Every single business with value can succeed with the right people at the rudder.
■ Be sellable. You cannot bump into a potential investor by telling them, we have potential here, there, and over there, too. You have value, for sure, but the potentiality of your value is not everywhere; it is a combination of the fusion between your product's potential and the ecosystem's potential to embrace it. Clarify those and you will sell.
■ Where are you going? Envision for your investor two next steps ahead of the current one. Have more than just your current strategic direction; know the next two.

And never doubt yourself when you explain it to an angel investor, etc. To get multiple stakeholders requires an incredible pitch, a good communicator, and a good presentation, explaining the situation and the potentiality of your company.

Believe me, an investor, a good one, the one that puts money where money grows, can read between the lines. They see more than what 99% of the population would see in a simple graph. In other words, the good investor is "the chosen one"—a winner among winners. You cannot hide the truth from him, and you cannot sell a good strategy and company direction if you do not have it. They will catch you out.

So, do not throw yourself onto the sharks if you do not have a good:

■ Clear value proposition.
■ Three key answers to why you are investable.
■ Proven evidence.
■ 10 common-sense first objections already answered. Memorise them, before exposing yourself, and above all your company, to the Q&A round after the speech.

When they ask, where are you going, and where do you expect to be in five years, you need no doubt. Truly, who knows where you will be? But do not present a range of possibilities. Present the most likely scenario. And have three as a backup: the best, worst and base. And you can give percentages for each to happen.

So please, be prepared, before being exposed. Prepare answers to the following:

The whys:

■ Why your healthtech and not the other? Differentiation proposal.
■ Why are you in the project? Sense of purpose.
■ Why are you worth it? Value proposal.

The whats:

■ What do you have to offer? Positive impact within the ecosystem. This is about giving an executive summary of the whole value dossier, key points.
■ What is your roadmap? Where are you going to be in three to five years?
■ What is your unicorn approach? What is the maximum version of your company, the 100% potential?

The wheres:

■ Where do you go? Vision objectives.
■ Where are your barriers and opportunities? Rule of the three to one; for every three key strengths you state, point at one improvement area.

The whos:

■ Who are you? Who is your board committee? And who do you need to onboard in the near future? Maybe a European fund, or who knows maybe a key talent for the next step. Sometimes a key talent is worth more than a capital injection of €3 million.
■ Show your true value, why "you", and who else is better than you?
■ European? US? Who are you? Because some investors discriminate by where you built yourself. Are you Silicon Valley? Or a European wanting to be a European company?

Above all, it is about getting yourself into the right mindset. You are not needy. You are valuable, and you are at the same level as anyone else. Position yourself as such when you ask for funds. Nothing is worse than wanting to invest in someone that thinks they do not deserve it. There is nothing less credible than gain confidence in investing with someone that does not think they deserve it. So put yourself at the same level as the investor that you have in front of you, and do not allow anyone to step on you because of money. Age is irrelevant, money is irrelevant, power is irrelevant.

Have in mind that investors not only invest in the product, but also in a team of people, as they are meant to be a high-performance team that will fly above the others. It is not about selling what you are not. It is about having confidence in yourself and your team and showing your maximum potential.

The key is to answer all of the mentioned questions before they are asked and have in mind this suggestions. It will give you the credibility that you need. Do not doubt it.

Team Building and Decision Making

Since everything will converge onto hubs of health, we need to build talent. But we also need to embrace the new talents—talents coming from healthcare, healthtech and other disruptive markets.

We are submerged in the "doing", but ultimately, we must step back, think carefully and then move forward—again doing less action but more directed to the business goals. To do so, use the brain of your team. You do no good making your team perform tasks a robot could (or a system optimised by digitisation). Reinvent, reconsider and rebuild the structure of your company so that every person adds value. Because they all do, you just have to position them correctly. Otherwise, you waste everyone's time, and you lose value and money.

Leaders sometimes presume people lack value or capability—but that is their failing, not the team member's. It is your job to get that talent out of them. And you need to invest time and effort in building up and developing this talent. I agree that each person is responsible for their development, but still, you are the one positioning them within your company, giving or withholding room to expand. So, get it right: make them the best version of themselves and you will gain their respect.

Look for entrepreneurial minds, the ones that propose rather than ask. The ones that envision opportunities and can really drive your company to the next level through innovation. Capacitate them, give them the tools, and they will give in return more than you would have ever expected.

Some leaders get obsessed that they need a particular talent from a particular region, school, or institution. They assume they cannot find it elsewhere. Seriously? We live in an age where anyone from any remote area in the world has access to the best knowledge and best tech schools and knowledge from any singular region in the world. So, rethink that assumption. You will find the best talent in the unlikeliest of places.

How to Take Challenging Decisions?

- Challenge your team to find and solve a problem impacting your business.
- Challenge your team to brainstorm divergent actions to solve problems. Here tools like "The six thinking hats" could be useful.[20] Or why not make a session with a Lego Coach, accredited by "Lego Serious Play",[21] to push the disruptive thinking of your team?
- Challenge your team to vote on the main solutions.

Sometimes this process will be easy. In many other cases, however, you will be forced to take a decision different from that proposed during the exercise. But it will be a decision conditioned and pushed by the talents of the exercise (Pharmaoffer, 2020).

We are all humans, and as humans we make mistakes and require improvement. Being an entrepreneur, and operating inside the healthcare world, means being exposed to hurting sensitivities. You constantly interact with new players, from members of your team to a healthcare

---

[20] "Six Thinking Hats" and the associated idea of parallel thinking provides a means for groups to plan thinking processes in a detailed and cohesive way, and in doing so to think together more effectively (Bono, 1985).
[21] Lego Serious Play. A powerful tool designed to enhance innovation and business performance. URL: https://www.lego.com/en-us/seriousplay

authority. What all of them have in common, aside from being human, is the "ego". And you are exposed to hurting the sensitive ego, all the time and worse than this without even being aware of it.

So, I must say, above all, stay humble.

Always.

Do not degrade yourself. But retain your integrity with your humility. This has to do with assertiveness, closeness and protecting yourself in the process of trying to not hurt "egos".

Hurting the "ego" of the person in front of you can mean losing an opportunity. Doors can open and close in a split second, and sometimes a smile is the difference between a successful and failed encounter.

In the healthtech environment, you are exposed to many different profiles. Yet these profiles are in your personal life, too. It is like a soccer team—the attackers score the goals, but the team cannot win without the defenders. So, embrace all the profiles regardless of age, seniority, gender, socioeconomic background, religion, personality, etc. To disrupt the healthcare model, you will need diversity of people and opinion.

Respect each person you meet. You never know who is who before meeting that person deeply. In most cases, you will not have time to because your interaction with this player will not last more than a single meeting. But you are now in the big league, so every interaction matters. You must apply *savoir-faire* and *savoir-être* i.e., knowing how to act and knowing which role to occupy. Occupying the right place in a social interaction means being proactive when it is necessary, practicing active listening, having initiative and high capability. Fight the battles you can win; know when to quit.

Your personal branding is also important. I remember once, a startup of seven intelligent young men came with a horizontal business model, and with a potential startup in a very early stage that wanted to open up their value and services in the healthcare field. In that moment they had a pipeline of stunning, valuable solutions and an amazing versatile capacity to adapt to the ecosystem. Consequently, I opened a few doors for them, so that they could start building their ecosystem and setting up their position in the healthcare environment.

The thing is, when I asked one of the contacts, I introduced the young men to how it went, they said: "please, tell these kids to tidy up themselves and iron their shirts the next time they come to an important meeting". This was someone with a successful career in the healthcare environment meeting extremely highly talented entrepreneurs, but the mistake was the dress code, which immediately hurt egos before the meeting started. This is not about judging either side but pointing out that both sides were judging each other without even noticing it—to the detriment of progress.

So, put yourself in a position of equality in every interaction that you have. It is not just about the clothes; it is not about the speech; it is about respecting yourself and making yourself respectable.

Chapter 9

Going Global

To be as close as possible to the patient, we need to look towards scalable new business models. Consider that in healthtech, the local approach is the new global, and global is at the same time the new local.

We stand before a turning point: start-ups are becoming scaleups. Localised digital strategies—geolocating microeconomies—will become part of our growth drivers and the foundation to scale. Our business models should think globally but act locally: target patients globally, but on a personalised, local, close-to-patient approach to care. Thus, while seeing the overall picture, remain next to the patient. The new healthcare model is about taking personal care of him, about the physician, the caregiver and all the stakeholders involved in the pathology solution taking his hand along the patient journey.

Yet we cannot speak about personalised and precision medicine if we do not consider the clusters of regionally diversified customers.

Our clear approach should be going global but with a multi-local business concept, prioritising localisation under the big global umbrella of geo-clustering. For example, WeChat has just launched a national epidemic dynamic page with functions such as medical popularisation, real-time epidemic statistics, and fever outpatient local mapping (Sohu, 2020) (Ren, 2021).

As another example of where healthcare localisation is important, consider the passage of the Affordable Care Act (ACA) (HealthCare.gov, 2021) or more commonly called "Obamacare". Healthcare exchanges have been created in all 50 states, each with their own structures for handling the administration of care.

Or specifically in the healthtech field, the Nigerian HiBlance[1] is an online emergency medical service to book an ambulance online, find closest medical centres, purchase emergency medical equipment online and get help making smart choices when seeking medical attention locally or internationally. Considering that Nigeria, unlike many developed countries in the world, lacks a proper national paramedic service, HiBlance was born to fill the local gap while ensuring more lives are saved daily.

Since we are starting to buy and pay for our wellbeing and QALYs, when you go to market in the new healthcare environment, you should consider different cultures and lifestyle standards. Language is preventing many healthtechs from scaling up their solutions to a global level. For

---

[1] HiBlance. URL: https://www.hiblance.com/

DOI: 10.4324/b23147-12

example, just 78.1% of the US population speaks English at home. This has been a daily challenge for HCPs when providing care to patients during the last century, and the challenge is still here in the digital age of disruption, limiting equal access to information, safety and quality.

We need to democratise information to breakthrough to the next healthcare era. With language especially, artificial intelligence and machine learning tools have much to offer us. Like retail, you should consider the global consequences of simple actions such as translating a slogan into different languages or the colour usage in your campaigns. This should be integrated into your core business goals and strategies.

Adaptation to various lifestyles and cultures is essential now that citizens are empowered to look after their own healthcare attitudes and habits, such as standardising good nutritional habits, physical activity habits, quality of sleep, mental health, social healthiness, and above all, lifespan extension and quality. This is "lifestyle medicine": early medicine that is ultimately a circular economy in the healthcare systems of the future.

If we can adopt this lifestyle approach to medicine, many attractive healthtech markets will emerge for us to scale into. Look at different geographies—Asian consumer groups; American; African; European—and choose which has the highest potential, the best culture for expansion for your particular product, and then localise your solution to it.

The 2000s saw many emerging countries in terms of technology, some of them starting from a point of nonexistence, and later on, popping up as strong new technology players. This is also impacting the global healthtech chessboard. Recent generations have brought them towards unified cultures, bringing oppohealthtechrtunities for brands and business concepts to enter these newborn markets.

We can also learn this local-global approach from the best practices in other fields such as beauty, retail, filming, and gaming communities, and bring all this know-how to healthcare. How can we reach across borders to find healthtech marketing success?

- Understand the community and deliver them culturally relevant content on an integrated digital marketing approach.
- Track continuous data that validates growth paths in terms of strategy and tactics implemented, building up credibility to engage customers in your brand's story.
- Next-best-action should be the centre of live tactics to create value, along with its alignment with strategic position in the ecosystem.
- Focus on country-specific leading digital channels. For example, if we consider China, the country-specific channels would be WeChat[2] the Chinese WhatsApp that connects a billion people; Weibo, considered the Chinese Twitter; or Youku Tudou,[3] the Chinese YouTube.

When you wish to localise, ask, what do they need in terms of the pathology healthcare coverage gaps? When and how?

Building our strategic position and ecosystem within new markets will be challenging, but still the method is the same and can be applied in any high-potential and emerging country that you strategically choose for expansion. Use common sense to decide which one would be an opportunity for your healthtech and avoid the markets of countries where you already know before joining them. Be prepared to learn-by-doing on a pathway full of obstacles and barriers.

---

[2] WeChat. Chinese multi-purpose messaging, social media and mobile payment app developed by Tencent. URL: https://www.wechat.com/
[3] Youku. URL: https://www.youku.com

Of course, legislation is a key concern to select the country, as some countries permit what would be impermissible in others; here, your own ethics play a role.

Through scalability, we must aim to reach a point where any patient can benefit from our healthcare solution no matter where they come from. This should be the main goal before selecting which countries and how to make the go-to-market and penetrate that particular segment. In other words, we need to think bigger and inversely towards the status quo—not by us going to the emerging markets, but by making the emerging markets come to us, having them embrace our solution because it covers the unmet needs of that particular health system.

The sort of data that we will collect for our healthtech is essential for the niche where we want to raise our company or start-up. Indeed, we need to design how we are going to use and manage the key data and artificial intelligence before we build the company, services and products in a certain region. All this data will and must be an essential part of the DNA and value of our healthtech and the skeleton on which our product and services pipeline are built.

We must create rich products using the data we will be able to collect, so the whole ecosystem can see the true value and potential of these products based on data insights.

In this chapter, we discuss cross border e-commerce and setting up the marketplace, that is, building healthcare ecosystems, in different environments.

The five-year standard process would be:

■ Test the market (1–2 years)
■ Extend the business model (3–4 years)
■ Online vs offline bridges face-to-face health model consolidated (5 years)

Yet each region will have specific needs and a unique ecosystem in which you must operate, so it is important to be flexible and undertake considerable research when going from local to global.

Looking Abroad

Global healthcare expenditure slowed by 2.6% in 2020 due to the lockdowns and the increase of telehealth and decrease of face-to-face visits to the doctor, among many other factors (Deloitte, 2021 global health care outlook, 2021).

But between 2020 and 2024, this trend is expected to revert through a rise at a 3.9% CAGR, considerably faster than the 2.8% recorded in 2015–2019 (Arjun, 2020) (Unit, 2020). This is mainly due to governments investing heavily in pandemic contingency and other remaining issues, such as the effects of an ageing population, or follow-up, that have been challenging the traditional system of health expenditure statistics (OECD, 2021). The fastest growth will be in Asia and Australasia (5.3%) and the transition economies of Central and Eastern Europe (5.2%) (Deloitte, 2021). And the sector's global health care spending share of GDP is expected to average up to 10.3% in 2021 and 2022 (Deloitte, 2021).

All in all, it is expected that by 2026, the global digital health market size will be around 657 billion US dollars (Statista, 2021). Yet, the global paradigm is unstable, and your company will not succeed or make profit everywhere. Thus, discovering the best environment for your company to mature means choosing the right country—one with a favourable legal and accelerator framework for your aims.

The International Health Regulations (IHR) (WHO, 2021) are an agreement between 196 countries and territories to work together for global health security. They are a commitment to develop and improve public health capacities that make the world ready to respond to emerging public health emergencies. The data presented in the last World Health Statistics 2020 report (WHO, 2021) shows that while certain regions are better prepared than others, no region currently achieved a score of more than 85 for any of the 13 indicators (WHO, 2021).[4] So around the world, there remains much room for improvement across these 13 core capacities, and therefore considerable opportunity for your healthtech to make an impact.

According to the WHO regions, this chapter presents a headline analysis of this worldwide framework to help you to choose where to locate or scale up your company. This is not 100% accurate given the nature of how quickly the sector moves, and there will be experts out there that can add to this. However, it will provide the groundwork for you to begin your research, indicating general areas of interest and potential within the wider view of a sustainable, global healthcare agenda.

From my point of view, all regions have pros and cons in terms of healthtech ecosystem particularities. And at the same time, all of them have local opportunities in which I would deeply think about camping out for a while to pilot your solution and boost your growth.

I have chosen the WHO standard territorial regions to discuss for healthtech opportunities.

■ **African Region (AFR):** Algeria, Angola, Benin, Botswana, Burkina Faso, Burundi, Cameroon, Cape Verde, Central African Republic, Chad, Comoros, Ivory Coast, Democratic Republic of the Congo, Equatorial Guinea, Eritrea, Ethiopia, Gabon, Gambia, Ghana, Guinea, Guinea-Bissau, Kenya, Lesotho, Liberia, Madagascar, Malawi, Mali, Mauritania, Mauritius, Mozambique, Namibia, Niger, Nigeria, Republic of the Congo, Rwanda, São Tomé and Príncipe, Senegal, Seychelles, Sierra Leone, South Africa, South Sudan, Eswatini, Togo, Uganda, Tanzania, Zambia, Zimbabwe.

■ **Region of Americas (AMR):** Antigua and Barbuda, Argentina, Bahamas, Barbados, Belize, Bolivia, Brazil, Canada, Chile, Colombia, Costa Rica, Cuba, Dominica, Dominican Republic, Ecuador, El Salvador, Grenada, Guatemala, Guyana, Haiti, Honduras, Jamaica, Mexico, Nicaragua, Panama, Paraguay, Peru, Saint Kitts and Nevis, Saint Lucia, Saint Vincent and the Grenadines, Suriname, Trinidad and Tobago, United States, Uruguay, Venezuela.

■ **South-East Asia Region (SEAR):** Bangladesh, Bhutan, North Korea, India, Indonesia, Maldives, Myanmar, Nepal, Sri Lanka, Thailand, Timor-Leste, Singapore.

■ **European Region (EUR):** Albania, Andorra, Armenia, Austria, Azerbaijan, Belarus, Belgium, Bosnia and Herzegovina, Bulgaria, Croatia, Cyprus, Czech Republic, Denmark, Estonia, Finland, France, Georgia, Germany, Greece, Hungary, Iceland, Ireland, Israel, Italy, Kazakhstan, Kyrgyzstan, Latvia, Lithuania, Luxembourg, Malta, Moldova, Monaco, Montenegro, Netherlands, North Macedonia, Norway, Poland, Portugal, Romania, Russia, San Marino, Serbia, Slovakia, Slovenia, Spain, Sweden, Switzerland, Tajikistan, Turkey, Turkmenistan, Ukraine, United Kingdom, Uzbekistan.

■ **East Mediterranean Region (EMR):** Afghanistan, Bahrain, Djibouti, Egypt, Iran, Iraq, Jordan, Kuwait, Lebanon, Libya, Morocco, Oman, Pakistan, Palestine, Qatar, Saudi Arabia, Somalia, Sudan, Syria, Tunisia, United Arab Emirates, Yemen.

---

[4] Note: List of the 13 indicators: legislation and financing, Coordination and focal point, Zoonotic events, Food safety, Laboratory, Surveillance, Human resources, Health emergency framework, Health service provision, Risk communication, Points of entry, Chemical events and Radionuclear emergencies. Source: https://www.who.int/data/gho/whs-2020-visual-summary

■ **Western Pacific Region (WPR):** Australia, Brunei, Cambodia, China, Cook Islands, Fiji, Japan, Kiribati, Laos, Malaysia, Marshall Islands, Micronesia, Mongolia, Nauru, New Zealand, Niue, Palau, Papua New Guinea, Philippines, Samoa, Solomon Islands, South Korea, Taiwan, Tonga, Tuvalu, Vanuatu, Vietnam.

Of course, there are many regions to leverage inside this large-scale classification, but there is not space to consider them all individually in this book. All these regions might constitute an accommodative ecosystem for your situation, model or lifecycle. So, you must evaluate the global framework according to your needs when searching for the right locality in which to scale and consolidate. Nevertheless, I will outline a few major countries and regions and their main global aspects that I believe could be leveraged.

Keep an open, inclusive mindset.

The starting point should always be the region's real healthcare needs.[5] It is essential that when we decide to land our healthtech in a region that we know where applicability would have a major social impact.

The African Region

Technology is transforming as for how healthcare is delivered in Africa, giving more people in remote areas access to better care. Likewise, easier access to data helps both doctors and policy-makers make better-informed decisions about how to continue to improve the system (Clausen, 2015).

Nonetheless, access is still the greatest challenge to healthcare delivery in Africa. Fewer than 50% of Africans have access to modern health facilities. Many African countries spend less than 10% of their GDP on healthcare. Also, there is a shortage of trained healthcare professionals from Africa because many of them prefer to live and work in places like the US and Europe (Clausen, 2015).

Most Africans, mostly the poor and those in the middle-income bracket, rely on under-funded public health facilities while a small minority has access to well-funded, quality private health care (UNDP, 2017). Varying wildly from country to country and region to region, public healthcare does exist (Aetna, 2021).

Kenya spends just 5.7% of GDP on healthcare, which is low by global standards (GamaPServer, 2021). Yet it is higher than that of some neighbouring countries like Sudan and Ethiopia. While Nigeria has a public health service financed through a national insurance scheme, that is improving, but it faces several difficulties including a low ratio of doctors at only 1 per 2000 inhabitants (low on a global scale but higher than most of its African neighbours) and an infrastructure struggling to cope. The country spends 3.7% of its GDP on healthcare: a figure well below global average but on par with many of the countries around it. A number of initiatives are improving life for inhabitants including family planning and immunisation programmes, and the country's prospects continue to change as its economy grows to become one of the largest in Africa. South Africa spends nearly 9% of its GDP on health care (on par with countries like Spain and Malta) but the doctor to population ratio is just under 1 to 1000, well below the world average (Aetna, 2021).

---

[5] And that you can easily have a global first-sight overview if you look at https://www.who.int/about/who-we-are/regional-offices and you contact the different regional offices and the publications for each region.

The other side of the African health sector is in a place of privilege, with a sudden explosion of healthtech funding (Africa, 2021). Kenya, Nigeria, South Africa and Egypt are the premium investment destinations.

AI in the hands of frontline health workers (FHWs) is already enabling them to better serve and bring top-notch medical technology and advice to their patients. An example is supporting communities of health workers in remote regions like one rural village in Western Kenya, isolated from the nearest hospital by several hours. An AI-enabled diagnosis app could ensure the proper reading and interpretation of the results of a blood test, verifying that a paediatric patient does not have malaria and does not need to be referred for care (USAID, 2021). This demonstrates how cutting-edge healthtechs can improve in-home care and democratise access to healthcare even for the most disadvantaged.

There is a huge potential in Africa if we consider the digitally proficient profile of the citizen itself.

No matter their cultural or economic condition, they move with ease in the technological field and can defend themselves easily through any app or tech solution that a single smartphone can allocate. Every day in Africa, 90,000 new users connect to the internet, and 22% of Africa's working age population are starting businesses (LinkedIn, 2021).

Africa's main problem is not the lack of investment, which has recently become huge. To help the healthcare market grow needs more than us as healthtechs developing solutions, which is just problem-solving via technology and often easily addressed. The big challenge of the region is to implement the solution in the field (McKinsey, 2020).

For example, a US company that wants to scale up an AI healthtech tool in the field in East Africa might find a big barrier is being unable to use US-based health data to develop accurate predictions or diagnoses for patients in low- to medium-income countries (LMICs) (USAID, 2021).

This difficulty in implementation means most healthtechs that go-to-market in Africa seem to lack B/C funding rounds. They easily get the first round A/B funds, but in this second phase, when they try to grow, while they had estimated a certain amount of investment to scale up and reach their goals, they end up having to invest three times more after the first phase as skyrocketing costs exceed their forecasted budget. So, devote more time to financial planning when launching in Africa.

Africa is one of the most attractive markets to set up our time to fly, if we account for three key issues:

■ Market particularities to build and implement a scalable and viable business model include poor access to healthcare, with most private consultancies owned by a healthcare professional which most patients cannot afford.
■ In Sub-Saharan Africa, there are fewer HCPs per 1,000 people than the worldwide average (Bank, 2021).
■ HCPs with whom you might interact are clinically oriented profiles more than business-oriented ones. This is how it should be, but still this sometimes slows down the adoption curve of healthtechs in their clinical practice.

This is also the reason why you should prioritise the supply of economically accessible solutions for the population: pathology support programs, training, diagnostic tests, etc.

Waiting lists and big crowded rooms in the medical attendance consultancies are an issue that prompted us to consider providing healthtech solutions that raise the quality of the healthcare system vs the quantity that currently operates.

Thus, if you are planning to start up or scale up in Africa, I would say, consider the investment in B/C phases as important from the very first moment. As mentioned before, you will need a lot of investment to go through the implementation in the field. Then multiply it by "n" because of the particularities of the status-quo ecosystem, difficulties in provisions with vendors, and bureaucracy—all this will necessitate a larger budget. This happens all over the world, but in Africa more.

Also remember the worldwide frameworks in regulatory and compliance and apply them locally within the different regions of Africa. This is because, although some of the regulations seem less restrictive than under other umbrella policies, you will want to be able to use sensitive data overseas. But you cannot if you are not compliant as a standard healthtech to play worldwide.

Be responsible and clever there: it can be a future problem operating in Kenya, rather than South-Africa, and not being compliant just because you are allowed not to be. This will not position you as a trustworthy compliant healthtech that can find barriers in the future healthcare ecosystem environment while trying to scale up the pilot technology. The National Agency for Food & Drug Administration and Control NAFDAC (Nigeria) in Africa would be the equivalent to the United States Food & Drug Administration USFDA in the US.

Still the technological emergence of the Africa Region is leading intercontinental initiatives, such as:

- EU-Africa via EuroAfrilink, which is creating touch points between the two continents.[6] Thus, Europe-Africa collaborations are close.
- USAID,[7] from the US perspective, also leads initiatives in the African Region. It has established a strategic plan for the region to address healthcare challenges and elevate the healthcare standard to the next milestone (USAID, 2021). It also has the Centre for Innovation and Impact (CII), which applies business-minded approaches to the development, introduction and scale-up of health interventions to accelerate impact against the world's most important health challenges.[8]

Some of the leading African Global Digital for Development Hubs that can aid you are:

- #DigitalDivide; #EUAU and #AfricaEuropePartnership.
- Digital Cooperation, constituting the African component of the Digital for Development (D4D) Hub; #D4Dhub.
- #TeamEurope will strive to accelerate human-centric, inclusive and sustainable digital transformation with African partners.
- The African Innovation and Entrepreneurship Centre (AIEC).
- A good starting point is Africa Health Business (AHB) (AHBS, 2021).[9]

---

[6] EuroAfrilink. URL: http://euroafrilink.com/
[7] USAID leads international development and humanitarian efforts to save lives, reduce poverty, strengthen democratic governance and help people progress beyond assistance. URL: https://www.usaid.gov/
[8] Center for Innovation and Impact (CII) URL: https://www.usaid.gov/cii
[9] https://www.africahealthbusiness.com/

The Americas—PAHO

The WHO, together with the Pan American Health Organization, has a whole strategic program to address the Americas' healthcare: "The Sustainable Health Agenda for the Americas 2018–2030" (WHO, 2021). You should consider it while enrolling in a healthtech project in the region. And it is also interesting to study the strategic health plan of the certain region if you are planning to set up your business there. It is mainly focused on universal access to the highest standards of health, Pan American solidarity, equity in health and social inclusion with a detailed action plan according to these pillars. This will help you align your value proposals to the real healthcare goals and SDGs of the different countries of the region.

The Americas have hot spots to leverage when we consider expansion in healthtech. Emerging countries of the south and centre contrast the northern world powers: the US and Canada.

The US

The U.S. is unique among advanced industrialised countries for having no universal healthcare coverage and no uniform health system. Only recently has it launched legislation mandating healthcare coverage for all. The US healthcare system is a hybrid, with funding coming from two sides: multi-payer universal health insurance and single-payer private insurance (DPE, 2016).

In the States, there is no NHS. If someone gets ill, they will probably need to pay for their treatment unless they have insurance. The US government does fund two kinds of health plans, though: Medicare and Medicaid.

Healthcare providers in the US comprise insurance companies, hospital systems, and independent providers. It is a collection of micro healthcare systems. Each one of them has different eligibility criteria, budget split and financial obligations by patients. There is a baseline federal-state system which varies across the country (Medicaid). There is also a national social insurance program for the elderly population (Medicare). And there is another system covering working people (tax-advantaged, employer-sponsored coverage). Meanwhile, millions of other working people obtain services through another system (state-level exchange plans). And still millions of households fall between eligibility criteria for these programs or cannot afford coverage, and so they remain uninsured (Butler, 2020).

Healthcare facilities are largely owned and operated by private sector businesses. 58% of community hospitals in the United States are non-profit, 21% are government-owned, and 21% are for-profit.

According to Global Entrepreneurship INDEX 2018 report, in the entrepreneurial field, North America's strongest areas are in Opportunity Perception and Product Innovation (Acs, Szerb, & Lloyd, 2017).

Besides, the US healthcare systems are pushing for innovation. California remains one of the world's epicentres of healthtech development.

While thinking of going-to-market in the US, as in many other regions in the world, you should consider how to address the inequality gap growing every day between those who can and cannot afford health. Remember this while introducing your healthtech solutions to the market, as this emerging challenge, with the years, could evolve not only into gaps between those with poor and good health, but also between those with better and worse genes.

Thus, New York (NY) focuses on helping those with financial challenges and who lack access to good-quality healthcare. ONENYCity 2050 is one of the city's key initiatives. It aims to rebuild the city through a stronger and fairer approach (NYC, New York City's Green New Deal.

Volume 5 of 9, 2021). One of its main pillars is "healthy lives", with a single purpose of reducing inequities in health outcomes (NYC, 2021). While preparing your value dossiers, it is essential that you consider their action plan and strategic lines of action.

Remaining challenges for the US that our healthtechs can help address concern the lack of integration of healthcare institutions ranging from independent hospitals, hospital chains or independent physicians' associations up to highly integrated and organised institutions as multispecialty medical groups integrated with hospitals and health plans (CAPP, 2021).

Some of the biggest medical associations in the US have their own specialised healthtech promotional divisions that assist with integration. Such is the case of the American Heart Association[10] with the "Centre for Health & Technology & Innovation".[11] This is a consortium that connects entrepreneurs, providers, researchers and payers to accelerate novel solutions across the health continuum.

From the other side, American HealthTech (HealthTech, 2021)[12] is one of the nation's leading electronic health records (EHR) providers for long-term care (LTC) facilities and helps in this integration of the US health institutions.

Another enabler is the prestigious association the MIT-Harvard Medical School. It leads the learn-bootcamp initiative (MIT, 2021), constituting a reference online program in entrepreneurial creativity and problem-solving, healthcare innovation and leadership for those that want to enter the field and facilitates the integration.

Canada

Canada has a decentralised, universal, publicly funded health system called Canadian Medicare. This means that Canada's national health insurance program provides coverage to all legal residents in Canada. Healthcare is funded and administered primarily by the country's 13 provinces and territories. Each has its own insurance plan, and each receives cash assistance from the federal government on a per-capita basis. To pay for excluded services, including outpatient prescription drugs and dental care, provinces and territories provide some coverage for targeted groups. In addition, about two-thirds of Canadians have private insurance (Fund, 2020).

There are 2,735 Healthtech startups in Canada (Tracxn, 2021) (Starups, 2021). Medtech Canada[13] is the national association representing Canada's Medical Technology Companies. Medtech Canada, in turn, works with the government to implement effective national and regional procurement strategies to ensure timely access to medical technology in the region.

It is easy to operate in Canada as you can get register your company to operate in the ecosystem within a few days. 70% of the healthcare system is public with a decentralised budget in 13 different regions, and 30% is private.

As in other countries like the US, in Canada there is still a lack of interoperability between health systems. Hospitals and centres of care such as doctor's private consultancies have their own isolated siloed health datasets. The value chain remains in a closed structure state, and on top, Canada's regional and federal governments administer healthcare in different ways (PWC, 2021).

In this line, the government has established a list of healthcare system challenges and opportunities and considerations on how to address them with the aid of healthtech (Medec, 2017). In any

---

[10] https://www.heart.org/
[11] https://ahahealthtech.org/
[12] https://www.linkedin.com/company/american-healthtech/
[13] https://medtechcanada.org/

case, to address the issue of fragmented and inflexible silo-based health systems, a proposed solution is collaborative planning and transformation. This will focus on total cost of care, long-term savings and overall value to break barriers around short-term cost-containment issues. The suggestion is to incorporate digital change at managing level to support the adoption of innovation and address cultural resistance to innovation. At the same time, the government wants to build collaborative and transparent working relationships involving public-private partnerships (PPPs) and finally enable shared risk management through new models to face the aversion to risk.

Healthtechs that address these challenges will do well. For example, Canadian BlueDot advances preventive medicine with direct impact on healthcare sustainability.[14] It is empowering responses to infectious diseases risk using human and artificial intelligence to predict outbreaks. It has a track record of accurately assessing outbreak risk, in 2016 predicting the spread of Zika virus to Florida six months before official reports, and on COVID-19, accurately predicting eight of the first ten cities to import the novel coronavirus.

Canada in turn has recently adopted international standards, such as the Classification of Health Interventions (CCI), Digital Imaging and Communications in Medicine (DICOM), Health Level 7 (HL7) (O'Connor, 2017), and other integrative frameworks which makes it easy for Canadian and global healthtech companies to develop products equally marketable in national as well as international markets (Perspective, 2018). Such is the case of Esight,[15] a Canadian healthtech with a patented eyewear device that helps people with vision loss to regain their sight. Because it is a nonsurgical device, the technology adoption is easy.

Latin America (LATAM)

As the region is home to more than 18,000 hospitals, Latin America offers plenty of choices for healthcare. In fact, Brazil is home to more hospitals than the US, while 41% of the top hospitals in Latin America are in Colombia. Some countries in Latin America provide free, high-quality healthcare. For example, the cost of healthcare in places such as Mexico, Colombia and Panama are significantly less than in the US, despite offering excellent quality of care. However, access to quality care in many other countries in Latam can prove challenging (Jantra, 2021).

Healthtechs that want to operate in Latin America are leading with solutions to four main issues: (1) the healthcare industry's low productivity, as Latam has one of the lowest indexes of 'provider to customer' ratios, and (2) the lack of standards in service quality. Besides, healthcare (3) needs to evolve from a reactive (treatment oriented) to a more proactive medical attention system (early diagnosis and prevention programs). There is also an overall need of higher quality of life currently with access limitations for a big part of the population. Such healthcare unmet needs will leverage the following barrier: 20% of Latam populations are rural, leaving millions neglected when it comes to medical care and treatment (Saldarriaga & Mejia, 2021).

Indeed, healthtech in Latam is a fragmented market, and new emerging healthtechs are already working on facing this gaps. Yet their own country's healthtech initiatives are also emerging to cover the remaining healthcare needs that stand uncovered by foreign technology either.

LAVCA surveyed 36 healthtech startups in Latin America on the impact of the COVID-19 pandemic on their businesses, on adoption of healthcare technology and on access to healthcare services (Lavca, 2021). The results indicate the healthcare sector itself, and its regulations, continues to present the most significant barrier to growth for these startups. As main regulatory

---

[14] BlueDot. URL: https://bluedot.global/
[15] Esight. URL: https://esighteyewear.com/user-stories/

barriers to growth, respondents said that (1) healthcare sector regulations, (2) data privacy regulations and (3) payroll were the top three concerns, followed closely by taxation and compliance regulations.

Brazil

Healthcare in Brazil is a constitutional right. It is provided by both private and government institutions. The Health Minister administers national health policy. Primary healthcare remains the responsibility of the federal government, elements of which are overseen by individual states. Brazil is facing healthcare equity barriers and moving towards a more democratised healthcare, with the help of healthtech.

Brazil represents 1.8% of the global IT market and 40.7% of the Latin American market (ABES, 2020). Indeed, in Latam emerging countries like the present analysed Brazil, Panama or Colombia set up an enabling environment for health technology that wants to scale up in these countries. They are promising but fragmented markets.

The digital health strategy plan for Brazil 2020–2028 (ESD28) includes a strategic plan and follow up (SAÚDE, 2020). The strategic plan seeks to integrate operative synergies between Supplemental Health and Private Health.

From one side, the Department of System Computing Health Single (DataSUS) constitutes an agency of the Executive Secretariat of the Ministry of Health, which has the mission of promoting modernisation through the Technology of Information to support SUS. From another side, the National Data Network initiative in Health (RNDS), part of the Connect SUS Program, establishes the concept of a standardised, modern platform with interoperable services, information, and connectivity that is, in itself, transforming health in Brazil.

The RNDS sets the following objective: "promote the exchange of information between the points of Health Care Network (RAS), enabling the transition and continuity of care in the public and private".

The seven priorities of the ESD28 action plan are: (1) governance and leadership for Brazil's strategic health plan ESD; (2) computerisation of three levels of attention: including the implementation of computerisation policies for health systems, accelerating the adoption of health systems and considering EHRs and hospital management as a part of the integration of health services and processes; (3) improvement in the support of healthcare; (4) empowering the user as protagonist; (5) improving the training and capacitation of human resources; (6) interconnectivity and the environment; and (7) innovation in the ecosystem.

The plan also hopes to promote interoperability with telehealth services, develop health monitoring initiatives with the capacity to process a large amount of health data in real time, to implement electronic prescription, improve access to health services, reduce waiting times and improve the efficiency of the distribution of resources in an intelligent way in health services.

Besides, Brazil is developing initiatives in IoMT, Big Data and secondary use of data. Real-time monitoring of population health conditions is another priority of the ESD28, as is the process of disease prevention and health promotion. The ability to measure objective value and perceived value by all healthcare stakeholders and the use of resources from translational research is also important. And so is the acceleration of the adoption curve of innovation in Digital Health by the health system (SAÚDE, 2020).

Anyhow, according to the recent publication of the Action Plan 4.0 of the Brazilian Chamber of Industry (DF, 2019), one of the main strategic lines of action in Brazil is to promote shared product development between big and start-up companies. The Brazilian Association of Software

Companies (ABES)[16] is helping the construction of a Brazil that is More Digital and Less Unequal because it believes that information technology plays a fundamental role for the democratisation of knowledge and the creation of new opportunities, aiming at a better quality of life for all, in an inclusive and equal way. In this line, for example, Dr. Consulta[17] constitutes a network of proprietary medical centres. It is Brazil's largest private medical service provider (Saldarriaga & Mejia, 2021), representing a disruptive healthcare system shift for the poorest (Crichton, 2018) and a big step forward towards democratising health allowing a more equitable and universal access healthcare system.

Another achievement for the country has been driven by the emerging needs of the COVID pandemic. This prompted a push for the legalisation of telemedicine in Brazil, permitting a big shift in the healthcare sector.

If you are planning to establish your healthtech company products or services, or maybe scaling up a healthtech information as a service or software as a service, you should consider these priorities for the Brazilian health authorities. For example, an emerging opportunity in Brazil for healthtech innovation is in the mental disorders field, as Brazil has five times less mental health professionals per capita than the US and 10 times less than the EU (Kapps, 2021), leaving an important space to cover in this field.

Besides, the pharmaceutical Novartis Biome[18] has been allocated in Brazil as the first innovation hub in Latin America, which is a valuable resource for healthtechs looking to operate in the region.

Southeast Asia

Southeast Asia boasts 9% of the world's population, at around 600 million people, with Indonesia having the region's largest population (and fourth largest in the world) and Brunei the smallest (Hashim, et al., 2012). The region is home to more than half a billion people spread over highly diverse countries, from economic powerhouses like Singapore to poorer economies such as Cambodia, Laos and Myanmar. Key regional health challenges in Southeast Asia are a focus point for a diverse set of countries to seek a common identity that permits homogeneous effective solutions for all the population (Summerskill & Horton, 2011).

National healthcare systems in Southeast Asia are facing mounting pressures from demographic and epidemiological transitions. And these are only being amplified by the rising demands of an increasingly educated and wealthy population for excellent healthcare. Although many medical practices remain conservative, they are impacted by new technologies and pharmacological therapies, which in turn encounter regulatory barriers mainly due to safety and quality problems (Hashim, et al., 2012).

Some of the most innovative and advanced forms of healthcare service PPPs have emerged in the region, for example, the restructuring or corporatisation of public hospitals in Singapore from as early as 1985 and the later Swadana (self-financing) hospitals in Indonesia.

Considering further growth and integration of the Association of Southeast Asian Nations (ASEAN), the region should prioritise enhanced regional cooperation in the health sector to share

---

[16] https://abessoftware.com.br/en/
[17] Dr. Consulta. URL: https://www.drconsulta.com/
[18] https://www.biome.novartis.com/innovation-hubs

knowledge and rationalise health systems operations and its good practices, leading to further public health gains for the region's diverse population (Hashim, et al., 2012).

The growing openness to healthtech innovations is a driver for the region's markets, as it addresses immediate unmet needs and access problems, and moves healthcare in Southeast Asia (SEA) closer to equity (Singapore E., 2020).

Demand for high-quality healthcare in SEA is expected to keep growing. In the region's largest six nations alone, public healthcare expenditure is projected to double to USD 740 billion between 2017 and 2025 (Singapore E., 2020) (PWC, 2017).

A challenging environment that leaves the healthtechs who want to make their way in the region in a situation of point to think.

India

Access to the public hospital system is free for all citizens with some lower copays in defined situations. The Indian health system is a hybrid model between various public and private health insurance companies that pay for health care. It also has almost entirely tax-financed public hospitals, with their use almost free for all Indians barring minor co-payments for some services.

The healthtech market in India currently accounts for less than 1% of the health market, representing about US $1.9 billion in 2020, and presenting an annual CAGR growth of 39%.

Since digital access to health care will be a key area for the country, government initiatives such as the National Digital Health Mission (NDHM), the 2020 Telemedicine Practice Guidelines, the Draft Electronic Pharmacy Rules, etc. create an enabling environment to push healthtech ecosystems in India. Digital pharmacy and B2B models are the two most important elements in the healthtech sector, representing 70% of the healthtech market. For their part, online diagnosis and teleconsultation are the subsegments with the most potential in healthtech, growing 66% and 73% respectively (Alliance, 2021).

Key drivers for healthtech in India are the need to (1) improve accessibility, mainly in remote areas; (2) increase internet penetration and the (3) need to address the increase in lifestyle diseases. Besides, much anticipated are healthtechs for enabling early diagnosis, prevention, and better disease management.

For this reason, in India, a scaling healthtech might focus on overall healthcare cost containment, as affordability is an issue. Through healthtech applicability in optimisation of resources, continuous digital skillset capacitation and leveraging efficiency in the health system small changes can occur which may mean major upgrades for the health system. In this line, public health authorities are supporting these initiatives with policy, for example improving the public's purchasing power for healthtech offerings like telehealth (Alliance, 2021).

Innovaccer[19] became India's first healthtech unicorn (Kampani, 2021) by enabling the analysis of healthcare cloud data and putting the patient in the centre to offer actionable insights to doctors, hospitals, and insurance companies.

All in all, health expenses in India still represent a great burden for the country, with health being even now an inaccessible luxury for many given the low penetration of health insurance coverage. An estimated 50 or 60 million Indians fall into poverty or unmanageable debt just to obtain healthcare when there is a crisis in the family making insurance measures a priority of the government (Kampani, 2021).

---

[19] https://innovaccer.com/

For this, among other reasons, the healthtech industry is expected to reach $50bn by 2033, becoming an attractive ecosystem in which to operate (Shah, 2021).

Singapore

Singapore has a universal healthcare system that is more regulated than that in China and India. It is affordable and overall has great healthcare outcomes. The system represents about 4% of GDP (Triage, 2014). Besides, primary care access in government hospitals system is affordable. It offers the possibility of premium services as private rooms and in some cases is free.

Singapore has a unique approach: all workers are mandated to put a percentage of their earnings into savings for the future. The Medisave account is 7–9.5% of wages depending on your age (Triage, 2014). The rule to have access to healthcare is that the working population is expected to include a part of the payroll to "save-for-the -future". This is where the Medisave account represents 7 to 9.5% of wages depending on the age of the taxpayer.

Government healthcare authorities help with decisions about investing in healthtechs, and their main policies are patient centred throughout the value chain. The country has an integrated primary care network of polyclinics, acute and tertiary hospitals and a national speciality centre focused on healthcare contingency costs that is open to investing in healthtech (NYC, 2021) (Singapore, 2019).

The National University of Singapore's Medical Engineering Research and Commercialisation Initiative (MERCI) is an institution of reference in the country, as it helps to develop cost-effective, innovative, and clinically evidenced healthtech products that can be adopted towards the progress of Singapore's healthcare system.

Singapore is a mirror of the salient trends in Southeast Asia, building on an already existing trend of general digitisation of healthcare systems and consumerisation of healthcare.

HealthTEC Singapore,[20] supported by the National Research Foundation (NRF) and hosted at the Institute for Health Innovation and Technology (iHealthtech), National University of Singapore (NUS), acts as a national resource in R&D and commercialisation by providing seed funding and facilitating licensing of locally developed technologies.

Singaporean start-ups are embracing internationalisation. A best-practice example is Holomusk,[21] founded in 2015. Today it is a leading global data science and digital health company building the world's largest real-world evidence (RWE) platform for behavioural health. Moreover, it recently in 2021, acquired Otsuka Health Solutions (OHS), a UK-based mental health, predictive analytics provider, deepening Holmusk's footprint in the UK and paving the way for Holmusk to expand its partnerships with health systems working to transform behavioural healthcare (NEWSWIRE, 2021).

Indeed, Singapore is a good opportunity for those healthtechs who want to scale. It has deep clusters of tech and marketing talent, financing networks, and a notorious ecosystem of start-ups involved with a lot of support from the country with private and public actors. (Singapore, 2019). For example, governmental agencies like Enterprise Singapore help start-up companies to go global. In the same way, the Scaler8[22] program helps Singaporean start-ups find their footing overseas (Desrosiers, 2020).

---

[20] https://www.healthtec.sg/about-us/
[21] Holomusk. URL: https://www.holmusk.com/
[22] Scaler 8. URL: https://scaler8.com/

Singapore's Nanyang Technological University (NTU)[23] is one of the world's top universities. Along with the progressive Lee Kong Chian School of Medicine, and Singapore's state-of-the-art health services, HealthTech NTU provides a place where excellence in health, science, engineering, business, and policy converge.

Thailand

Thailand has a network of public hospitals that offer universal health coverage to the country's citizens, managed by the Ministry of Public Health (MOPH) together with other non-ministerial government agencies. Being highly overloaded, it is complemented by private hospitals, especially in urban areas such as Bangkok, where some internationally recognised hospitals stand out, constituting Centres of Excellence for being "electronically smart" and for their early adoption of cutting-edge health technologies (Post, 2017). Thailand's private and public sectors have identified innovation and technology as the two primary drivers propelling the medical industry into a new age of success (TIR, 2019).

Therefore, Thailand is among the main destinations for health tourism in the world, from which its private hospitals benefit tremendously (Collective, 2021). This is even though there continue to be challenges for the country such as access to health for populations living in rural areas. Non-communicable diseases are the main cause of death in the country, along with other infectious diseases such as malaria and tuberculosis, and traffic accidents.

These challenges have spurred an emergent healthtech start-up scene in Thailand, paving the way towards accessible health care and education for the population (Collective, 2021). Examples are Brain Dynamics,[24] an impressive start-up successfully changing the lives of paralysed patients by providing computer interface technology to help them communicate; Medvine,[25] an online platform providing a one-stop solution for clinics by connecting them to suppliers and distributors of disposable medical equipment and products in Southeast Asia; and Chiiwii Live,[26] a mobile application offering real-time phone consultations for women needing minor healthcare services.

Besides, Healthtech Thailand 2021 is Thailand's first hybrid event showcasing the latest medical and health technological innovations (Tech, 2021), and is a sizeable place for healthtechs to gain exposure and make contacts in the country's healthcare ecosystem. This is a potential opportunity for you and your team to make first contact with the healthtech ecosystem in the country, to learn first-hand what is happening, and to open some doors or build strategic collaborations for your company.

Another critical driver for the development of the healthtech start-up and innovation ecosystem in Thailand is the recently created True Digital Park[27] allocated in the heart of Bangkok's emerging innovation District on Sukhumvit Road. All under one roof, start-ups, entrepreneurs, tech companies, investors, accelerators, incubators, academies, and government agencies co-exist in an interconnected ecosystem, and that can be a place to host your company or find partners and assistance.

---

[23] https://www.ntu.edu.sg/healthtech
[24] Brain Dynamics. URL: https://www.braindynamics.co.th/
[25] Medvine. URL: https://www.medvine.com/th-en
[26] Chiiwii Live. URL: https://www.chiiwiidoctor.com/
[27] True Digital Park. URL: https://www.truedigitalpark.com/en

Healthtech Thailand is a Facebook community of healthtechs operating in Thailand (Startup, 2021), and it a useful entry resource and cooperative environment for healthtechs that want to enter the market.

In Thailand, supportive government policies are often implemented. They include incentivising manufacturers of high-risk or deep technology devices owners, and they are some of the key growth drivers for the Thai healthtech community (Staff, 2020).

Europe

Europe is a paradise in terms of healthcare. Nearly all European countries have a universal healthcare coverage. Though some people refer to it as Europe's "free health care" system, in reality, it is not really free as everyone contributes and pays for healthcare as a society, typically through tax (Steves, 2021). This means that you have a right to universal, high-quality and free healthcare, no matter who you are or where you come from, at any hospital, in any member of the EU.

With 53 countries under the umbrella of the WHO European Region (WHO, 2020), it is another hub of technology and rapidly emerging innovation. The challenges stem from capacitating citizenship and infrastructures with technology adoption.

In the entrepreneurial field, Europe shows stable high scores in Technology Adoption and Internationalisation, and the region's average score on Start-up Skills has recently climbed into the same league (Acs, Szerb, & Lloyd).

In 2020, more than 14,200 patent applications were filed with the European Patent Office (EPO) in the field of medical technology, representing a 2.6% growth in patent applications compared to the previous year (EPO, 2021). The medical technology field accounts for 8% of the total number of applications, the highest among all the sectors in Europe. 38% of these patent applications were filed from EPO countries (including EU27, the UK, Norway and Switzerland) and 62% from other countries, out of which the majority of applications were filed from the US (39%) (Europe, 2021).

It is also an oasis for health datasets, as the region has very powerful public health systems that constitute a reference worldwide. The European Data Strategy (Commission, 2021) aims to make the EU a leader in a data-driven society. Creating a single market for data will allow it to flow freely within the EU and across sectors for the benefit of businesses, researchers and public administrations.

A first step in this mission is democratisation of datasets, and healthtechs will have considerable opportunity in this field.

An example is the innovative Copernicus Project owned by the EU. It builds on a constellation of satellites that makes a huge number of daily observations, taking advantage of a global network of thousands of land, air, and marine-based sensors to create the most detailed pictures of Earth. And most of data/information delivered by Copernicus is made available and accessible to any citizen, and any organisation around the world on a free, full, and open basis (EU C., 2021).

This means that you have full access and can link your health innovations to the Earth Observation (EO) data that EU Copernicus puts at your service and at the service of citizens for free, being able to add substantial real-time value to your innovations. For example, you can link a wearable healthtech device, improving its daily monitoring of pathology and its early diagnosis by expanding the inputs to include geolocating EO datasets such as location, radiation, temperature, and air quality, among others. The model can find correlations between the data and link early diagnosis with EO geolocation data, coming up with a more accurate diagnosis and creating a geoclustered map of incidence and prevalence for the pathology.

EU Copernicus puts at your service all its DIAS (Data and Information Access Service) platforms. These include (1) WEkEO, which is the EU Copernicus DIAS reference service for environmental data, virtual processing environments and skilled user support, a platform for all audiences; (2) CREODIAS (CREODIAS, s.f.), where you can find the Earth Observation oriented data, mainly from the EU Satellite Copernicus program; and (3) MUNDI (MUNDI, s.f.), another project where you can access, combine and manage Earth Observation data with a powerful and scalable platform.

All these platforms could be applied to our healthtechs products and services.

Such is the case of the winner of Copernicus Masters in 2019, an operational UV product: The Ajuma UV-Bodyguard. It transmits by Bluetooth data such as current UV Strength, UV dose in percentage, UV-Forecast or the next five days and UV-Tracks. So, the user can decide the healthier time to go out in the sun.

Another use case including geotagging and geotailoring is Asmawatch, an app that collects information provided by the users combined with the information provided by satellites. Its USP is to co-create with users in real time, and it crosses the datasets obtained from users with those of the EO data satellites of Copernicus. Another example could be a solution that gives the user personalised information on their location: air pollution, pollen and radiation, for example.

Further potential applications could be for climate-sensitive diseases. How is climate change affecting the environment and the morbidity of people? Climate and health sectors have related challenges. Solutions not only include hazard data. If we combine EO data with comorbidities, we can understand the risks and needs related to climate health risks like water quality. This would entail using datasets and applications on vector-borne diseases and correlating them to climate change, since they are strongly associated. For example, consider mapping mosquito-borne pathogens, such as malaria, dengue fever, and yellow fever, to climate-related geolocation information and mosquito populations to create an online disease risk assessment platform. You might then enable predictive medicine by tracking the migration of mosquito populations and numbers and anticipating surges in the disease in certain locations.

Or why not incorporate datasets from other disciplines, like urban areas or deurbanising areas, farming systems related to food and health, or frontier areas such as socio-ecological systems. This could help us anticipate what landscapes are likely to face the most healthcare challenges so we can prioritise responses.

For example, we could answer how climate change is impacting the food system and consequently our health by mapping the macro and micronutrients present in the cereals like protein content, zinc and iron in the crops. Iron intake is related to development of anaemia and zinc, for example, and is key in the development of immune system. Thereby, data from EO data in the different environments can help to control or at least foresee this impact in the nutrition status and health status of a population.

Additionally, AI4EU democratises the use of its repositories as a full AI catalogue (Catalog, s.f.). Using available tools, most have already been prepared to be linked to DIAS datasets. Healthtechs would be wise to investigate all these tools, which could offer many opportunities for geo-related healthcare innovation.

You can address key challenges by using the standard products in the catalogue of Copernicus for comparability. For example, the PASYFO application is an operational pollen product that works through an allergy symptom forecasting system developed together with the Finnish Meteorological Institute, Medical University of Vienna and University of Latvia.

How can we better use EO data and deep dive into policies? How can we integrate all these gold datasets into our healthtech products and services? The first step is to address the unmet needs, and work together by creating partnerships, with new users, new companies and new jobs, and finally by finding actionable decisions at not only a European level but also a worldwide level.

As the digital transformation of the economy accelerates, Europe remains a robust technology market. Medical technology returned to top spot with 14.295 applicants at the EPO (EPO, 2021)[28] (+2.6% of growth in 2020 vs 2019). Meanwhile, pharmaceuticals and biotechnology surged, up +10.2% (2020 vs 2019) and +6.3% respectively (2020 vs 2019) (EPO, 2019).

Today, 12% of the world's unicorns are from Europe (Europe, 2020). The latest winners of the Digital Europe's Future Digital Unicorn 2021 Awards were Interact Medical Technologies, Turkey, which produces AI-guided robotic exoskeletons to enhance the mobility of disabled and elderly people and to reinforce the performance of industrial workers. Another winner was Hungarian Oncompass Medicine[29], a personalised healthtech solution that uses an AI-based medical software to choose the right targeted cancer therapy for every patient.

The focus of Europe is to empower people with a new generation of technologies. We must now strengthen its digital sovereignty and set standards, rather than following those of others—with a clear focus on data, technology, and infrastructure.

The European Medicines Agencies network strategy to 2025 outlines six priority focus areas: (1) availability and accessibility of medicines, (2) data analytics, digital tools and digital transformation, (3) innovation, (4) antimicrobial resistance and other emerging health threats, (5) supply-chain challenges and (6) sustainability of the network and operational excellence (Agency, 2021) (Commission, 2020).

New trends of the European Commission pushed on social media include #DigitalServicesAct, #DigitalEU, and #DigitalMarketsAct. They prioritise the digitalisation of the different industries including medicine and health (Commission, 2021).

MedTech Europe[30] is the European trade association representing the medical technology industries, from diagnosis to cure. In the last years it focused on pushing for innovation, highlighting the need to develop actions to enhance its use and use the data it generates to improve the health system, with regard to COVID-19 but also around the detection, diagnosis and monitoring of other diseases (Fenin, 2021). It also considers that PPPs can contribute to the construction of this favourable environment, through EU investment programs in research and innovation such as Horizon Europe.

Germany

Germany has a universal system with two main types of health insurance. Most Germans (86%) get their coverage primarily through the national public system (GKV, 2021), with others choosing voluntary private health insurance (NYC, 2021). Germans have access to three major (mandatory) healthcare coverages: (1) health insurance, (2) accident insurance, and (3) long-term care insurance co-financed by employer and employee.

Germany's medical device sector is the largest in Europe and the third largest in the world, taking up 10.2% of global healthtech production after the US (39.6%) and China (11.1%)

---

[28] This is the ranking in each technology field of the main consolidated applicants at the EPO in 2020 (first-named applicant principle). It is based on European patent applications filed with the EPO in each technology field. It includes direct European applications and international (PCT) applications that entered the European phase. Applications by identifiable subsidiaries, not necessarily located in the same country, are allocated to the consolidated applicants.

[29] https://www.oncompassmedicine.com/

[30] MedTech Europe. URL: https://www.medtecheurope.org/

(Kent, 2019). And at the same time, it is the world's third largest manufacturing nation with 9.9% of worldwide medical technology production (GTAI, 2021).

Despite the big dimension of Germany's healthcare system, the country is prioritising a digital adoption. For this reason, the Digital Healthcare Act program is expected to be implemented in the country. It will make integrative cloud EHRs mandatory in pharmacies and hospitals in the near future and encourage electronic sick leave notices, e-prescriptions and other services that can be prescribed electronically. In essence, patient's in-home healthtech solutions will deal with new methods of treatment and screening (NUB). Healthtech apps, like those tracking blood sugar levels, will be available on prescription as statutory health insurance will pay for them (Billing, 2021)

Telehealth is expected to become a commodity channel, as for example Kry[31], the Swedish telemedicine company (known as Livi in the UK and France) that is now also active in Germany as well as, a symptom-checking app: Ada Health[32], a disruptive medical AI that simplifies healthcare journeys and helps people take care of themselves.

From another side, the Digital Healthcare Act will enable doctors to provide information on digital services in real time on their websites, facilitate bureaucratic procedures and automate prescription systems, appointment requests, sending and reading of results and so on. Healthtechs that can support such processes will thrive.

EIT Health Germany,[33] funded by the EU, is an accelerator for healthtech startups allocated in Germany, and a good source of funding for new players in the ecosystem.

The United Kingdom

The UK has a government-sponsored universal healthcare system called the National Health Service (NHS). The NHS consists of a series of publicly funded healthcare systems in the UK. It includes the National Health Services (England), NHS Scotland, NHS Wales and Health and Social Care in Northern Ireland. Citizens are entitled to healthcare under this system but have the option to buy private health insurance as well (Chang, et al., 2021).

In the UK, digital tech gross value added (GVA)[34] increased by 43% from 2010 to 2018 (Nation, 2021). This exemplifies how the digital field contributed and is still contributing to the economy of the country.

The NHS has a Five Year Forward View. Its core focus is to cover the unmet needs related to (1) healthcare and its quality, (2) funding and (3) efficiency (NHS, 2015).

New Care Models (NHS, 2021) (NHS, 2016) is leading the way in new forms of integrated care that will become blueprints for the NHS as a whole. It targets an integrated primary and acute care system by joining up different stakeholders to operate together, including:

1. General Physicians (GP).
2. Hospitals and the community.
3. Mental health services.
4. Multispecialty community providers.

---

[31] Kry. URL: https://kry.health/
[32] Ada Health. URL: https://ada.com/
[33] EIT Health Germany. https://eit-health.de/en/startups/
[34] Gross value added (GVA) is defined as output (at basic prices) minus intermediate consumption (at purchaser prices); it is the balancing item of the national accounts' production account (eurostat, 2021).

Initiatives intend to move from in-hospital care to in-home care by improving consideration for elderly communities, joining up healthcare and rehabilitation services with urgent and emergency care. The models pursue approaches to improve the coordination of services and reduce pressure on A&E departments, boost acute care collaborations, and link hospitals together to improve their clinical and financial viability.

Meanwhile, the best-practice healthtech-driven project, the 100,000 Genomes Programme,[35] is delivering results of their own and are setting the standard for NHS innovations yet to come. In this line, access to innovative treatments for patients in the UK enables adoption to strengthen the medical technology sector as an economic driver.

As an entrepreneur in healthtech in the UK, you should know that through the creation of Innovation into Action (NHS, 2015) and the NHS Innovation Accelerator Program (NHS, 2021), the UK is trying to fast-track innovation to give patients more access to emerging innovative technology as well as address the conditions and cultural change needed to scale these innovations and impacts across the system. This attempt will likely create an environment that bolsters the adoption of healthtech products and services, for those who consider scaling in the UK.

You can easily find quick-win steps for your healthtech and bridges of collaboration at Innovate UK,[36] where you can search for funding opportunities, register for online funding webinars, connect with innovation experts and more or find the right support you need.

The association of British HealthTech Industries[37] is the UK's leading industry association for healthtech, so enrol in it if you plan to enter the UK healthtech market.

On the other hand, the Tech Nation[38], a publicly and privately funded accelerator, can provide fuel for you as it extends a hand to founders, and scaling companies that want to add value to the healthcare system. They can help you with coaching, networking and relevant guidance to help you in your growth journey.

Some examples of thriving healthtechs in the UK include Birdie,[39] a UK healthtech founded in 2017. It is reinventing in-home elderly care with a complete software homecare solution. Its intuitive app is the operating system for the care community to deliver more coordinated, personalised and preventative care.

Working closely with the NHS, Medefer is another example.[40] It is now included in the NHS England Increasing Capacity Framework. Medefer is a Care Quality Commission registered provider, working in partnership with the NHS to provide a virtual outpatient service and deliver faster, better care for patients. It uses its software platform to review and manage General Physician (GP) referrals online by its team of UK-registered, specialist consultants, so patients do not have to wait for an in-hospital appointment any more.

Spain

Spain has a public universal coverage healthcare system ranked 7th best in the world in 2000 by the World Health Organization (WHO, 2000). And it is ranked 1st in the world for organ transplants (Govan, 2017) (Givan, 2016).

[35] The 100,000 Genomes Project is a now-completed UK Government project managed by Genomics England that is sequencing whole genomes from National Health Service patients.
[36] https://www.gov.uk/government/organisations/innovate-uk
[37] https://www.abhi.org.uk/
[38] TechNation. URL: https://technation.io/about-us/
[39] Birdie. URL: https://www.birdie.care/
[40] Quibim. URL: https://quibim.com/

In Spain, the Ministry of Economic Affairs and Digital Transformation (MINECO) is pushing for a countrywide, disruptive change vehiculated by technology in the healthcare system. It is led by the superior body, the Secretary of State for Digitalization and Artificial Intelligence (SEDIA), which is in charge of the functions related to the policy of promoting the digitisation of society and the economy in a way that is respectful of individual and collective rights, as well as the values of the Spanish legal system (BOE, 2020).

In defining the concrete action plans in accordance to the national AI strategy (Commission, 2021), the Spanish government takes stock of the priorities and policy recommendations of the R+D+i strategy in artificial intelligence (MICINN, s.f.), the Spanish Digital Agenda 2025 (Digital, 2021), and the Recovery, Transformation and Resilience plan (Crex, 2020). It is already developing a secure framework for interconnection databases and data management in the field of public health (Digital, 2021).

Through tractor projects that accelerate the adoption of new healthtech products and services, small and mid-size enterprises (SMEs) are growing and going global rapidly. Further, such projects are boosting their capacities for innovation and data-based decision-making. This aligns with the objective that national sectors benefit as much as possible from the European "data lakes" promoted by the European Data Strategy (Data Strategy, 2020) as well as from the sectoral initiatives of the Digital Europe program.

Digital Health constitutes one of the major transformational areas of the country (Digital, 2021). It is aiming towards prediction, personalisation, efficiency, effectiveness and quality of health by streamlining information systems and promoting the sharing and interoperability of data in a secure way, as well as contributing to the personalisation of the services provided. This leaves much opportunity for healthtechs specialising in this area. For example, Quibim[41] is a healthtech with its own ecosystem of specialised suites for every body part. They develop algorithms that extract data from medical imaging samples, such as X-ray, to find abnormalities, and Computed Tomography (CT) scans to detect biomarkers for early diagnosis, contributing to a more personalised and precision medicine.

Another example of a healthtech contributing to a transformational shift towards improved quality of care and efficiency in chronic patients is Medicsen.[42] It was announced as the winner of the virtual Healthtech South Summit (April 2020). It was founded to improve quality of life with chronic diseases. Its Medicsen Smartpatch is the first needle-free and wearable drug delivery device, and they strive to deliver the latest technological advances to the medical world in order to reduce pain and uncertainty.

Fenin[43] is the Spanish medtech federation. Fenin recently launched an initiative campaign #espiasdelaboratorio to promote the awareness of the importance of in vitro analysis data collection considering that it generates significant returns in terms of greater disease prevention, sizeable efficiency and quality of care, and better health outcomes, with a benefit to society as a whole. Therefore, healthtechs specialising in this area would find Spain to be an ecosystem that is highly supportive.

---

[41] Quibim. URL: https://quibim.com/
[42] Medicsen. URL: https://www.medicsen.com/en/
[43] Fenin. URL: https://www.fenin.es/

The Eastern Mediterranean

Political volatility is rife in the Eastern Mediterranean. During the last decade, at least 10 countries experienced occupation, internal conflict or a complex emergency. The recent economic recession has worsened the situation, forcing many governments to cut their social services budget—including health. The anti-government protests, uprisings, and armed rebellions—known as the Arab Spring—will probably impact health policies, programmes and population health (WHO, 2012).

The region has many divergences between the least developed low-income countries, middle-income countries and high-income countries. Such divergences are unavoidable, and they relate to key healthcare matters:

1. Financing of universal health coverage.
2. Health workforce capacity and balance.
3. Service provision and accessibility of primary health care services.
4. Implementation of essential service packages vs escalating costs and limited capacity for cost and cost-effectiveness analysis.
5. Health information, covering functioning, management and fragmentation.
6. Health technologies, specifically access to essential technologies and the capacity of regulatory authorities to guard the quality, safety and efficacy clinical health technologies and devices (WHO, 2012).

In the entrepreneurial field, the Middle East and North Africa demonstrate strength in product innovation and risk capital (Acs, Szerb, & Lloyd).

According to Al Masah, capital investment in the Middle East and North Africa (Mena) healthcare sector is booming. Over $144 billion will enter Mena-wide medical facilities by end-2020, with GCC nations contributing over half (Buller, 2020).

The advancement of the for-profit private health sector is reflected in the quality, responsiveness, and image of public health services. Large private health sectors are associated with higher out-of-pocket spending in most countries.

Access to basic health services continues to be a problem in most least developed countries or those in emergency situations. Reasons include (1) destroyed infrastructures, (2) lack of roads or security barriers, (3) lack of personnel, (4) lack of access to medicines or (5) inability to afford medical care. Therefore, many countries have introduced essential health packages at the primary health care level to jump over these obstacles.

Integration of care for noncommunicable diseases and mental ill health in the essential service package continues to be a challenge (WHO, 2012). Healthtechs that want to expand in the region should consider solving this challenge with their products and services pipeline.

Here are the healthcare priorities for the region, on which healthtechs can focus with considerable benefit:

■ To move towards universal and equal-access healthcare.
■ Advance health systems based on primary healthcare following the principles stated in the Qatar declaration (2008) (that aim to deliver high-quality primary care as a fundamental for the healthcare system, with the purpose of creating a system of integrated services with the patient in the centre).
■ To prioritise public healthcare programs, promoting communicable disease, noncommunicable disease, and maternal and child health-related programmes.

■ To ensure a versatile highly skilled, well managed, balanced, motivated and well distributed health workforce.
■ To maximise family practice programmes to improve primary care.
■ To improve efficiency, management and performance in the public network of hospitals (which currently consume 60–80% of the total healthcare budget) extending coverage for marginalised or poorer populations.

Priorities regarding to health technology in the region are the following:

1. To ensure access to essential technologies by launching national policies, improving regulatory authorities and procurement, promoting rational use and good manufacturing practices, and implementing best-practice governance initiatives.
2. To build effective technologies management by expanding the skillset of technology staff.
3. To strengthen national health information systems, by making them a priority to ensure that data is reliable, complete and timely, as well as accessible and properly used for decision making and operations. Equally important is to stimulate demand for truthful information and evidence.
4. To be prepared and responsive in emergencies and major disasters, with efficient resilience to more extensive and complicated situations.
5. To empower health systems to address social determinants, through practices that bring them closer to universal access and equity in multidisciplinary and multisector operations (for example: HIV/AIDS, noncommunicable diseases, road safety), and by promoting community-based initiatives that reduce poverty and improve health (WHO, 2012).

The WHO establishes a few areas in the region that we as healthtechs should consider addressing as priorities to bring value to the healthcare system and help strengthen it:

1. Improve analysis and recording of health system interventions and best practices.
   – With the development of healthtech products and services focused on achieving equity in health and its universal coverage.
   – Supporting the training of health systems collaborators and that in turn support the drafting of new health policies.
   – Establish PPPs that support the expansion of low- and middle-income countries, establishing basic service portfolios in countries such as Afghanistan, Iraq, Somalia, and South Sudan.
2. Development of new practices, tools and methodologies.
   – Generate optimised tools for early diagnosis, universal coverage and cost-effectiveness in primary care.
   – Focusing primary care on the patient and his humanisation in the family model.
   – Empower highly skilled caretakers (nurses).
   – Build a unique platform for the health system.
   – Launch guidelines that help the implementation of national plans, good workforce practices, autonomy of hospitals and continuous training as well as the provision of high-quality services.
3. High skillset and up-to-date training of the healthcare system workforce.
   – To develop a continuous training program for the workforce of the national health system and WHO's staff.
4. Advance universal access to health and community participation in this process through dialogue and understanding of the optimal policies to implement.

Universal access is an area with high potential to add value to the public health system like in other regions of the world. The region in general has high unmet needs that would be basic in other countries, although with the adequate implementation of health technology quick wins, achievements can be earned in record time. For more stable countries with fewer ups and downs, consider to supply back-to-basics essential health coverage for citizens. Though, while some barriers in Eastern Mediterranean region are obvious, the challenges and opportunities outweigh them.

Saudi Arabia

Saudi's healthcare sector is largely funded by public funds. And, in recent decades, the Kingdom of Saudi Arabia has made significant progress in improving its healthcare infrastructure and system (Saudi, 2021).

Saudi Arabia also offers a high-quality healthcare system, with world-class facilities and services. Recent reforms aimed at improving the quality of life in the Kingdom have opened opportunities for pioneers in different key sectors such as health (Saudi, 2021).

The Health Transformation Program is one of the priorities included in Saudi Arabia's Vision 2030 goals, by further digitising and innovating in the healthcare sector (Programs, 2021).

The program aims to transform the Kingdom's health sector to be more comprehensive, efficient and integrated. A new system focused on values, transparency and sustainability is desired, promoting public health and prevention. The intention is to expand the portfolio of digital health services and solutions, as well as improve the quality of health services.

By the end of 2025, the Kingdom wants 100% of the population to be covered by the unified EHR system and 88% of the population, including those in rural areas, covered by inclusive health services (Programs, 2021).

Alongside this, key objectives for the strategic health program for 2030 are (1) universal access, (2) improved quality and efficiency and (3) the promotion of prevention programs including road safety.

Some of the best-practices implemented in 2020 come from the Ministry of Health in Saudi Arabia expanding the country's telemedicine services by using advanced technology in health services. Examples include the booking of more than 67 million appointments through Mawidi and 8.6 million medical consultations developed through the Seha application.[44]

Mawidi is an innovative platform that provides technical solutions which use artificial intelligence to facilitate access to healthcare services and contribute to the objectives of Saudi Arabia 2030. E-health app Seha was introduced in 2018 and allows individuals to have face-to-face visual medical consultations with their doctors on their smartphones. A recent study (Alharbi, et al., 2021) provided evidence that the Seha app improved the delivery of healthcare in Saudi Arabia. Users of the app had a better health experience in terms of their perceived ease of access to healthcare services; their satisfaction with healthcare services; and the efficiency of the system, measured by the number of required doctor visits.

At the centre of Saudi Arabia's Vision 2030 plan, NEOM[45] is the Kingdom's smart city project. It has an opportunity to become the first healthtech capital of the world, and a global hub for innovation and cooperation in health and wellness technology (Mohammadian-Molina, 2020). The mentioned NEOM HealthTech Hub is establishing partnerships and collaborations with research

---

[44] Mawidi. URL: https://mawidy.com/en/
[45] NEOM. URL: https://www.neom.com/en-us

institutions like the Centre of Excellence for NEOM Research at King Abdullah University of Science and Technology.

Young, digitally native people in the region, represented in the Gulf Cooperation Council (GCC), reveal they are ready to adopt artificial intelligence (AI) and robotics for the coverage of unmet medical needs.

Some entities in Saudi Arabia play a fundamental role in consolidating the region as a global healthtech hub. Such is the case of the Future Investment Initiative Institute (FII), which is a key centre for coordinating policies and actions (Mohammadian-Molina, 2020). You should research these entities if you wish to operate in the region.

United Arab Emirates

The United Arab Emirates (UAE) has a comprehensive publicly funded healthcare service and a growing private healthcare sector that greatly raises the bar for quality of care. The health system undergoes federal and emirate regulation, with public health services administered by, for example, the Ministry of Health and Prevention, the Abu Dhabi Health Authority (HAAD), the Dubai Health Authority (DHA), and the Emirates Health Authority (EHA) (Embassy, 2021).

Building a consolidated and resilient healthcare industry is a key priority for the UAE United Arab Emirates (UAE).

While the UAE currently spends around 0.7% of GDP on R&D&i, it plans to invest more than double that before 2030 (Leadership, 2021). The aim is to become the next-generation global hub for biotechnology and life sciences, welcoming more next-gen medicine and healthtech companies with an ecosystem that encourages innovation.

An example of this entrepreneurial drive is healthtech start-up Astragene.[46] It is the Middle East's first molecular diagnostics manufacturing company and produces in-vitro diagnostic indicators, kits and instruments and provides customised AI solutions on every desktop to serve as Decision Support Systems for the important problems in a pathology.

Dubai Science Park is pushing to host more companies for their contribution to the progress of health. Indeed, the UAE is betting on the health technology industry and its support for science. It is expected that Dubai will position itself in a few years as a world reference medical centre alongside San Francisco, Seoul and Basel (Leadership, 2021).

In the same line, Sarjah Research Technology and Innovation Park (SRTI)[47] aims to coordinate and develop an innovation ecosystem that promotes R&D&i and supports their respective business activities and PPPs between industry, government and academia.

An example of this support to the healthtech community is that for Nabta Health.[48] Based in Sharjah Innovation Park, it is merging the best of digital and traditional healthcare to empower women to identify and manage noncommunicable diseases. It has established a partnership with the University of Sharjah to help accelerate its research and development (R&D) ambitions, planning to sign joint ventures so that they can continue innovating in the women's healthcare field (Buller, 2020).

---

[46] Astragene. URL: https://www.astragene.com/
[47] https://srtip.ae/
[48] https://nabtahealth.com/

Western Pacific Region

Over the past decade, countries in the WHO Western Pacific Region have advanced considerably and made commitments towards Universal Health Coverage (UHC). The Regional Committee has highlighted the need for universal health coverage based on the five pillars of high-performance health systems: (1) quality, (2) efficiency, (3) equity, (4) accountability, (5) sustainability and resilience (WHO, 2021). This invites the member countries to develop action plans with the objective of UHC and based on the 5 pillars.

Equity in healthcare is a priority objective that most countries in the region are yet to attain (Pacific, 2019). For example, some 60% of the population are without health coverage for essential services. And 20% of families allocate over 10% of their income for health coverage (WHO, 2021).

The Sustainable Development Goals (SDGs) promote "just, rights-based, equitable and inclusive" action to overcome current barriers and promote expansion, social development and environmental protection for everyone (General Assembly, 2015). If we want to drive progress towards health equity in Western Pacific Region, we must focus on helping to facilitate universal access to high-quality health. In addition, we must push to ensure equity in broader factors in the health field to achieve equitable sustainability, accounting for situational factors such as where people grow, live, and work as they get older (Pacific, 2019).

The SDGs recognise how important it is to track equity and monitor its progress. Target 17.18 sets out the need to "increase significantly the availability of high-quality, timely and reliable data disaggregated by income, gender, age, race, ethnicity, migratory status, disability, geographic location and other characteristics relevant in national contexts", especially for small island developing states (SIDS) and the least developed countries (LDCs) (WHO, 2020).

Finally, most of the health data in these countries exists only on paper. Without stronger digital health infrastructure and the data it produces, some cutting-edge AI tools cannot be applied across LMIC countries (USAID, 2021). As such, healthtechs aiming to digitalise this data could find considerable success.

Malaysia

Malaysia has universal coverage and an efficient public health system, which co-exists with a private one (Insurance, 2021).

Currently a middle-income economy, Malaysia is near to achieving high-income economy status (Mottain, 2021). Malaysia has high growth potential in healthtech. While the slow speed of mobile compared to other ASEAN countries could be a barrier, this situation is already being fixed thanks to latest government measures (Malaysia, 2021).

Malaysia has six times as many doctors per person than Indonesia, for example, meaning access to traditional health care is wide (Star, 2020). The healthtech ecosystem is favourable thanks to the support and investment initiatives promoted by the government. However, healthtechs are faced with some minor barriers such as staff training or lack of facilities and advanced devices that are essential for the progress of healthcare (Pharma, 2020).

The Ministry of Health in Malaysia has digitised and integrated EHRs from health facilities across the country and then enhanced its analysis further by applying AI predictive analytics tools to this data.

Malaysia, together with Brazil and India, has focused its model on predictive medicine, for example using AI to achieve early diagnosis and sustainability. Artificial Intelligence in Medical

Epidemiology (AIME) (LinkedIn, 2021)[49] is an AI-enabled platform that helps a country's Ministry of Health predict future outbreaks of diseases like Zika and dengue in a specific geography months before their possible occurrence and helps the Healthcare systems to prevent the outbreak.

Overhead, Malaysia and Sweden have come together to introduce the Digital Health Innovation Challenge. Launched 15 January 2021, the Innovation Challenge invites start-ups registered in Malaysia to identify solutions in solving healthcare challenges, especially related to non-communicable diseases (NCD) (DNA, 2021).

Authorities have introduced additional innovative measures like Industry4WRD[50] 2018-2025 national policy on Industry 4.0 in 2018, which laid out Malaysia's vision for the manufacturing sector for the next 10 years. The Industry4WRD policy is a national policy which aims to transform the manufacturing sector and related services. This policy consists of three visions in making Malaysia as: (1) a strategic partner for smart manufacturing and related services in the Asia Pacific; (2) primary destination for investment in the high technology industry (3) and a total solutions provider for cutting-edge technology. Such policy can support new health technology initiatives that want to make their way in the country.

However, you have to take into account that the Industry4WRD policy promotes the development of Malaysia's own products and services using innovative manufacturing capabilities based on technology (Government M., 2021).

In this line, Malaysia's MYR3bn Industry Digitalisation Transformation Fund offers companies an annual interest subsidy of 2% on the financing taken to upgrade their production technology (Healthcare, 2019).

Another interesting project is Digital Lifestyle Malaysia, which promotes and accelerates the development and adoption of digital applications and services. It includes the adoption of IoT infrastructures in internet-based business transactions to promote growth and better quality of life. The National IoT action plan aims to position Malaysia as the regional development centre for IoT of reference, with the mission of creating a national ecosystem that encourages the use and industrialisation of IoT, becoming a growth driver for the country's economy. It is expected that IoT will contribute MYR42.5 billion[51] by 2025 to the gross national income (GNI) of Malaysia (Malaysia.gov, 2021).

MyDIGITAL initiative (Yassin & Menteri, 2021) constitutes a bridge towards the new Malaysia Digital Economy Blueprint (MyDigital, 2021). With the initiative, it is expected that in 2025 the digital economy will contribute 22.6% to the country's GDP. The plan is to overcome the limiting barriers faced by the most disadvantaged groups to health services, among others (quality education and employment) due to the lack of access to the internet and smart devices (MyDigital, 2021). It calls for bringing medical facilities to remote villages (Sunil, 2021). Another objective is to provide opportunities to companies through governmental initiatives such as: (1) Information Security Governance, (2) Risk & Compliance Health Check Assessment and (3) cyber security empowerment programmes for Micro, Small and Medium Enterprises (MSMEs) in order to determine the level of cybersecurity and investment required (MyDigital, 2021).

---

[49] Artificial Intelligence in Medical Epidemiology. AIME. AIME offers data and analytics of global diseases using predictive platforms to steer the future of public health. URL: http://aime.life/

[50] https://www.malaysia.gov.my/portal/content/30610

[51] Malaysian ringgit is the currency of Malaysia. 1 MYR equivalence to approximately 0.24 USD (December 2021).

Among others, priority initiatives involving government health agencies are (1) the development of a favourable environment for rapid adoption of technology with healthtech products and (2) the acceleration of the use of the Malaysian Health Data Warehouse (MyHDW) with the inclusion of blockchain (MyDigital, 2021). These are important factors to consider if you intend start-up or scaleup in Malaysia.

Taiwan

The national health system in Taiwan (National Health Insurance) is made up of a mandatory single payer[52] social insurance plan that centralises all health funds. Today we can consider Taiwan to have achieved universal healthcare coverage for its citizens.

Taiwan is the modern version of China when it comes to healthtech. It is particularly open to digital innovation in health. A broadly known campaign by the country's disruptive Ministry of Digital states: "When we see IoT, let's make it an internet of beings. When we see "virtual reality", let's make it shared reality. When we see "machine learning", let's make it collaborative learning. When we see "user experience", let's make it about human experience. When we hear "the singularity is near", let us remember: the Plurality is here."

The Ministry of Science and Technology (MOST) is supporting the field of AI, founding four Research Centers for Innovation in AI. The sub-centre of the MOST AI Innovation Research Center at National Taiwan University (NTU) is the "All-Vista Healthcare Sub-Center". It aims to be a hub for biomedicine, promoting in-home medicine, and increasing people's quality of life. It is encouraging the development of early diagnosis through artificial intelligence that helps current medical practices with the retrospective analysis of large amounts of data such as EHRs, diagnosis registry or literature reviews, also diagnostic imaging. It aims to interconnect AI technologies and methodologies with their practical use to be implemented in real life (Highlight, 2019).

Being the national standards body in Taiwan, the BSMI is an agency you must consider. It bears responsibility for developing and operating a standardised system that is relevant and can effectively respond to regulatory and market needs, as well as keep pace with scientific and technological development (MOEA, 2019).

Taiwan's "5+2 Industrial Innovation Plan" which picks out "pillar industries" meant to transform Taiwan's industry, incorporates the (1) IoT (2) Biomedical, (3) Green Energy, (4) Smart Machinery, and (5) Defence. Added later were high-value (6) agriculture and the (7) circular economy (Ferry, 2017). It is good to know that the plan provides funding and capital-access for businesses in these sectors and will involve amending existing statutes and regulations that impede industrial transformation.

Since the recent approval by the Food and Drug Administration (FDA), the US has started using an AI system that will help doctors to read chest X-rays and thus more quickly detect COVID-19 infections. In the same line, in Taiwan, an AI-based diagnostic system, NTU Medical Genie, was developed jointly by a start-up called Taiwan Medical Imaging Co. and some medical institutions (Taiwan, 2021).

---

[52] Note: In a single payer healthcare system, rather than multiple competing health insurance companies, a single public or quasi-public agency takes responsibility for financing healthcare for all residents. That is, everyone has health insurance under a one health insurance plan, and has access to necessary services—including doctors, hospitals, long-term care, prescription drugs, dentists and vision care. However, individuals may still choose where they receive care (Christopher, 2016).

NTU Medical Genie is an AI Decision Support System for Precision Medicine (MAHC, 2021). The project aims to construct an AI clinical decision support system for precision medicine based on AI technologies at the National Taiwan University Hospital (NTUH) healthcare system.

"Asia IoT Alliance" (AIoTA)[53] is the first Taiwanese non-profitable organisation aiming to provide a platform that connects Taiwanese IoT providers across different industries, industrial chains and the global market. AIoTA has four core values: (1) to build the IoT industrial chain, (2) to promote international interaction, (3) to seize the opportunities of the border and (3) to engage alliance members. Besides, AIoTA promotes doing business with industrial chains, companies and the global market.

iXensor[54] is a pioneer in mobile health (mHealth) with its iXensor PixoTest, the first m-health camera-based blood test, allowing healthcare professionals to provide in-patient health check-ups (BBC, 2021). And its recent PixoTest® POCT COVID-19 Antigen Testing is a smart antigen testing solution—issuing test results to PixoHealth Pass App users—designed as an aid to managing the COVID-19 outbreak for corporations, manufacturers, schools, travel and hospitality industries (iXensor, 2021).

Biomed Taiwan[55] aims to transform Taiwan into a hub of biotech and medical R&D&i in Asia. One of the main goals of biomed Taiwan is to Build the Biomedical Corridor. This will encompass different innovators in a single biomedical corridor including all the key points of the biomedical value chain. Among them are (1) to improve the infrastructure and ecosystem of the industry, (2) strengthen and make laws and regulations transparent and (3) promote talent, capital and other areas to create a positive environment for acceleration of growth biotechnological and medical in the country.

The other two objectives are (1) entry to international markets to establish partnerships with global reference research centres, opening the doors to international talents and building new innovative R & D & I centres; and (2) to promote industries that support quality of life especially for the elderly with well-being solutions for aging populations, with precision and quality medicine.

If you are a healthtech entrepreneur planning to start-up or scaleup in Taiwan, the government might help you through the National Development Fund Start-up Angel Project. The project is specifically designed to support entrepreneurs with innovative business ideas who are planning to establish and run their own start-ups in the country and thereby ensure that companies with innovative capabilities and global potential could grow rapidly in Taiwan. Besides, the SMEs National Development Fund Investment aims to help SMEs that need financing for their business plans, international technology transfer or partnering projects and would like to receive private or public funds. (Bio.Taiwan, 2021).

Also, the Taiwan Venture Capital Association (TVCA) provides additional information and assistance to address your needs for funds.[56]

The push for the development of a favourable ecosystem to advance healthtech solutions in Taiwan is well known, with a continuous injection of talent and innovative technologies. In this line, the Taiwan AI Academy,[57] Taiwan AI Labs, and the Artificial Intelligence Academy Foundation[58] are Taiwan's representative institutions in the field of AI education and research.

---

[53] https://www.asiaiota.org/
[54] https://www.ixensor.com/ixensor_web/
[55] https://bio.taiwan.gov.tw/#events
[56] https://bio.taiwan.gov.tw/Entrepreneur/
[57] Taiwan AI Academy. Linkedin URL: https://www.linkedin.com/company/twaiacademy/?originalSubdomain=tw
[58] https://en.aiacademy.tw/foundation/

From the private perspective, consider Microsoft Taiwan Accelerating for start-ups,[59] Sparklabs taipei,[60] or Taiwan AI per Robotics Accelerator.[61]

Japan

Japan has a national health system with universal coverage of its citizens, with enrolment in either an employment-based or a residence-based health. It is financed mainly by taxes and individual contributions. In addition, it offers premium services including screening tests, prenatal care, and infectious diseases aid with a co-payment of 30%.

With more than 25% of the population categorised as elderly, the country is the oldest society in the world, a distinction that the United Nations Population Division predicts it will maintain until at least the middle of this century as the percentage of older people in its population grows even more (Japan, 2021).

In 2014, the Japanese government adopted its SAKIGAKE strategy to streamline the adoption of innovative medical products (pharmaceuticals, medical devices, and regenerative products) from Japan (Team, 2014) (Maruyama, et al., 2018). J-Start-up[62] supports the Japanese start-up ecosystem with over 10,000 start-ups to scaleup in global markets overseas.

Also, national, regional, and local initiatives support foreign investment and invite the establishment of foreign start-ups as healthtechs. An example of this initiative is Shibuya Start-up Support[63] with over 2,000 start-ups that want to establish and grow their business in Shibuya.

An example of a Japanese local municipality establishing an advanced health data platform is Hacarus[64], an AI start-up from Kyoto, Japan. Their AI Sparse Modeling based AI offers customers highly accurate predictions by taking advantage of its three main strengths: it does not require large amounts of data for training, can provide explainable solutions and has a lightweight design that offers high speeds and low power consumption in a variety of environments. Using 3D printing, Exiii[65] created Handiii,[66] which uses EMG sensors to develop a myoelectric prosthetic arm for people without arms at an affordable cost. The prosthetic arm is smartphone-connected to provide algorithmic reports for doctors or caregivers (Chin, 2021).

In between the top 20 companies filing AI-related patents, 12 are based in Japan, 3 are from the US and 2 are from China (WIPO, 2019). So, Japan is clearly an area that welcomes high-tech healthtechs.

Australia

Australia has a universal healthcare system called Medicare (Triage, 2014). It provides free inpatient care in public hospitals and access to most medical services and prescription drugs. There is also voluntary private health insurance, giving access to private hospitals and to some services the public system does not cover (NYC, 2021).

---

[59] https://www.microsoft.com/taiwan/mtcaccelerator/default.htm
[60] https://www.sparklabstaipei.com/program
[61] https://www.tairax.com.tw/index.aspx
[62] J-Startup. URL: https://www.j-startup.go.jp/en/about/
[63] Shibuya Startup Support. URL: https://shibuya-startup-support.jp/
[64] Hacarus. URL: https://hacarus.com/
[65] https://exiii.jp/wrist-dk2/
[66] https://ifworlddesignguide.com/entry/148430-handiii

The Australian Digital Health Agency focuses on putting data and technology safely to work for patients, consumers and the healthcare professionals who look after them. At the same time there is the Department of Health, which supports the Australian Digital Health Agency to deliver the "My Health Record" project under the umbrella My Health Records Act (Health, 2021), including its policy and governance. This ensures the regulation of My Health Records system operates optimally for citizens (digitalhealth.gov.au, 2021).

My Health Record, an initiative led by the Australian Government and the Australian Digital Health Agency My Health Record, is an Electronic Health Record management tool that brings together health information from the patient, his healthcare providers and Medicare.

A second phase is planned to use My Health Record data for research and public health soon.

Caretakers and pharmacists can add information to EHRs, and up to 2-years Medicare history can be added at their opening. A best-practice model, "My Health Record" helps achieve a more equitable medical care for all regions. For example, the project succeeds in making the Tjuntjunt area in Western Australia, a remote area, where telehealth and the use of "My Health Record" have transformed the provision of more equitable health care for the entire country.

Digital Health Agency's Practice Incentives Program (ePiP) digital health incentive is a Medicare-funded Telehealth initiative. It helps people to see specialists without having to move long distances by promoting the adoption of the cutting-edge health technologies by HCPs. This helps upskill HCPs, improving and adding value to their healthcare practice (Health, 2021).

In Australia, government regulatory bodies like the Health Technology Assessment Team reviews cutting-edge health technologies to make sure they have enough evidence in meeting (1) high quality standards, (2) safety, (3) efficacy, (4) effectiveness and (5) cost-effectivity standards stablished by health services (Health, 2021). And in the same line, the Office of the Gene Technology Regulator from the Australian Government Department of Health provides bureaucratic support to the Gene Technology Regulator in the performance of the functions under the Gene Technology Act 2000 (OGTR & Regulator, s.f.).

Another example of best practices in healthtech in Australia is the Provider Connect Australia project (digitalhealth.gov.au, 2021). This new technology maintains the accuracy of the healthcare service along with the contact details of nationwide physicians. It is expected to contain spending at a saving of $30 million a year by 2025. Provider Connect Australia (formerly SRA) cuts red tape for healthcare providers and improves the quality of healthcare information across the country's health ecosystem.

Australians can choose an electronic prescription over the traditional paper prescription, an important shift in response to COVID-19 (digitalhealth.gov.au, 2021). In this field, there is an emerging opportunity for clinical SaaS healthtechs, patient treatment compliance and management devices enhancing their products to provide innovative options and further disruption in the field when using electronic prescriptions for medicine supply.

These governmental shifts have created new disruptive private initiatives, ensuring the democratisation of healthtech throughout the country. One example is Butterfly iQ[67] from Butterfly Network. It is making more precise diagnoses at in-patient (in-office) check-ups, and in-emergency rooms and in-ambulances. Using ultrasound technology, considered to be the safest and most widely used medical imaging equipment, it does medical imaging inside the body and can detect the presence of anything from blood flow to tumours. The device has 13+ settings that can look at musculoskeletal, abdominal, aorta, bladder, cardiac, and paediatric abdomen; all these functions are FDA approved.

---

[67] Butterfly Network. URL:https://www.butterflynetwork.com/uk/

Clinic to Cloud[68] is another disruptive healthtech company in the line of the Australian peer Genie Solutions.[69] It operates in the specialist patient management market, which claims to have taken a lot of share off the market leader in its first few years.

Australia has initiatives such as the Industrial Digital Innovation Hub to attract foreign healthtechs, an Australasian initiative (Forum, 2021) involving a PPP alliance between the private Siemens and Royal Melbourne Institute of Technology (RMIT). Currently, it is connecting Australian and Vietnam campuses with the global industry.

You should also be aware of the Australian Healthtech Hub, which connects Australia's pharma, biotech and healthtech industry professionals and key industry stakeholders to create a diverse, inclusive, and resourceful network (Hub, 2021).

China

Over 95% of China's population is covered by a health insurance programme, including public, private and insurance programs. Besides, public health insurance is responsible for the payment of half of all medical costs. Urban Employee Basic Medical Insurance is financed mainly from employee and employer payroll taxes, with minimal government funding (Focus, 2020).

Also, in 2018, China spent approximately 6.6% of GDP on healthcare, which amounts to RMB 5,912 billion. 28% was paid by central and regional governments, 44% was financed by publicly funded health insurance, private health insurance, or social health donations, and 28% was paid out-of-pocket (Focus, 2020).

Every Chinese person is by law the owner of their own data, as in Europe with the GDPR rule (Tracxn, 2021).

China has set itself up as a promising country for healthtech start-ups and small and midsize enterprises (SMEs). China's second quarter of 2020 saw an investment peak for venture-backed healthcare companies. Led by MGI Tech, from Chinese genome sequencing BGI Group, there was $1 billion in investment in Series B round financing. Meanwhile, Chinese biopharma Mabwell raised $278 million in the Series A round, led by Shiyu Capital.

With $7.2 billion raised,[70] Shanghai leads the Chinese healthcare funding landscape. This is almost the same amount ($7.4 billion) as the second city in the world for venture-backed healthcare investment: San Francisco, which comes just after Cambridge, Massachusetts (SVB, 2021).

In essence, Chinese, the healthcare market still has plenty of room to grow due to the country's ongoing demographic shift, which is expected to rebound by 2030. The country's elderly population (over 65) is estimated to rise from 166 million in 2018 to 250 million by 2030 (Bermingham, 2019).

For the same date, the country aims to reach a life expectancy of 79 years, the same as in the United States today (Coppens, 2020) (macrotrends, 2021). If we consider that in 2020, life expectancy in China was 76.96 years (Commons, 2019), coming from a much lower rate of 66.84 back in the 1980 (Nations, 2017), it is a big shift in terms of QALYs.

Meanwhile, it is anticipated that as more people move to urban areas and the number of wealthy families increases, healthcare costs will also increase (Leng, 2019).

Even though Western countries spend 10 times more per capita in terms of health than China, the county's focus is in pushing for preventive healthcare, supporting for areas in primary care,

---

[68] Clinic to Cloud. URL: https://www.clinictocloud.com/
[69] Genie Solutions. URL: https://www.geniesolutionssoftware.com.au/
[70] Amout raised from 2 years 2018–2020 period.

e.g., diabetes, as it is one of the prevailing issues of a system more focused on tier 1 hospitals and centres of excellence (Leng, 2019).

The Healthy China 2030 Plan (PRC, 2021) (Bank, 2019) is a priority for the progress of the Chinese healthcare system and is implemented by the National Health Commission (NHC). With it, China is becoming a powerful country in healthtech innovation and implementing a totally new model of medical care that will track the patient 24/7.

The National Health Commission is the main national health agency or body in China. It (1) develops national health policies; (2) leads medical and healthcare reform and (3) coordinates public health, medical care, health emergency responses, and family planning services. The State Administration for Market Regulation (SAMR) oversees the China Drug Administration, which is responsible for drug approvals and licenses, and in healthtech, various bodies under SAMR ensure compliance in the field.

One of this institution's priorities, according to a document published on China's SAMR website, is that companies including healthtechs should not use data, algorithms or other technical means to hijack traffic or influence users' choices (Reuters, 2021).

Also in the healthcare field, the National Medical Products Administration (NMPA) is the Chinese agency for regulating drugs and medical devices (formerly the China Food and Drug Administration or (CFDA)).

The cyberspace affairs commission works with the National Health Commission (NHC) (China, 2021) and The Ministry of Science and Technology to regulate healthcare related personal information, including the collection, storage, uses and transmission of human genetic resources.

Chinese traditional medicine is seen as the internal state of the body as a whole. It aims to restore the harmony of the body by praxis of acupuncture, medicinal herbs and certain selected foods to recover from illness. Thus, it embraces a more holistic approach of perceiving the patient as a whole equilibrium rather than what we call medicine in Western countries, where we treat the illness specifically. In China, the State Administration of Traditional Chinese Medicine is also affiliated with the NHC too (Focus, 2020).

Some population-monitoring projects have been developed in China recently, one of them involving large parts of the country's infrastructure. Ping An insurance company monitors 300 million farmers collecting and uploading photos, which include facial recognition and artificial intelligence, and uploads them to the cloud for medical purposes. The idea is to use the conclusions a posteriori to improve the overall health of the population (Luo, 2019) (Olano, 2019).

On the start-up scene, there are 1,366 HealthTech startups in China (MedicalStartups, 2019). Hong Kong is a pillar in the introduction and promotion of innovations in healthtech globally, acting as a bridge of collaboration between China and the rest of the world. (Centre, 2021a).

Ping An Good Doctor, for example, constitutes one of the best practices operating in China, becoming China's largest online medical service platform. It operates along with iCarbonX, which combines genomics disciplines with other health inputs such as metabolites, bacteria and lifestyle behaviours to create a digitised form of life. Healthtechs that work towards this digitisation of life will do well in China.

Conclusion

How do we build a global sustainable health system? This is the new question of our age. Prevention and sustainability go hand in hand—the prognosis of health and early diagnosis will be integral to the beloved circular economy in healthcare.

We need more than innovation in startups to drive sustainability. We, the private and public sector, push and pull for disruption, but we need to consider the ecosystem: understand that public and private health goals can align and make it happen.

Resilience here is key. Along your journey, you will be presented with numerous rejections or roadblocks from different stakeholders in the ecosystem. But you must have faith and believe in you and in your healthtech's mission. Using your intelligence and the team you have built, research your way around such regulatory or policy-based obstacles. Remember that, above all, you have value to offer the patient, and that if you stop at the first "no" or first barrier of the ecosystem, then the patient is the one who loses. It is a path of constantly jumping over obstacles and seeking opportunities.

We must also bear in mind the responsibility that falls on us as healthtechs. It falls on our companies to help build the health systems of the future through health technology. And therefore, we must act accordingly, not only pushing innovation but also knowing how to ask for and receive help every step of the way. And I am not speaking only from a perspective of continuous fundraising, but rather embracing public-private collaborations, mentors, and even critics to build the new health systems of the future: new transversal systems accommodating multiple disciplines across multiple nations.

I see so many extraordinary and disruptive solutions every day. Although sometimes, when studying the business models, I wonder where is the "monetisation"?

Often, the social purpose and mission of the company and its members are so strong that they forget income and cashflow, ultimately slowing growth. Financials are so important: high rates of revenue, investment and treasury to operate.

I see many talented entrepreneurs create business models to meet a single unsatisfied need within the pathology, but right at the beginning they forget about the future sustainability of the project or its survival. I have even done this myself. Remember not only sustainable growth but also sustained over time. Business profitability is just as important as the social mission or purpose of the company because it also means viability and progress. And this is as crucial as the sense of purpose of the company, "the why".

DOI: 10.4324/b23147-13

And in the opposite way, it also happens that sometimes I run into entrepreneurs who are too focused on the business and its results, although they neglect the social purpose and why they are there. It is a matter of finding the balance.

With all the pool of accelerators, aid programs, grants, open datasets, loans, crypto-financials and millions of opportunities that we have around us to push our health technologies, it is just a matter of reaching out and grasping them.

And there is room for everyone, and there must be so that we can reach the next milestone in the healthcare system together. We need all the possible disruption and innovation and, at the same time, all the push and pull possible to create the space within the ecosystem for the adoption of these changes in the improvement of healthcare, universalising it and achieving its equity.

And when I ask myself, where are we going, I think that without a doubt the next step is the fusion of technology with health.

All this is emerging in the large health markets, which today present products and services that have achieved standardisation status: commodities. These are the healthtech disruptors that have best adapted and are affordable for each individual and health system, and they are training the client to make informed decisions about the products and services that can control their health condition. And they manage to bring health to the homes of every patient.

Consider marketplaces that operate on a big scale. Amazon Care,[1] for example, is making healthcare easy and covering the unmet need of habitual in-home sense healthcare. And so is Ali Healthcare.[2] Both, following the trend of thinking globally but acting locally, offer their private services locally, in the patient's home, though they operate globally. They are shaking up how the purchase of health is perceived. At the same time, they make decisions and offer health products and services before they are needed thanks to technology improving their services, offering an ad-hoc pipeline of solutions that might impact patients' QALYs.

We must remember preventive healthcare. This is the goal. Such is the case of the recent Tencent launched AI-powered symptom self-screening tool that helps users with suspected symptoms to obtain medical guidance. Tencent is also democratising its cloud computing, AI, and big data capabilities making them available as free technical support for virus mutation prediction, antiviral drug screening, and vaccine research (Tencent, 2020).

In the same line, Alibaba launched an online clinic service (Xinhua, 2020), a drug delivery service for chronic diseases, and an AI algorithm that can identify the image of coronavirus-infected pneumonia in 20 seconds, with an accuracy rate of 96% (Kharpal, 2020).

All in all, traditional health systems are no longer sustainable. With their conventional structures they cannot provide this premium healthcare and meet the necessary high standards to extend QALYs and QoL for their citizens. Validated products and services owned by private healthtechs, which in turn are offered in large umbrella marketplaces owned by different public governments, are beginning to democratise health, offering validated health and equity of access. And the next step will most likely be to integrate similar health marketplaces into our public health systems, where validated health technology solutions are offered to their citizens.

An example of this is the recently opened portal Digital Technology Assessment Criteria for health and social care (DTAC) (NHS, 2021). It speeds up the validation of healthtech apps and gives new baseline criteria for digital health technologies entering into the NHS and social care pipeline.

We live in a changing environment. All that we think will happen will not. Believe me. While forecasting the future is hard in many fields, when it comes to healthcare, it is even more difficult.

---

[1] Amazon Care. URL: https://amazon.care/
[2] Ali Healthcare. URL: http://www.aliihealthcare.com/

But we can follow big lines, like predictable medicine, which is inevitable.

We must realise the new trend of "no patient left behind", and this means also having "no nation left behind" or in other words a cross-border approach. The new digital edge is embracing free, equal and universal access to excellent healthcare.

But, of course, there is little sustainability in healthcare so far. To become sustainable, we must be smart—investing wisely and preserving patient empowerment. This means we must enable self-referral, behavioural change, data-driven self-diagnosis, personalised outreach, medical record collection, and AI-enabled self-care. In other words capacitate the patient to understand and manage his own healthcare condition.

Take, for example, CareVoice,[3] a free downloadable. The app makes it more convenient for users to choose the right medical providers and health insurance plans for themselves. Again, eZTracker[4] permits a patient to track if his medication is from a legitimate distributor and verifies this data for him. After scanning a product code, eZTracker uses blockchain technology to authenticate where a medicine was supplied, manufactured, distributed, and whether the product is from an authorised distributor. Both solutions take a sustainable approach to healthcare.

Patient empowerment is important, through capacitation in technology and pathology. We must provide patient training through e-learning platforms that impact pathology outcomes positively. This is the game-changing solution across many industries. While AI improves our thinking, we must preserve the human element in decision making—this again pursues informed: free, massive, high-quality, and equality-based healthcare decisions for everyone.

And what is an innovation now? It is a creation or ideation that has room to scale—a location to build, the right ecosystem in which to innovate.

We must act together on a global scale. We must take the best, the business leaders in healthcare, the talents in the business industry at all levels from the region, the country and the planet and create "task forces" to advance.

Many awesome solutions are going directly to the frontier. We need to stand on the centres of acceleration, rely on them, and permit them to help us. You will find in this industry many people who volunteer to be mentors, and some of them are brilliant. Take advantage of their help.

There exist hubs of expert volunteers that offer assistance freely, as is the case of Volunteers in Business Advice (VAE),[5] where highly skilled volunteers help entrepreneurs.

For those of us already established in the healthtech ecosystem, we must think of these newcomers like our own "safeguarded". They want to help the healthcare system. And what are they getting in return? We need mentoring programs for them not to fail at the first bump in the road. And we must ask leaders to mentor newcomers. All these senior people that have spent all their lives in the healthcare industries—allow them to help the newcomers through tutorship programs. They have the experienced knowledge and the seniority, while the youngsters have the push, the idea, the innovation and an awesome knowledge growing at the speed of light.

Problems and bureaucratic barriers to starting the entrepreneurship path are already being minimised and improved. In Europe, we have initiatives like the Funding and Tenders Portal (Commission, 2021) owned by the European Commission, where all the funding projects are published. In turn, open public institutions and accelerators are moving fast in improving how help is delivered and assigned. Consequently, and fortunately the few hinderers of progress, the ones that want to stay in the comfort zone, are side-lined.

---

[3] CareVoice URL: https://www.thecarevoice.com/

[4] eZTracker URL: https://www.eztracker.io/

[5] http://www.vaeassessoriaempresarial.org/

We as founders of new healthtechs need to create new armies of ambassadors inside and out-side our companies. And our new armies are our co-workers together with other stakeholders that are pushing for progress in the same field as ours and share the same mission, vision and values of the company. We need to rely on them and help them. Build solid human relationships in the ecosystem based on a deep, trustworthy networking. Co-work with them. Set up fusions and alli-ances to go further. It does not have to be in a formal meeting room; it can also be in an informal afterwork setting, a coffee or a work meal—it does not matter. What matters is to be open to receive your peers' views and opinions about your doubts and circumstances, and at the same time share feedback with theirs.

Some healthtech newcomers lose faith at the first turn because they have been fighting for on average 5 years for their solution to empower the patient, and they see they still lack room to estab-lish their strategic position in the ecosystem. We cannot afford this situation. As entrepreneurs, we need to keep faith on our healthtechs and preserve a constant state of open mindedness towards progress. Reconvert the business model learning-by-doing throughout the process. Sometimes, pre-seeds reconsider their business model while they are pushed to apply for funding, where the project is evaluated and tested—that does not constitute failure but an opportunity to improve.

We need to allow ourselves to be helped, push ourselves to network with our entrepreneur peer communities. For example, why not join hubs or communities of entrepreneurs like you? Because if we get lost along the way, you can easily be redirected. Healthtech is a very particular field, as I said before, with lots of opportunities but also challenges, and these challenges can be overcome in very different ways.

How are we reaching the next global milestone in 2030, or 2035 in the global spectrum of disparate countries?

First is by using common sense and second looking for support. Create economical PPP based on healthcare risk-sharing contacts means support. The contacts with their value judgements and the contracts public-private bridges of collaboration are already predefined in the public "strate-gic healthcare plans". The "who's" should be open access and freely accessible in a click through LinkedIn. And the contracts of public-private partnerships are already pre-settled too, created and standardised too: for example, on platforms like Public-Private Partnership Legal Resource Center[6] from the World Bank Group. So, it is a matter of taking the initiative and taking the first step.

Building digital health ecosystems means consolidating a network of alliances and getting them to work in an optimised way. This costs time and effort, as you must start from scratch most of the time, although taking advantage of a consolidated network of stakeholders that are already operating in the real world can be a good starting point and a great leap in level.

Thus, some of the ecosystems are already pre-created and settled where they are accessible for healthtechs to jump in and start to operate from day one of their origination. Some of these eco-systems grouped by pathology families are already created in a digital environment. There is no need for every healthtech to create an ecosystem from zero independently and alone with all the effort that entails. Be clever and invest your time wisely.

Us, together with all the small fishes—the Nemos of the sea—that have just started, full of colourful beauty and value, we cannot allow ourselves to be eaten by a big shark on the first turn. We need to push to consolidate a solid place-to-be inside the ecosystem in record time. This is possible in the digital field. Of course, it takes time, but less time than it used to in the mature

---

[6] https://ppp.worldbank.org/public-private-partnership/library/royal-north-shore-hospital-and-community-health-services-project-summary-contract

business models. When you start, you do not have the structure, the size nor the possibilities that a big fish has in a healthcare ecosystem. But we learn-by-doing at the speed of light, and we find drivers of growth along the path.

So, this why the healthcare authorities and governmental institutions around healthcare are enablers. They are building up these pre-created ecosystems, these platforms, these places-to-be, and they are increasingly doing so. They need to create these habitats, if we take a maritime ecosystem for example, so that the small fish can live and find cover. Then push yourself to grow in a sustainable and sustained way. Sometimes it is just about looking for and relying on the help available.

We need a healthcare system based on a proper and fair creation of an established and standardised method, where people can interact with the different stakeholders easily and digitally. And it must be facilitator, permitting entrepreneurs to expand beyond their limits and add value.

We as entrepreneurs need to embrace the support of the big structures required to play in the ecosystem. We need to deal with market access, legal, institutional relationships, finance and fintech. But to do this, we can get support that institutions are providing. These essential aids that public governmental bodies and big private parties as health insurances or pharmaceutical companies can provide are key.

Besides, new technologies permit all these areas to be available to us, at very low costs.

So with a wide number of accelerators available (In Chapter 8 we made an extended review of available accelerators), it is evident that governments together with the private sector are already preparing the umbrellas containing enablers and support to entrepreneurs. They are collecting and grouping digital corners built of similar entities, providing free services, and making digital clusters of interconnectivity and networking.

We need to push and pull for the metamorphosis and progress of the capacities of health systems, helping with technology to redesign national health systems, responding to the needs of patients and anticipating future health challenges.

The co-governance, cohesion and efficiency of the health systems will go through technological modernisation. In other words, health systems will see the renewal of medical devices and digital transformation. They will experience the strategic provisioning of all sorts of upgraded pharmacological and healthtech solutions, and the empowerment of patients to manage their own health conditions, the collection of anonymised high-value data that drives the research and development of optimised solutions, and finally the offering of high standards of personalised and precision medicine that cover to the real and unique unmet needs of each patient.

And just to finish I would say, you do not need to think of your healthtech as a single solution to a single unmet need. Instead think widely. Think of your healthtech as a hub of solutions covering the whole patient journey in addition to considering meeting the needs of the payer and the regulator. Do not think of a disruptive business model; think of a whole battery of disruptive business models, and of a battery of healthtech products and services that have room to become real and scale in the healthcare field.

It is just as simple as not going for one solution but going for ten instead and pushing "now" for the one that best fits in the ecosystem in which you are playing, the most promising MVP. Then later you push for the second one and so on.

And do not think that your positioning will last forever. You need to be prepared for constant change, for constantly reinventing yourself. I am a believer that we as humans we are "versatile" and can adapt to many different functions or activities, and it is time to embrace "continuous change" as the new normal.

To maintain a sustainable and sustained flight, keep in mind above all your major purpose, your "whys"—in that you will find both the constancy to excel and the drive to adapt. I leave you with a few key points:

- Equity, universal access, and excellent healthcare standards can be achieved with the help of technology, with sustainable development goals (SDG) as a roadmap to follow.
- Sustainability comes from early diagnosis and better prognosis of the pathology, requiring IoMT for tracking real time chronic pathologies, empowering the patients and predicting acute situations.
- Co-working, co-creating and continuous crowd-learning have key roles in healthtech innovation.
- We are continually addressing the trust between patients and the high standards of healthcare available.
- The "humanisation of the patient" is possible through digital innovation and technological disruptive solutions.
- To improve health outcomes, we need to lean on higher quality, borderless, open and anonymised data.
- "Information as a service" is the main way to achieve the democratisation of healthcare respectfully for disaggregated data to build equity-based healthtech solutions.
- Health data is the most sensitive link to the deepest human privacy, and we must respect it.
- We must cover the healthcare unmet needs of the patient on a real-time basis and preserve the lifestyle of each individual as much as possible.
- Think about how the synergy between different profiles of digital talent plays a key role, considering differences between highly qualified young and old talents, between men and women, between different social and cultural profiles—diversity generates wealth in teams and progress for all.
- Think how AI, robotics, blockchain are leading the disruption of healthcare and how we can elevate their uses and early adoption rates.
- PPPs are the new focus for progressing the healthcare ecosystems of the future.
- Patient-centric approaches using cloud technologies, optimised treatment management and in-home pharmacy and care deliveries are the new trends.
- New tendencies of personalised healthcare and telehealth include the follow-up of facial features for diagnosis, using e-learning synergic tools to empower the patient.
- We are aiming for fully integrated healthcare via tokenised health datasets, considering digital health diplomacy.
- Identify where to scale, not only considering the barriers, but mainly the social impact of your healthtech in the region.

I would like to thank all of you for joining me on such long journey with this book. Thank you for your time, and I look forward to your healthtech's contribution to the future of healthcare. We all deserve a better world, and we are here to make it possible. You have crowds of help and opportunities around you that are waiting for you to reach out. You can fly and maintain the flight. It is just a matter of bringing value, value and value above all. And even more important is to have by your side a strong personal environment with friends and family and trusted people who support you throughout the ups and downs of your flight.

Remember: the healthcare ecosystem needs our healthtech solutions; we are the drivers of progress for the healthcare systems of the future.

Bibliography

(ABHI), A. o. (2021). *Procuring for Outcomes in an Evolving NHS*. Recuperado el 07 de September de 2021, de https://www.abhi.org.uk/

(Editor), I. R. (2019). *Disruptive Technology: Concepts, Methodologies, Tools, and Applications*. IGI Global.

360, G. (2018). *Google Glass-Based Solutions Can Empower Autistic People in India: Brain Power*. Recuperado el 02 de September de 2021, de https://gadgets.ndtv.com/wearables/features/google-glass-based-solutions-can-empower-autistic-people-in-india-brain-power-1888036

Abbott, A. (2020). *Farewell to Europe's Horizon 2020*. Recuperado el 29 de August de 2021, de https://www.nature.com/articles/d41586-020-03516-6

ABES. (2020). *ABES Software*. ABES.

ABES. (2021). *ABES Software*. Recuperado el 05 de September de 2021, de https://abessoftware.com.br/en/

Academy, K. (2021). *For every student, every classroom*. Recuperado el 29 de August de 2021, de https://www.khanacademy.org/

Academy, T. A. (2021). *Taiwan AI Academy*. Recuperado el 08 de September de 2021, de https://en.aiacademy.tw/

Academy, T. A. (2021). *Taiwan Artificial Intelligence Academy Foundation*. Recuperado el 08 de September de 2021, de https://en.aiacademy.tw/foundation/

Accelerace. (2021). *Where Danish pre-seed startups come to scale up*. Recuperado el 09 de September de 2021, de https://www.accelerace.io/accelerator/

Accelerator, B. (2021). *The Gateway To Asia For HealthTech & MedTech*. Recuperado el 28 de August de 2021, de https://www.beaccelerator.com.tw/

Accelerator, O. (2021). *Open Accelerator is the fast track accelerator program dedicated to life sciences and digital health with a focus on CNS and respiratory diseases*. Recuperado el 09 de September de 2021, de https://www.openaccelerator.it/

Acs, Z. J., Szerb, L., & Lloyd, A. (s.f.). *Global Entrepreneurship Index powered by The Global Entrepreneurship and Development Institute (GEDI)*. Recuperado el OCTOBER de 2021, de GEDI: https://thegedi.org/tool/

Acs, Z.J., Szerb, L.; Lloyd, A. (2017). The Global Entrepreneurship and Development Institute. Global Entrepreneurship Index powered by GEDI. 2018, https://thegedi.org/wp-content/uploads/dlm_uploads/2017/11/GEI-2018-1.pdf

ada. (2021). *Go automation-first with Ada's AI chatbot*. Recuperado el 01 de September de 2021, de https://www.ada.cx/

Ada. (2021). *Health. Powered by Ada*. Recuperado el 06 de September de 2021, de https://ada.com/

Administration, U. f. (2021). *Coronavirus Treatment Acceleration Program (CTAP)*. Recuperado el 28 de August de 2021, de https://www.fda.gov/drugs/coronavirus-covid-19-drugs/coronavirus-treatment-acceleration-program-ctap

Administration, U. F. (2021). *Real-World Evidence*. Recuperado el 28 de August de 2021, de https://www.fda.gov/science-research/science-and-research-special-topics/real-world-evidence

Administration, U. f. (2021). *Software as a Medical Device (SaMD)*. Recuperado el 02 de September de 2021, de https://www.fda.gov/medical-devices/digital-health-center-excellence/software-medical-device-samd

Administration, U. f. (2017). *FDA approves pill with sensor that digitally tracks if patients have ingested their medication.* Recuperado el 01 de September de 2021, de https://www.fda.gov/news-events/press-announcements/fda-approves-pill-sensor-digitally-tracks-if-patients-have-ingested-their-medication

Aetna. (2021). *Diverse and growing, the African continent is home to a vast range of national identities and regional cultures.* Recuperado el 05 de September de 2021, de https://www.aetnainternational.com/en/about-us/explore/living-abroad/culture-lifestyle/health-care-quality-in-africa.html

Africa, D. (2021). *Disrupt Africa African Tech Startups Funding Report 2020 & Full Startup List.* Disrupt Africa.

Africa, O. (2021). *Accelerate innovative impact-driven start-ups in Africa to protect our Oceans.* Recuperado el 28 de August de 2021, de https://www.oceanhub.africa/

Agarwal, D. (2018). *An Introduction to AI at LinkedIn.* Recuperado el 03 de September de 2021, de https://engineering.linkedin.com/blog/2018/10/an-introduction-to-ai-at-linkedin

Agency, A. D. (2021). *My Health Record.* Recuperado el 08 de September de 2021, de https://www.myhealthrecord.gov.au/

Agency, A. D. (2021). *Practice Incentives Program eHealth Incentive (ePIP).* Recuperado el 08 de September de 2021, de https://www.myhealthrecord.gov.au/for-healthcare-professionals/practice-incentives-program

Agency, E. M. (2021). *About Us.* Recuperado el 06 de September de 2021, de https://www.ema.europa.eu/en/about-us/how-we-work/european-medicines-regulatory-network/european-medicines-agencies-network-strategy

Agency, E. M. (2021). *European medicines agencies network strategy to 2025.* Recuperado el 06 de September de 2021, de https://www.ema.europa.eu/en/documents/report/european-union-medicines-agencies-network-strategy-2025-protecting-public-health-time-rapid-change_en.pdf

Agency, E. M. (2021). *Technical workshop on real-world metadata for regulatory purposes.* Recuperado el 28 de August de 2021, de https://www.ema.europa.eu/en/events/technical-workshop-real-world-metadata-regulatory-purposes

AHA. (2021). *AI and the Health Care Workforce.* Recuperado el 04 de September de 2021, de https://www.aha.org/center/emerging-issues/market-insights/ai/ai-and-health-care-workforce

AHBS. (2021). *About AHBS.* Recuperado el 05 de September de 2021, de https://www.africahealthbusiness.com/

AIME. (2021). *Big Data for Big Insights.* Recuperado el 08 de September de 2021, de https://aime.life/

AIoTA. (2021). *AIoTA – Asia IoT Alliance.* Recuperado el 08 de September de 2021, de https://www.linkedin.com/company/%E4%BA%9E%E6%B4%B2%E7%89%A9%E8%81%AF%E7%B6%B2asia-iot-alliance/about/

AIOTA. (2021). *AIOTA mission.* Recuperado el 08 de September de 2021, de https://www.asiaiota.org/

Alfimtsev, A., Basarab, M., Devyatkov, V., & Levanov, A. (December 2015). A New Methodology of Usability Testing on the Base of the Analysis of User's Electroencephalogram. *Journal of Computer Sciences and Applications, 3* (DOI:10.12691/jcsa-3-5-1), 105–111.

Alharbi, A., Alzuwaed, J., & Qasem, H. (2021). Evaluation of e-health (Seha) application: a cross-sectional study in Saudi Arabia. *BMC Medical Informatics and Decision Making, 21*(https://doi.org/10.1186/s12911-021-01437-6), 103.

alihealthcare. (2021). *Health Care Made Easy.* Recuperado el 09 de September de 2021, de http://www.aliihealthcare.com/

AliveCor. (2021). *Check your heart.* Recuperado el 01 de September de 2021, de https://www.alivecor.com/kardiamobile/

All, H. F. (2021). *Health For All.* Recuperado el 28 de August de 2021, de https://www.healthforall.tw/

Alliance of Advanced Biomedical Engineering. (2021). *Internet of Medical Things Revolutionizing Healthcare.* Recuperado el 01 de September de 2021, de https://aabme.asme.org/posts/internet-of-medical-things-revolutionizing-healthcare

Alliance, A. (2021). *Agile 101.* Recuperado el 28 de August de 2021, de https://www.agilealliance.org/agile101/

Alliance, D. t. (2021). *Transforming Global Healthcare by Advancing Digital Therapeutics.* Recuperado el 02 de September de 2021, de https://dtxalliance.org/

Alliance, P. G. (2021). *Transitioning towards technology-led patient-centric remote care.* HealthTech Predictions 2021.

Al-Qemaqchi, N., & Abdullah, W. (2017). The Effect of Walkability on the Sustainable University Campuses A comparison between the old and new campuses of Sulaimani University. *Conference: 7th Engineering and 1st International Scientific Conference College of Engineering/University of Baghdad.*

Amazon. (2020). *Introducing the All-New Echo Family—Reimagined, Inside and Out.* Recuperado el 02 de September de 2021, de https://press.aboutamazon.com/news-releases/news-release-details/introducing-all-new-echo-family-reimagined-inside-and-out

Amazon. (2021). *Healthcare made easy.* Recuperado el 09 de September de 2021, de https://amazon.care/

Amazon. (2021). https://pharmacy.amazon.com/. Recuperado el 01 de September de 2021, de Pharmacy has never been this easy

Amazon. (2021). *Pillpack.* Recuperado el 01 de September de 2021, de https://www.amazon.com/stores/page/5C6C0A16-CE60-4998-B799-A746AE18E19B?ref_=ap_lp_main

Amazon. (Amazon). *Health Car Made Easy.* Recuperado el 28 de August de 2021, de https://amazon.care/

Amazon.com. (2021). *What Is Alexa?* Recuperado el 04 de September de 2021, de https://developer.amazon.com/en-GB/alexa

Ambler, S. W. (2008). Agile Software Development at Scale. *IFIP Central and East European Conference on Software Engineering Techniques*, págs. Springer, Berlin, Heidelberg, DOI: https://doi.org/10.1007/978-3-540-85279-7_1.

Andrus, D. (2015). *The Robo-Advisors of the Health Care World.* Recuperado el 02 de September de 2021, de https://www.thinkadvisor.com/2015/05/04/the-robo-advisors-of-the-health-care-world/

APA. (10 de September de 2021). *AMERICAN PSYCHIATRY ASSOCIATION.* Obtenido de Psychiatry: https://www.psychiatry.org/

App, M. (s.f.). *Medamom.com.* Recuperado el September de 2021, de https://www.medadom.com/

Apple. (2021). *Siri does more than ever. Even before you ask.* Recuperado el 04 de September de 2021, de https://www.apple.com/siri/

Arjun, K. (3 de March de 2020). China's giants from Alibaba to Tecent ramp up healthtech efforts to battle coronavirus. *CNBC.*

Association, A. H. (2021). *Hospital-at-Home.* Recuperado el 30 de August de 2021, de https://www.aha.org/hospitalathome

Astragene. (2021). *Middle East's first Molecular Diagnostics Manufacturing Company.* Recuperado el 07 de September de 2021, de https://www.astragene.com/

ATSDR. (2018). ATSDR; Agency of Toxic Substances and Disease Registry. https://svi.cdc.gov/map.html

Audia. (2021). *Automatic quality assurance for all your patient consultations.* Recuperado el 02 de September de 2021, de https://www.corti.ai/

Austin_SCCFinal. (2020). *The Smart City Challenge.* Texas: City of Austin.

Auyang, S. (1999). *Foundations of Complex-system Theories -In Economics, Evolutionary Biology, and Statistical Physics* (Revised ed. edition (28 August 1999) ed.). Cambridge University Press.

AWAK. (2021). *AWAK Technology.* Recuperado el 05 de September de 2021, de https://www.awak.com/

Babyl. (2021). *Welcome to Babyl.* Recuperado el 02 de September de 2021, de https://babyl.rw/

Badie, K. (2021). *Call for Applications: IBM Hyper Protect Accelerator 2021.* Recuperado el 28 de August de 2021, de https://community.ibm.com/community/user/ibmz-and-linuxone/blogs/kavon-badie1/2021/04/30/ibm-hpa-applications-2021

Badie, K. (2021). *Call for Applications: IBM Hyper Protect Accelerator 2021.* (IBM HPA Deck Video.mp4) Recuperado el September de 2021, de IBM Community: https://community.ibm.com/community/user/ibmz-and-linuxone/blogs/kavon-badie1/2021/04/30/ibm-hpa-applications-2021

Badve, S., & Kumar, G. (2019). *Predictive Biomarkers in Oncology.* Springer International Publishing.

Baily, S. (2020). *What is a Payer?* Recuperado el 28 de August de 2021, de https://remapconsulting.com/what-is-a-payer/

Bank, T. W. (2021). *Physicians (per 1,000 people) - Sub-Saharan Africa.* Recuperado el 05 de September de 2021, de https://data.worldbank.org/indicator/SH.MED.PHYS.ZS?locations=ZG

Bank, W. A. (2019). *Healthy China: Deepening Health Reform in China.* 9 International Bank for Reconstruction and Development/The World Bank and World Health.

Barcelona, C. (2021). *Hospital Clínic de Barcelona*. Recuperado el 04 de September de 2021, de https://www.clinicbarcelona.org/en/assistance/about-clinic

Barcelonahealth. (2021). *The mission of Barcelona Health Hub is to promote innovation in digital health and its transfer to the sector, linking startups, health organizations, companies and investors*. Recuperado el 09 de September de 2021, de https://barcelonahealthhub.com/

Barh, D., Carpi, A., Verma, M., & Gunduz, M. (2017). *Cancer Biomarkers Minimal and Noninvasive Early Diagnosis and Prognosis*. CRC Press.

Barnett, J., Vasileiou, K., Djemil, F. et al. (2011). Understanding innovators' experiences of barriers and facilitators in implementation and diffusion of healthcare service innovations: a qualitative study. *Journal name: BMC health Serv Res*. https://bmchealthservres.biomedcentral.com/articles/10.1186/1472-6963-11-342

Baselaunch. (2021). *Building the next generation of biotech ventures*. Recuperado el 28 de August de 2021, de https://baselaunch.ch/

Baselaunch. (2021). *Building the next generation of biotech ventures*. Recuperado el 09 de September de 2021, de https://baselaunch.ch/

Bayley Matthew, M., Sarah, C., Levine Ed, M., & Monisha, a. M.-P. (2021). *Hospital revenue cycle operations: Opportunities created by the ACA*. McKinsey & Company (healthcare).

BBC. (2021). *The Taiwanese medtech transforming healthcare*. Recuperado el 08 de September de 2021, de http://www.bbc.com/storyworks/future/transforming-taiwan/the-taiwanese-medtech-transforming-healthcare

Benevolent. (2021). *Unravelling the mysteries of disease*. Recuperado el 03 de September de 2021, de https://www.benevolent.com/

Bermingham, F. (2019). *China's population to peak in 2023, five years earlier than official estimates, new research shows*. Recuperado el 08 de September de 2021, de https://www.scmp.com/economy/china-economy/article/3008471/chinas-population-peak-2023-five-years-earlier-official

Berwick, D.M. (2003). Disseminating innovations in health care. *Journal of American Medical Association, 1965-1975*. https://pubmed.ncbi.nlm.nih.gov/12697800/

Besserer, D., Bäurle, J., Nikic, A., Honold, F., Schüssel, F., & Weber, M. (12 de November de 2016). Fitmirror: A smart mirror for positive affect in everyday user morning routines. *Proceedings of the Workshop on Multimodal Analyses enabling Artificial Agents in Human-Machine Interaction*, págs. 48–55.

Bhatia, B. (2020). *Negativity is biggest problem: don't be negative be positive*. BookRix.

Bijker, W., Leonards, C., & Wackers, G. (January de 2001). Research and technology for development (RTD) through a EU-APC policy dialogue: scientific background, methodology, and toolbox. *American Journal of Clinical Nutrition*.

Billing, M. (2021). *The new El Dorado for healthtech startups*. Recuperado el 06 de September de 2021, de https://sifted.eu/articles/germany-healthtech-revolution-telemedicine/

Bio.Taiwan. (2021). *BioMed Taiwan*. Recuperado el 08 de September de 2021, de https://bio.taiwan.gov.tw/Entrepreneur/

Bio.Taiwan. (2021). *Events*. Recuperado el 08 de September de 2021, de https://bio.taiwan.gov.tw/#events

Bipolar, M. (2017). *Mundo Bipolar*. Recuperado el September de 2021, de http://mundobipolar.org/

birdie. (2021). *Care with confidence*. Recuperado el 07 de September de 2021, de https://www.birdie.care/

Birenbaum, L. (2021). *Larry Birenbaum*. Recuperado el 29 de August de 2021, de https://ocw.mit.edu/give/our-supporters/larry-birenbaum/

BITSIGHT. (2021). *Gartner Report: The Urgency to Treat Cybersecurity as a Business Decision*. Recuperado el 04 de September de 2021, de https://info.bitsight.com/the-urgency-to-treat-cybersecurity-as-a-business-decision

Blog, T. M. (2021). *What is Programmatic Advertising? The Ultimate 2021 Guide*. Recuperado el 03 de September de 2021, de https://www.match2one.com/blog/what-is-programmatic-advertising/

Blokdyk, G. (2019). *Healthcare Value Chain a Complete Guide*. Emereo Pty Limited.

Bloom, D., & Canning, D. (2003). Health as Human Capital and its Impact on Economic Performance. *Geneva Papers on Risk and Insurance – Issues and Practice, 28* (DOI: 10.1111/1468-0440.00225).

Bloom, D.E., Canning, D., & Sevilla, J. (2004). The Effect of Health on Economic Growth. *World Development, 32(1), 1-13* (DOI: http://10.1016/j.worlddev.2003.07.002). Obtenido de The Effect of Health on Economic Growth

BlueDot. (2021). *A track record of accurately assessing outbreak risk.* Recuperado el 05 de September de 2021, de https://bluedot.global/

BOE. (2020). *Royal Decree 403/2020, of February 25, which develops the basic organic structure of the Ministry of Economic Affairs and Digital Transformation.* Recuperado el 07 de September de 2021, de https://www.boe.es/diario_boe/txt.php?id=BOE-A-2020-2739

Bono, E. d. (1985). *Six Thinking Hats.* Little Brown & Company.

Bonta, R. (2021). *California Consumer Privacy Act (CCPA).* Recuperado el 04 de September de 2021, de https://oag.ca.gov/privacy/ccpa

Bookmeds. (2021). *Bookmeds.* Recuperado el 01 de September de 2021, de https://bookmymeds.com/

Bragazzi NL. (2013). Children, adolescents, and young adults participatory medicine: involving them in the health care process as a strategy for facing the infertility issue. *PubMed* (DOI: 10.1080/15265161. 2012.760672.).

Bragazzi, N., & Puente, G. (2013). Why P6 medicine needs clinical psychology and a trans-cultural approach. *Healthy psychology Research* (https://doi.org/10.4081/hpr.2013.e5).

Brain, E. (2021). *Empowered Brain.* Recuperado el 02 de September de 2021, de https://brain-power.com/empowered-brain/

Breakthrough Designation. (s.f.). *Food and Drug Administration.* (FDA, Productor) Recuperado el October de 2021, de https://www.fda.gov/medical-devices/how-study-and-market-your-device/breakthrough-devices-program

Broadcasting, L. P. (2021). *Chasing European unicorns: how to become a tech innovation hub?* Recuperado el 04 de September de 2021, de https://eng.lsm.lv/article/economy/business/chasing-european-unicorns-how-to-become-a-tech-innovation-hub.a407224/

Brown, N., Williams, M., Renjen, P. (2022). Investing in Health Equity: Why Strong ESG Strategies Help Build a Healthier, More Inclusive World. World Economic Forum. In collaboration with the American Heart Association, Deloitte and Harvard T.H. Chan School of Public Health. https://www.weforum.org/reports/investing-in-health-equity-why-strong-esg-strategies-help-build-a-healthier-more-inclusive-world

Brown, S.-A. (2015). Building SuperModels: Emerging patient avatars for use in precision and systems medicine. *Frontiers in Physiology, 453* (DOI:10.3389/fphys.2015.00318).

Buller, A. (2020). *Raising the bar for women's healthcare.* Recuperado el 07 de September de 2021, de http://staging.wamda.com/index.php/2020/06/raising-bar-women-healthcare

Burches, E., & Burches, M. (2020). Efficacy, Effectiveness and Efficiency in the Health Care: The Need for an Agreement to Clarify its Meaning. *Allergy Department, ALERGOCONTROL SLP, Valencia, Spain, DOI: 10.23937/2643-4512/1710035*(Public Health and Community Medicine). Obtenido de https://clinmedjournals.org/articles/iaphcm/international-archives-of-public-health-and-community-medicine-iaphcm-4-035.php?jid=iaphcm

Burki, T. (2020). The online anti-vaccine movement in the age of COVID-19. *Lancet Digit Health,* págs. DOI:https://doi.org/10.1016/S2589-7500(20)30227-2. Obtenido de https://www.thelancet.com/journals/landig/article/PIIS2589-7500(20)30227-2/fulltext

Burroughs, A. (2021). *Language Processing Tools Improve Care Delivery for Providers.* Recuperado el 02 de September de 2021, de https://healthtechmagazine.net/article/2020/05/language-processing-tools-improve-care-delivery-providers

Busch, I., Moretti, F., Travaini, G., Wu, A., & Rimondini, M. (2019). Humanization of Care: Key Elements Identified by Patients, Caregivers, and Healthcare Providers. A Systematic Review. *The Patient - Patient-Centered Outcomes Research,* págs. pages461–474.

Busch, R. (2019). *The Cyber Patient: Navigating Virtual Informatics (HIMSS Book).* Productivity Press.

Butler, S. M. (2020). *Achieving an equitable national health system for America.* Brookings.

butterflynetwork. (2021). *Easy-to-use software with powerful features.* Recuperado el 08 de September de 2021, de https://www.butterflynetwork.com/uk/

Cahan, E., Hernandez-Boussard, T., Thadaney-Israni, S., & Rubin, D. (March de 2019). Putting the data before the algorithm in big data addressing personalised healthcare. *NPJ Digital Medicine*, págs. https://doi.org/10.1038/s41746-019-0157-2.

Canada, M. (2021). *Medtech Canada*. Recuperado el 05 de September de 2021, de https://medtechcanada.org/

Canadian Council of Social Development. (2010). *Community Vitality: A Report of the Canadian Index of Wellbeing*.

Cancer.Net. (2019). *Biopsy*. Recuperado el 02 de September de 2021, de https://www.cancer.net/navigating-cancer-care/diagnosing-cancer/tests-and-procedures/biopsy

CanopyLab. (2021). *The Future of Learning*. Recuperado el 04 de September de 2021, de https://canopylab.com/

Cao, Y., Romero, J., & Aspuru-Guzik, A. (Nov–Dec 2018). Potential of quantum computing for drug discovery. *IBM Journal of Research and Development, 62, 6* (DOI: 10.1147/JRD.2018.2888987.), 6:1–6:20.

CAPP. (2021). *CAPP Operations Are Paused*. Recuperado el 05 de September de 2021, de https://accountablecaredoctors.org/american-healthcare-whats-the-problem/?gclid=Cj0KCQjwxdSHBhCdARIsAG6zhlXIuthSPvPJal-IEYJLL-Ft6b7p9vWpQSk-OM6iU1dRv0VMyAlix8oaAjaLEALw_wcB

CAR. (2019). Centro de Alto Rendimiento de Sant Cugat del Vallès (Barcelona). https://www.csd.gob.es/es/csd/instalaciones/centros-de-alto-rendimiento-y-tecnificacion-deportiva/centros-de-alto-rendimiento/car-en-detalle/centro-2ahighperformance

Care, S. H. (2021). *Mammogram - Medical Test*. Recuperado el 02 de September de 2021, de https://stanfordhealthcare.org/medical-tests/m/mammogram.html

Carevoice. (2021). *Making health Insurance Moe Human*. Recuperado el 08 de September de 2021, de https://www.thecarevoice.com/

Caselli, S. (2009). *Private Equity and Venture Capital in Europe: Markets, Techniques, and Deals* (1st ed.). Academic Press.

Casey, E. (2010). Between Geography and Philosophy: What Does It Mean to Be in the Place-World? *Annals of the Association of American Geographers* (https://doi.org/10.1111/0004-5608.00266).

Catalog, A. (s.f.). *AI4Europe*. Recuperado el October de 2021, de AI-catalog: https://www.ai4europe.eu/research/ai-catalog

Catalyzer, S. (2021). *Catalyze Your Biomedical Research*. Recuperado el 09 de September de 2021, de https://www.smarthealthcatalyzer.com/

Cave, A., Kurz, X., & Peter, A. (April de 2019). Real-World Data for Regulatory Decision Making: Challenges and Possible Solutions for Europe. *Clinical Pharmacology & Therapeutics 106(1)*, pág. DOI: 10.1002/cpt.1426.

census.gov. (2020). Datacommons.org. Data Commons. Place Explorer. https://datacommons.org/place/country/USA?utm_medium=explore&mprop=count&popt=Person&hl=en ;Year: 2020

Centre, H. (2021a). *International HealthTech Forum 2021 – Keynote Speech & Panel Discussion*. Recuperado el 08 de September de 2021, de https://www.youtube.com/watch?v=LhFYDppQh00

Centre, H. (2021b). *International HealthTech Forum 2021 – Keynote Speech & Panel Discussion*. Recuperado el 09 de September de 2021, de https://www.youtube.com/watch?v=LhFYDppQh00

Cerner. (2021). *Fresh from Cerner Perspectives*. Recuperado el 04 de September de 2021, de https://www.cerner.com/

Cerner. (2021). *Population Health Management*. Recuperado el 04 de September de 2021, de https://www.cerner.com/solutions/population-health-management

Chang, J., Peysakhovich, F., Wang, W., & Zhu, J. (2021). *The UK Health Care System*. http://assets.ce.columbia.edu/pdf/actu/actu-uk.pdf.

Chebrolu, K., Ressler, D., & Varia, H. (2020). *Smart use of artificial intelligence in health care*. Recuperado el 01 de September de 2021, de https://www2.deloitte.com/us/en/insights/industry/health-care/artificial-intelligence-in-health-care.html

Chen, J., Alagappand, M., Goldstein, M., Asch, S., & Altman, R. (2017). Decaying relevance of clinical data towards future decisions in data-driven inpatient clinical order sets. *International Journal of Medical Informatics, 102* (https://doi.org/10.1016/j.ijmedinf.2017.03.006), 71–79.

Chiiwii. (2021). *Do you have any health problems?* Recuperado el 06 de September de 2021, de https://www.chiiwiidoctor.com/

Chin, B. (2021). *8 HealthTech Startups in Japan to Watch.* Recuperado el 08 de September de 2021, de https://hivelife.com/healthtech-startups-japan/

China, N. H. (2021). *News.* Recuperado el 08 de September de 2021, de http://en.nhc.gov.cn/

Christopher, A. S. (2016). *Single payer healthcare: Pluses, minuses, and what it means for you.* Recuperado el 08 de September de 2021, de https://www.health.harvard.edu/blog/single-payer-healthcare-pluses-minuses-means-201606279835

Clausen, L. B. (2015). *Taking on the Challenges of Health Care in Africa.* Recuperado el 05 de September de 2021, de https://www.gsb.stanford.edu/insights/taking-challenges-health-care-africa

Cloud_Clinic. (2021). *Practice Management Software that works for you.* Recuperado el 08 de September de 2021, de https://www.clinictocloud.com/

Cohrs, R., Martin, T., Ghahramani, P., & Bidaut, L. (2014). Translational Medicine definition by the European Society for Translational Medicine. *New Horizons in Translational Medicine* (DOI:10.1016/j.nhtm.2014.12.002).

Colantonio, S., Coppini, G., Germanese, D., & Giorgi, D. (2015). A Smart Mirror to Promote a Healthy Lifestyle. *Biosystems Engineering.*

Collective, T. (2021). *hottest healthtech startups in Singapore.* Recuperado el 06 de September de 2021, de https://techcollectivesea.com/2021/06/24/5-hottest-healthtech-startups-in-singapore/

Collective, T. (2021). *These healthtech startups in Thailand are making lives better.* Recuperado el 06 de September de 2021, de https://techcollectivesea.com/2019/09/12/these-healthtech-startups-in-thailand-are-making-lives-better/

Collier, K. (2012). *Agile Analytics: A Value-Driven Approach to Business Intelligence and Data Warehousing.* Pearson Education.

color. (2021). *A complete platform for healthcare delivery.* Recuperado el 04 de September de 2021, de https://www.color.com/

color. (2021). *About.* Recuperado el 04 de September de 2021, de https://www.crunchbase.com/organization/color-genomics

Commission, E. (2019). *The top healthcare accelerators in Europe.* Recuperado el 09 de September de 2021, de https://ec.europa.eu/eip/ageing/news/top-healthcare-accelerators-europe_en.html

Commission, E. (2020). *A pharmaceutical strategy for Europe.* Recuperado el 06 de September de 2021, de https://ec.europa.eu/health/human-use/strategy_en

Commission, E. (2020). *Europe fit for the Digital Age: Commission proposes new rules for digital platforms.* Recuperado el 04 de September de 2021, de https://ec.europa.eu/commission/presscorner/detail/en/ip_20_2347

Commission, E. (2020). *On Artificial Intelligence – A European approach to excellence and trust.* European Commission.

Commission, E. (2020). *Proposal for a Regulation of the European parliament and of the council.* European Commission.

Commission, E. (2020). *White paper on artificial intelligence: A European approach to excellence and trust.* European Commission.

Commission, E. (2021). *A Europe fit for the digital age.* Recuperado el 06 de September de 2021, de https://ec.europa.eu/info/strategy/priorities-2019-2024/europe-fit-digital-age_en

Commission, E. (2021). *EU Unicorns Call on Europe and Its Leaders.* European Commission.

Commission, E. (2021). *Europe's Digital Decade: digital targets for 2030.* Recuperado el 30 de August de 2021, de https://ec.europa.eu/info/strategy/priorities-2019-2024/europe-fit-digital-age/europes-digital-decade-digital-targets-2030_en

Commission, E. (2021). *European data strategy.* Recuperado el 06 de September de 2021, de https://ec.europa.eu/info/strategy/priorities-2019-2024/europe-fit-digital-age/european-data-strategy

Commission, E. (2021). *Exchange of electronic health records across the EU.* Recuperado el 04 de September de 2021, de https://digital-strategy.ec.europa.eu/en/policies/electronic-health-records

Commission, E. (2021). *Funding & tender opportunities.* Recuperado el 09 de September de 2021, de https://ec.europa.eu/info/funding-tenders/opportunities/portal/screen/opportunities/competitive-calls

Commission, E. (2021). *Overview.* Recuperado el 02 de September de 2021, de https://ec.europa.eu/health/md_newregulations/overview_en

Commission, E. (2021). *Overview.* Recuperado el 04 de September de 2021, de https://ec.europa.eu/health/md_sector/overview_en#new_regulations

Commission, E. (2021). *Questions and Answers – Digital Green Certificate.* Recuperado el 02 de September de 2021, de https://ec.europa.eu/commission/presscorner/detail/en/qanda_21_1187

Commission, E. (2021). *Recovery plan for Europe.* Recuperado el 30 de August de 2021, de https://ec.europa.eu/info/strategy/recovery-plan-europe_en

Commission, E. (2021). *Shaping Europe's digital future.* Recuperado el 04 de September de 2021, de https://ec.europa.eu/info/strategy/priorities-2019-2024/europe-fit-digital-age/shaping-europe-digital-future_en

Commission, E. (2021). *Spain AI Strategy Report.* Recuperado el 07 de September de 2021, de https://knowledge4policy.ec.europa.eu/ai-watch/spain-ai-strategy-report_en

Commission, E. (2021). *The Digital Services Act: ensuring a safe and accountable online environment.* Recuperado el 04 de September de 2021, de https://ec.europa.eu/info/strategy/priorities-2019-2024/europe-fit-digital-age/digital-services-act-ensuring-safe-and-accountable-online-environment_en

Commission, E. (2021). *The European Union – What it is and what it does.* Recuperado el 04 de September de 2021, de https://op.europa.eu/webpub/com/eu-what-it-is/en/

Commission, European. (2021). Questions and Answers - Digital Green Certificate. https://ec.europa.eu/commission/presscorner/detail/en/qanda_21_1187

Commons, D. (2019). *People's Republic of China.* Recuperado el 08 de September de 2021, de https://data-commons.org/place/country/CHN?utm_medium=explore&mprop=lifeExpectancy&popt=Person&hl=en

Congress, Library of. (2021). *Israel: Ministry of Health to Issue "Green Passports" to Those Who Vaccinate against or Have Recovered from Coronavirus.* Recuperado el 02 de September de 2021, de https://www.loc.gov/item/global-legal-monitor/2021-01-11/israel-ministry-of-health-to-issue-green-passports-to-those-who-vaccinate-against-or-have-recovered-from-coronavirus/

Consulta, D. (s.f.). *Dr. Consulta.* Recuperado el September de 2021, de https://www.drconsulta.com/

Consulting, I. (2021). *Health Data.* Recuperado el 01 de September de 2021, de https://gdpr-info.eu/recitals/no-35/

Control, C. o. (2016). *From Innovation to Implementation – eHealth in the WHO European Region.* World Health Organization.

Cook, D., Duncan, G., Sprint, G., & Fritz, R. (2018). Using Smart City Technology to Make Healthcare Smarter. *Proceedings of the IEEE,* (DOI:10.1109/JPROC.2017.2787688), 106(4), 708–722. https://pubmed.ncbi.nlm.nih.gov/29628528/

Coppens, P. (2020). *Is it time to revisit the trade-off between health and privacy?* Recuperado el 08 de September de 2021, de https://www.linkedin.com/pulse/time-revisit-trade-off-between-health-privacy-pascal-coppens/?trk=read_related_article-card_title

Corporation, C. (2021). *Cerner CEO: Data Will Drive Global Health Care Transformation.* Recuperado el 04 de September de 2021, de https://www.cerner.com/newsroom/cerner-ceo-data-will-drive-global-health-care-transformation

Cortez, D., Macedo, M., dos, J., Souza, D., Afonso, G., & Torres, H. (2017). Evaluating the effectiveness of an empowerment program for self-care in type 2 diabetes: a cluster randomized trial. *BMC Public Health,* págs. https://doi.org/10.1186/s12889-016-3937-5.

Costanza, F. (2020). *Managing Patients' Organizations to Improve Healthcare: Emerging Research and Opportunities (Advances in Healthcare Information Systems).* Business Science Reference.

Costco, P. (2021). *Costco Pharmacy.* Recuperado el 28 de August de 2021, de https://www.costco.com/pharmacy/warehouse-pickup

Coursera. (2021). *Learn Without Limits.* Recuperado el 29 de August de 2021, de https://www.coursera.org/

Courseware, M. O. (2021). *MIT Open Learning Library.* Recuperado el 29 de August de 2021, de https://ocw.mit.edu/courses/mit-open-learning-library/

Crawford, A., & Serhal, E. (2020). Digital Health Equity and COVID-19: The Innovation Curve Cannot Reinforce the Social Gradient of Health. *J Med Internet Res, 6* (DOI: 10.2196/19361.).

Crawford, M. (2016). *5 Lean Principles Every Engineer Should Know.* Recuperado el 29 de August de 2021, de https://www.asme.org/topics-resources/content/5-lean-principles-every-should-know

CREODIAS. (s.f.). *CREODIAS.EU.* Recuperado el October de 2021, de https://creodias.eu/data-offer

Crex. (2020). *Recovery, Transformation and Resilience Plan of the Government of Spain.* Recuperado el 07 de September de 2021, de https://creex.org/plan-de-recuperacion-transformacion-y-resiliencia-del-gobierno-de-espana/

Crichton, D. (2018). *Using tech and $100M, Dr Consulta transforms healthcare for the poorest.* Recuperado el 05 de September de 2021, de https://techcrunch.com/2018/06/19/dr-consulta-transforms-healthcare-for-the-poorest/

Crime, U. N. (2009). *Guidance for the Validation of Analytical Methodology and Calibration of Equipment used for Testing of Illicit Drugs in Seized Materials and Biological Specimens.* Recuperado el 04 de September de 2021, de https://www.unodc.org/unodc/en/scientists/guidance-for-the-validation-of-analytical-methodology-and-calibration-of-equipment.html

CrystalLinks. (2021). *Analysis Paralysis.* Recuperado el 01 de September de 2021, de https://www.crysta-links.com/analysisparalysis.html

Cukier, M. (s.f.). *University of Maryland. A. James Clark School of Engineering.* (U. o. Maryland, Productor, & News Story) Recuperado el October de 2021, de Study: Hackers Attack Every 39 seconds: https://eng.umd.edu/news/story/study-hackers-attack-every-39-seconds

CVS, P. (9 de September de 2021). *CVS Pharmacy.* Recuperado el 28 de August de 2021, de https://www.cvs.com

Danmark.dk. (2022). Danmark.dk. Work-life balance. https://denmark.dk/society-and-business/work-life-balance

Darwin, C. (1859). *On the Origin of Species by Means of Natural Selection.* London: W Clowes & Sons.

Darwin, C. (1873). *The Origin of Species (1872).* Recuperado el 28 de August de 2021, de https://en.wikisource.org/wiki/The_Origin_of_Species_(1872)

Darwin, C. (First Edition 1859). *On the Origin of Species by Means of Natural Selection,.* Recuperado el 28 de August de 2021, de https://en.wikisource.org/wiki/On_the_Origin_of_Species_(1859)

Das, R. (13 de November de 2018). Top 8 Healthcare Predictions for 2019. *Forbes.*

Das, R. (2019). *Top 8 Predictions That Will Disrupt Healthcare in 2020.* Recuperado el 29 de August de 2021, de https://www.forbes.com/sites/reenitadas/2019/12/04/top-8-predictions-that-will-disrupt-healthcare-in-2020/?sh=2c17f74e7f1e

Data Strategy, f. E. (19 de 2 de 2020). *Communication from the Commission to the European Parliament, the Council, the European Economic and Social Committee and the Committee of the Regions.* Recuperado el September de 2021, de A European Strategy for Data: https://ec.europa.eu/info/sites/default/files/communication-european-strategy-data-19feb2020_en.pdf

Data, O. W. (2021). *Life Expectancy.* Recuperado el 03 de September de 2021, de https://ourworldindata.org/life-expectancy#life-expectancy-has-improved-globally

Dataquest. (2021). *Learn the world's most in-demand data skills.* Recuperado el 29 de August de 2021, de https://www.dataquest.io/

Davoudi, A., Malhotra, K., Shickel, B., Siegel, S., Williams, S., Ruppert, M., ... Rashidi, P. (2019). Intelligent ICU for Autonomous Patient Monitoring Using Pervasive Sensing and Deep Learning. *Scientific Reports, 9*(https://doi.org/10.1038/s41598-019-44004-w).

de Jong BC, G. B. (2019). *Ethical Considerations for Movement Mapping to Identify Disease Transmission Hotspots.* Emerging Infectious Diseases.

De, D., Bharti, P., Technology, S. K., & Chellappan, S. (September - October de 2015). Multimodal Wearable Sensing for Fine-Grained Activity Recognition in Healthcare. *IEEE Internet Computing, 19*(5), 26–35. DOI: 10.1109/MIC.2015.72.

Deloitte. (2019). *AI Is Not Just Getting Better; It's Becoming More Pervasive.* Recuperado el 01 de September de 2021, de https://hbr.org/sponsored/2019/02/ai-is-not-just-getting-better-its-becoming-more-pervasive

Deloitte. (2021). *2021 global health care outlook.* Accelerating Industry change. Deloitte insights.

Deloitte. (2021). *2021 Global Health Care Outlook.* Recuperado el 05 de September de 2021, de https://www2.deloitte.com/global/en/pages/life-sciences-and-healthcare/articles/global-health-care-sector-outlook.html

Deloitte. (2021). *Disruptive and Sustaining Innovation*. Recuperado el 03 de September de 2021, de https://www2.deloitte.com/il/en/pages/innovation/article/disruptive_vs_sustaining.html

Deloitte. (2021). *Insights*. Recuperado el 04 de September de 2021, de https://www2.deloitte.com/us/en/insights.html

Deloitte. (2021). *The future of behavioral health*. Recuperado el 03 de September de 2021, de https://www2.deloitte.com/us/en/insights/industry/health-care/future-of-behavioral-health.html

Department, R. S. (26 de June de 2021). Global digital health market size 2019-2025 forecast. *Department Statista Research*. (Statista.com, Ed.) https://www.statista.com/statistics/1092869/global-digital-health-market-size-forecast/#statisticContainer.

Deshpande, S., & Warren, J. (2021). Self-Harm Detection for Mental Health Chatbots. *Public Health and Informatics,* (DOI:10.3233/SHTI210118).

Desrosiers, L. (2020). *Opportunities for HealthTech Startups in Singapore & Germany*. Recuperado el 05 de September de 2021, de https://www.germanaccelerator.com/blog/opportunities-for-healthtech-startups-in-singapore-germany/

Dexcom. (2021). *Meet the Dexcom G6 CGM System*. Recuperado el 29 de August de 2021, de www.Dexcom.com

DF, B. (2019). *PLANO DE AÇÃO DA CÂMARA BRASILEIRA*. Recuperado el 05 de September de 2021, de https://www.gov.br/economia/pt-br/centrais-de-conteudo/publicacoes/arquivos/camara_i40__plano_de_acaoversao_finalrevisada.pdf

Dhar, A., Delone, M., Ressler, D. (2018). Deloitte. Reimagining digital health regulation: An agile model for regulating software in health care. https://www2.deloitte.com/content/dam/Deloitte/us/Documents/public-sector/reimagining-digital-health-regulation.pdf

dHealth. (2021). *Public Blockchain Infrastructure for Healthcare*. Recuperado el 02 de September de 2021, de https://dhealth.network/

Digital, E. (2021). *Plana Espana Digital 2025*. Recuperado el 07 de September de 2021, de https://www.lamoncloa.gob.es/presidente/actividades/Documents/2020/230720-Espa%C3%B1aDigital_2025.pdf

Digital.gov. (2020). *Contact Center Technologies*. Recuperado el 03 de September de 2021, de https://digital.gov/resources/contact-center-guidelines/contact-center-technologies/

digitalhealth.gov.au. (2021). *Connecting Australia to a healthier future*. Recuperado el 08 de September de 2021, de https://www.digitalhealth.gov.au/

digitalhealth.gov.au. (2021). *Electronic prescriptions making telehealth easier for Australians*. Recuperado el 08 de September de 2021, de https://www.digitalhealth.gov.au/newsroom/media-releases/electronic-prescriptions-making-telehealth-easier-for-australians

digitalhealth.gov.au. (2021). *Provider Connect Australia - helping healthcare providers stay connected*. Recuperado el 08 de September de 2021, de https://www.digitalhealth.gov.au/newsroom/media-releases/provider-connect-australia-helping-healthcare-providers-stay-connected

digitalhealth.gov.au. (2021). *Provider Connect Australia - Helping healthcare providers stay connected*. Recuperado el 08 de September de 2021, de https://www.digitalhealth.gov.au/newsroom/events-and-webinars/provider-connect-australia-helping-healthcare-providers-stay-connected

DigitalMedical, M. d. (2021). RADAR Covid. DigitalMedical.

DNA. (2021). *Malaysia-Sweden collaborate to launch Digital Health Innovation Challenge aimed at finding healthtech solutions*. Recuperado el 08 de September de 2021, de https://www.digitalnewsasia.com/techwork/malaysia-sweden-collaborate-launch-digital-health-innovation-challenge-aimed-finding?__cf_chl_jschl_tk__=pmd_4d99bbb7e64cb43ef7e88881d8bd7fb397673e9a-1628256811-0-gqNtZGzNAo2jcnBszQi6

Dokter.Se. (2021). *Care app & health center*. Recuperado el September 02 de 2021, de https://doktor.se/

Donohue, K., & Zhang, Y. (2015). Sharing the Risk: Understanding Risk-Sharing Contracts from the Supplier's Perspective. *The Handbook of Behavioral Operations Management: Social and Psychological Dynamics in Production and Service Settings.*, pág. 10.1093/acprof:oso/9780199357215.003.0013.

Donovan, F. (2019). *Organizations See 878% Health Data Growth Rate Since 2016*. Recuperado el 02 de September de 2021, de https://hitinfrastructure.com/news/organizations-see-878-health-data-growth-rate-since-2016

Downing Peck, A. (22 de Sept. de 2017). Because of Expanded Numbers of Patients with High-deductible Health Plans, Patients Are Now Responsible for 30% of Hospital Revenues. *Dark Daily. Serving Clinical Labs & Pathology Groups, 7.*

DPE. (2016). *The U.S. Health Care System: An International Perspective.* Recuperado el 05 de September de 2021, de https://www.dpeaflcio.org/factsheets/the-us-health-care-system-an-international-perspective

Drees, J. (2020). *Cyberattacks on healthcare providers expected to triple next year: Black Book report.* Recuperado el 04 de September de 2021, de https://www.beckershospitalreview.com/cybersecurity/cyberattacks-on-healthcare-providers-expected-to-triple-next-year-black-book-report.html

Drummond, M., Federici, C., Busink, E., Apel, C., Kendzia, D., & Brouwer, W. (2020). Performance-based risk-sharing agreements in renal care: current experience and future prospects. *Taylor Francis Online, https://doi.org/10.1080/14737167.2021.1876566.*

Duhigg, C. (2013). *The Power of Habit: Why We Do What We Do, and How to Change (Inglés) 1st Edición.* RHUK.

Dynamics, B. (2021). *Power of Communication to You.* Recuperado el 06 de September de 2021, de https://www.braindynamics.co.th/

EADA, Liderazgo. (2018). Liderazgo de Alto Rendimiento: Dieta mental sana para CEOs. Growth; https://blogs.eada.edu/2018/08/02/liderazgo-de-alto-rendimiento-dieta-mental-sana-para-ceos/

EC. (2021). *Commitment between the EIC and the EIT.* Obtenido de https://ec.europa.eu/info/news/commitment-ensure-systematic-and-structural-cooperation-between-eic-and-eit-2020-sep-24_en

echalliance. (2021). *ECHAlliance 2020 Annual Report.* Recuperado el 04 de September de 2021, de https://echalliance.com/

econsult. (2021). *Digital solutions for NHS A&E waiting rooms.* Recuperado el 02 de September de 2021, de https://econsult.net/urgent-care

Education, I. C. (2020). *Conversational AI.* Recuperado el 01 de September de 2021, de https://www.ibm.com/cloud/learn/conversational-ai

e-estonia. (2021). *e-ambulance.* Recuperado el 02 de September de 2021, de https://e-estonia.com/solutions/healthcare/e-ambulance

e-estonia. (2021). *e-prescription.* Recuperado el 02 de September de 2021, de https://e-estonia.com/solutions/healthcare/e-prescription/

e-estonia. (2021). *healthcare.* Recuperado el 02 de September de 2021, de https://e-estonia.com/solutions/healthcare/e-health-record/

e-estonia. (2021). *Viveo Health conquers big markets with telemedicine.* Recuperado el 02 de September de 2021, de https://e-estonia.com/viveo-health-conquers-big-markets-with/

e-estonia. (2021). *We have built a digital society and we can show you how.* Recuperado el 02 de September de 2021, de https://e-estonia.com/

eHI, & Cerner. (2018). *Artificial Intelligence in Healthcare.* eHI; Cerner.

Einspänner-Pflock, J., Mark, D.-A., & Thimm, C. (2014). Computer-assisted content analysis of Twitter data. *Twiiter and Society,* 97–108.

EIT. (2021). *EIT Health Summit 2022.* Recuperado el 28 de August de 2021, de https://eithealth.eu/

EIT. (2021). *European Institute of Innovation and Technology (EIT).* Recuperado el 28 de August de 2021, de https://ec.europa.eu/programmes/horizon2020/en/h2020-section/european-institute-innovation-and-technology-eit

eit. (2021). *We help you to reach your goals!* Recuperado el 06 de September de 2021, de https://eit-health.de/en/startups/

eit-Health. (2021). *Accelerator.* Recuperado el 09 de September de 2021, de https://eithealth.eu/what-we-do/eit-health-accelerator-programmes/accelerator-assistance/

Elliott, T. (2013). *The Datification Of Daily Life.* Recuperado el 29 de August de 2021, de https://www.forbes.com/sites/sap/2013/07/24/the-datification-of-daily-life/

EMA, E. M. (2019). *HMA-EMA Joint Big Data Taskforce Phase II report: 'Evolving Data-Driven Regulation'.* European Medicines Agency.

EMA. (2021). *EMA Regulatory Science to 2025.* Recuperado el 06 de September de 2021, de https://www.ema.europa.eu/en/documents/leaflet/ema-regulatory-science-2025-five-goals_en.pdf

Embassy, U. (2021). *Health Care*. Recuperado el 07 de September de 2021, de https://www.uae-embassy.org/about-uae/health-care

EMIAS. (2021). *EMIAS*. Recuperado el 04 de September de 2021, de https://amp.ww.en.freejournal.org/44055412/1/emias.html

Empresarial, M. (2021). *Mundo Empresarial*. Recuperado el 28 de August de 2021, de https://www.monempresarial.com/2018/01/09/medicina-vanguardia-dafo/

emrify. (2021). *Be the CEO of Your Health*. Recuperado el 02 de September de 2021, de https://www.emrify.com/

Energy, O. o. (2017). *Consumer vs Prosumer: What's the Difference?* Recuperado el 30 de August de 2021, de https://www.energy.gov/eere/articles/consumer-vs-prosumer-whats-difference

ENISA. (2021). *Procurement Guidelines for Cybersecurity in Hospitals*. Recuperado el 04 de September de 2021, de https://www.enisa.europa.eu/publications/good-practices-for-the-security-of-healthcare-services

Enlihealthintel. (s.f.). *Enlihealthintel*. Recuperado el September de 2021, de www.linkedin.com: https://www.linkedin.com/company/enlihealthintel/

EPA. (10 de September de 2021). *EUROPEAN PSYCHIATRY ASSOCIATION*. Obtenido de Europsy: https://www.europsy.net/.

EPF. (2021). *Patient Empowerment*. Recuperado el 01 de September de 2021, de https://www.eu-patient.eu/policy/Policy/patient-empowerment/

EPO. (2019). *Welcome to the Patent Index 2019*. Recuperado el 06 de September de 2021, de https://www.epo.org/about-us/annual-reports-statistics/statistics/2019.html

EPO. (2021). *European patent applications*. Recuperado el 06 de September de 2021, de https://www.epo.org/about-us/annual-reports-statistics/statistics/2020/statistics/patent-applications.html#tab3.

EPO. (2021). *Welcome to the Patent Index 2020*. Recuperado el 06 de September de 2021, de https://www.epo.org/about-us/annual-reports-statistics/statistics/2020.html

eSight. (2021). *Empowering people with low vision*. Recuperado el 05 de September de 2021, de https://esighteyewear.com/int

Espin J, O. J.-B. (11 de November de 2010). [Innovative patient access schemes for the adoption of new technology: risk-sharing agreements]. *Gaceta Sanitaria, 6* (DOI: 10.1016/j.gaceta.2010.07.011), 491–497.

EU, C. (s.f.). *Copernicus*. Recuperado el October de 2021, de Access to data: https://www.copernicus.eu/en/access-data

eur-lex. (2020). Official Journal of the European Union. European Union. https://eur-lex.europa.eu/legal-content/EN/TXT/PDF/?uri=CELEX:32020R0561&from=IT

Europe, D. (2020). *21 European scale-ups nominated for DIGITALEUROPE's Future Unicorn Award 2021*. Recuperado el 06 de September de 2021, de https://www.digitaleurope.org/news/21-european-scale-ups-nominated-for-digitaleuropes-future-unicorn-award-2021/

Europe, M. (2020). *The European Medical Technology Industry in Figures*. MedTech Europe.

Europe, M. (2021). *MedTech Europe*. Recuperado el 06 de September de 2021, de https://www.medtecheurope.org/

Europe, M. (2021). *The European Medical Technology Industry in figures*. MedTech Europe.

Europe, M. (2021). *The Value of Diagnostic Information in Acute Respiratory Infections – Observations from the COVID-19 pandemic: Case Study*. Recuperado el 06 de September de 2021, de https://www.medtecheurope.org/resource-library/the-value-of-diagnostic-information-in-acute-respiratory-infections-observations-from-the-covid-19-pandemic-case-study/

EuroPriSe. (2021). *Contact EuroPriSe*. Recuperado el 04 de September de 2021, de https://www.euprivacyseal.com/EPS-en/Home

eurostat. (2021). *Glossary:Gross value added*. Recuperado el 06 de September de 2021, de https://ec.europa.eu/eurostat/statistics-explained/index.php?title=Glossary:Gross_value_added#:~:text=Gross%20value%20added%20(GVA)%20is,by%20industry%20and%20institutional%20sector.

Eurostat. (2021). *Hours of work - annual statistics*. Recuperado el 02 de September de 2021, de https://ec.europa.eu/eurostat/statistics-explained/index.php?title=Hours_of_work_-_annual_statistics

Evaluation Project, M. (2021). *About Us*. Recuperado el 01 de September de 2021, de https://www.measureevaluation.org/about.html

Evaluation, M. (2021). *Community-Level Program Information Reporting for HIV/AIDS Programs.* Recuperado el 01 de September de 2021, de https://www.measureevaluation.org/resources/tools/hiv-aids/clpir.html

Exeevo. (2021). *Hype Cycle for Life Science Commercial Operations, 2020.* Recuperado el 01 de September de 2021, de https://www.gartner.com/technology/media-products/newsletters/Omnipresence/1-24JNIG7W/gartner2.html?utm_source=No-Socis&utm_campaign=31529a6061-EMAIL_CAMPAIGN_2018_10_01_08_06_COPY_01&utm_medium=email&utm_term=0_0f6ba59d89-31529a6061-350543393

exiii. (2021). *Exos.* Recuperado el 08 de September de 2021, de https://exiii.jp/wrist-dk2/

Fauw, J., Ledsam, J., & Ronneberger, O. (2018). Clinically applicable deep learning for diagnosis and referral in retinal disease. *Nature Medicine, 24* (https://doi.org/10.1038/s41591-018-0107-6), 1342–1350.

FBI. (2021). *Intelligence Studies: Types of Intelligence Collection.* Recuperado el 02 de September de 2021, de https://usnwc.libguides.com/c.php?g=494120&p=3381426

FDA. (2021). *Proposed Regulatory Framework for Modifications to Artificial Intelligence/Machine Learning (AI/ML)-Based Software as a Medical Device (SaMD).* US. Food and Drug Administration.

fenin. (2021). *Espias de Laboratorio.* Recuperado el 07 de September de 2021, de https://espiasdelaboratorio.fenin.es/

fenin. (2021). *Spanish Federation of Healthcare Technology Companies.* Recuperado el 07 de September de 2021, de https://www.fenin.es/

Fenin. (2021). *The Health Technology Sector claims the integration of DiV information to improve the efficiency of the health system.* Recuperado el 06 de September de 2021, de https://www.fenin.es/resources/notas-de-prensa/841

Fernandes, H., Huising, R., & Peduzzi, M. (2021). *Role reconfiguration: what ethnographic studies tell us about the implications of technological change for work and collaboration in healthcare.* BMJ Publishing Group.

Fernando, J., & Mansa, J. (2021). *Compound Annual Growth Rate (CAGR).* Recuperado el 02 de September de 2021, de https://www.investopedia.com/terms/c/cagr.asp

Ferriss, T. (2011). *The 4-hour work week. Escape the 9-5, leive anywhere and joint the new rich.* Ebury Press.

Ferry, T. (2017). *The 5+2 Industrial Innovation Plan.* Recuperado el 08 de September de 2021, de https://topics.amcham.com.tw/2017/05/52-industrial-innovation-plan/

Fibricheck. (2021). *Why Should You Check your Heart Rhythm Regularly.* Recuperado el 04 de September de 2021, de https://www.fibricheck.com/

FitBit. (2021). *Take charge of your health with the latest from Fitbit.* Recuperado el 29 de August de 2021, de https://www.fitbit.com/

Flomics. (2021). *Better Health through sequencing diagnostics.* Recuperado el 08 de September de 2021, de https://www.flomics.com/

Flomics. (2021). *State-of-the-art molecular biology and data analysis.* Recuperado el 08 de September de 2021, de https://www.flomics.com/technology/

Flöther, D., Murphy, J., & Murtha, J. (2021). *Exploring quantum computing use cases for healthcare.* IBM.

fluicell. (2021). *Print tissues at will - with single-cell precision.* Recuperado el 03 de September de 2021, de https://fluicell.com/biopixlar-3d-single-cell-bioprinting/?gclid=CjwKCAjwmeiIBhA6EiwA-uaeFSYLvTxxJR_R8E0mgrXIeKjQItefY-5JTr5pCOC12KJySorLqROaBoCwIYQAvD_BwE

Focus, C.-B. B. (2020). *How does China Healthcare System Actually Work?* Recuperado el 08 de September de 2021, de https://focus.cbbc.org/how-chinas-healthcare-system-actually-works/#.YR5LD9MzZbU

Ford, D., & Joliet, J. (2020). *Payment Acceptance Will Never Be the Same After the COVID-19 Pandemic.* Recuperado el 28 de August de 2021, de https://www.gartner.com/doc/reprints?id=1-24F031AA&ct=201021&st=sb&utm_campaign=2020-12%20Gartner%20Reprint%20-%20Payment%20Acceptance%20Post-COVID-19&utm_medium=email&_hsmi=101544127&_hsenc=p2ANqtz-9xeIbYsBlvqRZsbiOB5PZ0dfvCinYNIhJAEjRdXT-Yvv2Za1UXyZ3dZH

Forum, A. M. (2021). *Industrial Digital Innovation Hub.* Recuperado el 08 de September de 2021, de https://i4amf.aigroup.com.au/siemens-and-rmit-establish-an-industrial-digital-innovation-hub-supported-by-federal-government-grant-connecting-australian-and-vietnam-campuses-with-global-industry/

Foundation, E. (2021). *Vagus Nerve Stimulation (VNS)*. Recuperado el 01 de September de 2021, de https://www.epilepsy.com/learn/treating-seizures-and-epilepsy/devices/vagus-nerve-stimulation-vns

Foundation, I. D. (2021). *User Interface Design*. Recuperado el 29 de August de 2021, de https://www.interaction-design.org/literature/topics/ui-design

Foundation, T. R. (2021). *Artificial Intelligence in Global Health*. Recuperado el 29 de August de 2021, de https://www.usaid.gov/sites/default/files/documents/1864/AI-in-Global-Health_webFinal_508.pdf

Foundation, T. R. (2021). *Artificial Intelligence in Global Health*. USAID.

Foundation, T. R. (2021). *Artificial Intelligence in Global Health - Defining a Collective Path Forward*. USAID From the American People.

Fountaine, T., McCarthy, B., and Saleh, T. (2019). The AI-Powered Organization; Publisher: Harvard business review. https://hbr.org/2019/07/building-the-ai-powered-organization. From the Magazine.

Fountaine, T., Saleh, T., & McCarthy, B. (2019). *Building the AI-Powered Organization*. Recuperado el 01 de September de 2021, de https://hbr.org/2019/07/building-the-ai-powered-organization

Fox, N., Ward, K., & O'Rourke, A. (06 de March de 2005). The 'expert patient': empowerment or medical dominance? The case of weight loss, pharmaceutical drugs and the Internet. *Soc Sci Med*, pág. DOI: 10.1016/j.socscimed.2004.07.005.

Freestyle. (2021). *Take the mystery out of your Glucose Levels*. Recuperado el 29 de August de 2021, de https://www.freestyle.abbott/us-en/home.html

FTC. (2016). Federal Trade Commission. Protecting America's Consumers; Developing a mobile Health app? Find out which federal laws you need to follow. https://www.ftc.gov/tips-advice/business-center/guidance/mobile-health-apps-interactive-tool#

Fund, T. C. (2020). *International Health Care System Profiles*. Recuperado el 05 de September de 2021, de https://www.commonwealthfund.org/international-health-policy-center/countries/canada

G4A, B. (2021). *Bayer G4A*. Recuperado el 28 de August de 2021, de https://www.g4a.health/

G4A. (2021). *Strategic Partners*. Recuperado el 09 de September de 2021, de https://www.g4a.health/about/strategic-partners

GAIA-X. (2021). *GAIA-X: Driver of digital innovation in Europe*. Recuperado el 04 de September de 2021, de https://www.data-infrastructure.eu/GAIAX/Navigation/EN/Home/home.html

Galanakis, M., Tsoli, S., & Darviri, C. (2016). *The Effects of Patient Empowerment Scale in Chronic Diseases*. Recuperado el 29 de August de 2021, de DOI:10.4236/psych.2016.711138

Gallup. (2021). *Behavioral Economics*. Recuperado el 04 de September de 2021, de https://www.gallup.com/services/170954/behavioral-economics.aspx

GamaPServer. (2021). *Per Capital Total Expenditute on Health*. Recuperado el 05 de September de 2021, de http://gamapserver.who.int/gho/interactive_charts/health_financing/atlas.html?indicator=i3

Garcia Perez, F.J. (2020). The need for a homogenised global legal framework in healthtech. https://www.med-technews.com/medtech-insights/the-need-of-a-homogenised-global-legal-framework-in-healthte/

Gardiner, R. (2008). The transition from 'informed patient' care to 'patient informed' care. *Stud Health Technol Inform*, *137*, pág. PMID: 18560085.

Gazette, S. A. (2020). *Royal Decree-Law 36/2020, of December 30, approving urgent measures for the modernization of the Public Administration and for the execution of the Recovery, Transformation and Resilience Plan*. Recuperado el 04 de September de 2021, de https://www.boe.es/diario_boe/txt.php?id=BOE-A-2020-17340

GBV. (2021). *Ping An Good Doctor One-Minute Clinics*. Recuperado el 02 de September de 2021, de https://www.global-benefits-vision.com/ping-an-good-doctor-one-minute-clinics/

GDPR. (2021). *Complete guide to GDPR compliance*. Recuperado el 28 de August de 2021, de https://gdpr.eu/what-is-gdpr/

GDPR. (2021). *What is GDPR, the EU's new data protection law?* Recuperado el 04 de September de 2021, de https://gdpr.eu/what-is-gdpr/

General Assembly, U. N. (2015). *Resolution adopted by the General Assembly on 25 September 2015*. Recuperado el 07 de September de 2021, de https://www.un.org/en/development/desa/population/migration/generalassembly/docs/globalcompact/A_RES_70_1_E.pdf

Gennari, P., & Navarro, D. (2019). Validation of methods and data for SDG indicators. *Statistical Journal of the IAOS*, *35* (DOI: 10.3233/SJI-190519), 735–741.

German Insurance Association (GDV). (2020). About German Insurance Association GDV. https://www.gdv.de/en/about-us/german-insurance-association-gdv--24324

Gillon, R. (1994). Medical ethics: four principles plus attention to scope. *BMJ*, *309* (DOI: 10.1136/bmj.309.6948.184.), 184–8.

GitHub. (2021). *pingbot*. Recuperado el 01 de September de 2021, de https://github.com/toricls/pingbot

Givan, F. (2016). *Global leader Spain carries out its 100,000th transplant*. Recuperado el 07 de September de 2021, de https://www.thelocal.es/20160225/global-transplant-leader-spain-reaches-its-100000th-transplant/

GKV. (2021). *Statutory health insurance*. Recuperado el 06 de September de 2021, de https://www.gkv-spitzenverband.de/english/statutory_health_insurance/statutory_health_insurance.jsp

Gläser, W. (2021). *Where does the term "VUCA" come from?* Recuperado el 28 de August de 2021, de https://www.vuca-world.org/where-does-the-term-vuca-come-from/

Glass. (2021). *Glass Enterprise Edition 2*. Recuperado el 02 de September de 2021, de https://www.google.com/glass/tech-specs/

Global, N. N. (2021). *Smart pens. Smarter care*. Recuperado el 29 de August de 2021, de https://www.novo-nordisk.com/our-products/smart-pens/novopen-6.html

glooko. (2021). *Powerful remote patient management for Better Care*. Recuperado el 29 de August de 2021, de www.glooko.com

GluCare. (2021). *How it Works*. Recuperado el 02 de September de 2021, de https://glucare.health/

Goasduff, L. (2020). *2 Megatrends Dominate the Gartner Hype Cycle for Artificial Intelligence, 2020*. Recuperado el 01 de September de 2021, de https://www.gartner.com/smarterwithgartner/2-megatrends-dominate-the-gartner-hype-cycle-for-artificial-intelligence-2020/

Gold, R. (2021). *Big Tech faces barrage of new rules*. Recuperado el 04 de September de 2021, de https://www.linkedin.com/news/story/big-tech-faces-barrage-of-new-rules-4992884/

Google. (2021). *Insights. Ideas. Inspiration*. Recuperado el 02 de September de 2021, de https://www.think-withgoogle.com/

gov.uk. (2021). *Innovate UK*. Recuperado el 07 de September de 2021, de https://www.gov.uk/government/organisations/innovate-uk

Govan, F. (2017). *How Spain became the world leader in organ transplants*. Recuperado el 07 de September de 2021, de https://www.thelocal.es/20170915/how-spain-became-world-leader-at-organ-transplants/

Government, H. (2020). *Genome UK. The future of healthcare*. OGL. Recuperado el 30 de August de 2021, de https://ec.europa.eu/info/news/commitment-ensure-systematic-and-structural-cooperation-between-eic-and-eit-2020-sep-24_en

Government, K. (2021). *Busan Eco Delta Smart city Pilot*. Recuperado el 01 de September de 2021, de https://smartcity.go.kr/en/

Gray, D. (2017). *Updated Empathy Map Canvas*. Recuperado el 29 de August de 2021, de https://medium.com/the-xplane-collection/updated-empathy-map-canvas-46df22df3c8a

Greenpeace East Asia. (2022). Greenpeace; Samsung, Xiaomi get Failing Grades in New Greenpeace Tech Ranking. https://www.greenpeace.org/eastasia/press/7095/samsung-xiaomi-get-failing-grades-in-new-greenpeace-tech-ranking/

Gross, O., & Gagnayre, R. (2014). What expert patients report that they do in the French. *Éducation théra-peutique du patient/Therapeutic patient education EDP Sciences*.

GTAI. (2021). *Medical Technology*. Recuperado el 06 de September de 2021, de https://www.gtai.de/gtai-en/invest/industries/life-sciences/medical-technology

Gualtieri, L. (2009). The Doctor as the Second Opinion and the Internet as the First. *ResearchGate*, (DOI:10.1109/ITI.2009.5196045).

Guardian, T. (2021). *Hospitals without walls:the future of healthcare*. Recuperado el 01 de September de 2021, de https://www.theguardian.com/society/2021/jan/02/hospitals-without-walls-the-future-of-digital-healthcare

Guide, W. D. (2021). *Prosthetic hand*. Recuperado el 08 de September de 2021, de https://ifworlddesign-guide.com/entry/148430-handiii

H2B. (2021). *Health2B Business Accelerator 2020*. Recuperado el 09 de September de 2021, de https://www. f6s.com/health2baccelerator2020

Hacarus. (2021). *Training programs for.* Recuperado el 08 de September de 2021, de https://hacarus.com/

Halim, A. (2019). *Biomarkers, Diagnostics and Precision Medicine in the Drug Industry: Critical Challenges, Limitations and Roadmaps for the Best Practices.* Academic Press.

Hashim, J., Chongsuvivatwong, V., Phua, K. H., Pocock, N., Teng, Y. M., Chhem, R. K., … Lopez, A. (2012). *Health and Healthcare Systems in Southeast Asia.* Recuperado el 05 de September de 2021, de https://unu.edu/publications/articles/health-and-healthcare-systems-in-southeast-asia.html

Hassan, S., Binte, S., & Zakia, U. (2020). Recognising Suicidal Intent in Depressed Population using NLP: A Pilot Study. *IEMCON 2020* (DOI:10.1109/IEMCON51383.2020.9284832).

Hastie, T. T. (2009). *The Elements of Statistical Learning* (2nd ed.). Springer-Verlag.

Hawkes, N. (2013). Hospitals without walls. *BMJ*, pág. 347.

Hayes, A., & Scott, G. (2021). *Venture Capital.* Recuperado el 04 de September de 2021, de https://www. investopedia.com/terms/v/venturecapital.asp

Hayhoe, T., Podhorska, I., Siekelova, A., & Stehel, V. (2021). *Sustainable Manufacturing in Industry 4.0: Cross-Sector Networks of Multiple Supply Chains, Cyber-Physical Production Systems, and AI-driven Decision-Making.* Addleton Academic Publishers.

Health, B. (2021). *Blueprint Health is a community of healthcare entrepreneurs helping build the next generation of healthcare IT companies.* Recuperado el 09 de September de 2021, de https://www.blueprint-health.org/

Health, D. o. (2021). *About Health Technology Assessment.* Recuperado el 08 de September de 2021, de https://www1.health.gov.au/internet/hta/publishing.nsf/Content/about-1

Health, D. o. (2021). *Implementing the Framework to guide the secondary use of My Health Record system data.* Recuperado el 08 de September de 2021, de https://www1.health.gov.au/internet/main/publishing. nsf/Content/eHealth-framework

Health, D. o. (2021). *Review of the My Health Records legislation.* Recuperado el 08 de September de 2021, de https://www.health.gov.au/resources/collections/review-of-the-my-health-records-legislation

Health, E. (2020). *Transforming healthcare with AI.* EIT Health.

Health, e. (2021). *High Value Care Forum.* Recuperado el 30 de August de 2021, de https://eithealth.eu/ project/high-value-care-forum/

Health, N. (2008). *Royal North Shore Hospital and Community Health Services Project - summary of contract.* Recuperado el 04 de September de 2021, de https://ppp.worldbank.org/public-private-partnership/ library/royal-north-shore-hospital-and-community-health-services-project-summary-contract

Health, N. (2021). *Personalised healthcare for women.* Recuperado el 07 de September de 2021, de https:// nabtahealth.com/

Health, T. D. (2021). *Telehealth.* Recuperado el 08 de September de 2021, de https://www1.health.gov.au/ internet/main/publishing.nsf/Content/e-health-telehealth

HealthBox. (2021). *Empower Healthcare Innovation at Your Organization.* Recuperado el 09 de September de 2021, de https://www.healthbox.com/

Healthcare. (2019). *Malaysia's medtech sector stages turnaround as investments pick up.* Recuperado el 08 de Septemberde2021,dehttps://healthcareasiamagazine.com/healthcare/news/malaysias-medtech-sector-stages-turnaround-investments-pick

HealthCare.gov. (2021). *Affordable Care Act (ACA).* Recuperado el 04 de September de 2021, de https:// www.healthcare.gov/glossary/affordable-care-act/

HealthIntent. (2021). Health Care Doesn't Stop Here. HealthIntent.

Healthily. (2021). *We are Healthily.* Recuperado el 02 de September de 2021, de https://healthily.com.au/

HealthIT. (2020). *Health Interoperability Outcomes 2030.* Recuperado el 29 de August de 2021, de https:// www.healthit.gov/topic/interoperability/health-interoperability-outcomes-2030

HealthIT.gov. (2020). *Strategy on Reducing Regulatory and Administrative Burden Relating to the Use of Health IT and EHRs.* HealthIT.gov.

HealthIt.gov. (2021). *What is the NHIN?* Recuperado el 04 de September de 2021, de https://www.healthit. gov/sites/default/files/what-Is-the-nhin-2.pdf

HealthKOS. (2021). *HealthKOS is the Leading Patient Engagement Solution.* Recuperado el 01 de September de 2021, de https://www.healthkos.com/

HealthTec. (2021). *About Us.* Recuperado el 05 de September de 2021, de https://www.healthtec.sg/about-us/

HealthTech, A. (2021). *American HealthTech.* Recuperado el 05 de September de 2021, de https://www.linkedin.com/company/american-healthtech/

HealthTech. (2021). *SaMD vs SiMD: What's the Difference?* Recuperado el 03 de September de 2021, de https://www.healthtechzone.com/topics/healthcare/articles/2020/06/29/445836-samd-vs-simd-whats-difference.htm

Healthtech. (2021). *The 10 biggest healthtech rounds of 2020.* Recuperado el 02 de September de 2021, de https://sifted.eu/articles/10-healthtech-rounds-2020/

Heart.org. (2021). *Let's Get Moving to Help Save Lives.* Recuperado el 05 de September de 2021, de https://www.heart.org/

HiBlance. (2021). *Hi Blance.* Recuperado el 04 de September de 2021, de https://www.hiblance.com/

Highlight, T. R. (2019). *Towards Smarter Medicine and Healthcare with AI.* Recuperado el 08 de September de 2021, de https://trh.gase.most.ntnu.edu.tw/en/article/content/15

HIMSS. (2021). *Certification: CAHIMS and CPHIMS.* Recuperado el 04 de September de 2021, de https://www.himss.org/resources-certification/overview?utm_source=google&utm_medium=cpc&utm_campaign=certification

HIMSS. (2021). *HIMSS Annual European Digital Health Survey 2021.* HIMSS.

H-ISAC. (2021). *Distributed Denial of Service(DDOS) Attacks.* H-ISAC.

Hodgson, T., Magrabi, F., & Coiera, E. (2018). Evaluating the usability of speech recognition to create clinical documentation using a commercial electronic health record. *International Journal of Medical Informatics, 113*(https://doi.org/10.1016/j.ijmedinf.2018.02.011.), 38–42.

Hoeppner, B., Hoeppner, S., Kelly, L., Schick, M., & Kelly, J. (2017). Smiling Instead of Smoking: Development of a Positive Psychology Smoking Cessation Smartphone App for Non-daily Smokers. *International Journal of Behavioral Medicine, 24*(https://doi.org/10.1007/s12529-017-9640-9), 683–693.

Holloway, S., Peterson, M., MacDonald, A., & Pollak, B. (2018). *From revenue cycle management to revenue excellence.* McKinsey & Company.

holmusk. (2021). *Behavioral health, reinvented.* Recuperado el 05 de September de 2021, de https://www.holmusk.com/

Hoy, M. B. (2018). Alexa, Siri, Cortana, and More: An Introduction to Voice Assistants. *Medical Reference Services Quarterly, 37* (DOI:10.1080/02763869.2018.1404391), 81–88.

https://www.medicineassistancetool.org/. (2021). *Worried About Affording Your Medicine? MAT is Here to Help.* Recuperado el 28 de August de 2021, de https://www.medicineassistancetool.org/

Huang, T.-K., Yang, C.-H., Hsieh, Y.-H., Wang, J.-C., & Hung, C.-C. (2018). Augmented reality (AR) and virtual reality (VR) applied in dentistry. *Kaohsiung J Med Sci, 34(4)* (DOI: 10.1016/j.kjms.2018.01.009.), 243–48.

Hub, H. I. (2021). *About us.* Recuperado el 08 de September de 2021, de https://www.healthindustryhub.com.au/about-us/

Hulsen, T. (2019). From Big Data to Precision Medicine. *Front Medicine (Lausanne), 34.* https://www.ncbi.nlm.nih.gov/pmc/articles/PMC6405506/

Hulsen, T. (2020). Sharing is Caring - Data Sharing initiatives in Healthcare. *International Journal of Environment Research & Public Health.* https://pubmed.ncbi.nlm.nih.gov/32349396/

Hu-manity. (2021). *Companies are using the Hu-manity.co Privacy Experience™ to promote privacy and build trust, transparency, and authenticity with customers across all channelsCompanies are using the Hu-manity.co Privacy Experience™ to promote privacy and build trust, tr.* Recuperado el 02 de September de 2021, de https://hu-manity.co/

Hwang, W., Lei, W., Katritsis, N., MacMahon, M., Chapman, K., & Han, N. (May de 2021). Current and prospective computational approaches and challenges for developing COVID-19 vaccines. *Advanced Drug Delivery Reviews, 172,* Pages 249–274.

I, M. (2021). *How do we Measure the "Value" in Value-Based care?* Recuperado el 28 de August de 2021, de https://www.ohe.org/publications/how-do-we-measure-%E2%80%9Cvalue%E2%80%9D-value-based-care

Iaione, C., Nictolis, E., & Suman, A. (December de 2019). The Internet of Humans (IoH): Human Rights and Co-Governance to Achieve Tech Justice in the City. *The Law & Ethics of Human Rights*, págs. https://doi.org/10.1515/lehr-2019-2008.

IBM. (2021). *Find out what factors help mitigate breach costs.* Recuperado el 04 de September de 2021, de https://www.ibm.com/account/reg/us-en/signup?formid=urx-46542

IBM. (2021). *The DeepQA Research Team.* Recuperado el 02 de September de 2021, de https://researcher.watson.ibm.com/researcher/view_group_subpage.php?id=2159

IBM. (2021). *Turn input into impact with an AI-led marketing strategy.* Recuperado el 02 de September de 2021, de https://www.ibm.com/thought-leadership/institute-business-value/report/ai-marketing-strategy

IBM. (2021). *Turn input into impact with an AI-led marketing strategy.* Recuperado el 03 de September de 2021, de https://www.ibm.com/thought-leadership/institute-business-value/report/ai-marketing-strategy

Ibrahim, H., Liu, X., Zariffa, N., Morris, A., & Denniston, A. (2021). Health data poverty: an assailable barrier to equitable digital health care. *Lancet Digital Health*, 3 (DOI:https://doi.org/10.1016/S2589-7500(20)30317-4).

ICU. (2020). ICU Management & Practice. *ICU Management & Practice, 20.* Obtenido de https://healthmanagement.org/c/icu/issue/volume-20-issue-1-2020-1

IDC. (2021). *IDC FutureScape: Worldwide IT Industry 2019 Predictions.* Recuperado el 04 de September de 2021, de https://www.idc.com/getdoc.jsp?containerId=US44403818

IFR. (2019). *Executive Summary World Robotics 2020 Industrial Robots.* Recuperado el 07 de September de 2021, de https://ifr.org/img/worldrobotics/Executive_Summary_WR_2020_Industrial_Robots_1.pdf

IMDA. (2021). *Accreditation@SGD.* Recuperado el 28 de August de 2021, de https://www.imda.gov.sg/programme-listing/accreditation-at-sgd

IMDRF. (2014). International Medical Device Regulators Forum. IMDRF. https://www.imdrf.org/sites/default/files/docs/imdrf/final/technical/imdrf-tech-140918-samd-framework-risk-categorization-141013.pdf

Initiative, T. T. (2021). *Inspiring Lives Free from Smoking, Vaping and Nicotine.* Recuperado el 01 de September de 2021, de https://truthinitiative.org/

Innovaccer. (2021). *Accelerate your transformation.* Recuperado el 05 de September de 2021, de https://innovaccer.com/

Innovation, C. f. (2021). *Engaging with the American Heart Association.* Recuperado el 05 de September de 2021, de https://ahahealthtech.org/

Innovation, S. V. (2021). *Transforming the Healthcare Industry.* Recuperado el 28 de August de 2021, de https://siliconvalley.center/education/standard-programs/transforming-the-healthcare-industry

Insights, H. (2020). *Artificial Intelligence.* Recuperado el 28 de August de 2021, de https://thehealthcare-insights.com/ge-healthcare-launches-a-new-startup-accelerator-for-artificial-intelligence-in-europe/

Institute, M. G. (2018). *Notes from the AI frontier: Modeling the impact of AI on the world economy.* McKinsey Global Institute.

Institutet, K. (2021). *Karolinska Institutet.* Recuperado el 28 de August de 2021, de https://ki.se/

Insurance, I. (2021). *Understanding Malaysia's Healthcare System.* Recuperado el 07 de September de 2021, de https://www.internationalinsurance.com/health/systems/malaysia.php

InTek. (2019). *What is Omnichannel Distribution: Types and Challenges Explained.* Recuperado el 30 de August de 2021, de https://blog.intekfreight-logistics.com/what-is-omnichannel-distribution-types-challenges-explained

Intellect. (2021). *Mental health made for everyone.* Recuperado el 29 de August de 2021, de https://www.intellect.co/

Intuitive. (2021). *Da Vinci Surgical Systems.* Recuperado el 01 de September de 2021, de https://www.intuitive.com/en-us/products-and-services/da-vinci/systems

Investopedia. (2021). *Spinoff.* Recuperado el 01 de September de 2021, de https://www.investopedia.com/terms/s/spinoff.asp#:˜:text=A%20spinoff%20is%20the%20creation,parts%20of%20a%20larger%20business.

i-PROGNOSIS. (2021). *The i-PROGNOSIS Approach.* Recuperado el 28 de August de 2021, de http://www.i-prognosis.eu/

IQ, P. (2021). *Translational Medicine 2020: What Does the Future Hold?* Recuperado el 30 de August de 2021, de https://www.pharma-iq.com/pre-clinical-discovery-and-development/articles/translational-medicine-2020-what-does-the-future

i-Scoop. (2021). *Industry 4.0 and the fourth industrial revolution explained.* Recuperado el 01 de September de 2021, de https://www.i-scoop.eu/industry-4-0/

ISO. (2021). *Members.* Recuperado el 03 de September de 2021, de https://www.iso.org/members.html

iXensor. (2021). *The Pioneer of Mobile Health.* Recuperado el 08 de September de 2021, de https://www.ixensor.com/ixensor_web/

iXensor. (2021). *Transform Rapid Testing Paradigm.* Recuperado el 08 de September de 2021, de https://www.ixensor.com/ixensor_web/pixotest-poct-covid-19-antigen-test/

Jacobs, J. (1 de December de 2011). *The Death and Life of Great American Cities: 50th Anniversary Edition.* Modern Library.

Jantra. (2021). *An overview of Latin American healthcare systems.* Recuperado el 05 de September de 2021, de https://www.pacificprime.lat/blog/an-overview-of-latin-american-healthcare-systems/

Japan, G. o. (2021). *An age of digital healthcare opportunity.* Recuperado el 08 de September de 2021, de https://cancerandageing.eiu.com/age-of-digital-healthcare-opportunity/

Johansson, V., Islind, A., Lindroth, T., Angenete, E., & Gellerstedt, M. (2021). Online Communities as a Driver for Patient Empowerment: Systematic Review. *JMIR Publications* (DOI: 10.2196/19910).

K,D. (2019). *The Value Flower: Defining Elements of Value in Health Care.* Recuperado el 28 de August de 2021, de https://www.linkedin.com/pulse/value-flower-defining-elements-health-care-ram-kumar-mishra-ph-d-/?trackingId=Mdt1vrCNmIMGd76ERX4O6w%3D%3D

Kagan, J. (2020). *Primary Account Number (PAN).* Recuperado el 02 de September de 2021, de https://www.investopedia.com/terms/p/primary-account-number-pan.asp

Kahneman, D. (2012). *Thinking, Fast and Slow.* Penguin Books Ltd.

Kahneman, D. (2013). *Thinking, Fast and Slow* (Reprint edition (2 April 2013) ed.). New York: Farrar, Straus and Giroux;.

Kaiboriboon, K., Lüders, H., Hamaneh, M., Turnbull, J., & Lhatoo, S. (2012). EEG source imaging in epilepsy—practicalities and pitfalls. *Nature Reviews Neurology, 8*(https://doi.org/10.1038/nrneurol.2012.150), 498–507.

Kampani, N. (2021). *Get ready to surf India's healthtech wave.* Recuperado el 05 de September de 2021, de https://www.fortuneindia.com/opinion/get-ready-to-surf-indias-health-tech-wave/105587

Kapps, M. (2021). *What's Spurring the Rise of Brazil's HealthTechs?* Recuperado el 05 de September de 2021, de https://latamlist.com/whats-spurring-the-rise-of-brazils-healthtechs/

Kaput, M. (2021). *What Is Artificial Intelligence for Social Media?* Recuperado el 03 de September de 2021, de https://www.marketingaiinstitute.com/blog/what-is-artificial-intelligence-for-social-media

Karantis360. (2021). *About Karantis360.* Recuperado el 02 de September de 2021, de https://karantis360.com/about-karantis360/

Kato H., Matsushita D. (2021). Changes in Walkable Streets during the COVID-19 Pandemic in a Suburban City in the Osaka Metropolitan Area. https://doi.org/10.3390/su13137442

Kelly, S. (2019). *SaMD will increase device innovation: Fitch.* Recuperado el 03 de September de 2019, de https://www.medtechdive.com/news/samd-will-increase-device-innovation-fitch/557006/

Kent, C. (2019). *5 things to know about Germany's gesund medical device market.* Recuperado el 06 de September de 2021, de https://www.medicaldevice-network.com/features/german-medical-device-market/#:˜:text=A%20well%2Dbuilt%20infrastructure,%25)%20and%20China%20(11.1%25).

Kharpal, A. (2020). *China's giants from Alibaba to Tencent ramp up healthtech efforts to battle coronavirus.* Recuperado el 08 de September de 2021, de https://www.cnbc.com/2020/03/04/coronavirus-china-alibaba-tencent-baidu-boost-health-tech-efforts.html

Kim, Y.-L. (2018). Seoul's Wi-Fi hotspots: Wi-Fi access points as an indicator of urban vitality. *Computers, Environment and Urban Systems, 72*(https://doi.org/10.1016/j.compenvurbsys.2018.06.004), 13–24.

Klappich, D., Muynck, B., Aimi, G., Titze, C., & Stevens, A. (2020). *Predicts 2021: Supply Chain Technology*. Gartner Research.

Komorowski, M., Celi, L., Badawi, O., Gordon, A., & Faisal, A. (2018). The Artificial Intelligence Clinician learns optimal treatment strategies for sepsis in intensive care. *Nature Medicine*, *24*(https://doi.org/10.1038/s41591-018-0213-5), 1716–1720.

Konnect, H. (2017). *Value Chain of Hospital*. Recuperado el 28 de August de 2021, de https://www.linkedin.com/pulse/value-chain-hospital-human-konnect/

Kopp, C. M., & Berry Johnson, J. (2020). *Seed Capital*. Recuperado el September de 2021, de https://www.investopedia.com/terms/s/seedcapital.asp

Kopp, C., & Drury, A. (2020). *Product Life Cycle*. Recuperado el 28 de August de 2021, de https://www.investopedia.com/terms/p/product-life-cycle.asp#:˜:text=The%20life%20cycle%20of%20a,new%20markets%2C%20or%20redesign%20packaging.

kore.ai. (2021). *Personalised Care: Virtual Assistants Trigger Innovation in Healthcare*. Recuperado el 01 de September de 2021, de https://kore.ai/solutions/industries/healthcare/

KroniKare. (2021). *iTHERMO*. Recuperado el 01 de September de 2021, de https://kronikare.ai/ithermo/

kry. (2021). *Great healthcare for all*. Recuperado el 06 de September de 2021, de https://kry.health/

Lab, H. V. (2021). *A global network helping teams disrupt healthcare*. Recuperado el 09 de September de 2021, de https://hvlab.eu/

Lab, N. Y. (2021). *New York Digital Health Innovation Lab*. Recuperado el 28 de August de 2021, de https://digitalhealth.nyc/

Lab, N. Y. (2021). *We are scaling innovation in health technology*. Recuperado el 09 de September de 2021, de https://digitalhealth.nyc/

Lacoste-Badie, S., & Droulers, O. (2014). Advertising Memory: The Power of Mirror Neurons. *Journal of Neuroscience Psychology and Economics*, *7* (DOI:10.1037/npe0000025), 195–202. Obtenido de DOI:10.1037/npe0000025

Lakdawalla, D., Doshi, J., Garrison Jr, L., Phelps, C., Basu, A., & Danzon, P. (February de 2018). Defining Elements of Value in Health Care-A Health Economics Approach: An ISPOR Special Task Force Report [3]. *Value Health*, pág. DOI: 10.1016/j.jval.2017.12.007.

Lakdawalla, D., Doshi, J., Jr, L., Phelps, C., Basu, A., & Danzon, P. (February de 2021). Defining Elements of Value in Health Care-A Health Economics Approach: An ISPOR Special Task Force Report. *Value Health*, pág. DOI: 10.1016/j.jval.2017.12.007.

Langley, G., Moen, R., Nolan, K., Nolan, T., Norman, C., & Provost, L. (2009). *The Improvement Guide: A Practical Approach to Enhancing Organizational Performance*. Jossey-Bass.

Lavca. (2021). *Healthtech Startups in Latin America*. Recuperado el 05 de September de 2021, de https://lavca.org/2021-startup-survey-healthtech/

Lawsofux. (2021). *Laws of UX is a collection of best practices that designers can consider when building user interfaces*. Recuperado el 29 de August de 2021, de https://lawsofux.com/

Lawson, J. (2019). *How Smart Technology Is Creating The Internet of Beings (IoB)*. Recuperado el 01 de September de 2021, de https://www.engineerlive.com/content/how-smart-technology-creating-internet-beings-iob

Layar. (2021). *AED4EU*. Recuperado el 02 de September de 2021, de https://www.layar.com/layers/sander1

Lazur, B., Sobolik, L., & King, V. (2020). *Telebehavioral Health: An Effective Alternative to In-Person Care*. Milbank Memorial Fund.

Leadership, T. (2021). *Can Dubai become the capital for next-gen healthtech startups?* Recuperado el 07 de September de 2021, de http://staging.wamda.com/index.php/2021/07/dubai-capital-gen-healthtech-startups

Lean. (2021). *What is Lean?* Recuperado el 29 de August de 2021, de https://www.lean.org/whatslean/

Learn, F. (2021). *This is Future Learning*. Recuperado el 04 de September de 2021, de https://www.futurelearn.com/

Lefebvre, H. (2005). *Rhythm Analysis: Space, Time, and Everyday Life*. London: Continuum.

LEGO. (2021). *LEGO® Serious Play*. Recuperado el 04 de September de 2021, de https://www.lego.com/en-us/seriousplay

Leng, S. (2019). *China's fragmented health care system under increasing pressure as nation rapidly ages*. Recuperado el 08 de September de 2021, de https://www.scmp.com/economy/china-economy/article/3013976/chinas-fragmented-health-care-system-under-increasing

Link, E. A. (2021). *Building Pathways to Connect Agribusiness Entrepreneurs.* Recuperado el 05 de September de 2021, de https://euroafrilink.com/

Link, E. A. (2021). *Partners.* Recuperado el 05 de September de 2021, de https://euroafrilink.com/partner-with-us/

LinkedIn. (2021). *AIME - Artificial Intelligence in Medical Epidemiology.* Recuperado el 08 de September de 2021, de https://www.linkedin.com/company/aime—artificial-intelligence-in-medical-epidemiology/about/

LinkedIn. (2021). *Empower your employees with skills. Strengthen your organization.* Recuperado el 29 de August de 2021, de https://learning.linkedin.com/

LinkedIn. (2021). *European Investment Bank (EIB).* Recuperado el 05 de September de 2021, de https://www.linkedin.com/posts/european-investment-bank_a-partnership-with-africa-activity-6815405367032344576-3gKS/

London, D. (2021). *Accelerator.* Recuperado el 09 de September de 2021, de https://digitalhealth.london/programmes/accelerator

Lorica, B., Armbrust, M., G. A., Xin, R., & Zaharia, M. (2020). *What is a Lakehouse?* Recuperado el 02 de September de 2021, de https://databricks.com/blog/2020/01/30/what-is-a-data-lakehouse.html

Luo, W. (2019). *China implements AI-driven facial recognition for its cows and pigs.* Recuperado el 09 de September de 2021, de https://www.heidi.news/sciences/reconnaissance-faciale-des-vaches-en-chine

macrotrends. (2021). *China Life Expectancy 1950-2021.* Recuperado el 08 de September de 2021, de https://www.macrotrends.net/countries/CHN/china/life-expectancy#:~:text=The%20current%20life%20expectancy%20for,a%200.22%25%20increase%20from%202018.

Madir, J. (2020). *HealthTech: Law and Regulation.* Cheltenham, United Kingdom: Edward Elgar Publishing.

MAHC. (2021). *NTU Medical Genie – AI Decision Support System for Precision Medicine.* Recuperado el 08 de September de 2021, de http://mahc.ntu.edu.tw/en/research_view.php?id=1

Mäkitalo, N., Taivalsaari, A., Kiviluoto, A., Mikkonen, T., & Capilla, R. (2020). On opportunistic software reuse. *Computing, 102*(https://doi.org/10.1007/s00607-020-00833-6), 2385–2408.

Malayasia.gov. (2021). *Industry4WRD: National Policy on Industry 4.0.* Recuperado el 08 de September de 2021, de https://www.malaysia.gov.my/portal/content/30610

Malaysia, F. (2021). *Unleashing the potential of HealthTech, EdTech in M'sia.* Recuperado el 08 de September de 2021, de https://focusmalaysia.my/unleashing-the-potential-of-healthtech-edtech-in-msia/

Malaysia.gov. (2021). *Digital Lifestyle Malaysia(DLM).* Recuperado el 08 de September de 2021, de https://www.malaysia.gov.my/portal/content/30796

Malaysia.gov. (2021). *National Internet Of Things (IoT) Strategic Roadmap.* Recuperado el 08 de September de 2021, de https://www.malaysia.gov.my/portal/content/30611

Markets, R. a. (2020). *World Healthcare Cloud Computing Market Analysis 2020: Key Player Profiles Including Carestream Health, GE Healthcare and Cisco.* Recuperado el 01 de September de 2021, de https://www.globenewswire.com/news-release/2020/05/11/2030832/0/en/World-Healthcare-Cloud-Computing-Market-Analysis-2020-Key-Player-Profiles-Including-Carestream-Health-GE-Healthcare-and-Cisco.html

Martech. (2020). *Report: Insights-led engagement for the mobile-first consumer.* Recuperado el 03 de September de 2021, de https://martech.org/report-insights-led-engagement-for-the-mobile-first-consumer/

Martin, M. (2020). *What Is a BCG Matrix?* Recuperado el 29 de August de 2021, de https://www.businessnewsdaily.com/5693-bcg-matrix.html

Martini, M., & Bragazzi, N. (2021). Googling for Neurological Disorders: From Seeking Health-Related Information to Patient Empowerment, Advocacy, and Open, Public Self-Disclosure in the Neurology 2.0 Era. *JMIR Publications,* (DOI: 10.2196/13999).

Martins, H. (2020). Digital Health Diplomacy in Chained Globalised Health Context. *HealthManagement. org, 20*(10).

Maruyama, Y., Kasai, M., Oyama, K., & Chikazawa, K. (2018). Experiences from Japan – SAKIGAKE Designation System for Regenerative Medical Products. *Cell and Gene Therapy Insights, 4* (DOI:10.18609/cgti.2018.045), 545–554.

Mastorakis, G., Mavromoustakis, C., & Pallis, E. (2015). *Resource Management of Mobile Cloud Computing Networks and Environments (Advances in Systems Analysis, Software Engineering, and High Performance Computing)* (1st ed.). U.S: Idea Group.

Mawidy. (2021). *Your doctor is with you wherever you are.* Recuperado el 07 de September de 2021, de https://mawidy.com/en/

McCarty, N. (2020). *What is Political Polarization?* Oxford University Press. Obtenido de https://whateveryoneneedstoknow.com/view/10.1093/wentk/9780190867782.001.0001/isbn-9780190867782-book-part-2

McDermott, J., Wang, J., Mitchell, H., Webb-Robertson, B.-J., Hafen, R., Ramey, J., & Rodland, K. (2013). Challenges in biomarker discovery: combining expert insights with statistical analysis of complex omics data. *Expert Opinion on Medical Diagnostics,* (https://doi.org/10.1517/17530059.2012.718329), 37–51.

McKenna, I. (2020). *How do we Measure the "Value" in Value-Based care?* Recuperado el 30 de August de 2021, de https://www.ohe.org/publications/how-do-we-measure-%E2%80%9Cvalue%E2%80%9D-value-based-care

McKesson. (2021). *McKesson Ventures.* Recuperado el 28 de August de 2021, de https://ventures.mckesson.com/

McKinsey Global Institute. (2018). Notes from the AI frontier: Modeling the impact of AI on the world economy. McKinsey Global Institute. chrome-extension://efaidnbmnnnibpcajpcglclefindmkaj/https://www.mckinsey.com/~/media/McKinsey/Featured%20Insights/Artificial%20Intelligence/Notes%20from%20the%20frontier%20Modeling%20the%20impact%20of%20AI%20on%20the%20world%20economy/MGI-Notes-from-the-AI-frontier-Modeling-the-impact-of-AI-on-the-world-economy-September-2018.ashx

McKinsey, e. (2020). *Transforming healthcare with AI.* McKinsey & Company.

McKinsey. (2020). *The next wave of healthcare innovation: The evolution of ecosystems.* Recuperado el 05 de September de 2021, de https://www.mckinsey.com/industries/healthcare-systems-and-services/our-insights/the-next-wave-of-healthcare-innovation-the-evolution-of-ecosystems

McKinsey. (2020). *The recovery will be digital.* McKinsey Global Publishing.

McKinsey. (2021). *Telehealth: A quarter-trillion-dollar post-COVID-19 reality?* Recuperado el 30 de August de 2021, de https://www.mckinsey.com/industries/healthcare-systems-and-services/our-insights/telehealth-a-quarter-trillion-dollar-post-covid-19-reality#

Medec. (2017). *The Innovation Dilemma: Achieving Value, Health Outcomes and Contributing to the New Economy.* Medec.

Medefer. (2021). *Medefer is a Care Quality Commission registered provider, working in partnership with the NHS to provide a virtual outpatient service and deliver faster, better care for patients.* Recuperado el 07 de September de 2021, de: https://medefer.com/

MedicalNewsToday. (2021). *Could 'mirror neurons' explain brain mechanisms of empathy?* Recuperado el 02 de September de 2021, de 324974

MedicalStartups. (2019). *Top 40 medical and healthcare startups in China.* Recuperado el 08 de September de 2021, de https://www.medicalstartups.org/country/China/

Medicine, B. (2018). *From hype to reality: data science enabling personalised medicine.* Recuperado el 28 de August de 2021, de https://bmcmedicine.biomedcentral.com/articles/10.1186/s12916-018-1122-7

Medicine, J. H. (2016). *Study Suggests Medical Errors Now Third Leading Cause of Death in the U.S.* Recuperado el 04 de September de 2021, de https://www.hopkinsmedicine.org/news/media/releases/study_suggests_medical_errors_now_third_leading_cause_of_death_in_the_us

Medicine, T. I. (2021). *he Charles Bronfman Institute for Personalised Medicine.* Recuperado el 02 de September de 2021, de https://icahn.mssm.edu/research/ipm/programs/biome-biobank

MedicinePlus. (2021). *What are genome editing and CRISPR-Cas9?* Recuperado el 02 de September de 2021, de https://medlineplus.gov/genetics/understanding/genomicresearch/genomeediting/

Medicsen. (2021). *The Painless Alternative to manage Chronic Diseases.* Recuperado el 07 de September de 2021, de https://www.medicsen.com/en/

MedlinePlus. (2021). *Pacemakers and Implantable Defibrillators.* Recuperado el 01 de September de 2021, de https://medlineplus.gov/pacemakersandimplantabledefibrillators.html

Medscape. (2021). *Simplify Your Professional Life. Use Medscape.* Recuperado el 04 de September de 2021, de https://www.medscape.com/features/mktg/public/register/ppc1?src=ppc_google_acq-brand_solo_lp2_englang-es-int&gclid=Cj0KCQjwxJqHBhC4ARIsAChq4auGctlrV4rqvqPd-BPqBe2EOi7sbZMgZPgP8k_W-Grt-l8TWPDdI_UaAlanEALw_wcB

MedTech Europe. *The European Medical Technology Industry in Figures, 2020.* https://www.medtecheurope. org/wp-content/uploads/2020/05/The-European-Medical-Technology-Industry-in-figures-2020.pdf

Medvine. (2021). *Medvine.* Recuperado el 06 de September de 2021, de https://www.medvine.com/th-en

Membrillo, A. (2021). *2021 Healthcare Marketing Trends to Watch.* Recuperado el 01 de September de 2021, de https://www.cardinaldigitalmarketing.com/blog/2021-healthcare-marketing-trends/

Merck. (2021). *Accelerator.* Recuperado el 28 de August de 2021, de https://www.merckgroup.com/en/research/innovation-center/accelerator.html

MICINN. (s.f.). *MICINN.* Recuperado el August de 2021, de Estrategia de Inteligencia Artificial: www. ciencia.gob.es/stfls/MICINN/Ciencia/Ficheros/Estrategia_Inteligencia_Artificial_IDI.pdf

Microsoft. (2021). *Microsoft HoloLens 2.* Recuperado el 02 de September de 2021, de https://www.microsoft.com/en-us/hololens

Microsoft. (2021). *Mount Sinai.* Recuperado el 02 de September de 2021, de https://customers.microsoft.com/en-us/story/858292-mount-sinai-health-system-health-provider-teams-hololens-remote-assist-dynamics-365

Mili, A., Zalila-Wenkstern, R., & Mittermeir, R. (January 1998). A Survey of software Reuse Libraries. *Annals of Software Engineering, 5* (DOI:10.1023/A:1018964121953), 349–414.

Miller, B. (Dirección). (2011). *Moneyball* [Película]. Recuperado el 28 de August de 2021, de https://www.euromoney.com/learning/blockchain-explained/what-is-blockchain#:˜:text=Blockchain%20is%20a%20system%20of,computer%20systems%20on%20the%20blockchain.

Ministry of Land, I. a. (2021). *Smart City Korea.* Recuperado el 01 de September de 2021, de Sejong 5-1 Living Area Smart City Pilot.: https://smartcity.go.kr/en/

Miotto, R., Danieletto, M., Scelza, J., Kidd, B., & Dudley, J. (2018). Reflecting health: smart mirrors for personalised medicine. *npj Digital Medicine*(https://doi.org/10.1038/s41746-018-0068-7).

MIT. (2021). *MIT–Harvard Medical School.* Recuperado el 05 de September de 2021, de https://learn-bootcamp.mit. edu/healthcare-innovation?utm_medium=sem&utm_source=google&utm_campaign=obhh&utm_term=healthcare%20tech%20startups&utm_content=aw-a&utm_term=healthcare%20tech%20startups&utm_campaign=Online+Healthcare+Innovation+Bootcamp+-+A/Dev

Mitchell, C., & Estevez, E. (2021). *IP Address.* Recuperado el 29 de August de 2021, de https://www.investopedia.com/terms/i/ip-address.asp

Mittra, J., & Milne, C.-P. (2013). Translational Medicine: The Future of Therapy? *Pan Stanford Publishing.*

Models, H. I. (2020). *CMS Announces Comprehensive Strategy to Enhance Hospital Capacity Amid COVID-19 Surge.* Recuperado el 30 de August de 2021, de https://www.cms.gov/newsroom/press-releases/cms-announces-comprehensive-strategy-enhance-hospital-capacity-amid-covid-19-surge

MOEA. (2019). *Annual Report of BSMI.* Bureau of Standards, Metrology and Inspection. Recuperado el 08 de September de 2021, de https://www.bsmi.gov.tw/wSite/public/Data/f1597022509889.pdf

Mohammadian-Molina, R. (2020). *Neom could become the first 'healthtech' capital of the world.* Recuperado el 07 de September de 2021, de https://www.arabnews.com/node/1707136/neom-could-become-first-%E2%80%98health-tech%E2%80%99-capital-world

Montagnon, E., Cerny, M., Cadrin-Chênevert, A., Hamilton, V., Derennes, T., Ilinca, A., Tang, A. (2020). Deep learning workflow in radiology: a primer. *Insights into Imaging, 11*(https://doi.org/10.1186/s13244-019-0832-5), 22.

Moorfields. (2021). *Moorfields Private Eye Hospital.* Recuperado el 28 de August de 2021, de https://www.moorfields-private.co.uk/

Mottain, M. (2021). *Malaysia on track to achieve high-income nation status.* Recuperado el 08 de September de 2021, de https://www.thestar.com.my/business/business-news/2021/05/22/malaysia-on-track-to-achieve-high-income-nation-status

Mtaccelerator. (s.f.). *Microsoft Accelerator.* (Microsoft, Productor) Recuperado el September de 2021, de Microsoft: https://www.microsoft.com/taiwan/mtaccelerator/default.htm

MUNDI. (s.f.). *MUNDI web Services.* Recuperado el October de 2021, de Mundiwebservices: https://mundiwebservices.com/

Muthuppalaniappan, M. (2021). Healthcare cyber-attacks and the COVID-19 pandemic: an urgent threat to global health. *International Journal for Quality in Health Care, 33* (https://doi.org/10.1093/intqhc/mzaa117).

MyDigital. (2021). *Malaysia Economy Digital Blueprint.* Recuperado el 08 de September de 2021, de https://www.epu.gov.my/sites/default/files/2021-02/Malaysia-digital-economy-blueprint.pdf

myHealthTeams. (2021). *We create social networks for millions of people living with chronic conditions.* Recuperado el 03 de September de 2021, de https://www.myhealthteams.com/

mySugar. (2021). *Your diabetes data, simply there.* Recuperado el 29 de August de 2021, de https://www.mysugr.com/en/

NACNS. (2021). *What is a CNS?* Recuperado el 28 de August de 2021, de https://nacns.org/about-us/what-is-a-cns/

Nation, T. (2021). *About us.* Recuperado el 07 de September de 2021, de https://technation.io/about-us/

Nation, T. (2021). https://technation.io/about-us/. Recuperado el 06 de September de 2021, de https://technation.io/about-us/

Nations, U. (2017). *World Population Ageing.* United Nations.

Nations, U. (2021). *Stop enforced disappearances.* Recuperado el 28 de August de 2021, de https://www.un.org/en/

NDRC. (2021). *China National Development and Reform Commission.* Recuperado el 28 de August de 2021, de https://www.ndrc.gov.cn/xxgk/zcfb/tz/202007/t20200715_1233793.html

Neom. (2021). *A Vision of a New Future.* Recuperado el 07 de September de 2021, de https://www.neom.com/en-us

Net, S. D. (2015). *Kenya launches telemedicine initiative for the poor.* Recuperado el 30 de August de 2021, de https://www.scidev.net/sub-saharan-africa/news/kenya-launches-telemedicine-initiative-poor/

Netatmo. (2021). *Live in a healthier home.* Recuperado el 29 de August de 2021, de https://www.netatmo.com/en-eu/aircare/homecoach

NEWSWIRE, C. P. (27 de April de 2021). *Cision PR Newswire.* Recuperado el September de 2021, de Holomusk Acquires Mental Health Analytics Provider Otsuka health Solutions to Expand its Footprint in the UK.: https://www.prnewswire.com/news-releases/holmusk-acquires-mental-health-analytics-provider-otsuka-health-solutions-to-expand-its-footprint-in-the-uk-301276565.html

NHS. (2009). *How To: Set an Audit Sample & Plan Your Data Collection.* UHBristol Clinical Audit Team.

NHS. (2015). *Innovation into action.* Recuperado el 07 de September de 2021, de https://www.england.nhs.uk/wp-content/uploads/2015/10/nhs-inovation-into-action.pdf

NHS. (2016). *New care Models: Vanguards - developing a blueprint for.* Recuperado el 07 de September de 2021, de https://www.england.nhs.uk/wp-content/uploads/2015/11/new_care_models.pdf

NHS. (2019). *Preparing the healthcare workforce to deliver the digital future.* NHS.

NHS. (2021). *A platform for sharing resources.* Recuperado el 04 de September de 2021, de https://learninghub.nhs.uk/home/login?returnUrl=%2Fconnect%2Fauthorize%2Fcallback%3Fclient_id%3Dlearninghubwebclient%26redirect_uri%3Dhttps%253A%252F%252Flearninghub.nhs.uk%252Fsignin-oidc%26response_type%3Dcode%2520id_token%26scope%3Dopenid%2520profile%2

NHS. (2021). *Acute Kidney Injury Programme – Think Kidneys.* Recuperado el 02 de September de 2021, de https://www.england.nhs.uk/akiprogramme/

NHS. (2021). *Digital Technology Assessment Criteria (DTAC).* Recuperado el 08 de September de 2021, de https://www.nhsx.nhs.uk/key-tools-and-info/digital-technology-assessment-criteria-dtac/

NHS. (2021). *Driving healthcare innovation.* Recuperado el 07 de September de 2021, de https://nhsaccelerator.com/

NHS. (2021). *New care models.* Recuperado el 07 de September de 2021, de https://www.england.nhs.uk/new-care-models/

NICE. (2021). *Evidence standards framework for digital health technologies.* Recuperado el 28 de August de 2021, de https://www.nice.org.uk/about/what-we-do/our-programmes/evidence-standards-framework-for-digital-health-technologies

Nikles, J., Daza, E., McDonald, S., Hekler, E., & Schork, N. (February de 2021). Editorial: Creating Evidence From Real World Patient Digital Data. *Frontiers in Computer Science,* pág. 10.3389/fcomp.2020.636996.

Nixi. (2021). *Nixi for Children.* Recuperado el 02 de September de 2021, de https://nixiforchildren.com/en/

Nnoaham, K., & Cann, K. (May 2020). Can cluster analyses of linked healthcare data identify unique population segments in a general practice-registered population? *BMC Public Health, 20* (DOI:10.1186/s12889-020-08930-z).

Novartis. (2021). *Hubs across the World*. Recuperado el 05 de September de 2021, de https://www.biome.novartis.com/innovation-hubs

Novartis. (2021). *The Novartis Biome*. Recuperado el 28 de August de 2021, de https://www.biome.novartis.com/

Novartis. (s.f.). Drones Deliver Medicines. Novartis https://www.youtube.com/watch?v=5EdHA62jrzE.

Novet, J. (2017). *Twitter is now using a trendy type of AI to figure out which tweets to show you*. Recuperado el 03 de September de 2021, de https://www.cnbc.com/2017/05/09/twitter-using-deep-learning-ai-to-rank-tweets.html

NSA. (2004). *NSA/CSS Freedom of Information Act Program*. NSA.

NSA. (2020). *2020 NSA cybersecurity year in review*. National Security Agency. United States of America: 2020 year in review.

NSA/CSS. (2021). *Policies*. Recuperado el 04 de September de 2021, de https://www.nsa.gov/news-features/declassified-documents/nsa-css-policies/

NSA-CSS. (2021). *National Security Agency Central Security Service*. Recuperado el 28 de August de 2021, de https://www.nsa.gov/

Ntoutsi, E, F., P, G., & U, e. a. (2020). Bias in data-driven artificial intelligence systems—An introductory survey. *WIREs Data Mining and Knowledge Discovery*(https://doi.org/10.1002/widm.1356).

NTU. (2021). *What We Do*. Recuperado el 06 de September de 2021, de https://www.ntu.edu.sg/healthtech

Nuance. (2021). *Document complete patient care—anytime, anywhere*. Recuperado el 02 de September de 2021, de https://www.nuance.com/healthcare/provider-solutions/speech-recognition/dragon-medical-one.html

Nunez, J. (2021). *'Neuromarketing' or how to use science to succeed in electronic commerce*. Recuperado el 02 de September de 2021, de https://elpais.com/economia/2020/12/22/nuevos_tiempos/1608627485_528341.html?ssm=TW_CC&s=08

NYC. (2021). *Healthy Lives*. NYC.

NYC. (2021). *New York City's Green New Deal. Volume 5 of 9*. Recuperado el 05 de September de 2021, de http://onenyc.cityofnewyork.us/

NYC. (2021). *NYCx Challenges*. Recuperado el 30 de August de 2021, de http://www.nyc.gov/html/nycx/challenges.html

NYC. (2021). *The Best Health Care System In the World*. Recuperado el 05 de September de 2021, de https://www.nytimes.com/interactive/2017/09/18/upshot/best-health-care-system-country-bracket.html?mtrref=undefined&gwh=1AD659426A679E8F1855C10B391E24A2&gwt=pay&assetType=PAYWALL

O'Connor, S. (2017). *What Is Interoperability, and Why Is It Important?* Recuperado el 05 de September de 2021, de https://www.adsc.com/blog/what-is-interoperability-and-why-is-it-important

OECD. (2021). *Health Expenditure*. Recuperado el 04 de September de 2021, de https://www.oecd.org/health/health-expenditure.htm

OGTR, & Regulator, O. o. (s.f.). *OGTR; Office of the Gene Technology Regulator*. (A. G. health, Productor) Recuperado el September de 2021, de Australian Government. DEpartment of health. Office of the Gene Technology Regulator.: https://www.ogtr.gov.au/

Olano, G. (2019). *AI to be more deeply integrated into insurance – Ping An*. Recuperado el 08 de September de 2021, de https://www.insurancebusinessmag.com/asia/news/breaking-news/ai-to-be-more-deeply-integrated-into-insurance–ping-an-190507.aspx

Olofin, B., Onyeabo, G., Olofin, O., Ejim, J., & Emeh, C. (May 2020). Health Information and Health Communication Technology: Impacts and Implications. *SSRN Electronic Journal* (DOI:10.2139/ssrn.3686187).

Omron. (2021). *Evolv*. Recuperado el 29 de August de 2021, de https://www.omron-healthcare.fr/fr/tensiometres/EVOLV.html

OnCompass. (2021). *Find the Best Personalised Cancer Therapy - Today*. Recuperado el 06 de September de 2021, de https://www.oncompassmedicine.com/

Oracle. (2021). Oracle. Oracle Crystal Ball Resources. https://www.oracle.com/applications/crystalball/resources.html#:˜:text=Oracle%20Crystal%20Ball%20is%20the,the%20critical%20factors%20affecting%20risk.&text=Comprehensive%20risk%20analysis%20and%20 optimization%20 enables%20 confident%20 strategic%20and%20 oper

Organization, W. H. (2021). *World health statistics 2021: monitoring health for the SDGs, sustainable development goals*. World Health Organization.

Organization, World Intellectual Property. (20 de October de 2021). *Innovation Perseveres: International Patent Filings via WIPO COntinued to Grow in 2020 Despite COVID-19 Pandemic*. Obtenido de www.wipo.int.

Osti. (2021). *Single cell analysis: the new frontier in 'Omics'*. Recuperado el 02 de September de 2021, de https://www.osti.gov/biblio/983315

Outlook, W. E. (2021). *World Economic Outlook*. Recuperado el 05 de September de 2021, de https://www.imf.org/en/Publications/WEO

OWASP. (2021). *Who is the OWASP® Foundation?* Recuperado el 04 de September de 2021, de https://owasp.org/

Owusu-Marfo, J., Lulin, Z., Asante Antwi, H., & Antwi, M. (2019). Electronic Health Records Adoption in China's Hospitals: A Narrative Review. *Nursing Informatics in Ghana*.

Ozturk, S., & Topcu, E. (2014). Health Expenditures and Economic Growth: Evidence from G8 Countries. *International Journal of Economics and Empirical Research*, 256–61.

Pacific., W. H. (2019). Health equity and its determinants in the Western Pacific Region. *WHO Regional Office for the Western Pacific*, págs. https://apps.who.int/iris/handle/10665/333944. License: CC BY-NC-SA 3.0 IGO.

PAGD. (2021). *Ping An Good Doctor (PAGD)*. Recuperado el 02 de September de 2021, de http://www.pagd.net/.

PAHO. (2021). *Why data disaggregation is key during a pandemic?* Paho.

Pandey, A., & Mann, M. (15 de June de 2000). Proteomics to study genes and genomes. *Nature*, págs. 837–46 DOI: 10.1038/35015709.

Panetta, K. (2016). *Artificial intelligence, machine learning, and smart things promise an intelligent future*. Recuperado el 04 de September de 2021, de https://www.gartner.com/smarterwithgartner/gartners-top-10-technology-trends-2017/

Paoli, A., & D'Auria, V. (2021). Digital Ethnography: A Systematic Literature Review1. *Italian Sociological Review, Verona, Vol. 11, Iss. 4S*, 243–267.

Parent, T. A. (2021). *The Asian Parent*. Recuperado el 03 de September de 2021, de https://sg.theasianparent.com/

Park, T. D. (2021). *Upcoming Events*. Recuperado el 06 de September de 2021, de https://www.truedigitalpark.com/en

Parmar, A. (2019). *China, other countries, beating US in digital health adoption*. Recuperado el 28 de August de 2021, de https://medcitynews.com/2019/06/us-lagging-behind-china-and-other-countries-in-digital-health-adoption/

Patientslikeme. (2021). *Heal Together*. Recuperado el 03 de September de 2021, de https://www.patientslikeme.com/

Patrick, C. (2021). *Medical Definition of No show*. Recuperado el 02 de September de 2021, de https://www.medicinenet.com/no_show/definition.htm

Patrick, D., Burke, L., Powers, J., Scott, J., Rock, E., Dawisha, S., … Kennedy, D. (Nov-Dec de 2007). Patient-reported outcomes to support medical product labeling claims: FDA perspective. *Value Health*, págs. 125–37.

Penn, N. (2021). *Uses For AI In Health Care Marketing*. Obtenido de Forbes Magazine: https://www.forbes.com/sites/forbesagencycouncil/2019/10/01/uses-for-ai-in-health-care-marketing/?sh=1508a0416f40

People, T. F. (2021). *109 Top Jack Welch Quotes On Winning And Leadership*. Recuperado el 30 de August de 2021, de https://quotes.thefamouspeople.com/jack-welch-1713.php

Perspective. (2018). *Canada is Ideally Positioned For The Healthtech Sector*. Recuperado el 05 de September de 2021, de https://perspective.ca/canada-ideally-positioned-health-tech-sector/

Peters, T., & Waterman Jr., R. (2004). *In Search Of Excellence: Lessons from America's Best-Run Companies.* Profile Books.

Pharma. (2020). *Growing HealthTech market in Malaysia offers myriad opportunities for domestic and foreign firms, says GlobalData.* Recuperado el 08 de September de 2021, de https://www.globaldata.com/growing-healthtech-market-in-malaysia-offers-myriad-opportunities-for-domestic-and-foreign-firms-says-globaldata/

Pharmaoffer. (2020). *The future of pharma: 5 Things that will change the pharmaceutical industry.* Pharmaoffer.

Pharmeasy. (2021). *Pharmeasy.* Recuperado el 01 de September de 2021, de https://pharmeasy.in/

Philips. (2019). *Technology and the democratization of healthcare.* Recuperado el 30 de August de 2021, de https://www.philips.com/a-w/about/news/archive/blogs/innovation-matters/20190925-technology-and-the-democratization-of-healthcare.html

Philips. (2021). *Big ideas are needed to drive change in healthcare.* Recuperado el 28 de August de 2021, de https://www.usa.philips.com/healthcare/innovation/philips-ventures

Phrma. (2017). *Barriers to Value-Based Contracts for Innovative Medicines.* Phrma.

Pigozzo, A., Macedo, G., Santos, R., & Lobosco, M. (2013). On the computational modeling of the innate immune system. *BMC Bioinformatics* (https://doi.org/10.1186/1471-2105-14-S6-S7).

Pontis, S. (2018). *Making Sense of Field Research: A Practical Guide for Information Designers* (1st edition ed.). Routledge.

Poppe, O., Sæbø, J., & Braa, J. (19 de February de 2021). WHO digital health packages for disseminating data standards and data use practices. *International Journal of Medical Informatics*, pág. https://doi.org/10.1016/j.ijmedinf.2021.104422.

Post, B. (2017). *The Healthtech Environment in Thailand.* Recuperado el 06 de September de 2021, de https://www.bangkokpost.com/business/1314743/the-healthtech-environment-in-thailand

Pouke, M., & Häkkilä, J. (17 de December de 2013). Elderly Healthcare Monitoring Using an Avatar-Based 3D Virtual Environment. *Int J Environ Res Public Health*, págs. 7283–7298 DOI: 10.3390/ijerph10127283.

Pouke, M., & Häkkilä, J. (2013). Elderly Healthcare Monitoring Using an Avatar-Based 3D Virtual Environment. *Int J Environ Res Public Health* (DOI: 10.3390/ijerph10127283), 7283–7298.

PPPLRC. (2008). *Royal North Shore Hospital and Community Health Services Project - summary of contract.* Recuperado el 09 de September de 2021, de https://ppp.worldbank.org/public-private-partnership/library/royal-north-shore-hospital-and-community-health-services-project-summary-contract

PPPLRC. (2021). *Are you financing or structuring public-private partnerships in infrastructure? PPPLRC can help.* Recuperado el 04 de September de 2021, de https://ppp.worldbank.org/public-private-partnership/

Prainsack, B. (2017). Personalised Medicine: Empowered Patients in the 21st Century? *JSTOR*(https://www.jstor.org/stable/j.ctt1pwtb48), 288.

PRC, N. H. (2021). *Healthy China Action Plan (2019 - 2030).* Recuperado el 08 de September de 2021, de http://en.nhc.gov.cn/HealthyChinaActionPlan.html

Press, N. A. (2002). The Future of the Public's Health in the 21st Century. *Institute of Medicine (US) Committee on Assuring the Health of the Public in the 21st Century.*

Pressbooks. (2021). *Introducing the key stakeholders: patients, providers, payors, and policymakers (the four p's).* Recuperado el 28 de August de 2021, de https://jln1.pressbooks.com/chapter/3-introducing-the-key-stakeholders-patients-providers-payors-and-policymakers-the-four-ps/

Prieto, L., & Sacristán, J. (2003). Problems and solutions in calculating quality-adjusted life years (QALYs). *Health Qual Life Outcomes*, 1: 80.(10.1186/1477-7525-1-80).

Programs, V. R. (2021). *Health Sector Transformation Program.* Recuperado el 07 de September de 2021, de https://www.vision2030.gov.sa/v2030/vrps/hstp/

Putrino, D. (2017). Constructing Your Idea. *SpringerLink* (DOI: 10.1007/978-3-319-71619-0_2).

PWC. (2017). *The Digital Healthcare Leap.* Digital health in emerging markets.

PWC. (2021). *Forging a path for healthtech in Canada means getting all stakeholders on the same page.* Recuperado el 05 de September de 2021, de https://www.pwc.com/ca/en/industries/technology/forging-a-path-for-healthtech-in-canada.html

Quibim. (2021). *We Speak Human.* Recuperado el 07 de September de 2021, de https://quibim.com/

Quotes, A. (2021). *Jack Welch*. Recuperado el 30 de August de 2021, de https://www.azquotes.com/quote/391460

Raghupathi, V., & Raghupathi, W. (2020). Healthcare Expenditure and Economic Performance: Insights From the United States Data. *Frontiers in Public Health*, pág. 156 DOI: 10.3389/fpubh.2020.00156.

Rally. (2021). *Agile With a Capital "A" Vs. agile With a Lowercase "a"*. Recuperado el 29 de August de 2021, de https://web.archive.org/web/20160105105258/https://www.rallydev.com/blog/engineering/agile-capital-vs-agile-lowercase

Rally. (2021). *Agile With a Capital "A" Vs. agile With a Lowercase "a"*. Recuperado el 28 de August de 2021, de https://web.archive.org/web/20160105105258/https://www.rallydev.com/blog/engineering/agile-capital-vs-agile-lowercase

Rantanen, L. (2020). *Barriers to high-tech SME internationalization: Finnish healthtech companies*.

Ready, R., & Burton, K. (2008). *PNL Para Dummies*. PNL Para Dummies.

Ready, R., & Burton, K. (2015). *NLP for Dummies*. Wiley Publishing.

RECOVER-E. (2021). *Welcome to RECOVER-E*. Recuperado el 28 de August de 2021, de http://www.recover-e.eu/

Reed, Z. (2021). *The Regulatory Aspects of AI/ML-based SaMD*. Recuperado el 03 de September de 2021, de https://www.medtechintelligence.com/feature_article/the-regulatory-aspects-of-ai-ml-based-samd/

Reeder, B., & David BS, A. (2016). Health at hand: A systematic review of smart watch uses for health and wellness. *Journal of Biomedical Informatics*, *63*(https://doi.org/10.1016/j.jbi.2016.09.001), 269–276.

Refolo, P., Minacori, R., Mele, V., Sacchini, D., & Spagnolo, A. G. (October de 2012). Patient-reported outcomes (PROs): The significance of using humanistic measures in clinical trial and clinical practice. *European Review for Medical and Pharmacological Sciences*, págs. 1319–1323.

Reiff, N., & Mansa, J. (2021). *Series A, B, C Funding: How It Works*. Recuperado el 04 de September de 2021, de https://www.investopedia.com/articles/personal-finance/102015/series-b-c-funding-what-it-all-means-and-how-it-works.asp

Ren, D. (2021). *WeChat's value surpasses Ferrari as Covid-19 pandemic upends businesses and buoys technology brands from Apple to Tesla*. Recuperado el 04 de September de 2021, de https://www.scmp.com/business/companies/article/3119292/wechats-value-surpasses-ferrari-covid-19-pandemic-upends

Reuters. (2021). *China issues draft rules banning unfair competition in the internet sector*. Recuperado el 08 de September de 2021, de https://www.thehindu.com/sci-tech/technology/china-issues-draft-rules-banning-unfair-competition-in-the-internet-sector/article35951284.ece

Review, M. T. (2021). *We tried out the Excelsior Pass, New York's state vaccine passport*. Recuperado el 02 de September de 2021, de https://www.technologyreview.com/2021/07/06/1027770/vaccine-passport-new-york-excelsior-pass/

RockHealth. (2021). *About Rock Health*. Recuperado el 09 de September de 2021, de https://rockhealth.com/about/

Rockstart. (2021). *About*. Recuperado el 09 de September de 2021, de https://www.rockstart.com/health/health-program/

Rodríguez, P., Graña, S., Alvarez-León, E.E., Battaglini, M., Darias, F. J., Hernán, M. A., … Lacasa, L.. (2021). A population-based controlled experiment assessing the epidemiological impact of digital contact tracing. *Nature Communications* (DOI:10.1038/s41467-020-20817-6), 587.

Rodziewicz, T., Houseman, B., & Hipskind, J. (2021). Medical Error Reduction and Prevention. *StatPearls Publishing*, pág. https://www.ncbi.nlm.nih.gov/books/NBK499956/.

Saeed, M., & Kersten, W. (2017). Supply chain sustainability performance indicators - a content analysis based on published standards and guidelines. *Logistics Research* (DOI:10.23773/2017_12).

Saldarriaga, M., & Mejia, P. (2021). *The Five Most Disruptive Healthtechs in Latin America*. Recuperado el 05 de September de 2021, de https://theorg.com/insights/the-five-most-disruptive-healthtechs-in-latin-america

Sara, G., Murray, R. M., & Wachter, R. J. (2020). *Discrimination By Artificial Intelligence In a Commercial Electronic Health Record—A Case Study*. Recuperado el 02 de September de 2021, de https://www.healthaffairs.org/do/10.1377/hblog20200128.626576/full/

Sasan, A. (2015). *Mobile Health: A Technology Road Map* (1st ed., Vol. 5). Springer.

Saúde, M. D. (2020). *Estratégia de Saúde Digital para o Brasil*. Recuperado el 05 de September de 2021, de https://bvsms.saude.gov.br/bvs/publicacoes/estrategia_saude_digital_Brasil.pdf

Saudi, I. (2021). *HealthCare And Life Sciences*. Recuperado el 07 de September de 2021, de https://invest-saudi.sa/en/sectors-opportunities/healthcare-life-sciences

Saudi, I. (2021). *Why Saudi Arabia*. Recuperado el 07 de September de 2021, de https://investsaudi.sa/en/why-saudi-arabia

Scaler8. (2021). *Navigate the German*. Recuperado el 05 de September de 2021, de https://scaler8.com/

Schueler, P. (2021). *Innovation in Clinical Trial Methodologies - Lessons Learned during the Corona Pandemic* (https://doi.org/10.1016/C2020-0-02117-1 ed.). Academic Press.

Schutzer M.D, S., Grady-Benson M.D, J., Libert, B., & Beck, M. (2017). *Healthcare urgently needs a Copernican Revolution*. Recuperado el 28 de August de 2021, de https://medcitynews.com/2017/04/healthcare-urgently-needs-copernican-revolution/

Schwartz, L. (2021). *Tel Aviv's symbiotic relationship with Silicon Valley*. Recuperado el 28 de August de 2021, de https://restofworld.org/2021/tech-hubs-tel-aviv/

Seedcamp. (2021). *Europe's Seed Fund*. Recuperado el 28 de August de 2021, de https://seedcamp.com/

Segment, T. (2021). *What is Data Orchestration & Why It's Essential for Analysis*. Recuperado el 28 de August de 2021, de https://segment.com/resources/data-strategy/what-is-data-orchestration/#:~:text=Data%20orchestration%20is%20the%20process,streamline%20data%2Ddriven%20decision%20making.

Sensely. (2021). *Increasing Access Lowering Costs Improving Health*. Recuperado el 02 de September de 2021, de https://www.sensely.com/

Serkel, M. M. (2021). *COVID-19: Up to Dh10,000 fine for breaking quarantine smartwatches*. Recuperado el 02 de September de 2021, de https://gulfnews.com/uae/government/covid-19-up-to-dh10000-fine-for-breaking-quarantine-smartwatches-1.1613463928939

Services, A. F. (2018). *Conceptualising a Data Infrastructure for the Capture, Use, and Sharing of Patient-Generated Health Data in Care Delivery and Research through 2024*. Office of the National Coordinator for Health Information Technology. Recuperado el 03 de September de 2021, de https://aspe.hhs.gov/conceptualising-data-infrastructure-capture-use-patient-generated-health-data

Services, U. D. (2017). *Software as a Medical Device (SAMD): Guidance for Industry and Food and Drug Administration Staff*. U.S Food and Drug Administration.

Services, US Department of Health and Human, (2020). cdc.gov. National Diabetes Statistics Report, 2020. https://www.cdc.gov/diabetes/pdfs/data/statistics/national-diabetes-statistics-report.pdf

Shah, P., Kendall, F., Khozin, S., Goosen, R., Hu, J., Laramie, J., ... Schork, N. (2019). Artificial intelligence and machine learning in clinical development: a translational perspective. *NPJ Digital Medicine*(https://doi.org/10.1038/s41746-019-0148-3).

Shah, R. R. (2021). *Unleashing the HealthTech Potential*. RBSA.

Shewan, D. (2020). *Pain Points: A Guide to Finding & Solving Your Customers' Problems*. Recuperado el 29 de August de 2021, de https://www.wordstream.com/blog/ws/2018/02/28/pain-points

Shortell, S., & Kaluzny, A. (2011). *Shortell and Kaluzny's Healthcare Management: Organization Design and Behavior*. Thomson Delmar Learning, Division of Thomson Learning.

Shrivastava, S., Shrivastava, P., & Ramasamy, J. (2014). Color coding: a tool to enhance the quality of health care in low resource settings. *Medicine* (DOI:10.4081/HLS.2014.4772).

Siemens. (2021). *Healthineers*. Recuperado el 01 de September de 2021, de https://www.corporate.siemens-healthineers.com/

Siemens. (2021). *Siemens Technology Accelerator*. Recuperado el 28 de August de 2021, de https://new.siemens.com/global/en/products/services/technology-accelerator.html

Siemens. (2021). *Smart hospitals. Environments built to heal*. Recuperado el 01 de September de 2021, de https://new.siemens.com/global/en/markets/healthcare/smart-hospitals.html?gclid=CjwKCAjw2ZaGBhBoEiwA8pfP_uSlXJGy2KRI-AjtmpMZgmrfoIXwnkhLCNbHbr1d02A38_w46qU1lxoC9R4QAvD_BwE

Simoni, G. D. (2018). *Five Ways to Use Metadata Management to Deliver Business Value for Data*. Recuperado el 02 de September de 2021, de https://www.gartner.com/en/documents/3878879/five-ways-to-use-metadata-management-to-deliver-business

Sinai, M. (2021). *Visiting Mount Sinai Hospital*. Recuperado el 28 de August de 2021, de https://www.mountsinai.org/locations/mount-sinai/your-visit/locations

Singapore, E. (2019). *Singapore's HealthTech Ecosystem*. EDB Singapore.

Singapore, E. (2020). *The HealthTech boom in Southeast Asia: Big strides and new opportunities for heal*. Recuperado el 05 de September de 2021, de https://www.edb.gov.sg/en/business-insights/insights/the-healthtech-boom-in-southeast-asia-big-strides-and-new-opportunities-for-healthcare.html

Singapore, E. (2021). *Growing Enterprises*. Recuperado el 05 de September de 2021, de https://www.enterprisesg.gov.sg/

Singapore, S. N. (2021). *Health*. Recuperado el 01 de Saptember de 2021, de https://www.smartnation.gov.sg/what-is-smart-nation/initiatives/Health

Singapore, S. N. (2021). *National Steps Challenge & the Healthy 365 app*. Recuperado el 01 de September de 2021, de https://www.smartnation.gov.sg/what-is-smart-nation/initiatives/Health/national-steps-challenge-and-the-healthy-365-app

Singh, A., Arora, J., Mittal, N. (2017). Healthcare Provider Annual Report 2017: Will the Real Value-Based Care (VBC) Please Stand Up. Everest Group. https://www2.everestgrp.com/reportaction/EGR-2017-12-R-2361/Marketing

Singh, K., & Misra, M. (2020). Corporate Social Responsibility as a tool for healthtech startups: Modelling enablers of healthcare and social support system to fight Coronavirus Pandemic. *11th International Conference on Computing, Communication and Networking Technologies (ICCCNT)* (DOI: 10.1109/ICCCNT49239.2020.9225687), 1–6.

Sissel, M. (2021). *Proposed Changes to Privacy Rule Won't Ensure Privacy*. Recuperado el 04 de September de 2021, de http://www.forhealthfreedom.org/Newsletter/September2010.html#Article3

Sit, J., Chair, S., Choi, K., Chan, C., Lee, D., Chan, A., ... Taylor-Piliae, R. (2016). Do empowered stroke patients perform better at self-management and functional recovery after a stroke? A randomized controlled trial. *PMC*, pág. DOI: 10.2147/CIA.S109560.

Slack. (2019). *Getting the most out of threads*. Recuperado el 03 de September de 2021, de https://slack.com/intl/en-in/blog/collaboration/getting-the-most-out-of-threads

Smartcities. (2020). *How Smart Cities Technology Can Help Improve Healthcare*. Recuperado el 01 de September de 2021, de https://innovation.engie.com/en/news/news/smart-cities/smart-cities-technology-healthcare/13698

Smartcity. (2017). *The Equitable City – A New Name For New York*. Recuperado el 30 de August de 2021, de https://www.smartcity.press/new-yorks-smart-city-initiatives/

SmartNation. (2021). *Transforming Singapore through Technology*. Recuperado el 29 de August de 2021, de https://www.smartnation.gov.sg/

Smith, T. T. (2016). *Examining Data Privacy Breaches in Healthcare*. Walden University.

Snyder, L., & Shen, Z.-J. (2019). *Fundamentals of Supply Chain Theory*. Wiley & Sons.

Soderlund, N., Lawyer, P., Larsson, S., & Kent, J. (2012). *Progress Towards Value-Based Health Care*. Recuperado el 28 de August de 2021, de https://www.bcg.com/publications/2012/health-care-public-sector-progress-toward-value-based-health-care

Sohu. (2020). *The National Health Commission and Tencent jointly released the "National Fever Clinic Map", and WeChat added a "Medical and Health" portal*. Recuperado el 04 de September de 2021, de https://www.sohu.com/a/369098592_220182

Solution, G. (2021). *Trusted Practice Management Software used by over 21,000 medical professionals*. Recuperado el 08 de September de 2021, de https://www.geniesolutionssoftware.com.au/

SparkLabs. (2021). *A mentorship driven mentorship program*. Recuperado el 08 de September de 2021, de https://www.sparklabstaipei.com/program

SPDR. (2021). *ESG Investing From Tipping Point to Turning Point*. SSGA.

Speer, M., & Delgado, M. (2017). Reminiscing about positive memories buffers acute stress responses. *Nature Human Behaviour*(https://doi.org/10.1038/s41562-017-0093).

SRTIP, & Park, S. R. (s.f.). *Sharjah Research Technology and Innovation Park P.O.* Recuperado el September de 2021, de SRTIP: https://srtip.ae/

Staff, A. (2020). *Thailand healthtech field set to grow: Report*. Recuperado el 06 de September de 2021, de https://www.businesstimes.com.sg/asean-business/thailand-healthtech-field-set-to-grow-report

Stanford Medicine. (2018). *The Democratization of Health Care*. Stanford Medicine 2018 Health Trends Report.

Star, T. (2020). *Miles to go for healthtech.* Recuperado el 08 de September de 2021, de https://www.thestar.com.my/business/smebiz/2020/07/25/miles-to-go-for-health-tech

Startup, H. T. (2021). *Healthtech Startup Thailand.* Recuperado el 06 de September de 2021, de https://www.facebook.com/HealthTechThailand/

Startupbootcamp. (2021). *Accelerating Innovators.* Recuperado el 09 de September de 2021, de https://www.startupbootcamp.org/

Startuphealth. (2021). *Together we can…* Recuperado el 09 de September de 2021, de https://www.startuphealth.com/

Starupbootcamp. (2021). *Accelerating Digital Health Innovation.* Recuperado el 28 de August de 2021, de https://www.startupbootcamp.org/accelerator/digital-health-berlin/

Starups, M. (2021). *Top 60 medical and healthcare startups in Canada.* Recuperado el 05 de September de 2021, de https://www.medicalstartups.org/country/Canada/

Statista. (2021). *Estimated healthcare IoT device installations worldwide from 2015 to 2020.* Recuperado el 02 de September de 2021, de https://www.statista.com/statistics/735810/healthcare-iot-installations-global-estimate/

Statista. (2021). *Global digital population as of January 2021.* Recuperado el 28 de August de 2021, de https://www.statista.com/statistics/617136/digital-population-worldwide/

Statista. (2021). *Number of active users of Fitbit from 2012 to 2020.* Recuperado el 29 de August de 2021, de https://www.statista.com/statistics/472600/fitbit-active-users/

Statista. (2021). *Number of unicorns in Europe as of April 2021, by country.* Recuperado el 04 de September de 2021, de https://www.statista.com/statistics/1094251/number-of-european-unicorns-by-country/

Statista. (2021). *Projected global digital health market size from 2019 to 2025.* Recuperado el 05 de September de 2021, de https://www.statista.com/statistics/1092869/global-digital-health-market-size-forecast/

Statistics, O. f. (2021). *Exploring the UK's digital divideExploring the UK's digital divide.* Recuperado el 01 de September de 2021, de https://www.ons.gov.uk/peoplepopulationandcommunity/householdcharacteristics/homeinternetandsocialmediausage/articles/exploringtheuksdigitaldivide/2019-03-04

Sterling, R., & LeRouge, C. (2019). On-Demand Telemedicine as a Disruptive Health Technology: Qualitative Study Exploring Emerging Business Models and Strategies Among Early Adopter Organizations in the United States. *J Med Internet Res* (DOI: 10.2196/14304).

Steves, R. (2021). *Medical Care in Europe.* Recuperado el 06 de September de 2021, de https://www.ricksteves.com/travel-tips/health/medical-care-in-europe

Stewart, C. (11 de May de 2021). *Value of healthtech startups in Europe in 2021, by segment.* Recuperado el October de 2021, de statista.com: https://www.statista.com/statistics/1234716/value-of-healthtech-startups-in-europe-by-segment/

Stewart, C. (2 de November de 2018). *U.S. Digital health Market Size by technology forecast 2014-2024.* Recuperado el October de 2021, de Statista: https://www.statista.com/statistics/938594/digital-health-market-size-forecast-united-states-by-technology/

Stewart, C. (24 de September de 2020). *Statista.com.* Recuperado el 2021 de October, de Statista: https://www.statista.com/statistics/1037970/global-healthcare-data-volume/

Stewart, C. (30 de March de 2021). *People's perception about the use of technology in response to COVID-19 in UK in 2020.* Recuperado el October de 2021, de https://www.statista.com/statistics/1221275/perceptions-around-the-covid-19-tech-response-in-the-uk/

Stocastic. (2021). *AI Support for Health Care.* Recuperado el 02 de September de 2021, de https://www.stocastic.com/

Sueiras, P., Romano-Betech, V., Vergil-Salgado, A., Hoyos, A., Quintana-Vargas, S., Ruddick, W., … Altamirano-Bustamante, M. (2017). Today's medical self and the other: Challenges and evolving solutions for enhanced humanization and quality of care. *PLoS ONE*, pág. https://doi.org/10.1371/journal.pone.0181514.

Sumathi, S., & Malini, R. (2010). Face recognition system to enhance E Health. *1* (DOI:10.1109/EDT.2010.5496604).

Summerskill, W., & Horton, R. (2011). *Southeast Asia.* Recuperado el 05 de September de 2021, de https://www.thelancet.com/series/health-in-southeast-asia

Sundhed. (2021). *Coronapas - COVID-19 test*. Recuperado el 02 de September de 2021, de https://www.sundhed.dk/borger/min-side/corona/covidpas/

Sunil, P. (2021). *Key highlights of the new Malaysia Digital Economy Blueprint, a part of the MyDIGITAL initiative*. Recuperado el 08 de September de 2021, de https://www.humanresourcesonline.net/key-highlights-of-the-new-malaysia-digital-economy-blueprint-a-part-of-the-mydigital-initiative

SVB. (2021). *Key takeaways*. Recuperado el 08 de September de 2021, de https://www.svb.com/china-healthcare-report

SVB_Financial. (2019). *HealthTech: Insights into an Emerging Industry -Valuable Exits Reinforce Growing Investments*. SVB_Financial.

Symplur. (2021). *#newhcvoices healthcare social media hashtag*. Recuperado el 03 de September de 2021, de https://www.symplur.com/healthcare-hashtags/newhcvoices/

Symplur. (2021). *Healthcare Hashtag Project*. Recuperado el 03 de September de 2021, de https://www.symplur.com/healthcare-hashtags/

System, M. S. (2019). *Icahn School of Medicine at Mount Sinai to Establish World-Class Center for Artificial Intelligence: Hamilton and Amabel James Center for Artificial Intelligence and Human Health*. Recuperado el 02 de September de 2021, de https://www.newswise.com/articles/icahn-school-of-medicine-at-mount-sinai-to-establish-world-class-center-for-artificial-intelligence-hamilton-and-amabel-james-center-for-artificial-intelligence-and-human-health

Taira. (2021). *Taira*. Recuperado el 08 de September de 2021, de https://www.tairax.com.tw/index.aspx

Taiwan, A. (2021). *CORONAVIRUS/Taiwan approves AI-based detection system for COVID-19*. Recuperado el 08 de September de 2021, de https://ai.taiwan.gov.tw/news/coronavirus-taiwan-approves-ai-based-detection-system-for-covid19/

Taiwan, F. (2021). *CORONAVIRUS/Taiwan approves AI-based detection system for COVID-19*. Recuperado el 08 de September de 2021, de https://focustaiwan.tw/sci-tech/202105300011

Talk, L. (2021). *Bell*. Recuperado el 03 de September de 2021, de https://letstalk.bell.ca/en/

Tardi, C. (2020). *80-20 Rule*. Recuperado el 01 de September de 2021, de https://www.investopedia.com/terms/1/80-20-rule.asp

Tasmanian. (2016). *HEALTHY TASMANIA FIVE YEAR STRATEGIC PLAN: One State, One Health System, Better Outcomes*. Government, Department of health and human services. Tasmania: Government of Tasmania. Recuperado el 29 de August de 2021, de https://www.healthtechhub.org/

Taylor, M. (2019). *These are the top healthtech accelerators in Europe*. Recuperado el 28 de August de 2021, de https://sifted.eu/articles/these-are-the-best-healthtech-accelerators-in-europe/

Team, B. (2020). *Rwanda will be the world's most advanced country for digital health*. Recuperado el 02 de Septemberde2021,dehttps://www.babylonhealth.com/blog/business/rwanda-will-be-the-worlds-most-advanced-country-for-digital-health

Team, G. (2020). *15 More Companies That No Longer Require a Degree—Apply Now*. Recuperado el 09 de September de 2021, de https://www.glassdoor.com/blog/no-degree-required/

Team, M. P. (2014). *Strategy of SAKIGAKE*. Ministry Project Team.

Teams, N.-H.-S. -H. (s.f.). *Home-stat*. Recuperado el September de 2021, de https://www1.nyc.gov/site/operations/projects/HomeStat.page

Tech, H. (2021). *About Us*. Recuperado el 06 de September de 2021, de https://www.healthtech-thailand.com/about-htt

Technology, F. P. (2021). *Hyllie: how Swedish prosumption could set a precedent for smart cities*. Recuperado el 01 de September de 2021, de https://power.nridigital.com/future_power_technology_dec20/hyllie_smart_city_prosumption

Tencent. (2020). *Tencent Open-sources Another AI-powered Tool to Help Conduct Preliminary Self-evaluation Regarding COVID-19 Infection*. Recuperado el 09 de September de 2021, de https://www.prnewswire.com/news-releases/tencent-open-sources-another-ai-powered-tool-to-help-conduct-preliminary-self-evaluation-regarding-covid-19-infection-301034933.html

The Rockefeller Foundation. (2018). *Artificial Intelligence in Global Health*. USAID FROM THE AMERICAN PEOPLE. The Rockefeller Foundation.

Thoring, K., Mueller, R.M., Badke-Schaub, P. (2015). Ethnographic Design Research With Wearable Cameras. Research Gate. https://www.researchgate.net/publication/273859828_Ethnographic_Design_Research_With_Wearable_Cameras

T-hub. (2018). *The Emerging World of Healthtech*. Recuperado el 28 de August de 2021, de https://t-hub.co/blog/the-emerging-world-of-healthtech/

Times, T. N. (2021). *Big Tech's Backlash Is Just Starting*. Recuperado el 01 de September de 2021, de https://www.nytimes.com/2020/07/30/technology/big-tech-backlash.html

timihealth. (2021). *timifit*. Recuperado el 02 de September de 2021, de https://timihealth.com/

TIR. (2019). *The Future of Medicine*. Recuperado el 06 de September de 2021, de https://www.spcr.cz/images/TIR_Newsletter_January2019_Final_-MEDICINE-A_HEALTH_OUTLOOK_FOR_INVESTORS.pdf

TMC. (2021). *TMCX*. Recuperado el 09 de September de 2021, de http://www.tmc.edu/innovation/innovation-programs/tmcx/

Tomašev, N., Glorot, X., & Mohamed, S. (2019). A clinically applicable approach to continuous prediction of future acute kidney injury. *Nature, 572*(https://doi.org/10.1038/s41586-019-1390-1), 116–119.

Top-Hashtags. (2021). *Hashtags for #healthtech in 2021 to be popular and trending in Instagram, TikTok*. Recuperado el 03 de September de 2021, de https://top-hashtags.com/hashtag/healthtech/

Topol, E. (2016). *The Patient Will See You Now: The Future of Medicine Is in Your Hands*. Basic Books.

Topol, E. (2019). *Deep Medicine: How Artificial Intelligence Can Make Healthcare Human Again*. Basic Books.

Topol, E. (2019). Preparing the healthcare workforce to deliver the digital future. An independent report on behalf of the Secretary of State for Health and Social Care February 2019; Publisher: NHS.

Topol, E. J. (2019). High-performance medicine: the convergence of human and artificial intelligence. *Nature Medicine*, 25, pages 44–56 (2019).

Toronto, S. (2021). *Toronto's Hub for StartUp Support*. Recuperado el 09 de September de 2021, de https://startupheretoronto.com/startup-support/

Tracxn. (2021). *HealthTech Startups in Canada*. Recuperado el 05 de September de 2021, de https://tracxn.com/explore/HealthTech-Startups-in-Canada

Tracxn. (2021). *HealthTech Startups in China*. Recuperado el 08 de September de 2021, de https://tracxn.com/explore/HealthTech-Startups-in-China

Tracxn. (2021). *HealthTech Startups in Singapore*. Recuperado el 05 de September de 2021, de https://tracxn.com/explore/HealthTech-Startups-in-Singapore

Triage, H. (2014). *Australian Health Care*. Recuperado el 08 de September de 2021, de https://www.youtube.com/watch?v=ylsO0VVy29U&list=PLkfBg8ML-gIngk82SUbTp6Og_KkYfJ6oF&index=3

Triage, H. (2014). Healthcare in Singapore. YouTube.

Truth, T. (2021). *Growing Wave of Quitters*. Recuperado el 01 de September de 2021, de https://www.thetruth.com

Twin, A., & Estevez, E. (2021). *Disruptive Innovation*. Recuperado el 03 de September de 2021, de https://www.investopedia.com/terms/d/disruptive-innovation.asp

Twin, A., & James, M. (2021). *Product Line*. Recuperado el 28 de August de 2021, de https://www.investopedia.com/terms/p/product-line.asp

Udemy. (s.f.). *Udemy*. Recuperado el October de 2021, de https://www.udemy.com/

UNDP. (2017). *Health care systems: time for a rethink*. UNDP.

UNESCO. (2020). *Global Investments in R&D*. UNESCO.

UNESCO. (2021). *Center of Excellence*. Recuperado el 04 de September de 2021, de http://www.unesco.org/new/en/natural-sciences/science-technology/basic-sciences/international-basic-sciences-programme/center-of-excellence/

Union, E. (2021). *European Union priorities for 2019-2024*. Recuperado el 04 de September de 2021, de https://europa.eu/european-union/about-eu/priorities_en

Union, European. (2021). Data Protection under GDPR. Your Europe. https://europa.eu/youreurope/business/dealing-with-customers/data-protection/data-protection-gdpr/index_en.htm

Unit, T. E. (October de 2020). World Industry Outlook: Healthcare and pharmaceuticals. *The Economist Intelligence Unit*.

Usability.gov. (2013). *Usability and Accessibility: Looking at User Experience through Two Lenses.* Recuperado el 29 de August de 2021, de https://www.usability.gov/get-involved/blog/2013/01/accessibility-and-usability.html

USAID. (2021). *Artificial Intelligence in Global Health.* Recuperado el 07 de September de 2021, de https://www.usaid.gov/sites/default/files/documents/1864/AI-in-Global-Health_webFinal_508.pdf

USAID. (2021). *Artificial Intelligence in Global Health.* The Rockfield Foundation.

USAID. (2021). *Center for Innovation and Impact (CII).* Recuperado el 05 de September de 2021, de https://www.usaid.gov/cii

USAID. (2021). *Vision for Health System Strengthening 2030.* Recuperado el 05 de September de 2021, de https://www.usaid.gov/global-health/health-systems-innovation/health-systems/Vision-HSS-2030

USAID. (2021). *Who We are.* Recuperado el 05 de September de 2021, de https://www.usaid.gov/who-we-are

VAE. (2021). *We promote illusions.* Recuperado el 09 de September de 2021, de http://www.vaeassessori-aempresarial.org/

Vega, E. (2003). Parallel trade. *Professional Pharmacy.*

Vilas, L. (2020). American Legacy Foundation Truth Singing Cowboy.

VisitPay. (2017). *The Self-Pay Gap: Growing Opportunity or Ticking Time Bomb?* VisitPay.

Viveo. (2021). *Your virtual clinic Fast, simple, secure.* Recuperado el 02 de September de 2021, de https://viveohealth.com/for-doctors/

Voser, S. (2018). *What is brand localisation and why is it so important for global success?* Recuperado el 28 de August de 2021, de https://www.yuqo.com/brand-localisation-why-important-for-global-success/

Voximplant. (2020). *What Are Voice Bots And How They Can Help You.* Recuperado el 03 de September de 2021, de https://voximplant.com/blog/what-are-voice-bots

VWO. (2021). *A/B Testing Guide.* Recuperado el 29 de August de 2021, de https://vwo.com/ab-testing/

W. Caves, R. (2004). *Encyclopedia of the city.*

W. E, D. (2004). *Critical Evaluations in Business and Management.* Routledge.

Walmart. (2021). *Walmart.* Recuperado el 28 de August de 2021, de https://www.walmart.com

Wang, F., Kaushal, R., & Khullar, D. (2020). Should Health Care Demand Interpretable Artificial Intelligence or Accept "Black Box" Medicine? *Annals of Internal Medicine, 172*(https://doi.org/10.7326/M19-2548), 59–60.

WeChat. (2021). *WeChat.* Recuperado el 04 de September de 2021, de https://www.wechat.com/

WEKEO. (s.f.). *Wekeo.EU.* Recuperado el October de 2021, de https://www.wekeo.eu/

Whitsel, L., Wilbanks, J., Huffman, M., & Hall, J. (2018). The Role of Government in Precision Medicine, Precision Public Health and the Intersection With Healthy Living. *Elsevier* (DOI: 10.1016/j.pcad.2018.12.002).

WHO. (2000). *Health Systems: Improving Performance.* Recuperado el 07 de September de 2021, de https://www.who.int/whr/2000/en/whr00_en.pdf

WHO. (2012). *Health systems in the Eastern Mediterranean Region:.* WHO.

WHO. (2018). *Circular Economy and Health: Opportunities and Risks.* Recuperado el 28 de August de 2021, de https://www.euro.who.int/__data/assets/pdf_file/0004/374917/Circular-Economy_EN_WHO_web_august-2018.pdf

WHO. (2020). *Core Health Indicators in the WHO European Region.* WHO.

WHO. (2020). *Health Equity and its Determinants in the Western Pacific Region.* WHO Western Pacific Region.

WHO. (2020). *WHO reports fivefold increase in cyber attacks, urges vigilance.* Recuperado el 04 de September de 2021, de https://www.who.int/news/item/23-04-2020-who-reports-fivefold-increase-in-cyber-attacks-urges-vigilance

WHO. (2021). *A Visual Summary.* Recuperado el 28 de August de 2021, de https://www.who.int/data/stories/world-health-statistics-2021-a-visual-summary

WHO. (2021). *Campaigns.* Recuperado el 01 de September de 2021, de https://www.who.int/campaigns/world-malaria-day

WHO. (2021). *Country Progress Towards Universal Health Coverage.* WHO.

WHO. (2021). *Current health expenditure (CHE) as percentage of gross domestic product (GDP) (%).* Recuperado el 28 de August de 2021, de https://www.who.int/data/gho/data/indicators/indicator-details/GHO/current-health-expenditure-(che)-as-percentage-of-gross-domestic-product-(gdp)-(-)

WHO. (2021). *Data and statistics.* Recuperado el 03 de September de 2021, de https://www.euro.who.int/en/health-topics/Health-systems/health-workforce/data-and-statistics

WHO. (2021). *Homepage.* Recuperado el 28 de August de 2021, de https://www.who.int/

WHO. (2021). *Joint External Evaluation Tool.* Recuperado el 05 de September de 2021, de https://apps.who.int/iris/bitstream/handle/10665/204368/9789241510172_eng.pdf?sequence=1

WHO. (2021). *The Sustainable Health Agenda For The Americas 2018–2030.* WHO.

WHO. (2021). *Triple Billion dashboard.* Recuperado el 05 de September de 2021, de https://www.who.int/data/triple-billion-dashboard

WHO. (2021). *Universal health coverage in the Western Pacific.* Recuperado el 07 de September de 2021, de https://www.who.int/westernpacific/health-topics/universal-health-coverage

WHO. (2021). *Universal health coverage.* Recuperado el 07 de September de 2021, de https://www.who.int/westernpacific/health-topics/universal-health-coverage

WHO. (2021). *WHO Regional Office.* Recuperado el 05 de September de 2021, de https://www.who.int/about/who-we-are/regional-offices

WHO. (2021). *World AIDS Day.* Recuperado el 01 de September de 2021, de https://www.who.int/campaigns/world-aids-day

WHO. (2021). *World Health Statistics 2020.* Recuperado el 05 de September de 2021, de https://www.who.int/data/gho/whs-2020-visual-summary

WHO. (2021). *World Health Statistics 2021.* Recuperado el 03 de September de 2021, de https://www.who.int/data/stories/world-health-statistics-2021-a-visual-summary

Wigmore, I. (2021). *black box AI.* Recuperado el 02 de September de 2021, de https://whatis.techtarget.com/definition/black-box-AI

Wikipedia. (2020). *Business model pattern.* Recuperado el 29 de August de 2021, de https://en.wikipedia.org/wiki/Business_model_pattern#:~:text=Business%20model%20patterns%20are%20reusable,creating%20a%20new%20business%20model.

Wikipedia. (2021). *100,000 Genomes Project.* Recuperado el 07 de September de 2021, de https://en.wikipedia.org/wiki/100,000_Genomes_Project

Wikipedia. (2021). *Analysis paralysis.* Recuperado el 01 de September de 2021, de https://en.wikipedia.org/wiki/Analysis_paralysis

Wikipedia. (2021). *Augmented reality.* Recuperado el 02 de September de 2021, de https://en.wikipedia.org/wiki/Augmented_reality

Wikipedia. (2021). *Behavioral medicine.* Recuperado el 30 de August de 2021, de https://en.wikipedia.org/wiki/Behavioral_medicine

Wikipedia. (2021). *Bluetooth low energy beacon.* Recuperado el 29 de August de 2021, de https://en.wikipedia.org/wiki/Bluetooth_low_energy_beacon

Wikipedia. (2021). *Dual-tone multi-frequency signaling.* Recuperado el 03 de September de 2021, de https://en.wikipedia.org/wiki/Dual-tone_multi-frequency_signaling

Wikipedia. (2021). *Growth hacking.* Recuperado el 03 de September de 2021, de https://en.wikipedia.org/wiki/Growth_hacking

Wikipedia. (2021). *Health care in the United States.* Recuperado el 05 de September de 2021, de https://en.wikipedia.org/wiki/Health_care_in_the_United_States

Wikipedia. (2021). *Health care system in Japan.* Recuperado el 08 de September de 2021, de https://en.wikipedia.org/wiki/Health_care_system_in_Japan

Wikipedia. (2021). *Health information technology.* Recuperado el 01 de September de 2021, de https://en.wikipedia.org/wiki/Health_information_technology

Wikipedia. (2021). *Healthcare in Brazil.* Recuperado el 05 de September de 2021, de https://en.wikipedia.org/wiki/Healthcare_in_Brazil

Wikipedia. (2021). *Healthcare in Germany.* Recuperado el 06 de September de 2021, de https://en.wikipedia.org/wiki/Healthcare_in_Germany

Wikipedia. (2021). *Healthcare in India.* Recuperado el 05 de September de 2021, de https://en.wikipedia.org/wiki/Healthcare_in_India#cite_note-Zodpey_et_al_2018-1

Wikipedia. (2021). *Healthcare in Taiwan.* Recuperado el 08 de September de 2021, de https://en.wikipedia.org/wiki/Healthcare_in_Taiwan#National_Health_Insurance

Wikipedia. (2021). *Healthcare in Thailand*. Recuperado el 06 de September de 2021, de https://en.wikipedia.org/wiki/Healthcare_in_Thailand

Wikipedia. (2021). *Information and communications technology*. Recuperado el 04 de September de 2021, de https://en.wikipedia.org/wiki/Information_and_communications_technology

Wikipedia. (2021). *International Health Terminology Standards Development Organisation*. Recuperado el 04 de September de 2021, de https://en.wikipedia.org/wiki/International_Health_Terminology_Standards_Development_Organisation

Wikipedia. (2021). *Kaizen*. Recuperado el 01 de September de 2021, de https://en.wikipedia.org/wiki/Kaizen

Wikipedia. (2021). *Languages of the United States*. Recuperado el 01 de September de 2021, de https://en.wikipedia.org/wiki/Languages_of_the_United_States

Wikipedia. (2021). *List of WHO regions*. Recuperado el 05 de September de 2021, de https://en.wikipedia.org/wiki/List_of_WHO_regions

Wikipedia. (2021). *Matriz BCG*. Recuperado el 04 de September de 2021, de https://es.wikipedia.org/wiki/Matriz_BCG

Wikipedia. (2021). *Microblogging in China*. Recuperado el 04 de September de 2021, de https://en.wikipedia.org/wiki/Microblogging_in_China

Wikipedia. (2021). *Minimum viable product*. Recuperado el 29 de August de 2021, de https://en.wikipedia.org/wiki/Minimum_viable_product#:~:text=A%20minimum%20viable%20product%20(MVP,feedback%20for%20future%20product%20development.&text=The%20concept%20can%20be%20used,developments%20of%20an%20existing%20product.

Wikipedia. (2021). *Moneyball (film)*. Recuperado el 04 de September de 2021, de https://en.wikipedia.org/wiki/Moneyball_(film)

Wikipedia. (2021). *Non-communicable disease*. Recuperado el 07 de September de 2021, de https://en.wikipedia.org/wiki/Non-communicable_disease

Wikipedia. (2021). *Omics*. Recuperado el 30 de August de 2021, de https://en.wikipedia.org/wiki/Omics

Wikipedia. (2021). *Organoid*. Recuperado el 03 de September de 2021, de https://en.wikipedia.org/wiki/Organoid

Wikipedia. (2021). *Pharmaceutical industry*. Recuperado el 03 de September de 2021, de https://en.wikipedia.org/wiki/Pharmaceutical_industry#Mid-1800s_%E2%80%93_1945:_From_botanicals_to_the_first_synthetic_drugs

Wikipedia. (2021). *Slogan*. Recuperado el 28 de August de 2021, de https://en.wikipedia.org/wiki/Slogan#:~:text=The%20Oxford%20Dictionary%20of%20English,and%20appealing%20to%20the%20audience.

Wikipedia. (2021). *Snowball effect*. Recuperado el 29 de August de 2021, de https://en.wikipedia.org/wiki/Snowball_effect

Wikipedia. (2021). *Sun Tzu*. Recuperado el 28 de August de 2021, de https://en.wikipedia.org/wiki/Sun_Tzu#:~:text=Sun%20Tzu%20is%20traditionally%20credited,Asian%20philosophy%20and%20military%20thinking.&text=His%20birth%20name%20was%20Sun,(Chinese%3A%20%E9%95%B7%E5%8D%BF).

Wikipedia. (2021). *Sustainable Development Goals*. Recuperado el 28 de August de 2021, de https://en.wikipedia.org/wiki/Sustainable_Development_Goals

Wikipedia. (2021). *Tokenization (data security)*. Recuperado el 01 de September de 2021, de https://en.wikipedia.org/wiki/Tokenization_(data_security).

Wikipedia. (2021). *Tokenization (data security)*. Recuperado el 02 de September de 2021, de https://en.wikipedia.org/wiki/Tokenization_(data_security)

Wikipedia. (2021). *Top-of-mind awareness*. Recuperado el 03 de September de 2021, de https://en.wikipedia.org/wiki/Top-of-mind_awareness

Wikipedia. (2021). *Translational medicine*. Recuperado el 02 de September de 2021, de https://en.wikipedia.org/wiki/Translational_medicine

Wikipedia. (2021). *Unboxing*. Recuperado el 02 de September de 2021, de https://en.wikipedia.org/wiki/Unboxing.

Wikipedia. (2021). *Virtual reality*. Recuperado el 02 de September de 2021, de https://en.wikipedia.org/wiki/Virtual_reality

Wikipedia. (2021). *Watson (computer)*. Recuperado el 01 de September de 2021, de https://en.wikipedia.org/wiki/Watson_(computer)

Wikipedia. (2021). *WeChat*. Recuperado el 04 de September de 2021, de https://en.wikipedia.org/wiki/WeChat

Wikipedia. (2021). *Word of mouth*. Recuperado el 01 de September de 2021, de https://en.wikipedia.org/wiki/Word_of_mouth

Wikipedia. (2021). *World Day for Cultural Diversity for Dialogue and Developmenthttps://en.wikipedia.org/wiki/World Day for Cultural Diversity for Dialogue and Development*. Recuperado el 01 de September de 2021, de https://en.wikipedia.org/wiki/World_Day_for_Cultural_Diversity_for_Dialogue_and_Developmenthttps://en.wikipedia.org/wiki/World_Day_for_Cultural_Diversity_for_Dialogue_and_Development.

Wikipedia. (2021). *World Health Day*. Recuperado el 01 de September de 2021, de https://en.wikipedia.org/wiki/World_Health_Day

Wikipedia. (s.f.). Obtenido de mHealth: https://en.wikipedia.org/wiki/MHealth

Williams, J., & Chowdhury, R. (2021). *Introducing our Responsible Machine Learning Initiative*. Recuperado el 03 de September de 2021, de https://blog.twitter.com/en_us/topics/company/2021/introducing-responsible-machine-learning-initiative

WIPO. (2019). *Artificial Intelligence*. WIPO.

Wire, B. (2017). *Brain Power Releases First Augmented Reality Smartglasses to Help People with Autism Increase Social, School, and Job Success*. Recuperado el 02 de September de 2021, de https://www.businesswire.com/news/home/20171107006113/en/Brain-Power-Releases-First-Augmented-Reality-Smartglasses-to-Help-People-with-Autism-Increase-Social-School-and-Job-Success

Wu, L., Wang, D., & Evans, J. (2019). Large teams develop and small teams disrupt science and technology. *Nature, 566*(https://doi.org/10.1038/s41586-019-0941-9), 378–382.

Xinhua. (2020). *Alibaba launches free online medical consultation to ease hospital pressure*. Recuperado el 09 de September de 2021, de http://www.xinhuanet.com/english/2020-01/26/c_138735604.htm

Yasmina Andreu, F. C. (2016). Wize Mirror - a smart, multisensory cardio-metabolic risk monitoring system. *Computer Vision and Image Understanding, 148*(https://doi.org/10.1016/j.cviu.2016.03.018.).

Yassin, B. H., & Menteri, P. (2021). *TEKS UCAPAN YAB TAN SRI DATO' HAJI MUHYIDDIN*. Recuperado el 08 de September de 2021, de https://www.epu.gov.my/sites/default/files/2021-02/Teks%20Ucapan%20Perasmian%20MyDIGITAL%20YAB%20PM_0.pdf

Yee Hii, M., Courtney, P., & Royall, P. (2019). An Evaluation of the Delivery of Medicines. *Drone*, pág. DOI:10.3390/drones3030052.

Youku. (2021). *Youku*. Recuperado el 04 de September de 2021, de: https://www.youku.com

Index

Note: Page references in *italics* represent figures and page references with "n" represent the notes.

Printed in the United States
by Baker & Taylor Publisher Services